AVENUE
MANHATTAN
MIDTOWN EAST
UNION SQUARE AND CHELSEA
GREENWICH VILLAGE
SOHO AND TRIBECA
THE EAST VILLAGE AND THE LOWER EAST SIDE
LOWER MANHATTAN
HARLEM AND THE HEIGHTS
THE OUTER BOROUGHS
QUEENS
BROOKLYN
BRONX
Hudson
East
Harlem
CHELSEA
GREENWICH
SOHO
TRIBECA
LITTLE ITALY
CHINATOWN
EAST VILLAGE
LOWER EAST SIDE
FINANCIAL DISTRICT
BATTERY PARK CITY
DUMBO
WASHINGTON HEIGHTS
TREMONT
MELROSE
HARLEM
General Post Office
Madison Square Garden
Penn Station
Empire State Bldg
Macy's
Public Library
Whitney Museum of American Art
Lower East Side Tenement Museum
One World Trade Center
South Street Seaport
Staten Island Ferry Terminal
Statue of Liberty
Ellis Island
Staten Island
Governors Island
Brooklyn Naval Yard
BROOKLYN BRIDGE PARK
Morris-Jumel Mansion
Yankee Stadium
General Grant National Memorial
Columbia University
New York Botanical Garden
Bronx Zoo
FORT TYRON PARK
HIGH BRIDGE PARK
RIVERSIDE PARK
MORNINGSIDE PARK
HUDSON RIVER PARK AND GREENWAY
WASHINGTON SQ PARK
TOMPKINS SQ PARK
GRAMERCY PARK
CITY HALL PARK
EAST RIVER PARK
Holland Tunnel
Brooklyn Battery Tunnel
Queens-Midtown Tunnel
Brooklyn Bridge
Manhattan Bridge
Williamsburg Bridge
George Washington Br.
Washington Br.
Franklin D. Roosevelt Drive
Harlem River Drive
Henry Hudson Parkway
Major Deegan Expressway
Grand Concourse
Grand Blvd and Concourse
McGuinness Blvd
Riverside Drive
Broadway
W 155th St
W 125th St

INSIGHT GUIDES

NEW YORK

CITY GUIDE

www.insightguides.com/USA

Walking Eye App

Your Insight Guide now includes a free app and eBook, dedicated to your chosen destination, all included for the same great price as before. They are available to download from the free Walking Eye container app in the App Store and Google Play. Simply download the Walking Eye container app to access the eBook and app dedicated to your purchased book. The app features an up-to-date A to Z of travel tips, information on events, activities and destination highlights, as well as hotel, restaurant and bar listings. See below for more information and how to download.

MULTIPLE DESTINATIONS AVAILABLE

Now that you've bought this book you can download the accompanying destination app and eBook for free. Inside the Walking Eye container app, you'll also find a whole range of other Insight Guides destination apps and eBooks, all available for purchase.

DEDICATED SEARCH OPTIONS

Use the different sections to browse the places of interest by category or region, or simply use the 'Around me' function to find places of interest nearby. You can then save your selected restaurants, bars and activities to your Favourites or share them with friends using email, Twitter and Facebook.

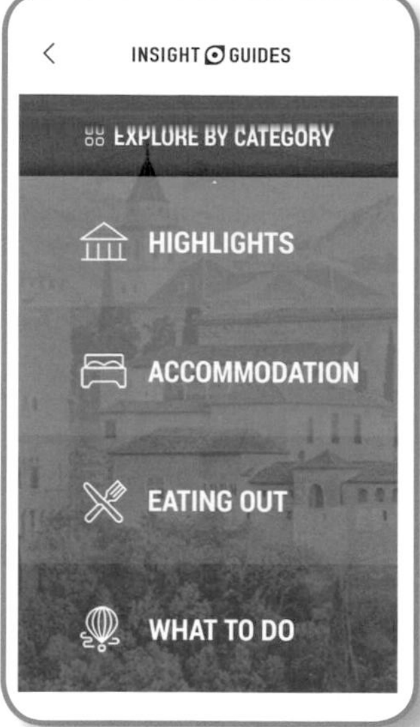

FREQUENTLY UPDATED LISTINGS

Restaurants, bars and hotels change all the time. To ensure you get the most out of your guide, the app features all of our favourites, as well as the latest openings, and is updated regularly. Simply update your app when you receive a notification to access the most current listings available.

TRAVEL TIPS & DESTINATION OVERVIEWS

The app also includes a complete A to Z of handy travel tips on everything from visa regulations to local etiquette. Plus, you'll find destination overviews on shopping, sport, the arts, local events, health, activities and more.

HOW TO DOWNLOAD THE WALKING EYE

Available on purchase of this guide only.

1. Visit our website: www.insightguides.com/walkingeye
2. Download the Walking Eye container app to your smartphone (this will give you access to both the destination app and the eBook)
3. Select the scanning module in the Walking Eye container app
4. Scan the QR code on this page – you will be asked to enter a verification word from the book as proof of purchase
5. Download your free destination app* and eBook for travel information on the go

* Other destination apps and eBooks are available for purchase separately or are free with the purchase of the Insight Guide book

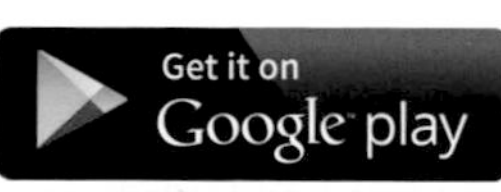

Introduction

History

Features

Insights

PHOTO FEATURES

MINI FEATURES

Places

Travel Tips

Maps

THE BEST OF NEW YORK CITY: TOP ATTRACTIONS

At a glance, everything you can't afford to miss when you visit the Big Apple, from high-energy Times Square and tall, iconic monuments to world-class museums and performance spaces.

◁ **Empire State Building.** This was the tallest structure in the world when it was completed in 1931; zoom up to the 102nd-floor observation deck for unsurpassed views of New York City. See page 173.

▷ **Brooklyn Bridge.** This iconic landmark opened to foot and hoof traffic in 1883 and has been an ideal place to view the skyline ever since. See page 86.

◁ **Museum of Modern Art (MoMA).** Look no further for a remarkable collection of 20th-century art. All the greats are here, displayed in a beautifully designed gallery. The sculpture garden sets Rodin, Picasso, and others amid trees and reflecting pools. See page 167.

▽ **Lincoln Center.** This is the cultural and intellectual hub of the city. Located on the Upper West Side, it's home to many giants of the performing arts, including the New York Philharmonic, the New York City Ballet, the New York Film Society, and the Metropolitan Opera. See page 222.

◁ **Metropolitan Museum of Art.** If you have time for only one museum, make it this treasure house, which has a collection of over 2 million pieces, from Native Americans to 21st-century couturiers. See page 208.

▽ **Times Square.** If there's a classic image of New York City, then it's surely the bright lights and billboards in the heart of Broadway's theater district. See page 160.

▽ **American Museum of Natural History.** The Hayden Planetarium is just one attraction here. Others include the world's tallest dinosaur, a 34-ton (31,000kg) meteorite, a life-size fiberglass blue whale, and an IMAX theater. Don't even think about doing it all in one visit. See page 226.

◁ **Statue of Liberty.** Unveiled in 1886, Lady Liberty was a gift to the US from France, a symbol of freedom and democracy after successful revolutions in both countries. See page 92.

▽ **Greenwich Village.** The artists have long been priced out, but the village still has great allure; there's a neighborhood feel to the area with its old brownstones, one-off stores, Italian bakeries, and small theaters. This is where many Manhattanites would live if they could. See page 129.

▽ **Central Park.** In the 1850s, the city's green lung was created to provide workers with a taste of nature, a function it retains today. See page 182.

THE BEST OF NEW YORK CITY: EDITOR'S CHOICE

The best luxury hotels, riverside walks, unique historic sites, family attractions, and money-saving tips to help you discover the real New York.

BEST HOTELS

The Algonquin. An all-time favorite, the site of theAlgonquin Round Table retains an atmosphere of oak-paneled, low-key elegance and charm. See page 164.

The Carlyle. On the Upper East Side, the Carlyle stakes its claim as one of the city's most luxurious hotels. Woody Allen plays at the Café Carlyle when he's in town. See page 201.

The Chelsea Hotel. A landmark to urban decadence and the former home of beatnik poets, Warhol drag queens, and punk Sid Vicious. Currently closed to guests, but still worth passing by to see the sign and the wrought-iron balconies. See page 148.

Hotel Gansevoort. The first luxury hotel in the Meatpacking District, with a rooftop bar and breathtaking views of the Downtown skyline. See page 139.

The Mercer Hotel. In the heart of SoHo, the Mercer attracts a stylish clientele, as does its fashionable restaurant, the Mercer Kitchen. See page 100.

Lobby of the Hotel Gansevoort, Meatpacking District.

ONLY IN NEW YORK

Stroll and spend. While away the afternoon in NoLita. Uncork some Champagne while getting a pedicure in a chic salon, eat Italian food, and shop in the one-off boutiques: think cute polka dots. See page 121.

Eat and drink. Sip a $10,000 Martini at the Algonquin, or try the "haute barnyard" cuisine downtown at Peasant. See page 164.

Be merry. Join pop stars, celebrities, and jovial shoppers for the annual lighting of the Christmas tree at Rockefeller Center. See page 176.

Sail the Statue of Liberty. Climb aboard a Circle Line tour or have brunch on a sleek 1929 sailboat. See page 92.

Moon over Manhattan. Take a late elevator to the top of the Empire State Building and watch the moon light up Gotham. See page 173.

Hang out with the in-crowd. Mingle with models and banter with butchers in the trend-setting Meatpacking District. See page 137.

Shop and skate. Take in the galleries, market, and small treasures of Chelsea, then don ice-skates for a spin around the Sky Rink at Chelsea Piers. See page 152.

Book some tickets. Catch at least one performance – opera, ballet or a Broadway show – at the Lincoln Center. See page 192.

Muse over music. Visit the home of jazz legend Louis Armstrong and find out why some called him "Dippermouth." See page 252.

Get sporty. Cheer on the Knicks or the Rangers at Madison Square Garden. See page 160.

Be artsy. Take the elevator to the top floor of the Guggenheim and make your way down the spiral ramp, taking in highlights of 20th-century art along the way. See page 210.

Do quirky history. Study a lock of George Washington's hair – and his tooth – at Fraunces Tavern Museum. See page 81.

BEST PARKS

The High Line. This innovative city park is located on an elevated train track once used to transport meat from the Meatpacking District to Chelsea. See page 140.
Central Park. The heart (some say the lungs) of Manhattan, is where residents and visitors alike come to stroll, picnic, play ball, skate or listen to a concert. See page 182.
Prospect Park. Lusher, denser, and greener than its Manhattan counterpart, this Brooklyn park occupies 585 acres (234 hectares). See page 247.
Bryant Park. This pretty midtown parks offers a welcome break from the hustle and bustle of Times Square and hosts outdoor film screenings in summer and an ice rink in winter. See page 164.

St Patrick's Cathedral.

The High Line.

CLASSIC NEW YORK

21. This former speakeasy is still a haunt of the powerful and the beautiful. See page 180.
The Russian Tea Room. Over-the-top and indefatigable, just like New York.
P.J. Clarke's. Sinatra preferred the back room, along with Louis Armstrong. Johnny Depp comes now.
White Horse Tavern. Dylan Thomas drank here. And then he died. See page 136.

Champagne at Sherry's bar, 1956.

NEW YORK FOR FREE

Culture in the Park. The Metropolitan Opera, the New York Philharmonic, and the Public Theater give free performances in Central Park during the summer months. See page 182.
Native American Art. is free to see at the George Gustav Heye Center of the National Museum of the American Indian in the US Custom House in Lower Manhattan. See page 79.
The Garment District. The Fashion Institute of Technology (Seventh Avenue at 27th St) shows off legendary costumes, textiles, and the work of well-known photographers in its fashion museum. See page 159.
Free Travel. Statue of Liberty views are still absolutely free on the Staten Island Ferry (see page 88), while Lower Manhattan has a free bus service known as the Downtown Connection. See page 88.
Free Flowers. The Brooklyn Botanic Garden (see page 248) is free to the public on Tuesdays and until noon on Saturdays, also weekdays in the wintertime, while the Queens (see page 252) is free from November through March.
St Patrick's Cathedral. Visit one of the most spectacular Catholic churches in the United States. See page 180.

NEW YORK FOR FAMILIES

Children's Museum of Manhattan. A kiddy kingdom with inventive interactive exhibits; let them touch everything. See page 219.

Carousels. The entire family can ride on New York's carousels. The one in Central Park has 57 hand-carved horses and operates all year round, while the carousels in Bryant and Prospect parks are seasonal. See pages 182, 164, and 247.

Central Park. From rowing in the lake and ice-skating on the rinks to swimming in the pool and exploring more than 20 playgrounds, the park is fun for everyone. See page 182.

Sony Wonder Technology Lab. Wondering how to entertain those bored pre-teens? Look no more. See page 196.

Books. Between the Scholastic Store, Books of Wonder and the Strand, you're sure to find something to read on the plane home. You may meet an author or two as well. See page 87.

Intrepid Sea, Air, & Space Museum. Explore an aircraft carrier, view fighter jets, and get an up-close at Space Shuttle Enterprise. See page 164.

Fabulous food. Inexpensive snacks don't come any easier. If you only try one NY specialty, make it Nathan's Famous hot dogs on Coney Island. See page 250.

Children's Museum of the Arts. Based in SoHo, this is a successful cross between a museum and a very lively community center. See page 101.

Brooklyn Children's Museum. The oldest kids' museum in the US. See page 250.

Bronx Zoo. The largest urban zoo in America. See page 260.

Celebrating the Christmas season at Rockefeller Center began in 1933. The most popular attraction is the Christmas tree, which is spectacularly illuminated from just after Thanksgiving until 12th Night, January 6th.

Trump Tower.

BEST WALKS

Fifth Avenue. Few streets evoke the essence of the city as powerfully as Fifth Avenue, with its iconic Empire State Building, rollicking Rockefeller Center, stylish shopping, and elegant St Patrick's Cathedral. See page 180.

Madison Avenue. Between 42nd and 57th streets lies the spiritual home of advertising, with a skyline bristling with gleaming glass towers and streets typically jammed with taxis. See page 189.

Times Square. New York's "Crossroads of the World," swirls with irrepressible energy from the masses of people and the eye-popping neon wattage. See page 154.

Battery Park Esplanade. Perfect for a summer's day stroll, this leafy riverside path runs for over a mile, with great views of the Hudson River and the Statue of Liberty. See page 76.

Brooklyn Heights Promenade. This elegant walkway has handsome townhouses on one side and views of Manhattan and the East River on the other. See page 244.

BEST FESTIVALS AND EVENTS

TriBeCa Film Festival. Mingle with the stars and see first-run films on the banks of the Hudson River. Every spring. See page 52.

Ninth Avenue International Food Festival. A street fair in May when Ninth Avenue, from 37th Street to 57th Street, is lined with food stalls. See page 163.

Feast of San Gennaro. A cheesy but boisterous 10-day festival in September where Little Italy shows off, and the air is heavy with garlic. See page 123.

Next Wave Festival. Some of the most innovative sounds around can be heard at the Brooklyn Academy of Music (BAM) every fall. This is definitely a hot ticket. See page 247.

St Patrick's Day. Watch the wearing o' the green on Fifth Avenue every March 17.

Thanksgiving Day Parade. Started in the 1920s, this is the longest-running show on Broadway, brought to you by Macy's.

New York City Marathon. Five boroughs, 26.2 miles, tens of thousands of runners, millions of spectators. Beyond inspiring. First Sunday in November. See page 205.

The annual Macy's Thanksgiving Day parade features reminders of what the holiday stands for.

View from the 86th floor of the Empire State Building.

BEST VIEWS

Empire State Building. The view from the 86th-floor Observatory of this Art Deco landmark is incomparable. See page 173.

Top of the Rock. Although not quite as iconic as the Empire State Building, nonetheless the observation deck on the 70th floor of the Rockefeller Center offers terrific views of Central Park. See page 176.

Brooklyn Bridge. For one of the best, and most famous, of all views of the East River and Lower Manhattan. See page 86.

Statue of Liberty. Climb up to the crown for great views of New York and the harbor. See page 92.

MONEY-SAVING TIPS

Theater Tickets. The **TKTS Booth**, at Broadway and 47th Street by Times Square, has discounted seats (25–50 percent off) for that night's performances. It's open Monday through Sunday 3pm–8pm (2pm opening on Tue) for evening performances, and Wednesday, Thursday, Saturday, and Sunday 10am–2pm for matinees. Near South Street Seaport in Lower Manhattan, another booth in the South Street Seaport sells discounted tickets for the following night's shows. That booth is open Monday through Saturday 11am–6pm and Sundays 11am–4pm. Arrive early.

Special Passes. A way to save on New York's buses and subways is to buy a **MetroCard** (http://web.mta.info/metrocard; save between 5–25 percent depending on how much you spend). Available for 30 days, 7 days or per ride. **CityPass** saves if you plan to visit attractions. Buy the pass at the first destination; then you have several days in which to visit five others. You also avoid most ticket lines. Savings of almost 45 percent; plus discounts on shopping. Go to www.citypass.com. The **New York Pass** is a similar scheme. Go to www.newyorkpass.com**.**

Shopping. All visitors can find great bargains at New York's **sample sales**, where designers sell off end-of-season clothes, or smaller sizes. See page 108.

Aerial of Midtown Manhattan.

Interior of Grand Central Station.

TICKET MACHINES
TRACKS 31 TO 42
WAITING ROOM

Central Park in winter.

Hudson Street, Greenwich Village.

NEW TO EVERYONE

No one would ever say that New York is a city with an identity crisis, but it is a place of shifting identities just the same.

Forget about newness for a moment. Forget about the new restaurant exceling in molecular gastronomy, the new gallery showcasing contentious contemporary art. The new of New York is only part of the story. What truly defines the city is how it reinvents itself.

Peace-loving bicycle, West Village.

To American colonists, it was the capital of a new nation, if only for a short time. One hundred years later, it was a den of corruption, run by the greed of Tammany Hall. Jump forward another century, and it was welcoming international diplomacy to the United Nations Headquarters.

This journey from fame to infamy and back again has played out time and again. The oyster beds of New York Harbor were the country's most productive at the end of the 1800s until the city's waterways became among country's most polluted a few decades later. These days, yearly swimming races are held in the Hudson and East rivers and there's talk of reintroducing the oyster. If we could set our watches to the financial cycle, we'd all be rich, but a place that has seen stock market crashes, construction booms, bankruptcy scares and multi-billion-dollar tech IPOs, comes to expect ups and downs. Crime rates go from historic highs to historic lows in barely a decade. Even the legendary Yankees have faced famine (though mostly they feast).

Street sign on Park Avenue.

It's no wonder that people looking to reinvent themselves flock here. Actors, chefs, even office drones test their mettle against the city. Yes, Sinatra's words still ring true about making it here, but it's more about emulating the city, trying on different masks and seeing which ones fit. No wonder the Halloween Parade is so popular.

What makes traveling to New York so exciting is the possibility of experiencing a bit of that reinvention yourself. After catching a performance at the Met, will you become an opera addict? Will your taste buds be won over by an ethnic cuisine you've always avoided? After seeing the speed and efficiency of the subways, will you advocate for public transportation in your hometown? Perhaps not, but at the very least you'll be curious to revisit New York, maybe years later, to witness the latest version of this always-evolving metropolis.

Guggenheim Museum.

NEW YORK, NEW YORKERS

New York gave us the phrase 'the melting pot,' and it's more diverse than ever, attracting those who yearn to fade into the crowd, to see their name in lights, or simply to find a home of like-minded souls.

The first thing that strikes a visitor about New Yorkers is the talk. Well-dressed men and women fearlessly walk through traffic while barking into cell phones. Groups huddle at rooftop bars, joyfully recounting adventures while dining and drinking alfresco. Vendors holler, assuring you their purses are genuine. Everyone has an opinion, a story to sell. All you have to do is listen.

Stock market and sculpture

In such a fast-moving, densely packed metropolis, there's a loud background to speak over, but more surprising is the range and depth of discourse. Intellectual voracity can be seen on the street at café tables with chessboards, and on the subway in the range of literature being read. You can feel the New Yorkers' lust for fact, knowledge, debate and opinion; you can barely heft it in the sheer weight of the Sunday *New York Times.*

Cerebral and cultural lives here have their rituals, temples, and haunts, like museum and gallery openings. It is not a minority thing hidden away in exclusive speakeasies, where entrance is gained by murmuring a secret password at a sliding door panel; it is the stock market and sculpture, poetry and particle physics – a polyglot landscape of lectures, plays, concerts, libraries, films, and, of course, parties. It is the casual association of great minds: Tom Wolfe stalking Brooklyn streets, Sonny Rollins practicing his sax on the Williamsburg Bridge.

Culture and intellect transform the individual, but they also give identity to the mass, to the city as a whole. In his book *The Art of the City: Views and Versions of New York,* Peter Conrad writes, 'Every city requires its own myth to justify its presumption of centrality,' and he cites annotators of New York from songwriter George M. Cohan to painter Saul Steinberg, whose famous cover for the *New Yorker* was of a world shrinking to the far horizon, away from a great, spreading Manhattan.

Outside the Lincoln Center.

Alexander Alland Jr, former chair of anthropology at Columbia University, said, 'The intellectual life is why I am a New Yorker. It's why I stay here. I spend my summers in Europe, and when they ask me if I'm an American, I say, "No, I'm a New Yorker." I don't know about everyone else, but for me that's a positive statement.'

Union Square Market.

New York's rise to intellectual prominence did not begin until the 1850s. Through the Colonial era and the early 19th century, New York was at best the third city in the US, behind Boston and Philadelphia, until the publishing industry decamped here. New York had a larger population, and publishers were seeking more customers. As seagulls follow great ships, writers, editors, and illustrators came in the publishers' wake.

Meanwhile, at the top of the New York economic scale, captains of commerce and industry began to endow museums and to support individual artists. At the bottom of the scale, each wave of immigrants enriched and diversified the intellectual community. City College, established in 1849, acted as the great pedagogue for those without wealth, and came to be known as 'the poor man's Harvard.'

URBAN WOODLAND

When Henry Hudson sailed up the river that bears his name, his first mate, Robert Juett, wrote: 'We found a land full of great tall oaks, with grass and flowers, as pleasant as ever has been seen.' New York still has over 29,000 acres (11,700 hectares) of parks, of which 10,000 acres (4,000 hectares) are in more or less their natural state. Peregrine falcons nest on Midtown skyscraper ledges, and coyotes prowl from Westchester County down into the Bronx.

Frederick Law Olmsted, the architect who laid out Central Park, wrote that 'the contemplation of natural scenes… is favorable to the health and vigor of men.'

Immigrants

The German influx of 1848, the Irish flight from famine, migrations of Jews, Italians, Greeks, Chinese, Koreans, and Vietnamese – all brought knowledge and culture to New York, making this American city cosmopolitan. In 1933, the New School for Social Research encouraged that rich resource by founding the University in Exile (now the Graduate Faculty of Political and Social Science) as a graduate school staffed by European scholars who escaped the Nazi regime. The international

Andy Warhol once said: 'When reporters asked the Pope what he liked best about New York, he replied "Tutti buoni" – everything is good. That's my philosophy exactly.'

dynamic continues with the Soviet Jews in Brighton Beach and the West Indians in Queens joined by the Southeast Asians of Queens' Elmhurst district. Nearly 20 percent of the Brooklyn population speaks Spanish at home, while a smaller number of people speak Russian, French or a French Creole, Chinese, Yiddish, Italian, Polish, Hebrew, or Arabic. Thousands of people speak Cantonese, Urdu, Bengali, Greek, Korean, and Albanian. There are more Greeks in New York than in any city but Athens, and more Dominicans than in any city but Santo Domingo.

Public schools offer bilingual instruction. In some neighborhoods, traffic signs, advertisements, and subway signs announce in two or three languages, most often in Spanish or Chinese, the city's unofficial second and third languages. City agencies must also provide information in Russian, Korean, Italian and French Creole. There are at least a dozen non-English newspapers published in the city itself and countless others imported. Driving tests can be taken and banking business done in other languages. Automatic cash machines offer transactions in Spanish, Chinese, and French.

The minority majority

Never in the American mainstream, New York is one of the few minority-majority cities, where the majority are from an ethnic minority. The promise for immigrants in New York is a place of opportunity. Some variation of the American dream still lives on these streets, and immigrants come eager to share in it. Once a migrant group gets into a line of work, others follow in the same trade. In recent years Koreans have dominated the grocery business, Chinese have manned the garment industry, and Indians or Pakistanis run newsstands. Greek coffee shops and Latino bodegas have joined the New York landscape, and every nationality turns the wheel of a yellow cab.

The New York mix is defined by immigration, and also by artists. New York's bards date

Charging Bull sculpture, Bowling Green Park.

> *New York taxis date from 1907, when John Hertz founded the Yellow Cab Company. He chose this color after reading a report stating that yellow was the easiest color to spot.*

back to at least 1855, when Walt Whitman published *Leaves of Grass.* The late Lou Reed, photographer Robert Mapplethorpe, novelist Jay McInerney, and filmmakers Woody Allen and Martin Scorsese, have all taken New York as their muse. These days, the works of authors like Jonathan Safran Foer or Paul Auster, singer Alicia Keys, comedian Tina Fey, and many other young luminaries, continue to craft the world's image of the city.

Greenwich Village became an urban version of the artists' colony, a home to creators of all stripes, the place that gave Eugene O'Neill one of his early stages in the 1920s (at the Provincetown Playhouse) and Bob Dylan a bandstand in the 1960s (at Folk City). Miles Uptown, Harlem was home to a black intelligentsia that included the writers Langston

Brooklyn Academy of Music.

Hughes (see page 234), James Weldon Johnson, and James Baldwin, plus the political theorist W.E.B. Du Bois and the photographer James Van Der Zee, whose record of his era appeared decades later in the album *Harlem on My Mind.*

Urban pioneers

When creative people discovered SoHo in the 1970s, it was hard to get a cab to stop there. Their presence led to the neighborhood's rebirth, and when it became too expensive for them, they moved to Alphabet City (avenues A, B, C, and D) on the Lower East Side of Manhattan, or across the East River to Greenpoint and Williamsburg, or to a part of Brooklyn called DUMBO, for Down Under Manhattan Bridge Overpass. Trendy stores, bars,

> *Gone are the days of graffiti-covered subway cars and prostitutes loitering in Times Square. Of the 25 largest cities in the US, New York consistently ranks as the safest.*

Everyone in New York is Irish on St Patrick's Day.

Artists' studios in Queens.

and restaurants followed, rents soared, and the artists scoped out new territories like Red Hook in Brooklyn and Astoria in Queens.

Pop culture and high culture are often indistinguishable. Tom Stoppard and Stephen Sondheim have regular Broadway hits, while a gospel version of *Oedipus at Colonus* sold out at the Brooklyn Academy of Music. Religion is a matter both of passion and of intellectual rigor. There are almost a dozen Roman Catholic colleges in New York City, an Islamic seminary on Queens Boulevard and *shtibels* – houses of study – where Hasidim pursue theology.

News nexus

The intellectual force of New York sends ripples far beyond the city. The principal network news in the United States originates not from the nation's capital, but from New York. One of the last major news magazines, *Time*, and two national newspapers, *The New York Times* and the *Wall Street Journal*, are published here, and most of the leading critics of theater, film, art, dance, and music make their pronouncements from Manhattan.

> *Walk through Central Park in the summer and you're sure to see games of softball, basketball, volleyball, soccer, tennis – even lawn bowling, croquet, and cricket.*

Without any of those publications, important as they are, New York intellectual life would pulse just as vigorously. Outwardly expressed in individual taste and style, it has little to do with celebrity or vogue. The intellectual sweep is an eclectic striving for search and discovery. So many New Yorkers share a biographical tale that has become mythic itself. With variations, the story goes like this:

An able young man or woman feels misunderstood, unappreciated, surrounded by what playwright Eugene O'Neill called 'spiritual middle-classers,' and yearns to escape from small-town minds, to be among people with a broader vision. Perhaps he yearns to reinvent himself, to shake loose the trappings of his youth. Perhaps she has a dream, an aspiration too great or too strange to realize on hometown

The Strand Book Store.

Alphabet City.

turf. So they come here. Whether or not dreams are realized, even in part, they come to feel the city has spoiled them for any other place. Despite, or even because of the pressure, the pace, and the grime, they discover a vigorous sense of being alive.

Rich stimulation

'New York draws the cosmopolite, the person who wants to be challenged the most, who needs the most varied and rich stimulation,' said a well-known Jungian analyst, Dr James Hillman. 'It is the person who is full of possibilities, but who needs New York to draw them out. You come to New York to find the ambience that will evoke your best. You do not necessarily know precisely what that might be, but you come to New York to discover it.

> *Although New Yorkers are known for their fast walking pace, a survey of urban walking speeds put them in eighth place. Singapore came first, followed by Copenhagen.*

'If there were a god of New York it would be the Greeks' Hermes, the Romans' Mercury. He embodies New York qualities: the quick exchange, the fastness of language and style, craftiness, the mixing of people and crossing of borders, imagination.' And cosmopolitan, in every sense, is what the Big Apple is. From the lines of sparkly clubbers and diners in SoHo and the Meatpacking District to the wild costumes in the Greenwich Village Halloween parade, New York is more than just a melting pot; it is a hothouse nursery for fantastic hybrids of talent and expression.

A great bookstore is a hub of imaginative activity, and in New York the Strand Book Store is arguably the best. In a former clothing store at Broadway and East 12th Street in Manhattan, the Strand carries some 2 million volumes of such variety that on a single table titles might range from *The Sonata Since Beethoven* to *Civil Aircraft of the World.*

Writers Anaïs Nin and Saul Bellow, painter David Hockney and poet/rock singer Patti Smith numbered among the Strand's regular customers. Smith was on both sides of the counter, as she also worked at the store.

New York has great window-shopping.

The complete city

So what stitches the fabric of reinvention and the rigors of intellectual life together? What draws the filmmakers, the flower vendors, and the restaurateurs to pack up and move here, and intellectuals to end their contemplations here? Back to Dr Hillman: 'New York is the city of rampant creativity, of abundant imagination, whether in advertising or the theater or the stock market. Any syndrome that might characterize another city is found in New York: manic energy, depression and hopelessness, the extreme excitement of the hysteric. Psychologically, New York is the complete city.'

New Yorkers *do* talk. They talk loud, and they talk a lot – enough to call it a defining characteristic. But here in New York, they also walk the walk.

FACTS THAT FIT

Biggest: Ahnighito, the biggest meteorite 'in captivity,' weighs 34 tons (31,000kg) and is on display at the American Museum of Natural History.

Smallest: a Morningside Heights couple claims to own the smallest apartment in the city, a 175-sq-ft (16-sq-meter) studio they bought in 2009 for $150,000.

Longest: after Broadway leaves the city, it becomes the Albany Post Road, and travels all the way to New York's state capital – a distance of 175 miles (282km).

Oldest: the oldest grave in New York is located in the back of Lower Manhattan's Trinity Churchyard, and dates from 1681.

Waterlogged: the record time for swimming the 28.5 miles (46km) around the island of Manhattan is 5 hours and 44 minutes.

Making the switch: Radio City's Rockettes use more than 1,300 costumes during their annual 90-minute Christmas Spectacular show.

Flipping the switch: Thomas Edison turned on New York's first public electric lights on Wall Street in 1882.

City shore: New York City has 14 miles (22.5km) of beaches. The best known is Coney Island, with its carnival rides and the original Nathan's hot-dog stand.

City core: New York City's nickname of 'the Big Apple' originated in the 1920s in a series of newspaper articles about horse racing.

DECISIVE DATES

1524
Italian explorer Giovanni da Verrazano sights the territory that is now New York, but doesn't land his ship.

1609
Englishman Henry Hudson weighs anchor on the island, then sails the *Half Moon* up the river that now bears his name.

1624
The Dutch West India Company sets up a trading post on the southern tip of the island at what is now Battery Park.

1626
The provincial director-general of the New Amsterdam settlement, Peter Minuit, purchases Manhattan from the Algonquin tribe for 60 guilders' worth of trinkets – the equivalent of $24 in today's currency.

Peter Stuyvesant.

1630s
Dutch farmers settle land in what is now Brooklyn and the Bronx.

1647
Peter Stuyvesant becomes director-general and soon suppresses political opposition.

The trial of Peter Zenger, 1734.

1653
Peter Stuyvesant builds a fence along what is now known as Wall Street to protect New Amsterdam from British incursion.

1660
Nearly half the population is foreign born. Irish-born Americans are the largest group in the city, then German-born Americans.

1664
In the first year of the sea war between England and Holland, Stuyvesant is forced to surrender the town to the British without a fight. New Amsterdam is renamed New York, after King Charles II's brother, James, the Duke of York.

1673
The Dutch recapture New York and rename it New Orange, again without fighting taking place.

1674
New York is returned to the British by the Anglo-Dutch Treaty of Westminster.

1690
With a population of 3,900, New York is now the third-largest town in North America.

1735
Newspaper publisher Peter Zenger is tried for slandering the British crown. He is acquitted,

establishing the precedent for freedom of the press.

1765
In accordance with the Stamp Act, unfair taxes are levied against the early colonists.

1770
Skirmishes between the Sons of Liberty and the British culminate in the Battle of Golden Hill, the first blood to be shed prior to the Revolutionary War.

1776
George Washington loses the Battle of Long Island, and British troops occupy New York until 1783.

1789
New York becomes the capital of the United States of America, but only retains this status for 18 months. George Washington is inaugurated as President of the United States at the site of the Federal Hall, Wall Street.

1790
A first official census reveals that the city of New York now has a population of over 33,000.

1792
A popular, open-air money market is established beneath a buttonwood tree on Wall Street.

1811
An important decision is made affecting the city's future appearance: all streets are to be laid out in the form of a grid.

1820
An official Stock Exchange replaces the outdoor money market that has been held on Wall Street.

1825
The economic importance of New York increases sharply as a result of the construction of the Erie Canal, which connects the Hudson River with the Great Lakes.

1835
Manhattan, between South Broad and Wall Street, is ravaged by the 'Great Fire.'

1857
William M. 'Boss' Tweed, elected to the County Board of Supervisors, launches a career of notorious corruption.

1858
Calvert Vaux and Frederick Law Olmsted submit plans for Central Park, which is to be the 'lungs' of the city.

The Great Fire of 1835.

The American Civil War.

1860
New York becomes the largest metropolis in the United States; in the previous 30 years, Brooklyn's population increased 10 times over.

1861
The Civil War begins, and many New Yorkers are recruited for the cause.

1863
The Draft Riots rage throughout New York, and it is believed that around 100 people are killed.

1869
The American Museum of Natural History opens.

1870s
William M. 'Boss' Tweed, of Tammany Hall notoriety, is arrested, tried, and taken to a jail he helped to build, before escaping to Spain.

1880
The Metropolitan Museum of Art opens.

1883
The Brooklyn Bridge opens, and there is a first gala performance by the Metropolitan Opera.

1886
The Statue of Liberty, a gift from France, is unveiled on Liberty Island.

1892
Ellis Island in New York Harbor becomes the point of entry for immigrants to the United States.

1898
New York's five boroughs are united under one municipal government.

1904
An underground subway system is established.

1911
The Triangle Fire alerts the public to the appalling living conditions of immigrants.

1913
Construction of the world's tallest skyscraper, the Woolworth Building, begins. It is superseded in 1930 by the Chrysler Building.

Constructing the subway.

1929
Wall Street crashes, and with it comes the end of the Jazz Age and the start of the Great Depression.

1931
After 14 months of construction, the Empire State Building opens ahead of schedule and is heralded as a great success.

1933
Fiorello LaGuardia is elected mayor and uses Federal money to fight the devastating effects of the Great Depression.

World War II poster.

1939
Ten years after its foundation by Abby Aldrich Rockefeller, the Museum of Modern Art moves into its new home on 53rd Street. The World's Fair opens in Flushing, Queens.

1941
The United States enters World War II.

1946
The United Nations begins meeting in New York. The permanent buildings on East 42nd–48th streets are completed six years later.

1959
The Frank Lloyd Wright-designed Guggenheim Museum opens. Work begins on Lincoln Center.

1970
Economic decline sets in, which continues until around 1976.

1973
The World Trade Center opens. With its 110-story Twin Towers, it is the tallest building in the world.

1975
Impending bankruptcy is avoided only by obtaining a bridging loan from the Federal government.

1977
A 27-hour power outage occurs, with widespread looting and vandalism.

1978
Ed Koch becomes mayor of New York and remains in office until 1989.

1982
The IBM building opens, followed by the AT&T building in 1983.

1986
Battery Park City opens.

1987
'Black Monday' on Wall Street. Shares suffer a 30 percent drop in value.

1990
David Dinkins becomes the first African-American mayor.

Remembering the fallen on September 11.

1993
A bomb explodes below the World Trade Center. Six people are killed and over 1,000 are injured.

1997
Mayor Rudolph Giuliani's 'zero tolerance' campaign is effective, and there are major declines in crime.

2001
Terrorists crash two planes into the World Trade Center's towers. Nearly 3,000 people are killed.

2003
Smoking is banned in bars and restaurants. There is another huge power outage, but this one is met with good spirits.

2004
The Time Warner Center in Columbus Circle opens.

2008
The global financial crisis begins on Wall Street, as banks fail and stocks plunge.

Citi Field.

2009
New baseball stadiums open for the Mets and the Yankees.

2011
Ten years after the terrorist attacks of September 11, 2001, the memorial opens. The Occupy Wall Street movement descends on Lower Manhattan.

2012
Hurricane Sandy cripples the subway and floods lower Manhattan, causing extensive damage.

2013
Mayor Bloomberg unveils CitiBike, Manhattan's first bike sharing program. Democrat Bill de Blasio is elected as the city's new mayor.

2015
One World Trade Center, the tallest building in the Western Hemisphere (1,776ft/541 meters), opens its Observatory to visitors. The Whitney Museum moves downtown to the Meatpacking District.

Immigrants arrive in the land of the free.

THE MAKING OF NEW YORK

In its youth New York was a small outpost of trade and politics. Through the immigration of people and ideas the city matured into an international center of finance, culture, and diplomacy.

It's hard to believe it all started as a small farm. For the Lenape, a grouping of Algonquin tribes concentrated around the Delaware and Hudson rivers, Manahatta (island of many hills) was a wild place of streams and pine, occasionally burned and used for seasonal crops. Local legend has it that Peter Minuit, an official for the Dutch, bought the island from a tribe of Lenape known as the Canarsie (or Canarsee) for a box of trinkets worth 60 guilders, about $24, which wouldn't buy a square inch of today's Big Apple. Minuit came to govern the small village in the area approximately where Bowling Green is now located. Foreign to the notion of land ownership, the Indians may not have understood the deal, but Minuit didn't understand tribal territory either, so the tribe he paid may not have had a claim to Manhattan at all.

Detail of the painting Purchase of Manhattan by Peter Minuit, 1626, by Alfred Friedericks.

New Amsterdam

Despite occasional skirmishes, relations between the Algonquin Indians and European settlers had been cordial, if not exactly friendly, but they deteriorated when the Dutch settled for good. Theft, murder, and land disputes turned into a cycle of savagery that led to the murder of a Native American woman and the Peach War of 1655.

The Dutch were not the first European arrivals. In 1524, Giovanni da Verrazano was struck by the Lower Bay's 'commodiousness and beauty,' but Europe paid no regard until Henry Hudson sailed under a Dutch flag into the natural harbor in 1609. Hudson traded, particularly in furs, and in 1621 the Dutch West India Company acquired exclusive trading rights to territory from Cape May (New Jersey) to New England. Trading posts were set along the coast and rivers, and about 50 Walloon Protestants were sent to settle Nut Island (Governor's Island) off the tip of Manhattan. Soon the camp spread to the southern end of Manhattan, which settlers named New Amsterdam.

The Walloons and Dutch were joined by convicts, slaves, religious zealots, and profiteers, with tribes coming to trade occasionally. In 1647, the company sent Peter Stuyvesant to tame the wild New Amsterdam. He cracked down on smuggling and tax evasion, and kept order with

George Washington en route to fight the British.

the whip and the branding iron. Stuyvesant got things done, but made few friends in New Amsterdam. In 17 years, he established a hospital, a prison, a school, and a post office. He also erected a barricade against the Indians and the British, from river to river on the site of what is now Wall Street, hence its present name.

Dutch to British

The thriving Dutch town was under pressure from the British on both sides, and in 1664 King Charles II sent four warships to seize New Amsterdam. Stuyvesant was ready for war, but the townspeople were happy for a chance to be rid of him. Without a shot fired, the English raised the Union flag and renamed the town New York, in honor of the king's brother. The Dutch retook the town about 10 years later in the Second Anglo-Dutch War, but quickly negotiated a return to British hands, again without bloodshed.

Director-general Peter Stuyvesant (1646–64) was known as 'Peg Leg' or 'Old Silver Nails' because of his wooden leg studded with nails.

The seeds of New York's independence were sown in 1765 with the Stamp Act, among a battery of legislation passed to assert King George III's authority and plump the royal coffers. The Stamp Act levied tax on everything from tobacco to playing cards and brought the cry, 'No taxation without representation.'

Angry mobs stormed a government stronghold and terrorized officials until the British repealed the act. A later tax on imported items like paper, lead, and tea followed in 1767, this time backed by the English army, the dreaded Redcoats. A battle of nerves rattled until January 1770, when the rebels and Redcoats fought the Battle of Golden Hill.

After Boston's example on April 22, 1774, New Yorkers dumped tea from an English cargo ship into the harbor. A year later, the 'shot heard 'round the world' was fired at Lexington, Massachusetts, and the American Revolution began. At the Declaration of Independence's reading in New York, a mob raced to topple King George III's statue in Bowling Green.

Erie Canal grain barges towed down the Hudson River to New York City, 1870s.

Legend has it the statue was melted into musket balls, then fired at the British troops.

General George Washington chased the British out of Boston, then came to New York, where he fared poorly. British troops beat Washington's fledgling army from Brooklyn through Manhattan, to a grim defeat at White Plains, New York. A brutal seven-year occupation followed, but in 1785, Washington returned to celebrate an American victory. Four years later he returned again, to place his hand on a Bible for the oath of office as America's first president. For the next 18 months, New York was the nation's capital.

The Wiechquaekeck Trail, an Algonquin trade route, ran all the way to the state capital at Albany, crossing the island of Manhattan diagonally. This is now Broadway.

Growing pains

A small town at the turn of the 19th century, New York's population was about 35,000. A yellow fever outbreak scared some residents off to the open spaces of Greenwich Village, but most occupied the crooked lanes south of Canal Street. The public debated the new Constitution; brokers traded in the shade of a buttonwood tree on Wall Street; five people died in a riot against Columbia University doctors who robbed graves for their anatomy labs; and buffalo were brought from the western territories. Politically, the town was split between Democrats, represented by Aaron Burr, who was Thomas Jefferson's vice-president, and Federalists, headed by Alexander Hamilton, the nation's first Secretary of the Treasury. In 1804 their years of feuding were settled in a duel when Burr shot and killed Hamilton.

The 350-mile (565km) Erie Canal from Lake Erie to Buffalo drew cargo from across the globe into the East River Harbor (now South Street Seaport). Business boomed, the population soared to 312,000 (1840), and real-estate prices rocketed. John Jacob Astor and Cornelius Vanderbilt grew rich on property and shipping.

By the 1850s, the *Evening Post* reported, 'The city of New York belongs almost as much to the South as to the North,' as Mayor Fernando Wood supported the 'continuance of slave labor

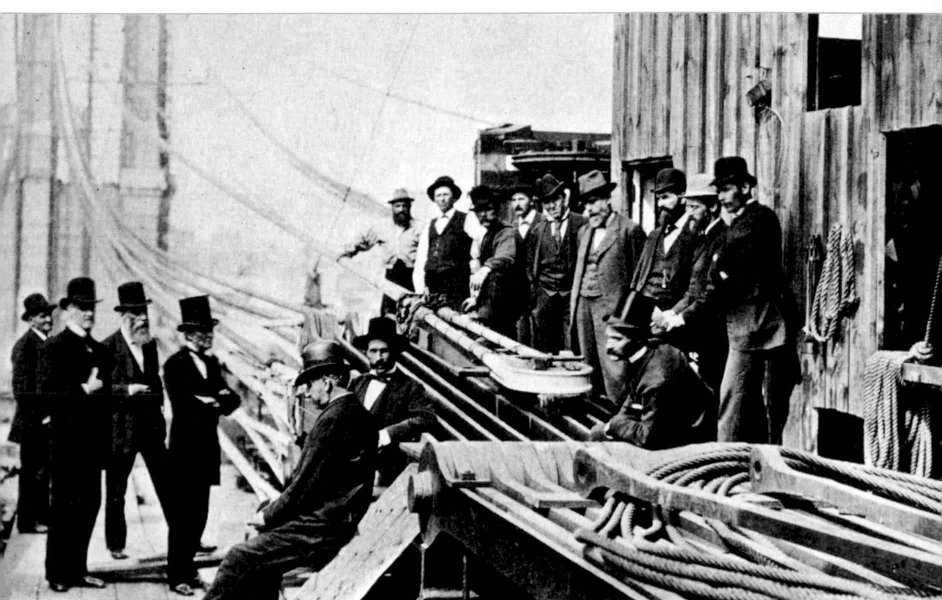

The opening of the Brooklyn Bridge.

and the prosperity of the slave master.' When civil war was inevitable, he proposed that the city declare itself independent to protect its business interests with the South.

In February 1860, Abraham Lincoln spoke at philanthropist Peter Cooper's free college. Lincoln's words and delivery riveted the audience, and copies of the Cooper Union address crossed the country. Lincoln won the November election without one Southern electoral vote, and five months later Confederate artillery bombarded Fort Sumter. At the Plymouth Church of Brooklyn, abolitionist minister Henry Ward Beecher shrieked for 'war redder than blood and fiercer than fire,' and that is what he got.

NEW YORK WORLD'S FAIRS

The American Institute Fair was held every year in New York City from 1829 until the end of the 19th century. This is frequently considered to be the first World's Fair, although it was quite small compared to later events. In 1829, 30,000 people attended, first at Niblo's Garden and then later at the Crystal Palace.

The Exhibition of the Industry of All Nations in 1853 was a World's Fair held in the wake of the highly successful 1851 Great Exhibition in London. It showcased industrial achievements and national pride.

The 1939–40 New York World's Fair, on the current site of Flushing Meadows-Corona Park, allowed visitors to take a look at 'the world of tomorrow.' More than 40 million people attended its exhibits in two seasons. It was the first exhibition with a futuristic theme, and one of the main purposes was to lift the spirits of the American people in the midst of the Great Depression.

The 1964–5 New York World's Fair was again held in Flushing Meadows-Corona Park. The Space Age was one of the major themes of this popular event, and more than 51 million people visited. General Motors updated their *Futurama* show for what proved to be the fair's most popular attraction. Many of the pavilions from 1964 have been renovated or reused, to the improvement of the area and the benefit of New Yorkers.

A woodcut illustrates the draft riots in New York, July 13–16, 1863.

Dark-horse presidential candidate Abraham Lincoln made an electrifying speech at a New York college in 1860. A year later, the Civil War started and tore the country apart.

In April 1861, Lincoln called for volunteers to put down the rebellious South, and New York sent 8,000 soldiers, including Irish and German regiments. Patriotism swung into vogue. Tiffany & Co. crafted military regalia and Brooks Brothers stitched uniforms.

Draft riots

The war dragged on, hopes of a speedy victory faded, New York's fighting spirit began to sag, and defeatism turned to rage when Lincoln enacted conscription in 1862. When it emerged that the wealthy could buy their way out for $300, the city erupted. One July morning in 1863, a mob of several thousand stormed the Third Avenue draft office, routed police, and torched the whole block. Over several days, an orphanage on Fifth Avenue was burned, 18 black men were lynched, mutilated and left hanging from lampposts, and Union Army regiments were recalled to quell the Draft Riots. (The period of the Draft Riots was dramatically realized in Martin Scorsese's *Gangs of New York*.)

Two years later the Civil War ended, and Lincoln's body was returned to the city to lie in state at New York's City Hall.

THE GREAT FIRE OF 1835

On the night of December 16, 1835, fire tore through New York's Downtown business district and burned for over 15 hours. Raging from the East River almost as far as Broad Street, more than 600 buildings, including the Merchant's Exchange and more than half of the city's insurance companies, were destroyed with a cost of over $20 million. The blaze spread, propelled by fierce winds, in just 15 minutes to 50 timber buildings. The volunteer fire department was disorganized and ill-equipped to take on the task, handicapped by lack of wells or hoses, and the East River being frozen. Fortunately, only two people died in the blaze.

After the Civil War, immigrants arrived from Europe. Italians crammed into Mulberry Street and Greenwich Village. Jews fled anti-Semitic pogroms in Russia, flooding the Lower East Side, and Chinese settled around Mott Street.

During the 1860s, the city was run by Tammany Hall, and Tammany Hall was run by William M. 'Boss' Tweed. A larger-than-life and highly corrupt figure, Tweed ran the city as his personal piggy bank and fiefdom (see page 42). In 1898, the five boroughs formed a single government, bringing New York City's total population to 3.4 million people.

By the end of the 19th century, J.P. Morgan was on the way to creating the first billion-dollar American company (US Steel), John D. Rockefeller struck pay dirt with Standard Oil, and Andrew Carnegie established Carnegie Hall, where Tchaikovsky conducted the opening gala.

Fashion and famine

Abandoning their Downtown haunts to the immigrants, the upper crust began a 50-year march up fashionable Fifth Avenue, leaving a trail of mansions in their wake. This is when the social elite came to be known as the 'Four Hundred,' from the 400 guests at Mrs William Astor's annual ball. While the Four Hundred gorged themselves at lavish parties, Downtown New York was as wretched as ever. Every day 2,000 immigrants poured into the new Ellis Island immigration station, packing tenements and sweatshops ever tighter. Despite work by reformers like photo-journalist Jacob Riis, it took a tragedy to spur change.

The Triangle Shirtwaist Factory Fire, 1911.

Death trap

On March 25, 1911, as the five o'clock bell rang, fire lapped the top floors of the Triangle Shirtwaist Company near Washington Square. Around 600 workers were inside, and stairways were locked or barred by flames. Girls jumped from the eighth and ninth floors, thudding onto the sidewalk. The blaze lasted only about 10 minutes, but over 140 workers, mostly Jewish or Italian women no older than 20, were killed. The two company owners were acquitted, but the tragedy did stimulate labor reforms.

BOSS TWEED AND TAMMANY HALL

During the 1860s, William M. 'Boss' Tweed was the most powerful politician in New York State. A man of voracious appetites, he ran the local Democratic Party as though it were his own. The root of Tammany power was the lower classes, who saw Tweed as one of them. He was a former bookkeeper and fireman who transformed into a Robin Hood figure, robbing the rich and cutting the poor in for a slice.

Tweed did do some good for the poor, but most of his energy went into lining his own pockets. City contracts were padded with extra funds, and a percentage of the total – sometimes the largest percentage – fattened Tweed's wallet. On one single morning, Tweed and his cronies raked $5.5 million on a contract for the New York City Courthouse (aka the 'Tweed Courthouse') in Lower Manhattan. After more than a decade as New York's uncrowned monarch and three years of litigation, Tweed was sent to Ludlow Street Prison, which, ironically, he had been responsible for building.

Hardly a typical jailbird, on one of the frequent visits to his Madison Avenue brownstone, Tweed ducked out the back and fled to Spain. He was recaptured and died in prison of pneumonia less than two years later.

World War I had little impact on New York City. American infantrymen, known as Doughboys, returned home to find business booming, the population growing, and an era of good feelings in the city. Prohibition was a dreary note to kick off the 'Roaring Twenties,' though the good times seemed better and the parties wilder now that drinking was taboo.

The free-spirited Twenties brought freethinkers, too. Cheap rents and an 'old quarter' atmosphere attracted writers, artists, and radicals to Greenwich Village. John Reed, Emma Goldman, Louise Bryant, and Edna St Vincent Millay advocated everything from communism to free love. Eugene O'Neill knocked 'em back at a speakeasy called the Hell Hole, and lit up the theater world at the Provincetown Playhouse.

The city may have been in a handbasket en route to hell, but New York kept on partying – and kept on spending, too. In the 1920s, the city's stock-buying binge didn't look like it would ever slow down; it didn't matter that trades were on credit, or that the city was being bilked of millions by Tammany Hall. As long

The Empire State Building under construction.

Prohibition backfired in Manhattan. Twice as many speakeasies were estimated to be in New York City after Prohibition began as there were legitimate bars before.

as the money kept rolling, the lights burned on Broadway, and Mayor Jimmy Walker was smiling, everything was OK. Gossip columnist and broadcaster Walter Winchell said, 'In the 1920s the American people were hell-bent for prosperity and riches. And they wanted a politician who was hell-bent only for re-election… a man who would respect the national rush to get rich, who would accept greed, avarice, and the lust for quick gain as a legitimate expression of the will of the people… Walker knew what the people wanted.'

Black Thursday

On October 24, 1929 – Black Thursday – the bottom fell out of the stock market, and the goodwill for Mayor Jimmy Walker went with it. The Great Depression hit New York hard; total income dropped more than half, unemployment leaped to 25 percent, and breadlines snaked along Broadway. Groucho Marx said the city was on the skids 'when the pigeons started feeding the people in Central Park.'

Before Walker could ride out a second term, his administration unraveled. Investigations into city government found a nest of corruption second only to the Tweed Ring. Governor Franklin D. Roosevelt reviewed the charges, and Walker knew he couldn't walk away without a political,

JIMMY AND THE JAZZ AGE

Presiding over Jazz Age New York was Mayor James Walker. In the 1920s, a blossoming of art and culture throughout the city, but especially in Harlem (known as the first Harlem Renaissance), filled the streets. Duke Ellington and Count Basie played the Cotton Club, Small's Paradise, and other ritzy after-hours clubs. Alcohol flowed, despite Prohibition. A gambler, lady's man, and former Tin Pan Alley songwriter, Walker left the running of the city to Tammany Hall hacks. Meanwhile, he played craps with reporters and flaunted his affair with a Broadway actress. When he raised his own salary by $10,000, Walker told critics, 'Think what it would cost if I worked full time.'

and personal, skinning. He resigned his office in 1932, and took the next ship to Europe.

About a year later, the new mayor in City Hall was Fiorello LaGuardia – a small, plump man with an animated face, a line in rumpled suits, and none of Walker's finesse. He was quick-witted, savvy, and determined to whip the city into shape. Hard-nosed and almost ruthless, but by turn paternalistic and warm, the man who ordered gangster Lucky Luciano off the streets read comics over the radio every Sunday. LaGuardia had critics, but for a city ravaged by the Depression, he was their closest thing to a savior. After his 1933 election, LaGuardia joined Franklin Roosevelt's New Deal, launching programs to revive the economy. His government built bridges, highways, and housing, and found work for artists and writers in the Federally funded Works Progress Administration.

At the same time, big projects begun in the 1920s came to completion. Art Deco changed the skyline of the city with the Chrysler Building in 1930, the Empire State Building and the Waldorf-Astoria Hotel in 1931, and Rockefeller Center in 1933. The 1939–40 New York World's Fair attracted more than 44 million people to Queens for the 'Worlds of Tomorrow,' at Flushing Meadows-Corona Park, where the Xerox copier, the electronic computer, and television premiered to the American public.

Effects of the Wall Street crash of 1929.

Former mayor Ed Koch.

In 1941, the US entered World War II, and the city was swept into the war effort. Actual and supposed German spies were arrested, Japanese families were incarcerated on Ellis Island, and blackouts were ordered – even the torch of the Statue of Liberty was turned off. In the basement of a Columbia University physics lab, Enrico Fermi and Leo Szilard experimented with atomic fission, groundwork for what was later called the Manhattan Project: the atomic bomb.

Postwar boom and bust

The postwar United Nations came to the city in 1947 and Idlewild (now Kennedy) Airport opened in 1948. New York had peace, a healthy economy, and the riches of technology. The glass-walled UN Secretariat Building brought a new sleek look to Midtown and kicked off the 1950s modernity. Glass-box skyscrapers lined Park and Madison avenues, then spread to the West Side and the Financial District. Birdland, the bebop nightclub named for saxophonist Charlie Parker, opened on Broadway, and Franklin National Bank issued the world's first credit card.

V-E Day in Times Square, May 7, 1945.

Then, as in many northeastern cities, came a postwar decline. The middle class moved to the suburbs, corporations relocated, and poor blacks and Hispanics flocked into a run-down city. Tensions were dramatized in the 1957 version of *Romeo and Juliet*, the musical *West Side Story*.

In the summer of 1964, a young black man was shot by police under questionable circumstances, and rioters in Harlem raged for six days. Gender and sexual politics also caught light in the '60s. In 1969, gay rights gained momentum from a police raid on the Stonewall Inn in Greenwich Village. The next year, legendary McSorley's Old Ale House was forced to admit women.

The Harlem riots passed, but the bitterness was unresolved. By 1975, the city was on the verge of bankruptcy, and was forced to go cap in hand to the Federal government. President Gerald Ford's response was summarized in the *Daily News*: 'Ford to City: Drop Dead.'

Ed Koch

In 1976, feisty mayor Edward Koch attempted another financial rescue – this time backed by a Federal government loan guarantee of $1.65 billion. A resurgence of corporate development fed capital into the economy, and the city climbed back onto its feet. Half-empty since their 1973 opening, the twin towers of the 110-story World Trade Center sparkled into life; in 1974, Philippe Petit tightrope-walked between the towers. Three years later, George Willig climbed the South Tower, and was fined one penny per story. Battery Park City and the South Street Seaport were developed in Lower Manhattan, and the 1977 Citicorp Building led to the growth of a forest of new skyscrapers. One UN Plaza, the 37-story AT&T (now Sony Tower) building, and the dark-glass IBM building personified the era.

New York acquired an international reputation for excess. In 1977, Studio 54 exemplified a sybaritic, cocaine-driven culture. A power failure that year led to widespread looting – in contrast to the community spirit around a major blackout in 1965, and the later massive Northeastern blackout in 2003. In December 1980, John Lennon, the former Beatle, was murdered outside his home, the Dakota building.

Broadway theatres began their shows an hour earlier to give tourists and out-of-towners a chance to get clear before the late-night mugging shift punched in. The gap between rich and poor widened and the legacy of homelessness was on almost every street corner. AIDS and drug abuse pushed the healthcare systems beyond their capacity, and racial conflicts erupted. Manhattan businesses and middle-class workers fled to the suburbs or New Jersey, further weakening the New York tax base.

Good times, bad times

Moguls like Donald Trump snatched up New York real estate like squares on a Monopoly board, and the glitz of conspicuous consumption was lionized on the pages of *Vanity Fair*, a long-defunct magazine revived by Condé Nast in 1983. But by 1987, the good times had turned sour even for the tycoons, with two of Wall Street's biggest share dealers heading for jail and the market taking a record one-day dive of 508 points. On the streets, the annual murder rate peaked at 2,245 and the number of citizens on welfare reached a new high. International terrorism arrived in 1993, when a car bomb in the World Trade Center killed six people.

In the 1993 mayoral election, an abrasive New York district attorney, former Department of Justice prosecutor Rudolph ('Rudy') Giuliani promised to get tough on crime. The first Republican mayor for two decades, he more than kept his promise, extending 'zero tolerance' on law breaking and police corruption, jaywalking, begging, graffiti, and non-recyclers. The policy didn't endear him to all, but it did win respect, and the crime rate fell, to make New York one of the safer big cities in the US. By 1997, the murder rate had fallen two-thirds from its 1990 high.

Former mayor Rudolph Guiliani

Business Improvement Districts (BIDS) sprang up across the city, construction boomed, and seedy areas like Times Square were cleaned up. The economy rebounded from the 1987–92 slump, and unemployment fell. Giuliani was returned for a second term in 1997 and his ambitions turned towards the US Senate, but in 2000 his luck ran out. Prostate cancer and a messy separation from his second wife forced him out of the contest, which was won by a Democratic candidate, Hillary Rodham Clinton.

GOVERNOR'S ISLAND

Local tribes called it Pagganck (Nut Island) when the Dutch purchased the tree-covered island off the southern tip of Manhattan in 1637. With 172 acres (70 hectares) of wooded land, it was a small piece of the pie in the battle between the British and the Dutch for control of the region, but when the British finally claimed victory, they reserved it for the 'benefit and accommodation of His Majesty's Governors.'

Defensive works were first built on the island during the American Revolution, when minute men fired on British troops from behind earthworks. After independence, the island became property of the United States Army, who established Fort Jay and Castle Williams, and the island became an important staging area during the War of 1812. It remained important during conflicts, first as a prison for Confederate soldiers in the Civil War, then as a supply center for the World Wars. The US Coast Guard took over in the 1966; for nearly 30 years it was home to thousands of officers and their families.

In 2001 the military decommissioned the base, and the island was proclaimed a National Monument. These days, following an extensive restoration programme, it is a summertime playground for sunbathers, bicyclists, and picnickers. Art shows, concerts, and food festivals fill the lawns and park areas on weekends. The island can be accessed via two free ferries from Brooklyn and Manhattan. Visit www.govisland.com for ferry schedules and information on events.

Terrorism

On the morning of September 11, 2001, four passenger planes were hijacked by terrorists. Two of the planes crashed into the World Trade Center's towers. New Yorkers and viewers around the world watched the towers collapse, killing 2,606 people, including 343 of the firefighters and 60 members of the police force who raced to the scene.

Smoke at 'Ground Zero' hung in the air for three weeks, and the wreckage smoldered for weeks after. More than 20,000 New Yorkers were displaced from their homes near the 16-acre (6.5-hectare) disaster area. Even criminals were subdued; the week following the attack, crime in Manhattan fell 59 percent.

Mayor Giuliani personified New York's resilience. His trademark abrasiveness turned to a straight-talking compassion and earned the town's trust. These qualities were called on again just nine weeks later when an American Airlines morning flight for Santo Domingo crashed in the Rockaway district of Queens. Terrorists were not blamed but, in a bitter twist, the crash site was home to many emergency workers who bore such a toll on 9/11.

Giuliani's popularity was such that he had only to endorse Michael Bloomberg as his successor to win the election for the Republican, self-made media mogul. Bloomberg, a political novice, put $41 million of his own money into the campaign. Known on Wall Street for his financial data empire, and in the gossip columns for glamorous female companions after his 1993 divorce, Bloomberg inherited daunting tasks. As well as the massive rebuilding program in Lower Manhattan, the city had an $8.7 billion budget shortfall, and New York's social services had already been ruthlessly pruned. Fears of a recession and the effects of the terror attack spiked unemployment numbers. Bloomberg enjoyed a high approval rating and, in 2009, he was re-elected for an unprecedented third term.

Back to the future

As always in New York, energy came and rejuvenation began. The Hudson River waterfront was revitalized, Governor's Island reopened as a retreat for visitors, the spectacularly reorganized Museum of Modern Art returned from Queens and opened its new building to great acclaim. The gleaming Time Warner complex rose over Columbus Circle, with the distinctive triangular facades of the green Hearst Tower climbing nearby to join it in 2006.

Baseball game at the Citi Field.

The destruction of the World Trade Center site.

The city took a blow with the 2008 financial crisis, but the construction picked back up almost immediately: new baseball stadiums opened for both the Mets and the Yankees in 2009; the Lincoln Center renovation was completed; and new skyscrapers such as the Bank of America Tower, One57, and 8 Spruce Street joined the increasingly cluttered skyline.

On the tenth anniversary of the 2001 attack, the 9/11 Memorial (see page 75) opened at the south side of the World Trade Center site. Architect Daniel Libeskind's plans to erect Freedom Tower stalled amid various controversies until the building was redesigned by David Childs and David Libeskind and renamed One World Trade Center. It finally opened in 2014.

Some credit is certainly due to Mayor Bloomberg's pro-development policies, but his three terms will also be remembered by major health initiatives that banned smoking and trans fats in restaurants, and transportation improvements that added bike lanes and a fledgling bike-sharing program. Many, however, complained that the income gap also expanded under his watch, prompting protestors from the Occupy Wall Street movement to descend on Lower Manhattan in late 2011, sparking an international movement.

Blizzards and thunderstorms have always been manageable annoyances for the city, but little could be done to prepare for what hit the city on October 29, 2012. Hurricane Sandy arrived at high tide and sent a storm surge that flooded low-lying parts of the city, filled the subways tunnels and knocked out the power for days. Even a year later, parts of Lower Manhattan, Staten Island and Queens were still recovering and new mayor Bill de Blasio inherited the responsibilities not only to redevelop, but also to plan for future unforeseen disasters. These came earlier than suspected, as soon after his inauguration in January 2014 the new mayor struggled with the fallout of ferocious snowstorms that paralyzed large areas of the city. New York is many things. Predictable isn't one of them.

200 ticker-tape parades have taken place in Lower Manhattan, along what is known as the 'Canyon of Heroes.' The Yankees, the Mets, and Nelson Mandela have all been honored.

A Tenement Life

A land of opportunity became a crowded corner of hardship for the immigrants who settled on New York's Lower East Side.

The Lower East Side went by many names: 'the typhus ward,' 'the suicide ward,' 'the crooked ward,' or simply 'Jewtown.' The irregular rectangle of tenements and sweatshops crammed between the Bowery and the East River were the New World's ghetto.

Between 1880 and 1920, more than 2 million Eastern European Jews came to the United States, and over 500,000 settled in New York City, mostly on the Lower East Side. With 330,000 people per square mile and primitive sanitation, yellow fever and cholera were constant threats, and child labor and exploitation were facts of life. Rents were extortionate. Families of six or seven often slept, cooked, ate, and worked in a small room – in hallways, in basements, in alleyways – anywhere they could huddle. It's baffling to imagine, and even more so to see. The Lower East Side Tenement Museum (see page 119) offers guided tours of apartments that replicate the look of life 100 years ago.

The 'needle trade' was a keystone of the economy, and piles of half-sewn clothes cluttered the rooms. Pay was by quantity, hours were long, and the pace was relentless. Sewing machines were typically whining by 6am and droned far into the night. Sweatshop workers were charged for needles and thread, for lockers and chairs, and fined for damaged material at two or three times its regular value. Wages were minimal – maybe $8 or $10 a week for a family of five or six people, or $14 or $15 for the exceptionally productive.

Writer Michael Gold remembered, 'On the East Side people buy their groceries a pinch at a time; three cents' worth of sugar, five cents' worth of butter, everything in penny fractions.' Compassion for friends had a high personal cost. 'In a world based on the law of competition, kindness is a form of suicide.' Danish photo-journalist Jacob Riis published a book in 1890 called How the Other Half Lives, exposing the appalling conditions in the tenements, and leading eventually to the reforms of the Tenement House Act in 1901.

Building a Community

At the center of the neighborhood was Hester Street market, where Jews sold meat, produce, or cheap clothes from pushcarts. The area was nicknamed 'the Pig Market,' probably, as Jacob Riis said, 'in derision, for pork is the one ware that is not on sale.' Eastern European Jews put a high value on education and political organization, and community members were active in the labor movement. Unions were regularly organized, but strike-busters were hired by the bosses to intimidate them with threats and violence. The East Side Socialists finally saw their candidate in Congress in 1914. Organizations like the Educational Alliance sponsored lectures and demanded libraries, Yiddish theater blossomed, and religious observances continued as they had in the old country.

An elderly woman smokes while doing handiwork in her small New York City tenement room, c.1890.

Visitors at the Guggenheim Museum.

Jimi Hendrix in New York in the 1960s.

CULTURE AND THE CITY

New York is both a breeding ground and an international showcase for art and artists of every kind. If you can make it here, they say, you can make it anywhere.

New York bristles with world-class performing arts venues, in Lincoln Center, Carnegie Hall, and Madison Square Garden, as well as the big-ticket theaters that cluster around Broadway. The Off-Broadway scene has become so big that it has spawned a thriving and energetic Off-Off-Broadway family.

Parks across the city offer free, fresh-air culture with outdoor performances of the New York Philharmonic, the Metropolitan Opera, and the Public Theater's Shakespeare in the Park. On every New York corner and subway platform, a dreamer or a talented student works the 'if I can make it here, I can make it anywhere' refrain – the 'if' being key to that kick-step off the city streets.

One-third of all American independent movies are made here, and great jazz was crafted in clubs like Birdland. Artists of all kinds have thrived in the Big Apple, from Edward Hopper in his Washington Square studio and Andy Warhol's Factory divas, to Bob Dylan and Jimi Hendrix, who was 'discovered' in a Village bar by British bass player Chas Chandler.

Louis Armstrong and Gary Crosby, Basin Street.

Live music

New York is famous for great jazz clubs, like the Blue Note and the Village Vanguard in Greenwich Village. Excellent up-and-coming bands of all kinds play at the CMJ Music Marathon and at BAM (Brooklyn Academy of Music), home to the innovative Next Wave Festival since 1982.

CBGB's on the Lower East Side, birthplace of Talking Heads and The Ramones, slammed its doors in 2006, and the Knitting Factory moved from TriBeCa to Brooklyn, but Sounds of Brazil (SOB) in SoHo is a lively world-music venue, the Mercury Lounge in the East Village showcases cutting-edge bands, and (Le) Poisson Rouge in the West Village books an eclectic mix of all of the above.

Cultural centers

The Upper West Side's cultural heart is the Lincoln Center for the Performing Arts (see page 222), the largest cultural center in the US. The Metropolitan Opera, the New York City Ballet, and the Philharmonic reside here, with concerts and recitals in Avery Fisher Hall

Enjoying an evening at the Lincoln Center.

and Alice Tully Hall. The Vivian Beaumont and Mitzi E. Newhouse theaters put on plays and, each September, the New York Film Festival opens at the Walter Reade Theater. Jazz at Lincoln Center, a few blocks downtown at the Time Warner complex, thrives under the artistic direction of Wynton Marsalis.

World-famous Carnegie Hall was opened to the public with Tchaikovsky's American debut in 1891, and later hosted Albert Einstein, Amelia Earhart, Winston Churchill, Frank Sinatra, The Beatles, and Elton John. Charles Dana Gibson drew the Gibson Girls and established *Life* magazine in a studio on the premises, and dancer Isadora Duncan lived at the hall. In the late 1950s, developers wanted the plot for office space, but violinist Isaac Stern led a group of citizens to save the site from the wrecker's ball.

In Studio 1011–12, Baroness Hilla von Rebay convinced Solomon Guggenheim to fund promising artists, and established the Guggenheim Foundation, with Alexander Calder and Wassily Kandinsky among the beneficiaries. The baroness's acquisitions formed the core of the Guggenheim collection, housed in the Frank Lloyd Wright building on Fifth Avenue.

Visual arts

Art auctions came to public attention in the 1990s when a Van Gogh sold for $82.5 million at Christie's (Van Gogh once wrote that he

BUYING BROADWAY TICKETS

The TKTS booth (www.tdf.org/tkts) in Times Square has discounted seats (25–50 percent off) for that night's performances. It's open Monday through Sunday 3pm to 8pm for evening performances (opens at 2pm on Tuesdays), Wednesday, Thursday and Saturday 10am to 2pm for matinees, and Sunday 11am to 3pm. A booth at the South Street Seaport opens daily at 11am and sells tickets for the same-day evening and next-day matinee shows. Lines form early and are long. Unsold tickets can often be bought at theater box offices an hour or so before show time. The Times Square Visitor Center on Broadway Plaza, between 44th and 45th streets, also sells theater tickets.

In the summer, movies and music aren't confined to theaters and clubs. Free outdoor film screenings and concerts take over in Madison Square Park, Bryant Park, and other moonlit venues.

wished his paintings were worth what he had spent on the paint). Experts said the auction frenzy was a blip, but in 2004 Picasso's *Garçon à la Pipe* fetched $104 million at Sotheby's. And in one dizzying week in 2007, Andy Warhol's *Green Car Crash* fetched $71.7 million at Christie's, while Mark Rothko's *White Center* sold for $72.8 million at Sotheby's. More works by Picasso, as well as Cezanne and Munch, have all sold for prices over $100 million in the years since. In 2015 Modigliani's Nu couché fetched a record $170.4 million at Christie's.

The Metropolitan, the Guggenheim, and others line 'Museum Mile' (see page 210) along Fifth Avenue. The Metropolitan, along with the Museum of Modern Art on West 53rd Street, are the biggest and best. The Frick, once a private Fifth Avenue mansion, shows fine Rembrandts and Vermeers. The New York Public Library on 42nd Street exhibits art in a grand setting, its Reading Room providing an office for many writers.

Moving pictures

Once upon a time in New York, Radio City Music Hall was to movies what Lincoln Center is to ballet and opera. Now it's an Art Deco treasure, and even the ladies' powder room is worth visiting. Designed by a showman who was known for lavish silent-film theaters, S.L. 'Roxy' Rothafel's Radio City opened for vaudeville shows in 1932 as a 'palace for the people.' Radio City is still an exciting place to see a special screening or catch a gig.

Movie lines often wind around the block in Manhattan, providing eavesdropping and people-watching opportunities. (And, no, the skinny, nervy guy waiting ahead of you isn't Woody Allen.) Space is precious in the city, and multiplex theaters can make movie-going seem like standing in line to watch a TV screen. The Angelika Film Center on West Houston Street in Soho, though, has six screens, an espresso bar, and an atmosphere as good as the coffee. The Film Forum on West Houston Street features revivals, obscurities, and director series, as do the Museum of Modern Art, Anthology Film Archives, and the Museum of the Moving Image, aptly located by the Kaufman Astoria film studio complex in Queens.

The Walter Reade Theater and Elinor Bunin Monroe Film Center, home of the Lincoln Center Film Society and the New York Film Festival, screens foreign and independent films, as do Brooklyn Academy of Music's BAM Rose Cinemas. Downtown, the IFC Center opened in 2005 in the Village's historic Waverly Theater, while every spring, the TriBeCa Film Festival, co-launched by actor Robert De Niro, is the high-profile, hot-ticket event at which to be seen and to attend the latest screenings.

Dance

New York's dance boom began in the 1960s, with an infusion of funding and the defection of Russian superstars Rudolf Nureyev, Mikhail

Nu couché by Amedeo Modigliani for sale at auction in Christie's New York

The TriBeCa Film Festival is a highlight of New York's spring events.

Baryshnikov, and Natalia Makarova. The legendary George Balanchine handpicked the New York City Ballet company, putting them through almost superhuman training. 'Mr B' said, 'Dancers are like racehorses; they need a jockey on their backs.' Balanchine, who designed much of the performance space at the Lincoln Center's New York State Theater, died in 1983. The American Ballet Theater occupies the Lincoln Center's Metropolitan Opera House when the opera is out of season. ABT began with a more classical repertory than the New York City Ballet but, under Mikhail Baryshnikov's artistic direction, welcomed contemporary choreographers like Twyla Tharp.

The Dance Theater of Harlem, founded in 1969, performs both classical and contemporary

TRIBECA FILM FESTIVAL

First established in 2002 by Robert De Niro and producer Jane Rosenthal, the TriBeCa Film Festival has rapidly become a major fixture in the moviemakers' calendar. The impetus of the project was originally intended to lead a Downtown regeneration in response to the 2001 terrorist attacks, but within five years (in an event that had climate change as a major theme and was opened by the former vice-president Al Gore), more than 200 titles were screened to an enraptured and ready audience.

The first festival drew crowds of more than 150,000 people, and at least $10 million was raised in charity for local TriBeCa merchants. The next year, the crowds doubled, donations grew almost fivefold, and screenings featured outdoor shows along the banks of the Hudson River.

Many well-known films have gotten their start at the TriBeCa Film Festival. Paul Greengrass's acclaimed *United 93* premiered at the festival, as did *Mission Impossible III*. In 2011, the festival achieved another first, hosting the premiere of a video game, the decidedly cinematic LA Noire. The TriBeCa Film Festival is so successful that *New York* magazine began to wonder if the festival isn't getting too big, and that isn't something New Yorkers often wonder.

repertories. Other venues for dance, particularly modern dance, range from the Joyce Theater in Chelsea to the Ailey Center and the City Center, both in Midtown West.

Off-Broadway theater dates back to the Greenwich Village production of four one-act plays by Eugene O'Neill in 1916.

Theatrical stories

In 1901, the glare of electric signs earned the theater district of Broadway the name of the Great White Way. Taking in Seventh Avenue and several side streets, it enjoyed its heyday before the arrival of talking pictures and long before television. By the 1970s and 80s, the streets were dirty with drugs, pornography, and prostitution, but Times Square today is a twinkly tourist mecca of theaters, hotels, megastores, and restaurants.

The Shubert Theatre (1913) and Shubert Alley are named for the Shubert brothers, who built dozens of venues. The Palace on West 47th Street was a vaudeville theater until the 1930s, whose boards were trodden by Sarah Bernhardt. Now it's a prime venue for lavish musicals like the latest revival of *Annie*, as well as one-off gigs. The Belasco Theatre, founded in 1907 by flamboyant playwright-actor-director David Belasco, was famously haunted by his ghost until the 1970s production of *Oh! Calcutta.* Perhaps the nudity spooked the spook.

Today, Broadway is in exuberant health. Excellent drama draws crowds, but the big noise is the musicals. Successful musicals often have longer runs, to make back their bigger investments. The original *A Chorus Line* opened in the 1970s and ran for 6,137 performances, before being overtaken by *Cats*, which yowled for more than 20 years. Recent hits like *The Book of Mormon* should fill seats for years to come.

Off-Broadway venues are a feeding ground for the bigger theaters and a cultural force in themselves. The Lucille Lortel, the Cherry Lane, and the Public Theater: time to take a bow.

Broadway has over 40 prominent theater houses.

HOLLYWOOD ON THE HUDSON

Plenty of celebrities call New York home, but in movies set in the urban jungle, the glittering stars are the skyscrapers, brownstones, streets, and parks.

Ever since *The Lights of New York* was released in 1927, the city and its landmarks have been illuminating the big screens of the world's celluloid consciousness. King Kong atop the Empire State Building is an enduring image – although the 1976 remake was a disaster (Peter Jackson's 2005 resurrection of the story with Naomi Watts fared better).

The Empire struck back when New York writer-director Nora Ephron made *Sleepless in Seattle*, itself a pastiche of the 1957 three-hankie weepie *An Affair to Remember*. Director Spike Lee portrayed life uptown in *Mo' Better Blues* and across the East River in Do the Right Thing and *Crooklyn*. The city was turned into a maze of paranoia and hallucination in Darren Aronofsky's *Black Swan* and has been bruised and battered countless times, recently and spectacularly in Marvel's The Avengers.

Fonda and Redford went *Barefoot in the Park*, and Scorsese's *Raging Bull* rampaged around Greenwich Village, while his Taxi Driver patrolled the seedy corners of Times Square. *How to Marry a Millionaire* was set in the apartment of sassy dames Monroe, Grable, and Bacall at 36 Sutton Place South. Oliver Stone has visited *World Trade Center*, as well as *Wall Street* not once, but twice. And Woody Allen may be filming in Europe or on the West Coast these days, but his decades of celebrating the Upper East Side are a vital part of cinematic history. The number of films made here each year continues to rise, so there's no *Escape from New York* to Hollywood just yet.

Naomi Watts atop the Empire State Building in the 2005 remake of King Kong.

Carrie Bradshaw and friends in Sex and the City.

Will Smith in I Am Legend.

Breakfast at Tiffany's opening scene.

Ben Stiller in Night at the Museum.

THE WORLD'S BIGGEST BACKLOT

When Harry Met Sally.

First-time visitors taking a stroll through Madison Square Park may recognize the Flatiron Building at the park's south end, but not necessarily because of its iconic architecture. 'That's the *Daily Bugle* building from *Spider Man*,' they might point and say. It seems every block of the city been immortalized on celluloid (or, these days, in pixels). Forget booking a walking tour, just take to the streets and you'll be transported to the world's biggest backlot. Grab a pastrami sandwich at Katz's, the deli from *When Harry Met Sally*. Relive the opening scene from *Breakfast at Tiffany's* at the iconic store on the corner of Fifth Avenue and 57th. Hop over to Brooklyn Heights and take in the storefronts and brownstones from *Moonstruck*. Kids will demand a visit to the American Museum of Natural History to see if they can harness the magic of *Night at the Museum*. Out-of-towners won't find Grand Central Terminal and Central Park to be the dens of filth and crime depicted in Neil Simon's *The Out-of-Towners*, but they'll recognize the clock atop the information booth, the Bethesda Fountain, and countless other symbols of the city. When budgets are tight, Toronto sometimes stands in for the Big Apple, but if Hollywood is making a true New York film, there's no substitute for the real thing.

Under attack in Cloverfield.

Pancakes in Midtown.

DINERS, DELIS, AND DEGUSTATION

You can get a hot dog for around a dollar, or a double-truffle hamburger for 100 times that price. This is New York, where the only culinary dilemma is too much choice.

New York is, and always was, a great place to eat. From bagels to corned-beef sandwiches, Italian fine dining to curbside fast food, and from sashimi to sauerkraut, the breadth of cuisines is matched only by the range of prices. It's easy to feast well for a few dollars on a hot dog or banquet at Per Se for – if not a king's, then at least a royal sommelier's – ransom.

Food and fashion

Fashion and trends are vital in all that is New York, and celebrity chefs have left the town peppered with famous-name kitchens (some now leftovers as their famous founders cook up franchises and offshoots elsewhere, like Miami and Las Vegas). Meanwhile, the appetites for star-chef servings are increasingly fed by restaurateurs from out of town, and from as far afield as London, Paris, and Italy.

The styles and chefs may be international but the ingredients may not be. The local and sustainable food movements have become so entrenched in the city that seasonal menus detailing where the ingredients were sourced are a regular occurrence. Cookshop, Blue Hill, and Telepan are just a few outlets leading the charge among what have come to be known as 'farm-to-table' or 'greenmarket' restaurants. Vegetarian dishes have graduated from a regular option to a mainstay, with vegan diets increasingly available, while 'free' – as in 'lactose-free' and 'gluten-free' – is sprinkled over many menus.

To guarantee you're eating local, visit one of the city's greenmarkets. None is more important than the Union Square Greenmarket. Every Monday, Wednesday, Friday, and Saturday, sidewalks fill up with stands hawking local foods. In the winter, start the day with cider and cinnamon donuts; during the summer, there's lemonade and fruit-filled pastries. Or come for a lunchtime picnic, and pick up bread, wine, locally cured meats, and cheese.

Dining out on the Lower East Side.

The first visible signs of food are often at street corners, on silver carts. In the morning, many New Yorkers grab their breakfasts here on the way to the office, so don't be afraid to give these vendors a go. The coffee is good and the bagels make a quick meal. For a snack or lunch on-the-go, skip the soggy pretzels, charcoal-burned ears of corn, and over-boiled hot dogs. There are better

Tradition dies hard. While Manhattan restaurants open, close, and are forgotten in the blink of an eye, two classics – Le Cirque and the Russian Tea Room – couldn't stay shuttered.

options. *Empanadas* (South American savory pastries), chow fun noodles, wholegrain pancakes, chocolate-truffle cookies, or mango ices are also right there at the curb, often prepared quite well.

You'll find convenient sandwich shops, corner bodegas, and soup stands selling to people who try to eat without messing up their shirts, but you'll also see tiny storefronts catering to the latest food fad. Competition and rent can be ruthless – Vietnamese *bánh mì* sandwiches might be all the rage one moment, then all of a sudden it's meatballs or dumplings that everybody craves. Some trends die quicker than others. Southern barbecue and gourmet hamburgers are here to stay, while the cupcake and fried chicken crazes are a fading memory.

Fast and slow

Pizzas range from street-corner slices, often made with a crunchy semolina flour, to the Sullivan Street Bakery, where the slice is about the only thing they have in common. Jim Lahey is a passionate campaigner of 'slow food' and applies the principles he learned in Tuscany (using only high-grade flour and wild yeast, plus fresh, all-natural ingredients) to the no-frills pizzas sold in his bakeries. His signature slice is the seductively simple pizza *pomodoro*, with a thin tomato puree.

Some of the world's finest and most expensive restaurants – Per Se, Le Bernadin, and Masa to name but a few – are in Midtown. Many Manhattan mainstays are here too, with the longevity prize going to the excellent centenarian Oyster Bar at Grand Central Terminal. For Midtown dining, it pays to do some homework. While spontaneity is fun farther downtown, in Midtown it's best to make reservations, especially to dine before or after the theater.

Restaurants here, especially the more expensive ones, occasionally have formal dress codes. Men are suited (or at least jacketed) and women are groomed for a glamorous night on the town. Many Midtown restaurants are closed Sundays, and for lunch on Saturdays, as their corporate customers have gone.

The Meatpacking District is good for both dining and posing, even if the patrons are often wafer-thin models who don't look as if they eat, ever. Prepare to eat late, and stay up even later. The nearby Chelsea Market, at Ninth Avenue

Sardi's is an old-school, theatrical experience.

Chelsea Market.

and 15th Street, is a dreamland for food fetishists – a dozen or so bakeries, meat markets, kitchen suppliers, and other stores of a gastronomic bent, all based in former warehouses.

Once SoHo gained recognition as an artistic center, people began streaming here in search of 'the scene.' The prices often reflect SoHo's chicness, but there's no need to go hungry, or to pay through the nose. You can shell out $40+ for a steak at Balthazar, but you can also eat for plenty less at Snack.

Famous diners

Robert De Niro is one of TriBeCa's most famous diners. The actor moved here in 1976, and began investing in restaurants: Nobu, Locanda Verde, and the Tribeca Grill. To avoid these movie-star prices, head for the reasonably priced neighborhood bistro Landmarc, finishing off with ice cream from Blue Marble in the All Good Things Market. De Niro promoted his 'hood as a cool area in which to hang out, and it still is.

The once-mean streets of the Lower East Side are now very much the domain of hipsters. Get a taste of the area's heritage as an enclave of immigration with a visit to Katz's Delicatessen. To watch Uptown elegance melding with young and hip Downtown, head for Acme on Great Jones Street, or try Morimoto or Buddakan in the Meatpacking District.

Tiny restaurants like Degustation and Momofuku Ko offer a front-row view of the action. Diners sit at a bar and chat up the chefs as they prepare intricate dishes directly behind it.

Around the world and back

Ethnic food can often be found in pockets around the city. The stretch of Ninth Avenue north of the Port Authority is awash with Thai eateries, while 32nd Street between Fifth Avenue and Broadway – otherwise known as Korea Way – boasts over a dozen specialists in *bibimbap* and *kimchi*. Near 28th Street and Lexington, just south of Murray Hill, is 'Curry Hill,' a collection of reasonably priced Indian restaurants. This is to say nothing of Little Italy and Chinatown.

It's no surprise that immigrants pack their recipes when they depart for New York, and even if there isn't a particular block, they always find at least one storefront to share their delicacies. Eats from around the world are easily found in this part of town. Utensils are not required when you sit down for an Ethiopian feast at Meskerem in Greenwich Village. Jacketed waiters hover at your table, slicing from huge cuts of meat at the rodizio-style Brazilian behemoth Churrascaria Plataforma (316 W. 49th Street). Tsampa in East Village will give you a Himalayan take on noodles and dumplings, there's always ilili for Lebanese, and Peruvian delights are on offer at Lima's Taste (122 Christopher Street). Name a country and New York just may offer a local purveyor of its signature dish.

CULINARY CELEBRATIONS

No one could possibly sample every pork rib, chocolate truffle, and slice of sashimi in the city. That doesn't mean people don't give it a shot at the food festivals that are held nearly every week. Conglomerations of stands, sometimes offshoots of major restaurants, take over streets, parks, and convention centers.

Some festivals are à la carte, while some offer tickets that grant all-you-can-eat (and drink) privileges. The major ones include the Ninth Avenue International Food Festival in the spring, the Barbecue Block Party in summer, and the New York Wine and Food Festival in the fall.

FOOD ON THE MOVE

In a more cosmopolitan world, it is less likely New York has a monopoly on any one thing, but the city can still claim dominance in some quintessential dishes.

It's hard to resist the smell of grilled kabobs (kebabs) at the city's food markets.

The variety of food on offer is one of the reasons why dining in New York is so appealing. Sure, the peanuts and kabobs (kebabs) you may see being sold from carts aren't masterpieces, but there's nothing like eating them while walking down Fifth Avenue. The legendary H&H Bagels may have closed up its storefront, but Murrays has taken up the mantle and makes some of the world's finest bagels. When it comes to pizza, contentious would be a mild word to describe the debate over who tosses the best, but classics like Di Fara, Grimaldi's, Lombardi's, Johnny's, and Patsy's usually get a vote, while new places like Adrienne's Pizzabar and Kesté are entering the contest.

For an egg cream (a mixture of chocolate, milk and sparkling water), few do it better than Gem Spa in the East Village. Grab a dozen oysters and a bowl of Manhattan clam chowder at the Grand Central Oyster Bar. For years, Junior's was the place to get a New York cheesecake, but these days many swear by Artisanal. People make pilgrimages for the hot dog at Nathan's Famous in Coney Island and stand in line for burgers at Corner Bistro in Greenwich Village. Are they the best around? Taste them and decide.

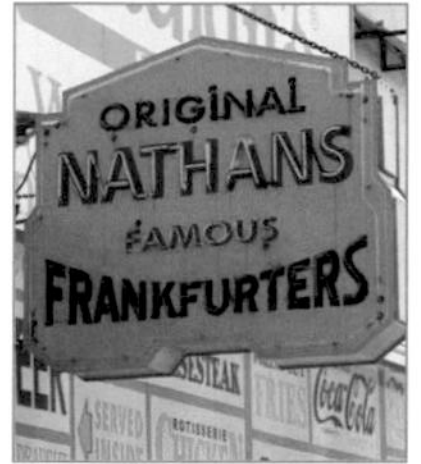

Nathan's has been selling its famous hot dogs in Coney Island since 1916.

The stand-up coffee bar at Dean & Deluca (560 Broadway) is a good place for a snack.

With food carts to be found along the city's streets and in its squares and parks, lunch is never far away.

Pretzels and hot roasted chestnuts make the perfect holiday treat.

KEEP ON TRUCKING

The Wafels & Dinges truck serves sweet Belgian-style waffles all around the city.

In recent years, a fleet of food trucks has sprung up, moving daily to feed food-loving office workers in largely un-foodie neighborhoods. Other major American cities have their own food-truck scenes, but few can compete with the variety in New York.

So just what can you eat from a truck? Many serve sweets, including the vegan Cinnamon Snail (www.cinnamonsnail.com) and Treats Truck (www.treatstruck.com), a cart that sells the all-American classics: chocolate chip cookies, brownies, and Rice Krispie squares. Wafels & Dinges (www.wafelsanddinges.com) serves – you guessed it – Belgian waffles. There are fancy ice-cream trucks, including Van Leeuwen (www.vanleeuwenicecream.com).

There are also plenty of savory foods – look for Salvadorian pupusas (www.elolomega.com), lobster rolls (http://lukeslobster.com/nauti), schnitzel (www.schnitzelandthings.com), burgers (www.lacensebeef.com), and even kimchi tacos (http://korillabbq.com). Since there are no seats at which to eat these purchases, most people stake out space on public park benches.

To track down a particular food truck, check out the info on the Midtown Lunch website (www.midtownlunch.com), or follow your individual favorites on their websites, Twitter, or Facebook.

Try El Olomega for the best Salvadorian pupusas – corn tortillas filled with cheese, pork, chicken, and jalapeños, and finished off with tasty salsa and pickled cabbage.

Aerial view at dusk in central Manhattan.

Rush hour on Fifth Avenue.

A typical street of brownstones in New York.

521

Washington Square Park.

INTRODUCTION

A detailed guide to the entire city, with principal sites clearly cross-referenced by number to the maps.

Manhattan is divided into three areas: Midtown, Uptown, and Downtown. Midtown and Uptown are criss-crossed by a street grid system where avenues travel north and south, and streets travel east and west.

Midtown East is best known for the Grand Central Terminal, the United Nations headquarters, and the Chrysler Building; while Midtown West is home to Times Square, Rockefeller Center, and the Museum of Modern Art. Cool, elegant Uptown is epitomized by the Upper East Side – between 82nd and 104th streets are cultural treasures so lavish that they have earned this stretch the name Museum Mile. The Upper West Side is both more towering and more family-oriented, evidenced by the taller buildings and baby carriages. At the top end of Manhattan are Harlem and Washington Heights, which have been undergoing a renaissance for over a decade.

West Village.

Downtown is more of a challenge to navigate, as its smaller streets do not follow a pattern and it uses names instead of numbers. At the northern edge are Gramercy Park and Chelsea. Farther south it's Greenwich Village, Chinatown, and the Lower East Side. To the east is Alphabet City, with avenues A, B, C, and D, plus NoHo (North of Houston) and NoLita (North of Little Italy), making a large-scale map of this area look like a bowl of alphabet soup.

Shoppers on Broadway.

The southern part of Downtown is the center of financial New York, where Wall Street banks keep tabs on the money before the Meatpacking District soaks it up again in its high-end restaurants and boutiques. Don't forget the outer boroughs, which are covered near the end of the book.

All together, the city covers a whopping 300 sq miles (776 sq km). With a little time, a sturdy pair of shoes, and a MetroCard, you are sure to see enough to convince you this is more than a place. It's a pulsing and evolving masterpiece.

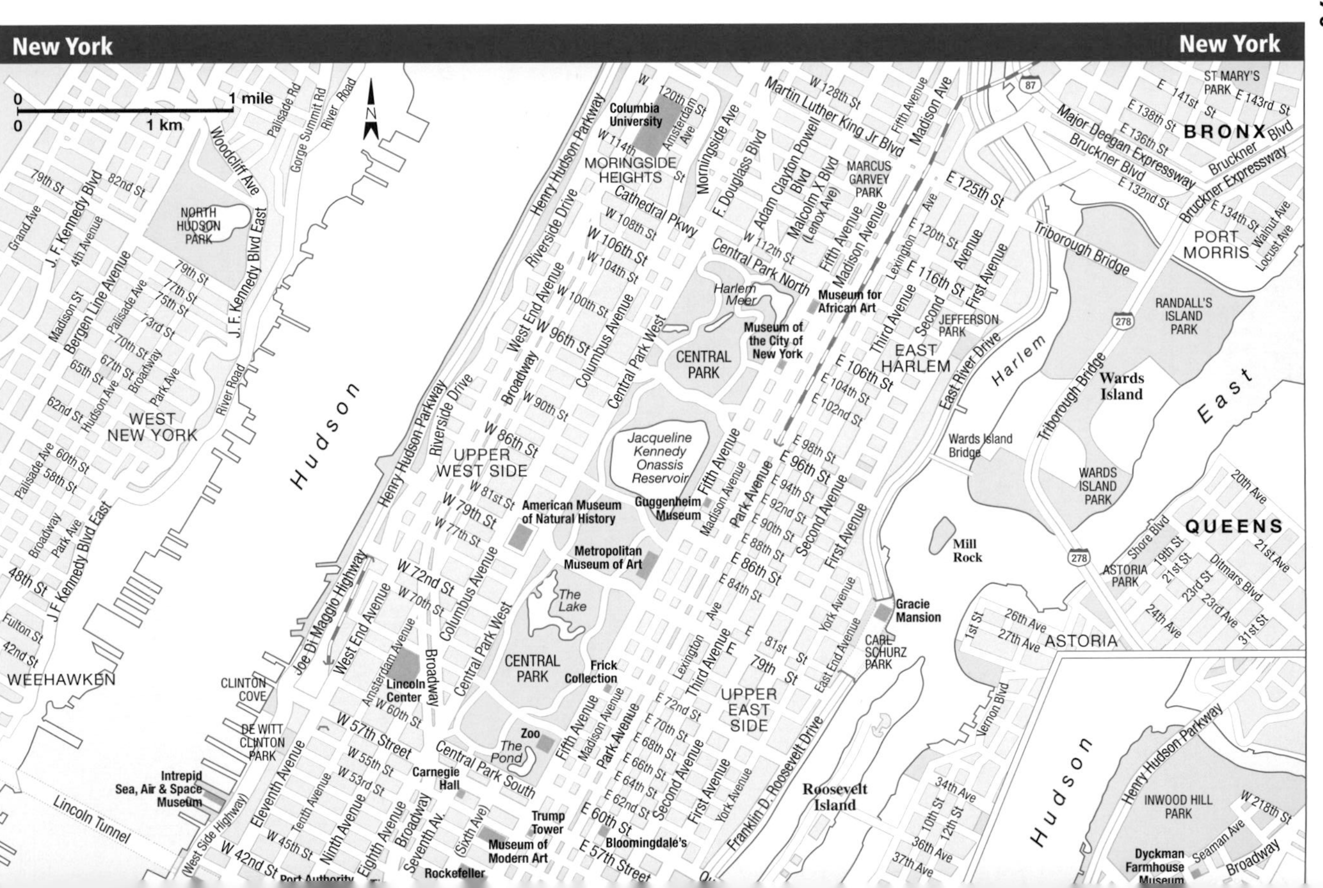
BRONX
ST MARY'S PARK
E 143rd St
E 141st St
E 138th St
E 136th St
E 134th St
E 132nd St
Bruckner Blvd
Bruckner Expressway
Major Deegan Expressway
Walnut Ave
Locust Ave
PORT MORRIS
RANDALL'S ISLAND PARK
Wards Island
WARDS ISLAND PARK
Triborough Bridge
278
87
East
Harlem
QUEENS
20th Ave
21st Ave
Ditmars Blvd
23rd Ave
24th Ave
31st St
23rd St
21st St
19th St
Shore Blvd
ASTORIA PARK
ASTORIA
26th Ave
27th Ave
1st St
Vernon Blvd
34th Ave
36th Ave
37th Ave
12th St
10th St
Mill Rock
Wards Island Bridge
East River Drive
E 125th St
E 120th St
E 116th St
First Avenue
Second Avenue
Third Avenue
Lexington Ave
JEFFERSON PARK
EAST HARLEM
E 106th St
E 104th St
E 102nd St
E 98th St
E 96th St
E 94th St
E 92nd St
E 90th St
E 88th St
E 86th St
E 84th St
E 81st St
E 79th St
UPPER EAST SIDE
Gracie Mansion
CARL SCHURZ PARK
York Avenue
East End Avenue
Roosevelt Island
Franklin D. Roosevelt Drive
Madison Ave
Fifth Avenue
W 128th St
Martin Luther King Jr Blvd
MARCUS GARVEY PARK
Madison Avenue
Malcolm X Blvd (Lenox Ave)
Adam Clayton Powell Blvd
W 112th St
Museum for African Art
Museum of the City of New York
Central Park North
F. Douglass Blvd
Morningside Ave
Harlem Meer
CENTRAL PARK
Jacqueline Kennedy Onassis Reservoir
Guggenheim Museum
Park Avenue
Columbia University
W 120th St
Amsterdam Ave
W 114th St
MORNINGSIDE HEIGHTS
Cathedral Pkwy
W 108th St
W 106th St
W 104th St
W 100th St
W 96th St
W 90th St
W 86th St
W 81st St
W 79th St
W 77th St
W 72nd St
W 70th St
Central Park West
Columbus Avenue
Henry Hudson Parkway
Riverside Drive
West End Avenue
Broadway
UPPER WEST SIDE
American Museum of Natural History
Metropolitan Museum of Art
The Lake
Frick Collection
E 72nd St
E 70th St
E 68th St
E 66th St
E 64th St
E 62nd St
E 60th St
E 57th Street
Bloomingdale's
Trump Tower
Museum of Modern Art
Zoo
The Pond
Central Park South
Carnegie Hall
(Sixth Ave)
Seventh Av.
Rockefeller
Lincoln Center
Amsterdam Avenue
W 60th St
W 57th Street
W 55th St
W 53rd St
W 45th St
W 42nd St
Eighth Avenue
Ninth Avenue
Tenth Avenue
Eleventh Avenue
Port Authority
Joe Di Maggio Highway
(West Side Highway)
CLINTON COVE
DE WITT CLINTON PARK
Intrepid Sea, Air & Space Museum
Lincoln Tunnel
Hudson
INWOOD HILL PARK
Dyckman Farmhouse Museum
W 218th St
Seaman Ave
Henry Hudson Parkway
River Road
Gorge Summit Rd
Palisade Rd
Woodcliff Ave
J. F. Kennedy Blvd East
NORTH HUDSON PARK
79th St
77th St
75th St
73rd St
70th St
67th St
65th St
62nd St
60th St
58th St
48th St
42nd St
82nd St
Park Ave
Broadway
Hudson Ave
Palisade Ave
Bergen Line Avenue
Madison St
4th Avenue
J. F. Kennedy Blvd
Grand Ave
Fulton St
WEST NEW YORK
WEEHAWKEN
0
1 mile
1 km
N

Hudson
HUDSON RIVER PARK AND GREENWAY
CHELSEA
High Line
Post Office
Madison Square Garden
Penn Station
Macy's
Public Library
Empire State Building
Chrysler Bldg
United Nations
Queens-Midtown Tunnel
McGuinness Blvd
George Washington Br.
WASHINGTON HEIGHTS
Henry Hudson Parkway
Harlem River Drive
Major Deegan Expressway
TREMONT
BRONX
Bronx Zoo, New York Botanical Garden
Whitney Museum of American Art
GREENWICH VILLAGE
MADISON SQUARE PARK
GRAMERCY PARK
UNION SQ PARK
WASHINGTON SQ. PARK
EAST VILLAGE
TOMPKINS SQ PARK
Merchant's House Museum
SOHO
Holland Tunnel
East
Hudson
HIGH BRIDGE PARK
Harlem
Morris-Jumel Mansion
JOHN MULLALY PARK
Yankee Stadium
Franklin D. Roosevelt Drive
EAST RIVER PARK
LOWER EAST SIDE
Lower East Side Tenement Museum
LITTLE ITALY
CHINATOWN
TRIBECA
BATTERY PARK CITY
One World Trade Center
National September 11 Memorial and Museum
CITY HALL PARK
New York Stock Exchange
Castle Clinton
FINANCIAL DISTRICT
South Street Seaport
Williamsburg Bridge
Manhattan Bridge
Brooklyn Bridge
BROOKLYN BRIDGE PARK
DUMBO
BROOKLYN
Brooklyn Naval Yard
Flushing Avenue
RIVERSIDE PARK
General Grant National Memorial
Columbia University
MORNINGSIDE PARK
HARLEM
MELROSE
Grand Concourse
Brooklyn Battery Tunnel
Staten Island Ferry Terminal
Ellis Island
Statue of Liberty
Staten Island
Governors Island

The Freedom Tower.

LOWER MANHATTAN

Lower Manhattan is where New York began. Now it's an area of high finance and poignant memories, revitalized parks and glimmering new skyscrapers.

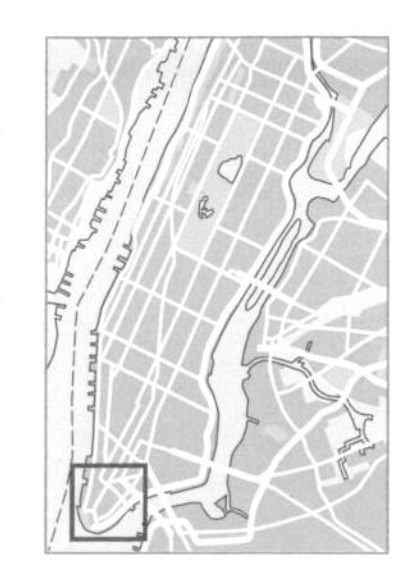

Below Chambers Street and the Brooklyn Bridge is the original New York, where the Dutch and the English first settled, the country's first hotel was built, the first president was sworn in, and the city's first theatrical opening night took place. Clipper ships bound for the California Gold Rush sailed from Lower Manhattan's piers in the 1850s, and by 1895 the first skyscraper stood 20 stories above lower Broadway.

Financial powerhouses

Over a century later, New York's financial powerhouses and city government areas are bracketed by outdoor havens like the South Street Seaport and Battery Park. Some of the landmark office buildings on or near Wall Street have been converted to high-tech business-use and residential apartments.

But Manhattan's oldest neighborhood also has some of its most moving history, being the site of two memorials to modern tragedies. Just as events in the 20th century shifted the area from a maritime economy to one of financial commerce, so too, have events early in the 21st century changed the face of Lower Manhattan once again. The changes have been absorbed with typical New York energy – adapting and reconstructing, facing the future, without missing a beat.

PLACES OF PILGRIMAGE

Between West Street and Trinity Place is the site of the former World Trade Center. Rising an impressive 110 stories into the sky, the Twin Towers were the most prominent structures in a 16-acre (6.5-hectare), seven-building complex that took 17 years to complete. It was a classic piece of 1970s architecture, and the view

Main Attractions

9/11 Memorial and One World Trade Center
Battery Park City
Castle Clinton
Wall Street
City Hall
Brooklyn Bridge
South Street Seaport

Map

Page 74

On the Brooklyn Bridge.

from the South Tower's 107th-floor Observation Deck was one of the best in the city.

On September 11, 2001, a day few will forget, 2,606 New Yorkers died as the result of suicide terrorist attacks. Nearby St Paul's Chapel (see page 84) offered aid in the crisis, and acted as an unofficial spot where grief-stricken families could mourn their loss.

The grounds of the World Trade Center have changed dramatically in subsequent years. The complex of seven towers is still under construction, but its centerpiece **One World Trade Center**, a 1,776ft (541-meter) skyscraper packed with state-of-the-art technology, was completed in 2014. Now the tallest building in the western hemisphere, it offers breathtaking views over the city from the One World Observatory deck and the ONE Dine restaurant on the 101st floor (https://oneworldobservatory.com; daily 9am–8pm; until midnight in summer). Elevators take visitors to the 102nd floor in less than 60 seconds, complete with floor-to-ceiling LED displays recreating the development of New York City's skyline from the 16th century to the present

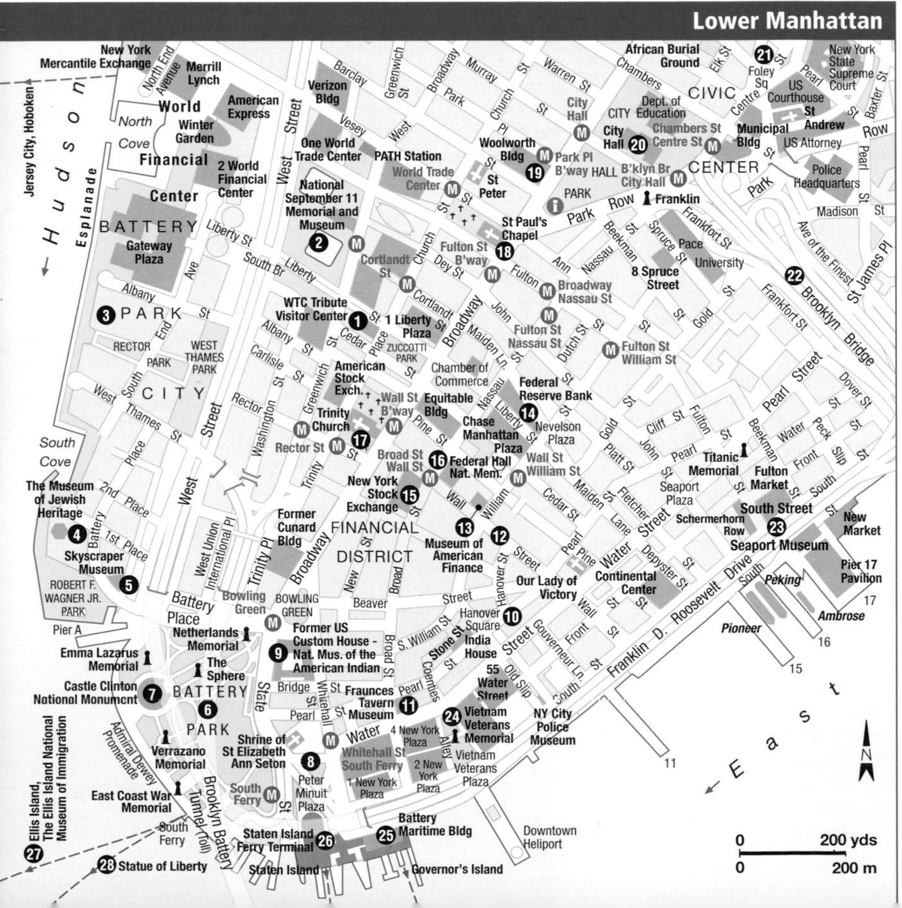

day. At the southern end of the site, a tribute center now provides a space for all to share memories and to remember. At the base is a stunning memorial to the victims.

Tribute WTC Visitor Center

Address: 120 Liberty Street (between Greenwich and Church streets), www.tributewtc.org
Telephone: 212-393 9160
Opening Hours: Mon–Sat 10am–6pm, Sun until 5pm
Entrance Fee: suggested donation, charge for guided tours
Subway: World Trade Center/Rector Street

The **WTC Tribute Visitor Center** ❶ is a project of the September 11th Families' Association, a non-profit organization set up in the aftermath of the tragedy to allow those most affected to stay in touch. The purpose-built center is comprised of five themed galleries: a running documentary on life before the attack has testimonies from former employees and local residents describing life as part of the WTC community, while other galleries focus on the day's events as they unfolded, and the subsequent rescue and cleanup operation.

The center is undeniably moving, and no matter how many documentaries are aired on television, little can prepare visitors for the stark reality of salvaged items, including a battered, but instantly recognizable airplane window, or the variety of faces that peer out from the wall of 'missing people' posters. A rolling list of names provides an intense reminder of the scale of the loss, while a collage of personal photos and mementoes ensures that we remember the victims' lives and not just their deaths.

Ultimately, the center is a tribute not only to the lives lost, but to those coping with being left behind. A wall in the final gallery allows visitors to add their thoughts and wishes for the future.

National September 11 Memorial & Museum ❷

Address: One Liberty Plaza (entrance at Greenwich and Albany streets), www.911memorial.org
Telephone: 212-312 8800
Opening Hours: memorial daily 7.30am–9pm, museum Sun–Thu 9am–8pm, Fri–Sat till 9pm
Entrance Fee: charge
Subway: World Trade Center/Rector Street

After years of designs, speculation, and unfortunate delays, the **9/11 Memorial** opened exactly 10 years after the attacks (the accompanying Museum took a few more years). All visitors must make reservations to visit and tickets can be purchased up to 3 months in advance. Do not wait until the last minute, as slots fill up far in advance.

The 9/11 Memorial.

The Firefighters' Monument at the Tribute WTC Visitor Center.

Brookfield Place, originally known as **World Financial Center**, with its towers and elegant waterfront **Winter Garden**, was repaired after structural damage during the attacks. It features stores, restaurants, and regular arts events held in the Winter Garden.

Battery Park City ❸ is a huge, 92-acre (37-hectare) development stretching along the Hudson River, and is highly desirable residential property. A third of the area around Battery Park City is public space, and linked to Manhattan's riverfront expansion by scenic walkways that meander north to TriBeCa and beyond. Running alongside the Hudson River is the pretty, green, and leafy **Battery Park Esplanade**, which stretches for more than a mile. It's a fine place to stroll and reflect (look out for the skateboarders). There are also benches that offer relaxing vantage points for enjoying the splendid views over the Hudson River and across to the Statue of Liberty.

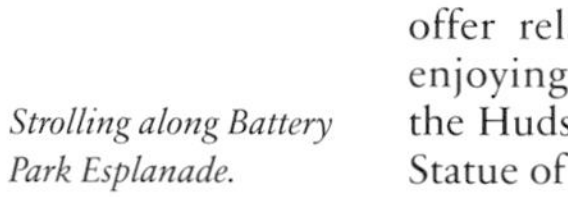

Strolling along Battery Park Esplanade.

The Museum of Jewish Heritage.

Another tribute to the past lies on the southwestern tip of Manhattan Island.

The Museum of Jewish Heritage ❹

Address: 36 Battery Place (at 1st Place), www.mjhnyc.org
Telephone: 646-437 4202
Opening Hours: Sun–Tue and Thu 10am–5.45pm, Wed until 8pm, Fri 10am–3pm (until 5pm during Eastern Standard Time)
Entrance Fee: charge
Subway: Bowling Green/Rector Street

With more than 2,000 photographs, artifacts, and original documentaries, the museum provides an insight into the experiences of Jewish people through the Holocaust and into the present day. Over a decade ago, the building was extended by a new wing with a digitally equipped performance center that runs a program of film, theater, music, and the spoken word. Steven Spielberg contributed video testimonies from Holocaust victims compiled while directing *Schindler's List*.

Beyond the museum, pathways wind through **Robert F. Wagner Jr Park**, which has attractive landscaped gardens, deck-topped brick pavilions, and places to sit with fine views of New York Harbor. Here are opportunities to meditate on the Jewish Museum's aim, which is to provide a thoughtful and moving chronicle of history, keeping the memory of the past alive and offering hope for the future.

Skyscraper Museum ❺

Address: 39 Battery Place (at West Street), www.skyscraper.org
Telephone: 212-968 1961
Opening Hours: Wed–Sun noon–6pm
Entrance Fee: charge
Subway: Bowling Green/Rector Street

Visitors with an interest in modern architecture may enjoy this celebration of tall buildings in this, the most vertical of modern cities. Through exhibitions, programs, and publications, this small museum explores skyscrapers as objects of design, products of technology, sites of construction, investments in real estate, and places of work and residence. The interior itself is a dazzling example of the form, with mirrored floor and ceiling offering a bewildering perspective.

EARLIEST NEW YORK

At the island's tip, **Battery Park** ❻ is where New Amsterdam was first settled by Europeans, and New York's history began. Named for the battery of protective cannons that once stood here, this is famously where Manhattan begins, or ends – as the song goes, 'The Bronx is up but the Battery's down.' The park, as well as having wonderful views and many memorials, now contains a lovely natural garden, the **Bosque**. Fritz Koenig's huge bronze sculpture *The Sphere* had stood for more than 30 years in the World Trade Center Plaza, and withstood the tons of metal and concrete crashing down on top of it on 9/11. In 2002, the battered globe

Inside the Museum of Jewish Heritage.

TIP

Romantics should look at Manhattan by Sail (www.manhattanbysail.com; tel: 212-619 6900), which offers a variety of trips on a 1929 double-masted schooner called the Shearwater, including harbor cruises that sail close to the Statue of Liberty and Ellis Island. There's a bar on board, or you can book for the excellent brunch cruise.

was moved to Battery Park. There is constant talk of plans to move it closer to the 9/11 Memorial, but for now it sits at the foot of a rose bed called Hope Garden. An eternal flame burns in memory, and it is a fine spot for contemplation.

Castle Clinton ❼

Address: Battery Park, www.nps.gov/cacl
Telephone: 212-344 7220
Opening Hours: daily 7.45am–5pm
Entrance Fee: free
Subway: Bowling Green/South Ferry

Built as a fort to defend against the British in the War of 1812, Castle Clinton was renamed Castle Garden in 1823 and became the city's premier place of amusement, where Samuel Morse gave his first public telegraph demonstration and Swedish singer Jenny Lind made her American debut in a tumultuously acclaimed concert in 1850 (for which some wealthy New Yorkers paid a then-unheard-of $30 a ticket). Not long after, the area was joined to the mainland by landfill and served as the New York State Immigration Station, where more than 8 million immigrants were processed between 1855 and 1890.

For two years, potential settlers were processed on a barge moored in the Hudson, but when the new headquarters opened on Ellis Island in 1892, the tide of immigration shifted. Home to the New York Aquarium until 1941, Castle Clinton was made a national monument in 1950 and opened to the public in 1975. The only time the fort has been breached was when Battery Park was overwhelmed by tides during 2012's Hurricane Sandy, but it reopened in 2013 after repairs.

Saints and Sails

Peter Minuit Plaza ❽, east of Battery Park, is named for the first governor (director general) of New Amsterdam. The flower-shaped New Amsterdam Plein and Pavilion, a gift to New York from the Netherlands, houses a pleasant café and an information center, and glows at midnight with an array of colors. In a tiny park nearby, a plaque commemorates some of the city's lesser-known arrivals: 23 Sephardic Jews, dropped off by a French ship in 1654, who founded

Castle Clinton, built as a defensive fort, is the place to buy tickets for the ferry to the Statue of Liberty.

A display at the National Museum of the American Indian.

New Amsterdam's first Jewish congregation, Shearith Israel.

Turn left on State Street, once lined by wealthy merchants' houses, to come to the **Shrine of St Elizabeth Ann Seton** (7 State Street; www.setonheritage.org), in the only 1790s Federal-style mansion still standing here, now surrounded by giant glass towers. The chapel by the shrine is dedicated to the first American-born saint, who founded the Sisters of Charity in 1809 and was canonized in 1975 by Pope Paul VI.

Herman Melville, author of *Moby Dick*, was born in a house near 17 State Street, where **South Street Seaport Museum** (www.seany.org; tel: 212-748 8600; Tue–Sun 11am–5pm; charge) offers a glimpse into the nautical heritage of the city. Visitors can tour the country's largest collection of six privately maintained historic vessels, including the 125-year-old 279ft (85-meter) wrought-iron sailing ship *Wavetree*; the four-masted wooden-decked 377ft (115-meter) *Peking*; and the tugboat *W.O. Decker*.

On the other side of State Street from Battery Park, the former **US Custom House** was designed by Cass Gilbert and built in 1907. A magnificent example of Beaux Arts architecture, with a facade embellished by ornate limestone sculptures that represent four of the world's continents and 'eight races' of mankind, this grand edifice also has striking Reginald Marsh murals on the rotunda ceiling inside.

And, in what could seem an ironic twist, this spot, where Peter Minuit is believed to have given goods to the value of $24 to local Indians for the purchase of Manhattan Island, is now a major museum to tribal culture.

A costume from the National Museum of the American Indian.

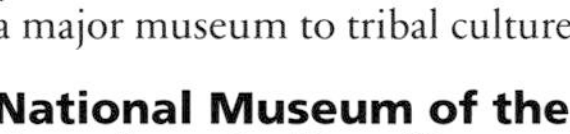

National Museum of the American Indian 9

Address: George Gustav Heye Center, 1 Bowling Green, www.nmai.si.edu
Telephone: 212-514 3700
Opening Hours: daily 10am–5pm, Thu until 8pm

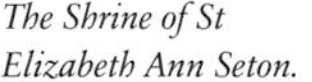

The Shrine of St Elizabeth Ann Seton.

EAT

For a choice of cafés and restaurants, head for cobblestoned Stone Street, said to have been the first paved street in New York City. This tiny alley, tucked away in the concrete canyons of Lower Manhattan, is situated off Hanover Square, between South William and Pearl streets.

Entrance Fee: free
Subway: Bowling Green
Operated by the Smithsonian Institution, the museum details the history and cultural legacy of America's native peoples through artifacts, costume, artworks, and online resources. The glass-cased exhibits seem dwarfed by the grand surroundings of the Custom House, but the museum is a worthy achievement nevertheless, and often presents music and dance performances in addition to its permanent displays.

Bowling Green and Hanover Square

Give a pat to Di Modica's *Charging Bull*, a statue forever linked to bullish Wall Street. He digs in his hooves at the northern end of **Bowling Green Park**, New York's first public park. Then wander up Beaver Street to Broad Street, or take a quick detour back to State Street before following Pearl Street to **Hanover Square** ❿.

The square burned to ashes in the Great Fire of 1835, one of many fires that destroyed virtually all remnants of Dutch New Amsterdam. According to one eyewitness who was watching from Brooklyn, 'The sparks from that fire came over the river so thick that the neighbors... were obliged to keep their roofs wet all night.' The square recovered to become a thriving commercial center, and includes **India House** (1 Hanover Square), an 1850s Italianate brownstone that's been home to a private club (at lunchtime) for maritime movers and shakers since 1914.

Captains of industry have dined at **Delmonico's**, at the corner of Beaver and William streets, since the 1830s, when two Swiss brothers established the city's first formal French-style restaurant. Stop and admire the impressive marble columns at the entrance, reputedly shipped over from Pompeii, or venture inside for a drink and a bit of market eavesdropping.

Bowling Green was New York's first public park.

Samuel Fraunces opened his tavern in 1763 as the Queen's Head, but changed the pub's name due to mounting anti-British sentiment.

Fraunces Tavern Museum ⓫

Address: 54 Pearl Street (at Broad Street), www.frauncestavernmuseum.org
Telephone: 212-425 1778
Opening Hours: Mon–Fri noon–5pm; Sat–Sun 11am–5pm
Entrance Fee: charge
Subway: Wall Street/Broad Street

Farther south, at the corner of Pearl and Broad streets, is one of Old New York's oldest buildings. Built in 1719 for a French Huguenot merchant, the house was extended and made into a tavern by Samuel Fraunces in the 1760s. The New York Chamber of Commerce got its start over a few mugs of ale here, and George Washington gave an emotional farewell address to his officers in 1783 in the Long Room. The tavern was restored to its 18th-century appearance and opened again in 1907.

The wood-paneled tavern is still an atmospheric bar-restaurant, with dining rooms for private rental. On the two floors above is the intriguing **Fraunces Tavern Museum**, where exhibits include a lock of Washington's hair, the Long Room complete with period furniture, a fragment of one of Washington's teeth (not, contrary to legend, wooden), and a shoe that belonged to his wife, Martha. The cases housing the exhibits were built by Tiffany & Co. in 1907.

WALL STREET

Walk north on William Street (its twists and turns a reminder of when it was known as Horse and Cart Street) to **Wall Street** ⓬, traditional hub of the financial world, where the narrow stone canyons are lined by towering banks, brokerage houses, and law offices.

A worldwide symbol of wealth, power, and deal-making, remembered for traumatic scenes during the 1929 stock market crash, the street took its name from the 17th-century wall – or, more accurately, a wooden blockade built by the Dutch as protection against the threat of Indian and

FACT

Waterfront development has transformed the banks of Manhattan along the Hudson River and East River from a parade of rotting piers into miles of recreation and relaxation. The work spread downtown, funded by the Lower Manhattan Development Corporation. New public spaces full of greenery have been established at the revitalized Coenties Slip, Old Slip, Peck Slip, and Burling Slip. It is all contributing to a 2-mile (3km) -long promenade where you can walk, jog, bike, or just sit and look out toward Brooklyn.

The New York Stock Exchange.

TIP

The Federal Reserve Bank offers free guided tours lasting an hour, Monday through Friday at 1pm and 2pm. For security reasons, you must book the tour in advance; bring your e-ticket and photo ID (such as a passport); and arrive 30 minutes before the tour begins.

English attacks. The country's first stock exchange began just in front of **60 Wall Street** in 1792, when 24 brokers gathered beneath a buttonwood tree. The building at **55 Wall Street** is a massive columned landmark that dates to 1841 and served as the original Merchants' Exchange, and later as headquarters for the influential First National City Bank.

Financial history

A few buildings south at the corner of William Street is the former Bank of New York, founded by Alexander Hamilton in 1784 and the new home of the **Museum of American Finance** ⓭ (48 Wall Street; www.moaf.org; tel: 212-908 4110; Tue–Sat 10am–4pm; charge). Affiliated with the Smithsonian, the museum is dedicated to the trading and financial industries, with a collection of antique stocks and bonds, ticker tape from the 1929 crash, and memorabilia from the era of the robber barons, a group that included Messrs Carnegie, Frick, and Rockefeller.

Following William Street to Maiden Lane will lead to **Nevelson Plaza**, with seven tall abstract sculptures by the late Louise Nevelson, a longtime New York resident.

Money may not be art, but there's a lot of it at the **Federal Reserve Bank** ⓮ (33 Liberty Street, entrance at 44 Maiden Lane; www.newyorkfed.org; tel: 212-720 6130), west of Nevelson Plaza. Constructed in 1924, this imposing edifice is said to house nearly a quarter of the world's gold reserves (as well as wheelbarrows-full of old and counterfeit cash). Tours are available, but security is tight and visits must be booked ahead.

Easy Street

Double back to Wall Street and the corner of Broad Street, where the **New York Stock Exchange** ⓯ was constructed in 1903, its building fronted by an impressive facade of Corinthian columns. Since 9/11, the Stock Exchange's Visitors' Gallery is no longer open for spectators to observe the speculators. The exchange has an annual trading volume of over $5 trillion.

The Greek temple-style **Federal Hall National Memorial** ⓰ (26

Federal Hall National Memorial.

Wall Street was named for the wooden barrier that was erected by the Dutch against the English in the mid-1600s.

Wall Street; www.nps.gov/feha; tel: 212-825 6990; Mon–Fri 9am–5pm; free) is, however, open to the public. It's on the site of the original Federal Hall, where on April 30, 1789, George Washington was sworn in as the first President of the United States (there's an impressive statue of him on the steps); it later became a branch of the US Treasury Department. Today it's run by the National Park Service and includes historical memorabilia, plus the suit that George Washington wore at his inauguration.

Trinity Church ⓱

Address: 89 Broadway (at Wall Street), www.trinitywallstreet.org
Telephone: 212-602 0800
Opening Hours: Mon–Fri 7am–6pm, Sat 8am–4pm, Sun 7am–4pm
Entrance Fee: free
Subway: Wall Street/Rector Street

At the very top of Wall Street where it meets Broadway, pretty Trinity Church is a serene survivor of early New York. First established in 1698, the present 1846 church is the third one built on the same site. **Trinity Church graveyard** contains some of the oldest graves in the city – including that of Alexander Hamilton, the

Trinity Church is a slice of Old New York.

US's first Secretary of the Treasury, who owned a house at 33 Wall Street and was killed in a duel with Aaron Burr. A small **museum** offers a look at the original charter, among other historic artifacts.

Two blocks to the west is the building of the **China Institute in America** (100 Washington Street, entrance from 40 Rector Street; www.chinainstitute.org; tel: 212-744 8181; daily 10am–5pm, Tue–Wed until 8pm; free). It houses displays on the history of Chinese art and contemporary art exhibitions.

St Paul's Chapel ⓲

Address: 209 Broadway (between Fulton and Vesey streets), www.trinitywallstreet.org
Telephone: 212-602 0800
Opening Hours: Mon–Sat 10am–6pm, Sun 7am–6pm
Entrance Fee: free
Subway: Fulton Street/Broadway

The churchyard at St Paul's.

St Paul's Chapel, part of the Trinity Church Parish, is situated five blocks north on Broadway, between Fulton and Vesey streets. Built in 1766, this Georgian-style landmark is the only church left from the Colonial era, when luminaries like Prince William (later King William IV) and Lord Cornwallis worshiped here. George Washington's personal church pew is also preserved.

Although it is located just one block east of the World Trade Center, remarkably, the building was not damaged on September 11, 2001, and was used as a shelter for many of the volunteers and workers who helped in the aftermath. The chapel is now the site of a permanent 9/11 exhibit: '*Unwavering Spirit: Hope and Healing at Ground Zero*,' honoring the eight-month-long volunteer effort of its parishioners during and after the tragedy.

CITY HALL AREA

The handsome, gargoyle-topped **Woolworth Building** ⓳ (233 Broadway), designed by architect Cass Gilbert, was known in its heyday as the 'cathedral of commerce.' From 1913 until 1930, when the Chrysler Building was completed, its 60 stories and soaring height of almost 800ft (245 meters) made it the tallest building in the world. The Gothic Revival tower cost five-and-dime baron Frank W. Woolworth $13 million, and was officially opened by President Woodrow Wilson, who pushed a button in Washington that successfully lit up all of the floors. The top floors have been converted into luxury apartments, including a $110-million penthouse. The building features in Baz Luhrmann's film adaptation of *The Great Gatsby* as a Nick Carraway's work place.

Turning around, you will get a close up view of one the skyline's newest stars, **8 Spruce Street** (aka New York by Gehry or The Beekman Tower). A creation of the inimitable Frank

Protesters at Occupy 2.0 in Duarte Square.

Gehry, this skinny 76-story curiosity undulates as if it were made of water. As one of the world's tallest residential towers, it is a spectacular addition to the evolving Downtown landscape.

Since 1910, New York has honored everyone from Teddy Roosevelt to Nelson Mandela (and, of course, the New York Yankees many, many times) with ticker-tape parades that conclude at handsome **City Hall** ⓴. At the junction of Broadway and Park Row, this French Renaissance/Federal-style edifice has been the seat of city government since DeWitt Clinton was mayor in 1812, and was co-designed by French architect Joseph-François Mangin, responsible for the Place de la Concorde in Paris.

Protests and politicking

City Hall Park, a triangular, tree-shaded former common in front of City Hall, has played an important role throughout the city's history: as the site of public executions, almshouses for the poor, and a British prison for captured Revolutionary soldiers. It's also where Alexander Hamilton led a protest against the tea tax in 1774, and where, two years later, George Washington and his troops heard the Declaration of Independence for the very first time.

Behind City Hall stands the former New York County Courthouse, dubbed on its completion in 1878 the **Tweed Courthouse**. This was after the revelation that 'Boss' Tweed and his Tammany Hall cronies (see page 42) had pocketed some $9 million of the final $14 million construction costs.

After extensive refurbishment, the courthouse is now the home of the New York City Department of Education and a New York City public school. Tours can be arranged by appointment (selected Fridays at noon; tel: 212-788 2656 or email tours@cityhall.nyc.gov).

TIP

Stockbrokers and other technophiles can be seen tapping their tablets in City Hall Park and more than a dozen other places, taking advantage of Lower Manhattan's free wireless hotspots. For a map, log on to www.downtownny.com/programs/free-public-wifi.

OCCUPY WALL STREET

On weekends and evenings Lower Manhattan has long had a reputation as a quiet and empty place, but in recent years, the volume of people and voices has increased, due in large part to a growing sense of discontentment.

In 2010, protestors filled Park Place in opposition to the construction of the Cordoba House (now known as Park51). Proposed as a community center for Muslims, it was quickly dubbed the 'Ground Zero Mosque.' What started as a small movement became a national debate, with politicians and pundits of all types arguing whether a Muslim organization should be built so close to the World Trade Center site. By the time Park51 opened in late 2011, the debate had fizzled out and the public hardly noticed. Attention had turned to a newer, bigger issue.

When thousands of disillusioned young people began camping out in Zuccotti Park in September 2011, no one could have predicted that their protest of corporate greed known as 'Occupy Wall Street' would quickly catch on worldwide. That debate still rages, though protesters are less visible (only 100 returned to Zuccotti Park to mark the second anniversary of the protest). One message, however, remains clear: As a crucible for political movements and discussions, New York is as essential as ever.

Past sumptuous **Surrogate's Court** (31 Chambers Street), with its eight Corinthian columns, **Foley Square** ㉑ is named for another Tammany Hall politician. It's also the site of worthy civic structures like the 1936 Cass Gilbert-designed **United States Courthouse** (1 Foley Square), and the **New York State Supreme Court** (60 Centre Street), built in 1913, where New Yorkers are summoned for jury duty.

When workers were excavating the foundations of a new Federal courthouse building, the skeletons of African slaves were discovered. Now a city, state, and Federal landmark, the **African Burial Ground** (www.nps.gov/afbg; Tue–Sun 10am–4pm; free) is commemorated by a memorial at the corner of Duane and Elk streets.

The **Municipal Building** (1 Centre Street), slightly to the south, is an enormous, ornate 1914 McKim, Mead, & White confection. In the second-floor civil wedding chapel you can tie the knot in about five minutes (after the proper preliminaries, of course).

In the lobby of the Municipal Building, **City Store** (http://a856-citystore.nyc.gov; Mon–Fri 10am–5pm) is a place for unusual gifts (manhole cover cufflinks or genuine New York taxi medallion, anyone?) and can provide a wealth of information on the city.

Cyclists on the Brooklyn Bridge.

THE BROOKLYN BRIDGE

The Brooklyn Bridge was the inspiration of engineer John Augustus Roebling. The span of almost 1,600ft (488 meters), from City Hall across the East River to Brooklyn's Cadman Plaza, was the world's longest ever conceived. Steel-cable suspension, used for the first time, gave unmatched stability and strength, as well as a striking image.

Construction began in 1867 and took 16 years to complete. Building was marred by tragedy. Two years into the project, Roebling was killed by a docking ferryboat. His son, Washington Roebling, took over, but like many other workers, fell victim to the bends during riverbed excavation. An invalid the rest of his life, Roebling Jr monitored the works by telescope as his wife, Emily, supervised the project. When the bridge opened in 1883, 12 people were trampled to death in a panic, fearing a collapse.

Despite its beginnings, the Brooklyn Bridge was dubbed the 'new eighth wonder of the world,' and has inspired artists ever since. The walk across the bridge is indeed a wonder, and residents of Brooklyn employed downtown often prefer it to the subway, even if it means leaving a little early for work.

BRIDGE AND HARBOR

For one of the best of all views of the **East River** and Lower Manhattan, walk down Frankfort Street or along Park Row. Both lead to the pedestrian walkway that leads onto the **Brooklyn Bridge** ㉒, one of the world's first suspension bridges. As the pointed arches of the bridge's great Gothic towers come into view, recognition is immediate, for this is another icon of New York that has etched itself into the world's visual vocabulary.

Alternatively, walk toward the East River along **Fulton Street**, to the place from where (until the Brooklyn Bridge was built) ferries carried New Yorkers to Brooklyn, from the Fulton Street pier. In the 1800s, this part of town was the center of New York's maritime commerce, where spices from China, rum from the West Indies, and whale oil from the Atlantic were bought and sold, where ships were built, and where sailors thronged to enjoy a seedy red-light district. All that ended after the Civil War, when the old East River port fell into a decline, and big ships no longer sailed here.

South Street Seaport ㉓

Address: Fulton Street (at South Street), www.southstreetseaport.com
Telephone: 212-732 8257
Opening Hours: Mon–Sat 10am–9pm, Sun 11am–9pm
Entrance Fee: free, charge for some attractions
Subway: Fulton Street/Broadway-Nassau

South Street Seaport bills itself as a 12-block 'museum without walls.' Near the **Titanic Memorial Lighthouse**, at the corner of Fulton and Water streets, **Schermerhorn Row** is lined by the last surviving Federal-style commercial buildings in the city, part of a block of early 19th-century warehouses.

Cannon's Walk is another block of restored buildings, between Fulton and Beekman streets. Around the corner on Water Street is **Bowne and Co.** (211 Water Street), a 19th-century printing shop that is the current home of the seaport museum's offices.

Hurricane Sandy devastated the area in 2012, but an ambitious revitalization program of the iconic waterfront Pier 17, featuring state-of-the-art sustainable buildings, open spaces, shopping areas, restaurants and a rooftop entertainment venue, is scheduled for completion in 2017. Until then visitors can enjoy temporary attractions such as the Seaport Studios (http://seaportstudios.com) and the Seaport Culture District, featuring exhibitions, art installations and projections organized by several cultural institutions, including the Guggenheim Museum.

In summer, step aboard one of the one-hour **Downtown Liberty Harbor Cruises**, operated by Circle

TIP

Driving to Brooklyn? It's a prettier ride over the bridges, but consider taking the Brooklyn Battery Tunnel (aka the Hugh L. Carey Tunnel). There's an $8 toll per vehicle, but access is easy from the West Side Highway near Battery Park, and you avoid the oft-congested interior of Downtown.

Ellis Island Immigration Museum.

TIP

There are dozens of stops on the free, seven-days-a-week Downtown Connection bus service in Lower Manhattan. Buses run from near South Street Seaport to Battery Park City, via Battery Park, from 10am to 7.30pm, roughly every 10 minutes on weekdays and 15 minutes on weekends (www.downtownny.com).

Line (www.circlelinedowntown.com; tel: 800-836 6666) from the piers.

The Seaport Museum's impressive collection of **historic vessels** used to occasionally conduct elegant cruises around Manhattan. They can now be seen at Pier 16.

Back toward Battery Park

The last few sites extend around the tip of the island, offering wonderful views along the way. South of South Street Seaport – past Pier 11, and just beyond **Old Slip**, a landfilled inlet where 18th-century ships berthed to unload their cargo – is a park where stranded sailors used to congregate. Today, at the foot of a brick amphitheater near the corner of Coenties Slip and Water Street, is a monument to other young men.

A 14ft (4-meter) monument erected by the city in 1985, the **Vietnam Veterans Memorial** ㉔ is made of green glass etched with excerpts of letters written to and from soldiers in Vietnam. It is movingly illuminated at night. The nearby **New York City Police Museum** (www.nycpolicemuseum.org) is yet to reopen following damage caused by Hurricane Sandy in 2012.

A few blocks away, the rusting **Battery Maritime Building** ㉕ (11 South Street), a steel landmark Beaux Arts structure built in Whitehall Street in 1909, is the boarding point for ferries to **Governor's Island** (www.govisland.com) each spring and summer. The island is the site of corporate parties and special events that the public can join.

On the next pier down from the Maritime Building is the refurbished **Staten Island Ferry Terminal** ㉖ (1 Whitehall Street; http://nyc.gov/statenislandferry for schedule). The 25-minute cruise to Staten Island not only offers close-up views of the Statue of Liberty, but is also free, making it the best bargain in town. There are rumors the ferry will be forced to charge in future because of its huge costs. In the meantime, however, the shiny new terminal and a new fleet of ferries make this a trip you really should make.

Another essential cruise departs a little farther around the waterfront. **Ferries** leave for Ellis Island and the

South Street Seaport.

Statue of Liberty a few steps from the East Coast War Memorial in Battery Park. Tickets and schedule information are available from **Statue Cruises** (http://statuecruises.com; tel: 877-523 9849), or at Castle Clinton. Buy tickets well in advance.

Ellis Island 27

Address: Ellis Island, www.nps.gov/elis
Telephone: 212-363 3200
Opening Hours: check website
Entrance Fee: charge
Subway: South Ferry/Whitehall Street

Ellis Island (see page 94) was known as the 'Island of Tears' because of the medical, mental, and literacy tests applicants had to undergo in the 32 years that it served as gateway to the United States. Today, it is a national monument and one of the city's most popular tourist destinations (although Hurricane Sandy damage left it closed for over a year). The **Ellis Island National Museum of Immigration** tells the story of the immigrants' journey to America and their struggle for survival once they arrived. The displays include photographs and videos of immigrants recounting their stories. Outside the museum, a promenade offers wonderful views of the Statue of Liberty and the Manhattan skyline.

Statue of Liberty 28

Address: Liberty Island, www.nps.gov/stli
Telephone: 212-363 3200
Opening Hours: Ferries daily approx. 9am–5pm
Entrance Fee: charge, including additional charge for crown access
Subway: South Ferry/Whitehall Street

The Statue of Liberty (see page 92) was completed in France in July 1884, and arrived in New York Harbor in June of 1885 on board the French frigate *Isère*. In transit, Lady Liberty and her crown, torch, tablet, and other accessories were reduced to 350 pieces and packed in 214 crates, but it took only four months to reassemble the statue in its entirety. On October 28, 1886, the dedication took place in front of thousands of spectators. Visitors today can climb to the crown for unforgettable skyline and Hudson River views.

The Staten Island ferry.

Looking up at the World Trade Center

It was once a monument to commerce and a symbol of bravado. It became the site of the worst terrorist attack on American soil. Now it is a place of remembrance and hope.

On the morning of August 7, 1974, New Yorkers gathered in the streets of Lower Manhattan and did something that only tourists are inclined to do. They looked up at the skyscrapers in awe. A diminutive Frenchman, aptly named Philippe Petit, had strung a cable between the two tallest buildings in the world, and he was 'dancing' his way across the tightrope at a height of over 1,300ft (396 meters). The World Trade Center, barely a year old at the time, was now not only a center of international commerce, but the site of the world's most audacious stunt.

A visitor to the 9/11 Memorial Preview Site in New York.

Thirty-seven years later, New Yorkers looked up again. Only the audacity they witnessed this time was even more unbelievable and far more sinister. The two towers were on fire, ignited by jet fuel from two terrorist-piloted planes that crashed into them. In a matter of hours, they would be piles of rubble. The rubble would bury more than 2,600 people. It was impossible to know what might come next.

On September 11, 2011, exactly ten years after the devastating attacks, families of the victims gathered for the dedication of a memorial. They ran their fingers over names inscribed in bronze panels. They stood in the shade of white oak trees and watched water cascade 30ft (9 meters) into the reflecting pools that sit in the deep footprints of the two towers. They had heard about this for years, but actually seeing it was different. Somber, powerful, cathartic, it was so many things. The next day, the memorial opened to the public and the first visitors took in the haunting and beautiful tribute to the fallen.

With an accompanying museum – underground, built around the surviving foundations of the Twin Towers, the memorial is now complete. The design, however, reminds of the void, not just in the skyline, but in the lives of everyone affected by the attacks. To limit the crowds and give each visitor ample time to explore, the memorial distributes passes via an online reservation system. They also recommend multiple visits to see the changing reflections in the water at different times of day. Because that's what the site is ultimately about: reflection.

One World Trade Center

Even as they reflect on the past, New Yorkers are looking up once more. Standing a patriotic 1,776ft (541 meters) tall, the building that during its initial construction was known as The Freedom Tower has finally joined the family of skyscrapers that make up the world's most recognizable skyline. The road to completion was longer than many might have hoped, but for a structure of such stature – in height, but also in historical importance – the job had to be done right.

Designed by David M. Childs, the glimmering tower consists of 2.6 million square feet (234,000 square meters) of space, 55,000 of which have been designated as lower-level retail space. A 1,000-seat performing arts center from the mind of Frank Gehry will stage dance programmed by the Joyce Theater. At the top, visitors are afforded the finest, and highest, view of the city from the observation deck, while the soaring spire doubles as a communications antenna. The observatory features three dining options (including a fine-dining restaurant ONE) and interactive exhibits. On their way up, the Sky Pod elevators' high-definition monitors display 500 years of Lower Manhattan history.

Back on the ground, at the northeast corner, subways and the PATH train will arrive and depart from the World Trade Center Port Authority Trans-Hudson Transportation Hub, a stunning white structure with a glass ceiling and a ribbed exterior. Its creator, Santiago Calatrava, was inspired by the image of a child releasing a dove from a pair of hands. The hub will mirror this action every September 11th, when the glass ceiling will retract and expose the grand pavilion to the open air.

And the transportation hub is not the only new neighbor. Five other new skyscrapers are under construction: 1,329ft (405-meter) 2 World Trade Center, with its four diamond shaped peaks; 3 World Trade Center will welcome retailers and trading firms into its 2.8 million sq ft (241,547 sq meters) of office space; and 5 World Trade Center, which will sit on the former site of the Deutsche Bank building that was irreparably damaged in the attack. Two of the towers have been completed: 4 World Trade Center (2013), the seat of its owner, Port Authority; and 7 World Trade Center, finished in 2006.

All the buildings have been built with safety and sustainability as a top priority, far exceeding building codes and employing state-of-the-art technology and materials to achieve LEED certification. Opening dates vary, but some unveilings occurred in 2013, 40 years after the original World Trade Center first had people putting their hands to their brows and looking skyward.

Names of the victims from the September 11, 2001 terrorist attacks.

THE STATUE OF LIBERTY

A potent icon in the United States for more than 125 years, the Statue of Liberty is still the most evocative sight in New York City.

Like millions of other immigrants, Italian-born writer Edward Corsi's first glimpse of America was the heroic figure of Lady Liberty, her hand thrust skyward with a torch to light the way. He wrote: 'Looming shadowy through the mist, it brought silence to the decks of the *Florida*. This symbol of America – this enormous expression of what we had all been taught was the inner meaning of this new country – inspired awe in the hopeful immigrants.'

Partly because of the statue's significance as a symbol of freedom and democracy, security measures have been implemented since 9/11. Visitors are screened before boarding the ferry, and backpacks and large bags are not permitted. Most visitors buy a pedestal ticket (available via www.statuecruises.com), which grants access to the statue's base and its museum. A few hundred daily crown tickets are available for those who plan ahead and are able to climb the steep steps to the top of the crown. Please note that many restrictions apply to crown tickets, including minimum age and height requirements.

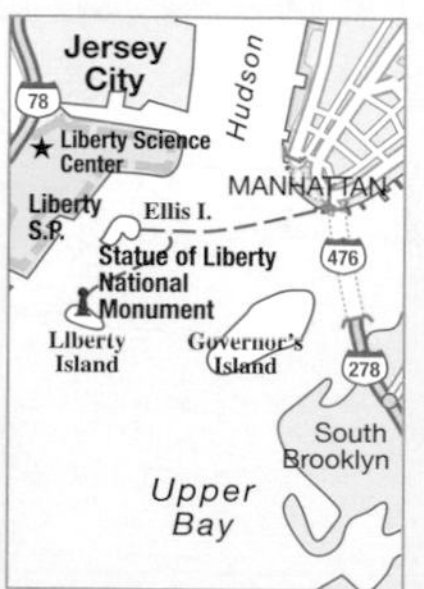

The Essentials

Address: www.nps.gov/stli
Tel: 212-363 3200
Opening Hours: ferries from 8.30am–3.30pm; seasonal variations; reservations required for crown access.
Entrance Fee: free; charge for crown access
Transportation: Statue Cruises, Battery Park, www.statuecruises.com

The city skyline wouldn't be complete without Lady Liberty gracing the harbor. Be aware that she might be smaller than she appears in many photographs.

The tablet that Liberty holds in her left hand reads (in Roman numerals) 'July 4, 1776,' the date of America's independence from Britain.

A GIFT FROM FRANCE

FRANK LESLIE'S ILLUSTRATED NEWSPAPER

A newspaper of the day depicts the construction of the statue.

The Statue of Liberty was a gift from the people of France to the United States to symbolize the spirit of successful revolutions in both of their countries.

In 1865, Edouard-René Lefèvre de Laboulaye, an intellectual, politician, and admirer of America, suggested to a young sculptor named Auguste Bartholdi that he make a large monument in honor of French and American brotherhood. By 1874, enough money had been raised by the French – through lotteries, subscriptions, and entertainment – to construct the statue. Funding for the pedestal was slower to materialize in the United States, however, and it took a concerted campaign from Joseph Pulitzer through his newspaper, *The World*, to raise the necessary finance.

Gustave Eiffel, who later built the Eiffel Tower, designed the ingenious framework that supports the thin copper skin. In 1885 Bartholdi's statue, called *Liberty Enlightening the World*, was shipped to the US, and was formally dedicated in a ceremony on October 28, 1886.

There are 25 windows in Liberty's crown, which symbolize gemstones found on earth. The seven rays of the crown represent the seven seas and continents of the world.

The statue is situated on 12-acre (5-hectare) Liberty Island, which is owned by the Federal government. The observation platform in the pedestal allows great views of New York and the harbor.

ELLIS ISLAND

More than 100 million Americans trace the history of their families' US citizenship back to the Grand Hall of Ellis Island.

Visitors arrive by boat in front of the Ellis Island Immigration Center's main building, exactly as thousands of hopeful migrants did during the center's operation from 1892 to 1954. The grand red-brick exterior and the high, vaulted ceiling of the Great Hall were meticulously restored and reopened in 1990, after nearly four decades of decay since the facility's closure. The reconstruction effort was driven mainly by public subscription, to which more than 20 million Americans donated. In addition to historic exhibits, Ellis Island houses an archive of records of the millions of immigrants who were processed through its halls, as well as the Wall of Honor, where the names of all the people who passed through are displayed.

Unfortunately, the island was another victim of Hurricane Sandy and some facilities are closed due to major repairs. At the time of writing the upper (second and third) level exhibitions are open, including dioramas of Ellis Island through time, peak immigration years, the immigrant experience, and a restored dormitory room. Visitors are led through recently restored structures that were run by the United States Public Health Service and served as the island's hospitals. Note that visitors must be over 13 years old to join the hospital tour.

Crates and other baggage items on display at the Ellis Island Immigration Museum.

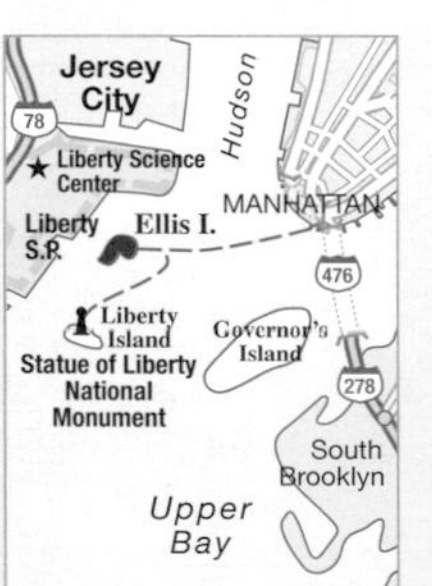

The Essentials

Address: www.nps.gov/elis
Tel: 212-363 3200
Opening Hours: daily 8.30am–3.30pm, seasonal variations
Entrance Fee: free, but fee for ferry
Transportation: Statue Cruises, Battery Park, www.statuecruises.com

The American Immigrant Wall of Honor is the largest wall of names in the world. It has over 700,000 immigrants' names inscribed.

The tiling of the Great Hall is a legacy of Rafael Guastavino (1842–1908), himself an immigrant from Catalonia in northern Spain. Already a successful builder when he came to the US, his specialty was Catalan vaulting. His work can also be seen over the Oyster Bar at Grand Central Terminal.

Reliving history: on January 1, 1892, the first immigrant processed at Ellis Island was Annie Moore. Annie arrived from Ireland on the SS Nevada, on her 15th birthday.

A NEW LIFE IN THE NEW WORLD

The Great Hall, where potential immigrants were processed.

The promise of a new life called to more than 22 million people from all over the world. Among these were Irving Berlin, Bob Hope, and the singing von Trapp family, all of whom entered the United States via the immigration center on Ellis Island. Applicants were taken through a selection process intended to sift out the physically and mentally infirm and the criminal, who were returned to the ships on which they came. These unfortunates gave the island its nickname: the Island of Tears.

Families wishing to research their genealogical history need only consult www.nps.gov/elis, pick up the How to Trace Your Immigrant Ancestor booklet available at the Ellis Island information desk, or visit the American Family Immigration History Center on the island.

The Ellis Island National Museum of Immigration, with the recently opened Peopling of America Center, is operated by the Statue of Liberty-Ellis Island Foundation and the National Park Service. The immigration archive, compiled from passenger manifests of ships docking at the island during its operation, is also available online at: www.ellisisland.org.

Sunshine and shopping on SoHo's Prince Street.

SOHO AND TRIBECA

Stylish boutiques, good food, landmark buildings, and an independent film scene contribute to Manhattan's lively and constantly evolving hubs of style.

Main Attractions
West Broadway
Wooster Street
New York City Fire Museum
Mercantile Exchange Building
Tribeca Film Center
Harrison Street
Washington Market Park

Map
Page 98

SoHo, an acronym for **So**uth of **Ho**uston, is bordered by Canal Street to the south, Lafayette Street to the east, and Sixth Avenue (Avenue of the Americas) to the west. When Abraham Lincoln made his first campaign speech at nearby Cooper Union, the area was the center of the city's most fashionable shopping and hotel district. By the end of the 19th century, however, the narrow streets were filled by factories, their imaginative cast-iron facades masking sweatshop conditions so horrific that the City Fire Department dubbed the entire region 'Hell's Hundred Acres.'

Temples of industry

The neighborhood could have been razed to the ground in the 1960s if local artists hadn't started moving into the old lofts, and the city hadn't changed zoning laws to allow them to do so legitimately.

Around the same time, determined conservationists established the **SoHo Cast Iron Historic District** to protect the appearance of these elaborate 'temples of industry.' As a result, apartments are now too expensive for all but the most successful (or those who got in when prices were low), and most of SoHo's remaining art galleries have relocated above street level to avoid the exorbitant rents. Others have absconded completely – to Chelsea or Brooklyn.

If SoHo is no longer the artists' neighborhood of old, it does maintain a New York combination of grit and blatant commercialism, where burly men unload trucks right by outrageous window displays, and double-decker tour buses lumber and wind slowly through the cobblestoned streets.

Young diners at the Tribeca Grill.

Soho and Tribeca, East Village and the Lower East Side

SoHo is a shopper's paradise.

THE STREETS OF SOHO

The main drag is **West Broadway** ❶, lined by stores offering everything from jewelry to quirky household wares. On Saturdays in particular, it's packed with crowds of tourists loaded down with shopping bags. From Houston to Canal is a generous selection of designer and top-end boutiques including US giants Ralph Lauren, and DKNY, interspersed with European designers such as Prada, which is housed in a Rem Koolhaas-designed building.

At the end of a hard day's credit-card abuse, the best-dressed shoppers head to the **Soho Grand Hotel** (310 West Broadway, at Grand and Canal streets, www.sohogrand.com). When it opened in 1996, this was the first new hotel in this part of town since the mid-1800s, when the fashionable American House Hotel stood at the corner of Spring Street, and the white-marble St Nicholas on Broadway and Broome held gala polka parties.

Rising 15 stories above the neighborhood, the Soho Grand manages to fit in with the 'temples of industry,' thanks to its industrial-chic decor and cozy bar and lounge, a meeting place for fashion and entertainment-industry types. It's also one of the few hotels where pets are not only welcome, but are as pampered as their owners (witness the dog statues in the foyer). If you check in without an animal, you can request a complimentary bowl of goldfish.

Prince Street ❷

Cutting across the top of West Broadway, **Prince Street** has all but forsaken galleries and turned into prime shopping territory, and the surrounding streets have been swift to follow suit.

Housed in an attractive former post-office building at the corner of Prince and Greene streets, **Station A** (103 Prince) is Apple's suitably stylish retail temple. Fight your way through the crowd to iPods, iPads, iMacs, or whatever the latest product is. Check your email on one of the display models while you're there or

TIP

TOAST stands for the TriBeCa Open Artist Studio Tour, when over 100 artists throw open their doors. This four-day event is usually held in spring. Details can be found at www.toastartwalk.com.

Vintage shops are plentiful.

TIP

It seems obvious, but it can confuse even the most seasoned SoHo pilgrim. West Broadway and Broadway are two different streets that run parallel to each other. Always double check your destination's address or you might end up on a corner, scratching your head.

check out the upstairs theater, where free seminars are held on how to get the best from your tech toy.

The Romanesque Revival-style building on the opposite corner dates from the same period, but a century or so later has been transformed into the small, luxurious **Mercer Hotel** (www.mercerhotel.com). Beneath it is a highly acclaimed basement-level restaurant, the **Mercer Kitchen**.

Broadway and beyond

Once home to the city's most elegant stores, and later to textile outlets, discount stores, and delis, the stately cast-iron buildings on Broadway below Canal Street reacquired cachet in the 1980s, first as museums, then as galleries, and then as stores like Crate & Barrel and Banana Republic. A Downtown **Bloomingdale's** (504 Broadway; www1.bloomingdales.com) has added more shopper traffic to the busy sidewalks.

Despite the presence of Bloomies and a handful of upscale stores, the SoHo stretch of Broadway is best seen as West Broadway's younger, more mainstream cousin. Here you can find stores selling the latest jeans, sneakers, and casual daywear. Recent imports H&M, Topshop, and Uniqlo are proving particularly popular with SoHo's young trendsetters looking for style on a budget.

A 1904 cast-iron confection called the **Little Singer Building**, designed by Ernest Flagg (and now home to swank, multimillion-dollar apartments), stands across Broadway from **Dean & Deluca** ❸ (560 Broadway; www.deandeluca.com), at the opposite corner of Prince Street. Dean & Deluca has been described by the *Washington Post* as 'a combination of Paris's Fauchon, London's Harrod's Food Halls, and Milan's Peck all rolled into one,' and presents food as art: a cornucopia of fruits, vegetables, and imported gourmet grocery specialties. This has proved to be so successful a formula that Dean & Deluca stores have branched out. The stand-up coffee bar is stocked with delectable pastries, and is a perfect place for a quick snack – although if you arrive before 10am, expect a long line of pre-work coffee drinkers.

If the Harry Potter novels made J.K. Rowling a billionaire, evidence that it did just as much for her US

CASTELLI'S GALLERY

Leo Castelli's gallery at 420 West Broadway (now DKNY) gave a shop window to the 1960s and 1970s Pop Art movement, and a massive boost to the SoHo arts scene. Leo and his wife Ileana first had a gallery in Paris in 1935, but as World War II broke out they decamped to New York. It wasn't until 1954, when Leo saw some of Robert Rauschenberg's work, that he re-entered the art world, wanting only to work with art that inspired him with 'pure enthusiasm.' He started on the Upper East Side, opening a gallery in 1957 that showcased the work of Rauschenberg, Jasper Johns, and Frank Stella. In the 1960s, the Pop Art movement exploded, and Castelli championed these and many other groundbreaking artists. His gallery relocated to 420 West Broadway in 1971, and was instrumental in making SoHo the center of the New York art scene. For the next 28 years, Castelli launched major exhibitions and bestowed major gifts, including giving Rauschenberg's Bed to MoMA in 1988 when it was valued at $10 million (he bought it in 1958 for a mere $1,200). When he died in 1999, Castelli's collection returned to the Upper East Side, and can be visited at 18 East 77th Street (www.castelligallery.com; tel: 212-249 4470).

A New York minute at the Roxy Tribeca.

publisher **Scholastic Books** is their huge and colorful bookstore at 555 Broadway (http://store.scholastic.com). Aisles of kids' books, arts and crafts, and free Saturday events make this a good family stop.

Walking east on Prince leads to Lafayette Street, where urbanites can pick up hip-hop-influenced street wear from stores such as Wesc or Brooklyn Industries.

Children's Museum of the Arts ❹

Address: 103 Charlton Street (between Greenwich and Hudson streets), www.cmany.org
Telephone: 212-274 0986
Opening Hours: Mon noon–5pm, Thu–Fri noon–6pm, Sat–Sun 10am–5pm
Entrance Fee: charge
Subway: Spring Street/Canal Street

A successful cross between a museum and a particularly lively day-care center, the Children's Museum aims to encourage tiny artists through inspiration – it has a collection of 2,000 works of children's art from around the world – and through interactive exhibits and artist-led classes for kids. Group activities are tailor-made for specific age groups – for example, the 'WEE Arts' program allows children aged 10 months to five years to explore art (or make a mess) using Play-Doh, paints, and a variety of other child-friendly materials, while for older kids, a highlight are classes that teach the basics of puppetry, podcasting, and filmmaking.

Prada is housed on the premises of the former Guggenheim Museum.

Bloomingdale's Department Store.

TIP

SoHo may be the place to score a pair of designer boots, but there are plenty of the hiking variety as well. Outdoor outfitters Eastern Mountain Sports, The North Face, Patagonia, and REI all have locations shoulder-to-shoulder with the boutiques.

Flora and Miss Lizzie

Back on Broadway, the **Haughwout Building** ❺ is the palazzo-style structure near Broome Street. The Haughwout is one of SoHo's oldest – and most striking – cast-iron edifices. Designed by John Gaynor, it was constructed in 1857 as one of the country's first retail stores, complete with its first elevator.

Named after a Revolutionary War general, **Greene Street** ❻, like Mercer and Wooster streets, runs parallel to West Broadway and Broadway. In the late 19th century this was the center of New York's most notorious red-light district, where brothels with names like Flora's and Miss Lizzie's flourished behind shuttered windows. Now the same windows attract a very different sort of browser – gazing longingly over summer dresses in bright, '80s-influenced colors at Anna Sui (484 Broome St; www.annasui.com).

As befits one of the SoHo Cast Iron Historic District's prime thoroughfares, Greene Street also offers a rich concentration of this uniquely American architecture at its best, including (at the Canal Street end) the city's longest continuous row of cast-iron buildings.

At the corner of Broome Street, the 1872 **Gunther Building** is particularly worthy of notice. Before continuing, stop and admire the cream-colored architectural 'king' of cast-iron splendor at **72–76 Greene Street**, just opposite. This impressively ornate structure was designed and built by Isaac Duckworth in 1873.

Wooster Street arts scene

For more shopping and a selection of SoHo's few remaining galleries (which seem to hop from street to street on a regular basis), walk across to stone-cobbled **Wooster Street** ❼. The long-established **Dia Center for the Arts** has moved onto Chelsea with everybody else, but they maintain a presence at 141 Wooster Street with the *New York Earth Room*, a room interior filled with real earth, by Walter De Maria (Wed–Sun noon–6pm, closed 3–3.30pm; free). The Dia Center also has a major gallery space at Beacon in the Hudson Valley.

In addition to galleries, this end of Wooster also has the ever-popular and

The Children's Museum of the Arts.

Something for everyone at Dean & Deluca.

experimental **Performing Garage** (33 Wooster, http://thewoostergroup.org/blog, tel: 212-966 9796), which has presented the Wooster Group's unique brand of theater, dance, and performance art since 1967.

Food for thought

John Broome was a successful merchant who imported tea and silk from China at the end of the Revolutionary War, so he might have appreciated the fresh produce and other goods sold at the **Gourmet Garage** (489 Broome, at Wooster Street, www.gourmetgarage.com), an indoor market serving the restaurant trade and SoHo locals.

In general, Broome Street is one of SoHo's least jazzed-up thoroughfares, unless you count the ornate Calvert Vaux-designed edifice at No. 448, built in 1872. A lunch treat awaits a little farther on at the corner of West Broadway in the characterful **Broome Street Bar**. Situated in a pretty 18th-century house, the Broome Street Bar with its friendly staff has been serving sandwiches, soups, and burgers at its wooden tables since SoHo was involved in the arts scene.

Crossing West Broadway, you're on the fringe of the South Village, where chic little shoe salons and boutiques nestle among places like the **Birdbath Bakery** (http://thecitybakery.com) on Prince between West Broadway and Thompson Street, which, until very recently, had been run as the Vesuvio Bakery by the same family since the 1920s. Vesuvio had locals lining up for its freshly baked bread, and now Birdbath follows in its footsteps with a focus on organic and sustainable baked goods. There are six other locations in New York.

One of SoHo's remaining refreshment stops should provide the stamina for a detour down Thompson to Spring Street, then west across Sixth Avenue to the New York Fire Department's museum, on one of Spring Street's last blocks before it meets the river.

Colorful fire escapes in SoHo.

The New York Mercantile Exchange Building on Harrison Street.

The New York Fire Museum.

New York City Fire Museum 8

Address: 278 Spring Street (at Varick and Hudson streets), www.nycfiremuseum.org
Telephone: 212-691 1303
Opening Hours: daily 10am–5pm
Entrance Fee: charge
Subway: Spring Street

It's worth the walk to Engine Company No. 30's former headquarters to visit this charming museum. The restored fire house's original features include the brass sliding pole and apparatus doors, providing a perfect setting for one of the country's largest collections of firefighting apparatus and memorabilia. Highlights include the shiny red antique hand- and horse-pulled wagons – especially popular with children. A special extension houses a permanent 9/11 exhibit, with powerful images from that sad day.

Canalside

Back on West Broadway, SoHo comes to a halt at **Canal Street** 9, where stores sell plastic odds and ends, rubber tubing, neon signs, household appliances, and barrels of peculiar industrial leftovers. It's all mixed together in a bedlam of hot-dog carts and street vendors displaying old books, bootleg CDs and DVDs, purses, and, from time to time, a few bona fide treasures.

TRIBECA

In the late 1970s, artists in search of lower rents migrated south from SoHo to TriBeCa – the **Tri**angle **Be**low **Ca**nal – which runs south of Canal Street to Chambers Street, and west from Broadway to the Hudson River. Called Washington Market in the days when the city's major produce businesses operated here (before they moved to Hunt's Point in the Bronx), this part of the Lower West Side is one of Manhattan's most pleasant neighborhoods.

Now an eclectic blend of renovated commercial warehouses, Corinthian columns, condo towers, and celebrity restaurants, TriBeCa was where artists like David Cale or Laurie Anderson showed their early works, at venues like the Alternative Museum and Franklin Furnace (now exclusively at www.alternativemuseum.org and www.franklinfurnace.org respectively).

Today's TriBeCa scene has more to show in the culinary than in the fine arts, but its largely residential atmosphere makes a pleasant change of pace from SoHo's tourist-packed streets. A block south of Canal, the Roxy Hotel Tribeca, rising from the triangle bordered by Sixth Avenue, Walker and White streets, looms over one of the area's oldest survivors: an 1809 brick house at **2 White Street**, just off West Broadway, which dates back to an earlier era when this was one of the city's original residential enclaves.

Grand designs

The newly refurbished, boutique The **Roxy** Hotel (www.roxyhotelnyc.com), younger sister to the Soho Grand, keeps the residential tradition alive with its hip, trendy hospitality. Features for glamorous guests include an atrium lounge and 201 ergonomically designed rooms, with extra-large windows and great amenities.

The handsome **Clocktower Building** at 108 Leonard Street (also 346 Broadway) – named for its ornate tower – is the former New York Life Insurance Building, which was remodeled by Stanford White in 1898. After more than 40 years of operation, the famous Clocktower Gallery closed its doors in 2013. The building is now undergoing a major conversion to contain luxury residential condominium units, while former resident **AIR, Art International Radio** – the internet-based radio station that showcases music, interviews with artists, and 'audio art' – has now moved their headquarters and studios to 159 Pioneer Street.

On the corner of Thomas Street and West Broadway, two blocks below Leonard Street, a red neon sign spells out 'Cafeteria,' but don't be fooled. This 1930s mock-stone building has housed **The Odeon** (www.theodeonrestaurant.com), one of Downtown's hippest restaurants, since it opened in 1980. Unlike many trendy spots, it shows no signs of fading away and is still a favorite with the cognoscenti, especially late into the night.

Duane and Staple

Below Thomas is **Duane Street**. Named for New York's first post-Revolution mayor, it meets Hudson Street at tiny triangular **Duane Park** ⑩ – all that's left of a farm that the city bought for $5 in 1795.

Staple Street, a narrow strip of cobblestone where 'staple' produce was once unloaded, connects the park with the ornate-brick, former **Mercantile Exchange Building** ⑪, on the corner of Harrison and Hudson streets.

The neighboring 1920s **60 Hudson, the** former **Western Union Building** ⑫ soars 24 stories above the rest of the neighborhood like a layered missile, and is made of 19 different shades of brick. Its lobby, where even the letterboxes are marvels of Art Deco artistry, is also stunning. Unfortunately you can no longer

TIP

Brandy Library (www.brandylibrary.com), 25 North Moore Street at Varick, appeals to an upscale crowd who like their couches low and their drinks long. To complete the sophistication, cigar smokers can light up on the heated terrace.

The exterior of the Angelica Theater.

TIP

Need to recharge? Slip into Bliss spa at its flagship SoHo location (568 Broadway at Prince Street; www.blissworld.com; tel: 877-862 5477) for premium pampering. There are other locations around town, too.

walk through it to West Broadway, but you can still get a good glimpse through the gate by the main doors.

Greenwich and Harrison

Greenwich Street is where much of TriBeCa's new development is centered, but you can still find authentic early remnants – like the 19th-century lantern factory between Laight and Vestry streets, which now houses million-dollar lofts.

The corner of Greenwich and Franklin streets is the place where actor Robert De Niro transformed the old Martinson Coffee Factory into the **Tribeca Film Center** ⓭ (www.tribecafilmcenter.com). On the first floor is the **Tribeca Grill**, co-owned by actor Robert de Niro and chef Drew Nieporent. Many come here in the hope of seeing De Niro or film-biz luminaries from the upstairs offices. Chances are, the closest you'll get to a sighting is one of De Niro's dad's paintings on the walls, and while you do occasionally see people talking 'back-end' and reading scripts, most of the clientele are regular business types and star-struck tourists. The food, however, rarely disappoints.

The late 18th- and early 19th-century brick houses on **Harrison Street** look incongruous, like a stage set in the shadow of **Independence Plaza**'s gargantuan 1970s apartment towers, but like the house on White Street, they're evocative survivors of TriBeCa's residential beginnings.

Neighborhood parks

Opposite the big line of condo dwellings stretching between Duane and Chambers streets, **Washington Market Park** ⓮ (www.washingtonmarketpark.org) has a thick grassy meadow to stretch out on, and even a fanciful gazebo to daydream in. P.S. 234, The Independence School – its wrought-iron fence embossed with Spanish galleons in full sail – is across from the park, and worth noting.

From Chambers and West Street, you can reach **Hudson River Park** (www.hudsonriverpark.org) via a pedestrian bridge that stretches across the West Side Highway. Walkways and bike paths extend north along the river beyond Pier 25, and south to connect to Battery Park City. If you continue south, there's a scenic riverside walk, complete with views of the Statue of Liberty.

Morgan Freeman, speaking at the Tribeca Film Festival.

HOUSTON STREET

The border between SoHo and the West Village is Houston Street. Pronounced '*how-stun*,' it was named for William Houstoun, a delegate from Georgia who married the daughter of Nicholas Bayard III, a prominent New Yorker and grandson of an original mayor. The city's three major art-house cinemas – Film Forum, The Angelica, and Landmark Sunshine – are situated on the street (the Anthology Film Archives is one block north). Also marking the point where numbered streets begin, it is a heavily trafficked, and not particularly attractive, thoroughfare. Still, years of construction have made it safer and easier to negotiate, and the stores, bars, and restaurants keep opening.

Hudson River Park, Greenwich Village.

SHOPPING

Sinatra might not have approved of these alternate lyrics, but they certainly ring true: If you can't buy it here, you can't buy it anywhere.

New York institution Bloomingdale's takes up an entire block on Third Avenue in the Upper East Side (there's also a branch in SoHo). Bloomies is full of everything you could ever need, and a lot you don't but want to buy anyway. Most of the top designers are here.

For anyone who rates shopping as one of life's greater imperatives, New York is the place to be. Manhattan has every kind of shop imaginable. In terms of orientation, a general rule of thumb is that the big department stores are in Midtown. Many of these are opulent – including Barneys and Bergdorf Goodman. Uptown and in Midtown you'll also find stores with world-famous names, like the popular Apple boutique on Fifth Avenue.

The more quirky stores are downtown. Greenwich Village, SoHo, NoHo and the Meatpacking District are places where stylish shoppers go to find the latest fashions from up-and-coming designers, as well as vintage pieces. And the style goes beyond clothing: ABC Carpet and Home offers a mix of luxurious home decor, and more unusual finds. Even the bath goods – like those at Kiehl's – are coveted.

Some purchases don't always have a long shelf life, but are worth every cent. World-class chocolate shops like Kee's, legendary cheesemongers like Murray's, and oenologists like Astor Wine & Spirits can offer expert advice on consumable gifts for friends, family, or yourself. So go ahead, take the plunge – just don't forget that sales tax of around 8 percent.

A clock stands at the entrance to the Nat Sherman tobacconist store in Midtown, at 5th Avenue and 42nd Street.

SoHo's Dean & Deluca stocks gourmet food and fine wine, wonderful cheeses, charcuterie, chocolate, and freshly ground coffee. The prices aren't low, but neither is the quality.

THE PRICE IS RIGHT

Thanksgiving shoppers hit the sales at Macy's.

You can buy anything in New York, but smart shoppers know how to get the best for less. New York City's biggest shopping period starts the day after Thanksgiving (known as 'Black Friday') through to New Year's Day. During this time, you may find sales (particularly early on the morning of Black Friday) along with festive holiday decorations and, at the department stores, magnificently decorated windows that draw crowds so big they need to put up velvet ropes.

Other than that, the best months for sales are February and August, as the stores clean out their inventory to make way for the next season's wares.

Savvy shoppers who don't like to wait for sales often frequent New York's bargain houses, including Century 21. Here, the clothing won't be well lit and lined up on elegant displays – in fact, you may have to dig through bins, and often you won't find items in a variety of colors or sizes. For some shoppers, it's a frustrating prospect – but for diehard deal hunters, it's great to know there's a bargain waiting if they are willing to look.

A muppet peeks out of a shopping bag in a toy store.

If the prices of the high-end stores are too intimidating, don't be afraid to window-shop.

The perfect souvenir.

Lower East Side folk.

THE EAST VILLAGE AND THE LOWER EAST SIDE

From historic synagogues on the Lower East Side to the trendy shops in NoLita; from dim sum in Chinatown to cutting-edge clubs in Alphabet City – this is Manhattan's melting pot.

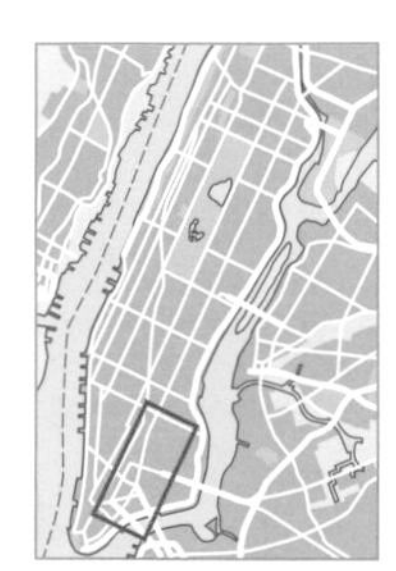

Main Attractions

Merchant's House Museum
Astor Place
St Mark's Place
Tompkins Square Park
Alphabet City
Lower East Side Tenement Museum
New Museum of Contemporary Art
Little Italy
Chinatown

Map

Page 98

Bordered by 14th Street to the north and Houston Street to the south, and roughly centered between Third Avenue and Avenue B, the **East Village** is a place that stays up late, where fashion and politics have always been more radical than elsewhere in the city, and whose residents have included Beat icons like Allen Ginsberg and William Burroughs, as well as Yippies, Hell's Angels, and punk rock pioneers.

Beneath its scruffy avant-garde surface, the East Village is also a neighborhood of immigrants, with Ukrainian and Puerto Rican social clubs next to cutting-edge boutiques, and free health clinics not far from expensive co-op buildings. Like other Downtown neighborhoods, old and new are juxtaposed here in an ever-changing mosaic.

EAST VILLAGE

At the beginning of the 20th century, lower Broadway around 9th Street was part of the 'Ladies' Mile' of fashionable retailing that extended north to 23rd Street. Later, it was just a dingy pause away from SoHo (when that area was still known as SoHo), but all that changed when Tower Records and other consumer meccas moved in. Unofficially known as **NoHo** (**No**rth of **Ho**uston) (15), this stretch of the East Village includes Broadway from Astor Place down to Houston Street, a place crowded with fashion, art, and design stores.

Some interesting home-furnishing shops and clothing boutiques also tempt along Lafayette Street, and trendy restaurants call out from the side streets like Bond and Great Jones, a two block stretch between East and West Third Street that was immortalized in a Don Delillo novel of the same name and contributed to

NoHo knitwear.

The exterior of the Merchant's House Museum.

Merchant's House Museum interior.

the immortalization of Jean-Michel Basquiat, who died in his studio at #57.

Merchant's House Museum ⓰

Address: 29 E. 4th Street (at Lafayette Street and the Bowery), www.merchantshouse.org
Telephone: 212-777 1089
Operating Hours: Fri–Mon noon–5pm; Thu till 8pm
Entrance Fee: charge
Subway: Astor Place

A block up from Great Jones Street on West 4th Street (just above Lafayette), drop in and see the city as it used to be at the 'Merchant's House,' a compact Greek Revival-style brick townhouse built in 1832. The same family, the Tredwells, lived here for generations until Gertrude Tredwell died in 1933, in the house where she was born. Their furnishings and personal effects have been preserved as they would have looked in the 19th century.

This is a good opportunity to see how wealthy New Yorkers lived – a nice companion to the slightly later Theodore Roosevelt Birthplace near Gramercy Park (see page 143). Visitors are free to walk around the house, and a booklet provides information on its history and the Tredwell family. There are guided tours at 2pm and Thu at 6.30pm.

NoHo arts

A detour east along 4th Street will take you to the slightly shabby **La MaMa** experimental theater (74A East 4th Street; http://lamama.org; tel: 212-475 7710). A pioneer of the avant-garde since 1961, the theater has three performance spaces and an art gallery.

Continuing north on Lafayette Street, **Colonnade Row** was originally a group of nine columned homes, built in 1833 when this was one of the city's most elegant neighborhoods. Only four of the houses still stand: current occupants include the perennially stylish **Indochine** restaurant at No. 430 and the **Astor Place Theatre** (No. 434), where the Blue Man Group (www.blueman.com) is currently resident.

Across the street is the **Public Theater** ⓱ (www.publictheater.org; tel: 212-539 8500), a red-brick, five-theater complex that originally housed the

Astor Library. Since its founding by Joseph Papp in 1967, the theater has been the host of Shakespeare in the Park (with free performances in Central Park during the summer), as well as more contemporary productions – from the world premiere of *Hair* to *A Chorus Line* to *Bring in 'Da Noise, Bring in 'Da Funk* – that have gone on to be bit hits on Broadway.

For great and eclectic live music, spend an evening in **Joe's Pub** (425 Lafayette Street; www.joespub.com; tel: 212-967 7555), an intimate venue, bar, and satellite of the Public Theater. You can have dinner here, too.

Around Astor Place

Lafayette ends at **Astor Place** ⓲, where a large Kmart reflects a departure from the Village's counterculture roots. The area's most notable landmark, besides the handsome **Astor Place subway kiosk** and the glassy condo building by Gwathmey Siegel, is the giant black cube by Tony Rosenthal called ***The Alamo***. One of the first abstract sculptures installed on city property, it stands at the intersection of Astor Place, St Mark's Place, and Lafayette Street. Tourists like to give it a spin (push it and see), but it goes largely unnoticed by local workers as they hurry by.

The imposing brown Italianate **Cooper Union Foundation Building** ⓳, between Third and Fourth avenues, opened in 1859 as one of the country's earliest centers of free education (only recently financial strains have forced them to charge for tuition). Now well known as an art school (varied exhibitions; www.cooper.edu; tel: 212-353 4100), this is also where Abraham Lincoln gave the popular speech said to have launched his presidential campaign.

A statue of the schools' founder-philanthropist Peter Cooper by Augustus St-Gaudens, who was a student here, stands behind Cooper Union at **Cooper Square**, where Third and Fourth avenues converge at the top of the Bowery. **41 Cooper Square** is the address and name of the school's newest center for classrooms, studios, and labs. Designed by Thom Mayne, it's a remarkable piece of modern architecture, full of slanted steel planes, creases, grids, and twists.

KIDS

It's only 8 acres (3 hectares), but Sara Roosevelt Park – bordered by Canal, Chrystie, Houston, and Forsyth streets – is a hidden sanctuary with basketball, volleyball, and handball courts, soccer fields, five playgrounds, and a community garden.

41 Cooper Square.

The cast-iron Astor Place subway kiosk is one of New York's finest.

St Mark's Historic District

Walking from the Cooper Union to Third Avenue, you'll come across Stuyvesant Street, which veers off at an angle toward Second Avenue. **St Mark's Bookshop** (www.stmarksbookshop.com; tel: 212-260 7853), at the corner of Third and Stuyvesant, is a long-established store stocked with obscure new fiction, art books, and political tomes – its peaceful aisles provide a refreshing break.

The red-brick Anglo-Italianate houses on Stuyvesant Street and on East 10th Street form the heart of the **St Mark's Historic District**. The handsome home at 21 Stuyvesant is the **Stuyvesant-Fish House**, a national historic landmark built by former Dutch governor Peter Stuyvesant's great-grandson by marriage, Hamilton Fish, which is now owned by the Cooper Union.

St Mark's-in-the-Bowery ⓴

Address: 131 E. 10th Street (at Second Avenue), http://stmarksbowery.org/welcome
Telephone: 212-674 6377
Opening Hours: daily, times vary
Entrance Fee: free
Subway: Astor Place/Third Avenue

The second-oldest church building in Manhattan (after St Paul's Chapel), St Mark's was nearly destroyed by fire in 1978, and was restored with the help of local residents. It has suffered a little again in the intervening years and is in need of attention, but when you consider its age this is hardly surprising. St Mark's has a long history of liberal religious thought – a reflection of the neighborhood that manifests itself in such longstanding community programs as the Poetry Project – and holds art shows in the parish hall.

East Village North

Continuing on 10th Street into the East Village, toward First Avenue, the **Theater for the New City** (www.theaterforthenewcity.net; tel: 212-254 1109) on First Avenue was founded in 1971 as a venue for experimental Off-Broadway productions. Today it continues to put on new plays, as well as providing a performance space for theater groups that don't have their own.

If you feel the need for an energy rush, there's espresso and pastries

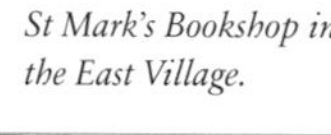

St Mark's Bookshop in the East Village.

LOISAIDA

Puerto Rican poet Bittman 'Bimbo' Rivas wrote, 'I dig the way you talk, I dig the way you look.' The object of his affection was the Lower East Side, or as he referred to it, *Loisaida*. The name stuck, and when an influx of Puerto Ricans arrived in New York in the 1940s–1960s, this is where they came. They called themselves Nuyoricans and by the 1970s they had established the Nuyorican Poets Cafe (www.nuyorican.org), where Rivas read his poetry, and Loisaida Inc (www.loisaidafestival.org), which aimed to combat poverty, drugs, and violence in the community. Nuyoricans are now scattered in communities throughout the boroughs, but the spirit still remains in Alphabet City, where the Loisaida Festival is held every Memorial Day weekend.

at **Veniero** (http://venierospastry.com) on 11th Street near First Avenue, testimony to an Italian enclave that flourished here in the early 1900s. You can't miss the red neon sign (even though a few of the letters have ceased working); once inside choose from a toothache-inducing array of tiny Italian pastries to take out, or sit down and enjoy one in the high-ceilinged café.

Not far away, **St Nicholas** ㉑ Carpatho-Russian Orthodox Greek Catholic Church (http://stnicholaschurchnyc.org) is a reminder of this ethnic and religious melting pot. Originally built for a predominantly Episcopal parish as St Mark's Chapel, inside it has tiled walls and a beamed ceiling dating from 1894.

Over on 9th Street, Performance Space 122, better known as **P.S.122** (First Avenue at 9th Street; www.ps122.org; tel: 212-477 5829), is a multi-arts organization set up to nurture young and mid-career artists. The East Village has been a center for live performances ever since Second Avenue was lined by Yiddish theaters in the 1890s; a reminder of those times is the venerable **Orpheum Theater** (www.orpheum-theater.com) situated at 126 Second Avenue.

Velvet Underground

St Mark's Place ㉒, a continuation of 8th Street between Third Avenue and Avenue A, is the East Village version of Main Street. In the 1960s, this was the counterculture center of the East Coast, where Andy Warhol presented Velvet Underground 'happenings' and, later, barefoot freaks tripped out at the Electric Circus. It's now a gentrified condo/retail center of stores and residences.

The Fillmore East, which presented the East Coast's most psychedelic concerts, is also gone, but St Mark's Place is still one of the city's liveliest thoroughfares. Sidewalk cafés and restaurants heave with customers, and the bazaar-like atmosphere is augmented by street vendors selling T-shirts, leatherwear, jewelry, and bootleg CDs and DVDs.

Shop for retro, punk, or retro-punk gear here, then pause for refreshment around the corner – down Third Avenue to East 7th Street – at a true drinking-man's pub.

McSorley's Old Ale House ㉓

Address: 15 E. 7th Street (between Second and Third Avenues)
Telephone: 212-474 9148
Opening Hours: Mon–Sat 11am–1am, Sun 1pm–1am
Subway: Astor Place/8th Street

McSorley's has been in business since the 1850s, although women weren't allowed inside until more than a century later. This was a favorite New York hangout of the Irish writer Brendan Behan, among other luminaries. The décor hasn't changed much over the past 150 years – there's still sawdust on the floor and standing-room only at the bar – but space *has* been made for a ladies' bathroom.

McSorley's Old Ale House dates from 1854.

EAT

A short time ago, Vietnamese bánh mì sandwiches were all the rage. Savory concoctions of meat, pâté, pickled veggies, and cilantro, they could be found in almost every neighborhood. Bành Mí Zòn, at 443 East 6th Street (www.banhmizon.com), is one of the few to survive the craze. Rightfully so: they're fantastic.

Every last patch of wall is covered with photos, posters, cartoons, and other curios; eagle-eyed patrons might spot an original wanted poster for Abraham Lincoln's assassin. As with New York's other remaining 19th-century saloons, McSorley's can be a bit of a tourist trap, but it's so much a part of the area's history that it still has its regulars – all of whom must abide by the McSorley motto: *Be Good, Or Be Gone*.

Music legends

Back on St Mark's, the block between Second and Third is lined by a motley array of music stores, tattoo parlors, and places to get piercings in a variety of body parts. CBGB-OMFUG, previously at 315 Bowery, was the city's coolest (and filthiest) live-music venue and the birthplace of the New York punk scene. The club was forced to close at the end of 2006 – joining the roll call of local businesses forced out by rising property prices. In 2008, the space reopened as a John Varvatos clothing boutique (www.johnvarvatos.com). The poster- and sticker-covered walls were left intact, and are behind glass.

Down the block, Daniel Boulud's brasserie DBGB (www.dbgb.com) has an excellent selection of sausage and beer.

Cheap and spicy

Once upon a time you could find just about any cuisine in the East Village for next to nothing. Many of the neighborhood's old stalwarts have been forced on, making way for new (more expensive) restaurants. However, if cheap and spicy is your preference, you can't do much better than head for **'Little India'** **24**, a strip of Indian restaurants on 6th Street between First and Second avenues. In the evening the air is filled with enticing smells, and visitors drift from menu to menu in the attempt to make a decision. All the restaurants here are inexpensive, most stay open pretty late, and some have live Indian music on weekend evenings.

Farther east on 6th Street is Avenue A, and a café-lined stretch that continues to **Tompkins Square Park** **25**. Formerly reclaimed swamp that was used as a drill ground and recruiting

Alphabet City market.

camp during the Civil War, it was later the center of the *Kleine Deutschland* (Little Germany) community that thrived here 100 years ago. The park was an infamous gathering place for hippies and runaways in the 1960s, and became a focal point for conflicts between homeless activists and police in the 1980s. Today, however, it's a generally peaceful place, frequented by young mothers with kids and neighborhood folk exercising their pets in the dog run. Many of the homes have been renovated (the 19th-century row houses on 10th Street are a good example), fueling a hike in rents as in other 'reclaimed' parts of the city, and creating resentment from the locals fighting to stay in the area.

Alphabet City

Nowhere is this urban reclamation more evident than in the area known as **Alphabet City** ㉖ (Avenues A, B, C, and D). For decades the very name was synonymous with crime and little punishment, but now slums and barbed wire have been supplanted by bars and restaurants with a young, hip clientele.

Tiny community parks have been divested of drug dealers and twinkle at night with fairy lights, while former bodegas have metamorphosed into fashion boutiques with SoHo prices. Avenue A in particular is on the up, and although still a little rough around the edges, now wears its graffiti like a badge of honor. **The Museum of Reclaimed Urban Space** (155 Avenue C; www.morusnyc.org; Tue and Thu–Sun 11am–7pm) offers tours of community gardens, activists centers and squats, led by local historians and activists (Sat–Sun at 3pm). The visit to the museum and the tours are good occasions to see how the local community has changed its neighborhood for the better.

As in other cutting-edge neighborhoods, though, it's wise to exercise a degree of caution, and here it's easy – just follow the alphabet. Avenues A, B, and C are fine anytime. Avenue D is fairly safe until midnight, but just for now it's an idea to avoid it after that.

Dining possibilities in the area are seemingly limitless, but an inexpensive stalwart has always been **Veselka** (144 Second Avenue at 9th Street ; http://veselka.com; open 24 hours), a survivor of the neighborhood's Eastern European past, where specialties include home-cooked *pierogies*, *blintzes*, and *borscht*, along with standard diner fare.

LOWER EAST SIDE

Technically, this area starts east of Tompkins Square Park, where Avenue C unofficially becomes Loisaida Avenue (*Loisaida* is Puerto Rican Spanglish for 'Lower East Side'). But the traditional Lower East Side, with its Jewish-immigrant roots still in place, is south of East Houston Street, bordered by the Bowery and the East River. This is where the narrow streets are lined by tenements dating back 150 years.

These days you'll see stores with Jewish names and Chinese or Hispanic owners, a reminder that this

Tompkins Square Park.

Jewish temple on the Lower East Side.

neighborhood has always welcomed new arrivals. Modern newcomers are the bohemian-minded bars, clubs, and shops thriving along Ludlow, Orchard, and other streets, a trend that was kicked off in 1993 when **Mercury Lounge** – one of the city's best small music venues – kicked open its doors at 217 East Houston Street (www.mercuryloungenyc.com; check out listings in *Time Out New York* or the *Village Voice*).

Today, you can shop for exotic foods from family stores that have been here for decades, then stroll along next door for a just-off-the-runway outfit – evidence of the gentrification of an immigrant neighborhood, but also of the vibrancy of change.

Delis and designers

Walk along East Houston to the top of **Orchard Street** ㉗ to reach a favorite Lower East Side retail destination. Serious shoppers may want to stop first at **Katz's Delicatessen** (205 East Houston, near Ludlow Street; http://katzsdelicatessen.com) for a little sustenance. The menu here has hardly changed since opening day in 1898 – and their pastrami sandwich has long been a New York culinary landmark.

New customers include the many construction workers currently working on the apartment blocks and fashionable hotels that are springing up in the area.

Once crowded with peddlers selling old clothes and cracked eggs, today the top of Orchard from East Houston to Rivington is being heavily redeveloped, with stylish new stores selling an intriguing mix of marked-up second-hand clothing, bespoke jewelry, street-smart sneakers, and designer clothes.

The crowning glory of this upscale takeover is **The Hotel on Rivington** (www.hotelonrivington.com), by Ludlow Street – a 21-story glass tower with unrivaled views over the Lower East Side. Bouncer-like doormen guard the entrance to the über-designed interior, and sharply dressed urbanites toy with Asian-fusion at **CO-OP**. The arrival of this hotel loudly proclaimed the Lower East Side's new status of cool, and more hotels are planned for the future.

Three blocks west of The Hotel, proof of the area's continuing role as a center for immigrants is the 19th-century **University Settlement House** (www.universitysettlement.org) on Eldridge Street (at Rivington). The first settlement house in the US, the organization continues to provide advice and assistance to local immigrants and low-income residents today.

Along Orchard Street

Farther south along Orchard Street, the lifestyle stores and boutiques give way to the Lower East Side's famous discount premises, selling bargain fashions, fabrics, linens, and shoes. The scene is frenetic at times, and bargaining is encouraged, but make sure you know what you want beforehand to ensure you get a good price.

THE ABCS OF PUNK ROAD

The West Village had established itself as the cool and mellow testing grounds for folk troubadours and masters of jazz. At the other end of the island, an opposite movement was taking place. Stressing attitude over musicianship, the pioneers of punk claimed the East as their own in the 1970s and 80s, congregating around the Bowery, St Mark's Place and Tompkins Square Park. Many trace the origins back to the Velvet Underground's 'happenings' and the high-energy rock of the New York Dolls, as well as Iggy Pop and The Stooges, but punk didn't really take off until 1976, when the Ramones came barreling into the limelight with a style that was like a revved up version of the Beach Boys. Legendary club CBGB anchored the scene, showcasing Patti Smith, the Misfits, and The Cramps. The Sex Pistols, The Clash, and other imports from London joined in, giving the aggressive style an international flavor.

By the 80s the tide began turning toward New Wave acts like Blondie, Talking Heads, and Devo. Some say the Tompkins Square Park Riot of 1988, where police clashed with young 'punks,' marked the end of the punk era, but even today you can catch some descendants of punk music in clubs like the Mercury Lounge.

Outside the Lower East Side Tenement Museum.

Old favorites include Giselle (http://giselleny.com) at 143 Orchard, with four floors of discounted women's fashion (labels include Escada, Laurel, and Valentino); Ben Freedman (www.benfreedman.com) at 137 Orchard, for 75 years the purveyor of bargain men's apparel; and Sam's Knitwear at 93 Orchard, where Polish immigrant Sam Goldstein has provided vintage and modern suits to snappily dressed men since 1965.

Head west on Delancey Street for some old-world comfort food at **Sammy's Roumanian Steak House** (175 Chrystie Street, just north of Delancey; www.sammysromanian.com), a memorable, if not inexpensive, place to feast, and where a traditional pitcher of chicken fat comes with every meal. On a corner of Delancey is a well-known tribute to the area's first immigrant families.

Lower East Side Tenement Museum ㉘

Address: 108 Orchard Street (at Delancey and Broome streets), www.tenement.org
Telephone: 212-982 8420
Opening Hours: tours daily, check hours on the website
Entrance Fee: charge
Subway: Delancey Street/Essex Street

This museum is dedicated to the story of what life was like for poor immigrants in New York at the end of the 19th century. The address at 108 Orchard is the visitors' center and the starting point for tours of the tenements, which can only be visited with a guide.

Tours cover different themes, but all last one hour, during which visitors explore the recreated apartments of families who lived in the cramped quarters at 97 Orchard Street – each arranged to provide insight into the families' ethnic backgrounds and daily lives. What is remarkable is the imagination and resilience with which they sought to combat poverty and assimilate into New York society. The museum's tours are very popular,

Katz's Delicatessen.

A sewing machine on display at the Lower East Side Tenement Museum.

so be sure to book in advance. From April to December the museum also conducts weekend walking tours of the Lower East Side.

Designer tenement

The **Blue Moon Hotel** (www.bluemoon boutiquehotel.com) on Orchard) has tried to bridge the gap between the tenement experience and the area's modern-day desirability by converting a traditional tenement building, empty since the 1930s, into a fashionable hotel. Many of the building's original features have been restored, and items recovered during the renovation – including newspapers and Yiddish sheet music – have been put on display. Room prices are *very* contemporary, though.

Back up Ludlow you'll find Il Laboratorio del Gelato (www.laboratoriodelgelato.com), an artisanal maker of Italian-style *gelati*, with surprising flavors like wasabi and rose petal. Or around the corner, on Broome, you'll see the trendy Babycakes vegan bakery (www.erinmckennasbakery.com). Sadly, as in other parts of the city, soaring rent prices are forcing many of the traditional stores and eateries to close; the Tenement Museum publishes a list of all surviving specialty food shops in the area. One of the biggest local legends, Guss' Pickles, closed in 2009 (though The Pickle Guys at 46 Essex Street are doing a pretty good job filling the void; www.pickleguys.com). Despite the ongoing gentrification, this neighborhood (especially the trendy Broome Street) has preserved its original spirit and successfully posed as the Lower East Side at the beginning of the 20th century in the popular series *The Knick*, directed by Steve Soderbergh.

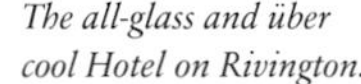

The all-glass and über cool Hotel on Rivington.

Living history

The Lower East Side's Jewish population produced an extraordinary number of famous actors and comedians. Oscar-nominated actor Sam Jaffe was born in an apartment at 97 Orchard Street – the 1863 tenement now run by the Tenement Museum – while a couple of blocks south, Grand Street's Seward Park High School (at Ludlow Street) counted Tony Curtis and Walter Matthau among its graduates. The high school closed in 2006, and has been divided up into five different schools, offering courses in a variety of fields.

In the 19th century, the area's substandard working and living conditions (ably chronicled by Jacob Riis) were instrumental in spawning anarchist and socialist movements. Emma Goldman preached her gentle anarchism on the Lower East Side, radical newspapers such as the *Jewish Daily Forward* flourished, and settlement houses offering immigrants health and education assistance were established.

Landmark buildings

The faces of Karl Marx and Friedrich Engels peer from a frieze above the entrance to the landmark building at **173 East Broadway** (between Pike and Rutgers) where the old *Daily Forward* was published, which has been converted into condos. A block south, the glorious red-brick **Henry Street Settlement** (265 Henry Street; www.henrystreet.org), founded in 1893 as the country's first volunteer nursing and social-service center, continues to serve the immigrant community and offers classes, health clinics, and after-school clubs.

Religion played an important role in the lives of immigrants. Although many of the synagogues in the area are no longer used, the **Eldridge Street Synagogue** (www.eldridgestreet.org, tel: 212-219 0302; charge), an 1887 Moorish-style landmark close to Division Street, has been the recipient of a 20-year restoration. Guided tours are available Sun–Thu 10am–5pm and Fri 10am–3pm on the hour,.

NOLITA 29

Dubbed **NoLita**, for **No**rth of **L**ittle **Ita**ly, the retail heart of this area, with its good-looking, arty residents and one-off (but pricey) fashion boutiques, is Mulberry Street, particularly between Houston and Kenmare. The best way to enjoy NoLita is simply to stroll around and drink in its exuberant atmosphere – a laid-back mix of the traditional and the trendy – before stopping off for a drink and a tasty tidbit in one of the watering holes on Elizabeth or Mott streets, now also with their share of fashionable stores.

St Patrick's Old Cathedral 30, (http://oldcathedral.org) on the corner of Mott and Prince streets, was the seat of New York's Catholic archdiocese until 1879, when the 'new' St Patrick's Cathedral on Fifth Avenue was completed. Construction of the cathedral began in 1809, was interrupted by the War of 1812, and was eventually finished three years later. It was rebuilt in 1868 after being destroyed by fire, and remains a unique landmark.

Across Mott Street from the cathedral graveyard, a plaque on the wall of a red-brick Victorian building explains that this was the School of the Children's Aid Society, created for the care and education of immigrant children. Designed in 1888 by Calvert Vaux, the English architect who also designed Jefferson Market Library and helped create Central

TIP

The Lower East Side Business Improvement District (LES BID) has a visitor center at 54 Orchard Street (between Hester and Grand streets; www.lowereastsideny.com; daily), with information on the area, walking tours, and discounts at many neighborhood businesses.

The Rice to Riches rice pudding bar, NoLita.

City of Immigrants

Getting started may be tough, but Lady Liberty's legendary call still beckons far across the globe.

The US Census Bureau estimated in 2012 that there were 8,491,079 people living in New York. Of these, more than 35 percent were born outside the United States, and more than 30 different regions of the globe were represented in the population. The common term 'melting pot' was first used by Israel Zangwill, an immigrant himself, to describe the masses huddled on the Lower East Side.

The New York migrant groups challenge city planners: the standard four-part categories – white, black, Hispanic, Asian – are hopelessly inadequate for the kaleidoscope of culture, race, and nationality of the people who live in the city. There's as much diversity within ethnic groups as there is between them, and the social and political splits within a group are often the most divisive.

Dancers perform in the Cinco de Mayo Parade.

A sample of Asians, for example, is as likely to include Koreans or Indians as it is Chinese immigrants, and they are just as likely to come from vastly different socio-economic backgrounds. Foreign-born blacks may resemble African-Americans, but black immigrants include French-speaking Haitians, plus English-speaking Barbadians, Trinidadians, and Jamaicans, Senegalese and Ghanians.

Among Latino groups, bound together as they are by a common language, are deep-rooted cultural differences. Mexicans and Chileans, Cubans and Puerto Ricans keep their cultural distinctions in the city's neighborhoods, just as they did back home. Little wonder, then, that the 2 million Latinos, easily the city's largest ethnic group, have yet to consolidate a unified political voice.

Syncretism

In the end, it doesn't really matter where people come from: They are here, and more arrive every day. New York's immigrants don't boil into a homogeneous cultural stew; they keep their identities and languages, and build new institutions and alliances. Nor is New York an example of pluralism – a multiethnic society where everyone has an equal say.

That tag is far too static, and doesn't account for the dynamism, or for the possibilities of confrontation and conflict. The right term for New York's cultural mix is probably syncretism – a continuous state of cultural collision, blending, and overlapping, where groups and individuals influence each other to create something new.

New York is a city of immigrants, and has been since the Dutch shared the town with English, French, and Scandinavian settlers, as well as with free Africans, black slaves, and Native Americans. The give-and-take – and often the push-and-shove – between cultures is what gave the city its vitality and a rough-cut worldliness.

Although immigrants come from farther away and speak languages never heard by New Yorkers 300 years ago, the same explosive energy still runs through the city today.

Park, it's now one of NoLita's most coveted apartment blocks.

Farther south on Centre Street are more desirable apartments; one in particular is the **Police Building**. This Beaux Arts edifice served as a police headquarters until 1973 (the current doormen do not look unlike the building's former employees).

New Museum of Contemporary Art 31

Address: 235 Bowery (at Prince Street), www.newmuseum.org
Telephone: 212-219 1222
Opening Hours: Wed–Sun 11am–6pm, Thu until 9pm
Entrance Fee: charge
Subway: Bowery/Broadway-Lafayette Street

In contrast to the Beaux Arts beauties around it, the New Museum of Contemporary Art is designed to make an emphatic statement in this historic neighborhood. Consisting of a series of cubes and rectangles, like a giant stack of boxes, the building provides a spectacular purpose-built home for the museum, which highlights the latest contemporary art and design.

The location of the New Museum follows a timeline of New York artistic trends. From its beginnings in 1977 on Fifth Avenue, it moved to SoHo during the 1980s, then followed SoHo's artists to Chelsea. The museum's arrival on the Lower East Side seals the status of the neighborhood as a center of innovative creativity. This is now even more true with the opening of the museum of the **International Center of Photography** (250 Bowery Street, www.icp.org), which has a permanent collection of over 135,000 photographs – including the archives of *Life* magazine. It includes real gems, so if you're interested in photography make sure to find out what's on while you're in New York. It also has a gallery, a media lab, and areas for research at Mana Contemporary in Jersey City.

LITTLE ITALY 32

Crowds – led along by tantalizing food stands and raucous games of chance – are an integral part of what draws visitors to the streets of Little Italy. Mulberry Street from Canal to East Houston becomes a lively pedestrian mall during the 10-day **Feast of**

TIP

A walking tour isn't exactly 'rock-and-roll' but the East Village Rock Tour is undeniably fun, with visits to the former homes of Joey Ramone, Iggy Pop, and Madonna. Visit www.rockjunket.com or call 212-209 3370.

Corner of Mulberry and Broome streets, Little Italy.

TIP

To save a few dollars while enjoying some lager or cabernet, seek out restaurants without liquor licenses. Most will let you bring your own, and there are over 20 in the East Village and Lower East Side alone. Filter your restaurant search results with 'BYOB' at http://nymag.com.

San Gennaro (www.sangennaro.org) held in September.

This area has been an Italian neighborhood since the 1880s, when large numbers of immigrants arrived in New York, mainly from southern Italy. The most pleasant part is along **Mulberry Street**, north of Canal, where the atmosphere changes from boisterous to almost mellow, and the sidewalks are lined by cafés and social clubs.

Buon appetito!

Little Italy used to be about the food, but now it is mostly a touristy spot and shrinking by the day. Good Italian restaurants are hard to find, but **Umberto's Clam House** (www.umbertosclamhouse.com), now back on Mulberry Street after a short stint on Broome, is a classic. The restaurant's first Mulberry Street location was where gangster Joey Gallo met an abrupt and bloody end over dinner in 1972.

Walking north on Mulberry past the headquarters of the Society of San Gennaro, you come to one of the oldest houses in Little Italy, a small white Federal-style building erected in 1816 for Stephen Van Rensselaer, a member of one of New York's oldest families. Originally at 153 Mulberry Street, the entire house was moved to its present site at No. 149 in 1841.

At the corner of Grand and Mulberry, **E. Rossi and Co.** has gifts, novelties, and religious relics to browse through, before it's time to sample the delicacies at **Ferrara**, (www.ferraranyc.com) a pastry shop and café since 1892.

CHINATOWN ㉝

One of the largest Chinese-American settlements in America, Chinatown got its start in the 1870s, when Chinese railroad workers drifted east from California in the wake of anti-Asian sentiment. Once squeezed into a three-block area bordered by Mott, Pell, and the Bowery, today's Chinatown encompasses around 40 blocks, swinging around Little Italy to Houston Street. Although Chinatown is now a little faded in some areas, half of its appeal is in negotiating the vendors, tourists, and residents that fill its busy streets.

Chinatown's heart lies south of Canal, where Worth Street, East Broadway, and the Bowery meet at **Chatham Square** ㉞. Though the square is named after William Pitt

An exhibit at the Museum of Chinese in America.

The New Museum of Contemporary Art.

– the Earl of Chatham – the **Kim Lau Memorial Arch** was built in honor of a Chinese-American pilot who died in World War II.

Nearby **Confucius Plaza** (35) is a lightly dilapidated concrete high-rise with apartments, stores, and a school. A bronze statue of the philosopher Confucius stands in front, facing the square.

Tucked in among all the Chinese banks lining the Bowery is a remnant of old New York: built in 1785, **No. 18 Bowery –** or the Edward Mooney house, after its first owner, a prosperous meat wholesaler – is a Federal-style house and the oldest surviving row house in Manhattan; it is now occupied by offices. There is, of course, a McDonald's with a pagoda-style entrance and Chinese signage. Another striking Bowery landmark is the domed building at 58 Bowery that has housed banks since it was built in 1924.

Long-ago gangland

Walk west to **Columbus Park** – a pleasant space with basketball courts, benches, and a children's play area – to reach the bottom of busy **Mulberry Street**, one of Chinatown's two main thoroughfares, the other being **Mott Street**. In the mid-19th century, this was part of the notorious Five Points slum district, evoked at length in Martin Scorsese's 2002 epic, *Gangs of New York*, where street gangs ran rampant and squatters' huts formed an equally notorious shantytown (later cleared to make way for Columbus Park).

The best place to learn about the neighborhood is at an old (1900s) school building on the corner of Mulberry and Bayard, now the Chinese community museum.

Museum of Chinese in America (36)

Address: 215 Centre Street (between Howard and Grand streets),

TIP

Here we go 'round Mulberry Street... If you head for Little Italy and walk north looking for NoLita (North of Little Italy), you'll end up in NoHo. NoLita is a misnomer: the neighborhood is really 'NoSLita,' the Northern Section of Little Italy, but this doesn't sound nearly as cool.

Essex Street Market.

www.mocanyc.org
Telephone: 212-619 4785
Opening Hours: Tue–Sun 11am–6pm, Thu until 9pm
Entrance Fee: charge, free on first Thursdays
Subway: Canal Street

Founded in 1970, when the area's population began to explode, this tiny museum features a permanent exhibit on the Chinese-American experience, with many items donated by residents or salvaged from demolitions. It also has a research library and a gift shop, and organizes regular walking tours (Sat at 1pm) and lectures. Gallery highlight tours every Saturday at 3pm are free with admission to the museum.

Shiny restaurants

From the museum, walk south to Canal Street and turn left. As you enter Chinatown, you'll pass stands selling fruit, vegetables, and snacks, including leaf-wrapped packets of sticky rice. Crowded with vendors hawking Taiwanese DVDs and stores stocked with designer 'knock-offs,' this is a scene that feels far removed from the rest of Manhattan. From Canal Street, turn south down Mott Street to find shiny Singapore-style restaurants with marble facades and plastic signs. These are part of the 'new' Chinatown built by recent, wealthier immigrants from Hong Kong and Shanghai; some are excellent, and surprisingly cheap.

Signs of the 'old' Chinatown are still visible, however, especially at the **Chinese Community Center** (www.ccbanyc.org), which first opened on Mott Street in 1883. Next door, in the **Eastern States Buddhist Temple** 37, there's a multi-armed statue of the Goddess Kuan-Yui. The air is thick with the scent of sweet incense.

Farther along, the **Church of the Transfiguration** (www.transfigurationnyc.org) was built for a Lutheran congregation in 1801 and was sold to the Roman Catholic Church in 1853. Today it offers Catholic services in Cantonese and runs a school for local children.

Chinese New Year celebrations.

Turn right down **Pell Street** and you'll see the shop-front facade of the **First Chinese Baptist Church** (http://e.nycbc.org). Ting's Gift Shop on the corner of Doyers Street and Pell is the perfect place to pick up trinkets and knickknacks. Nearby is the headquarters of the Hip Sing Association, one of Chinatown's many *tongs*, or fraternal organizations. From the 1870s until the 1930s, these groups were involved in often-violent disputes that were sensationalized as '*tong* wars' by the non-Chinese press.

Doyers Street

The narrow lane off to the right is the most crooked street in Manhattan; in the 1600s it was a cart track leading to one of the first breweries. Later, **Doyers Street** became an important communications center, where men gathered to get the latest news from China and to drop off letters and money for home with the small shopkeepers whose premises served as combination banks and post offices.

In keeping with this tradition, the current Chinatown post office was built on the site of the old brewery. Nearby is the **Nom Wah Tea Parlor**, the neighborhood's oldest restaurant. Unlike many places in the area, it generally closes early (around 9pm, Fri–Sat 10pm), but has some of the best dim sum in Chinatown. The interior is much as it was in 1921 when it opened, with sagging red-leather banquettes, linoleum floor, and ceiling fans. Prices are as old-fashioned as the décor.

Food and festivals

Food is one of the main attractions of Chinatown and, with hundreds of restaurants to choose from, the hardest part is picking where to eat. Options range from the extremely cozy New Malaysia Restaurant (http://newmalaysia restaurant.com) on Bowery to the Golden Unicorn (www.goldenunicorn restaurant.com) on East Broadway, where house specialties are served in luxurious surroundings, or the Peking Duck House (www.pekingduckhousenyc.com) on Mott Street, a favorite of former New York mayor Ed Koch.

For a deeper taste and sense of Chinese culture, visit the **Asian-American Arts Centre** (111 Norfolk Street; www.artspiral.org; by appointment only), which has a vast archive of Asian visual culture in the United States from 1945 to the present day. For many years, the **Asian-American Dance Theatre** presented traditional and contemporary dance productions here, too.

Chinese New Year combines feasts, dance, and music, and begins with fanciful parades. The festivities start around the end of January, and go on for several days, usually into February, but the street decorations tend to hang around a little bit longer.

EAT

Although it's possible to find good Chinese food anywhere in New York, one of the best places is the Nom Wah Tea Parlor (1 Doyers Street at Chatham Square; http://nomwah.com; tel: 212-962 6047). Serving dim sum in a tiny space, this is the oldest teahouse in Chinatown.

Shopping in Chinatown.

Summer entertainment in Washington Square Park.

GREENWICH VILLAGE

Greenwich Village was once a true bohemian neighborhood; now is the domain of the rich and fashionable, with quiet streets lined with multimillion-dollar homes and glitzy nightlife in the Meatpacking District.

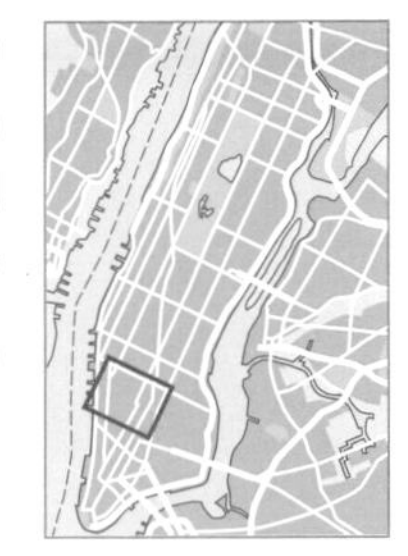

Main Attractions
- Washington Square
- Grace Church
- Washington Mews
- Hudson Street
- Bleecker Street
- Bedford Street
- Meatpacking District
- West 14th Street

Map
Page 130

Writers and poets, artists and radicals, runaway socialites, and others seeking freedom from conventional lifestyles have long flocked to Greenwich Village, spot lit most famously by poets and musicians of the 1950s and 60s.

Today, as other neighborhoods set the trends, New Yorkers often think of 'the Village' as one big tourist attraction. Untrue. A commercial element exists, serviced by double-decker tour buses, but many streets are as quietly residential as they were in the 18th and early 19th centuries, when the village of Greenwich was first settled by pioneers fleeing illness and epidemics at the tip of the island.

Success and the city

Spiraling real-estate prices have forced out all but the most successful, but the Village (both Greenwich and the West Village) is still where many people would choose to live: witness the 'Gold Coast' on West 9th Street or the buildings facing the Hudson River, which are home to celebrities and financiers.

Bordered by 14th Street to the north, the Hudson River to the west, and Broadway to the east (where the East Village begins), this is where the offbeat and the fashionable mingle with ease, and where the annual Halloween Parade is a riotous spectacle attended by both.

AROUND WASHINGTON SQUARE

Walking south on Fifth Avenue, **Washington Arch** rises in the distance. Designed in wood by Stanford White to commemorate the 1889 centennial of the first president's inauguration, the imposing marble arch from 1918 is the entrance to **Washington Square ❶**, the symbolic heart of Greenwich Village.

Victorian houses near Washington Square.

MacDougal Street, Greenwich Village.

Booksellers and collectors

A walk east from the square and then north up Broadway will lead you to the **Strand Book Store** (www.strandbooks.com; tel: 212-473 1452; daily 9.30am–10.30pm, from 11am on Sunday, rare books room closes at 6.15pm). Dusty and delightful, the Strand was started in 1927 and is the perfect place to track down that elusive edition.

Grace Church ❷, just to the south, is one of New York's loveliest ecclesiastical structures. Built in 1846, its exterior white marble, now a muted gray, was mined by convicts from the infamous Sing Sing prison in upstate New York.

Turn right at 10th, and walk toward Fifth Avenue crossing **University Place**, which runs parallel to Fifth for several blocks, to West 12th Street, where a block-shaped building houses the **New School for Social Research** (www.newschool.edu), which offers classes in everything from Arabic to screenwriting.

At Fifth Avenue and 12th Street, the **Forbes Building used to** hold the late Malcolm Forbes's collections of art, photography, jewelry and other objects from his estate's vast holdings, but is due to reopen as an academic center in summer 2016.

The nearby **Salmagundi Club**, at 47 Fifth Avenue, is the country's oldest artists' club, founded in 1870. Its

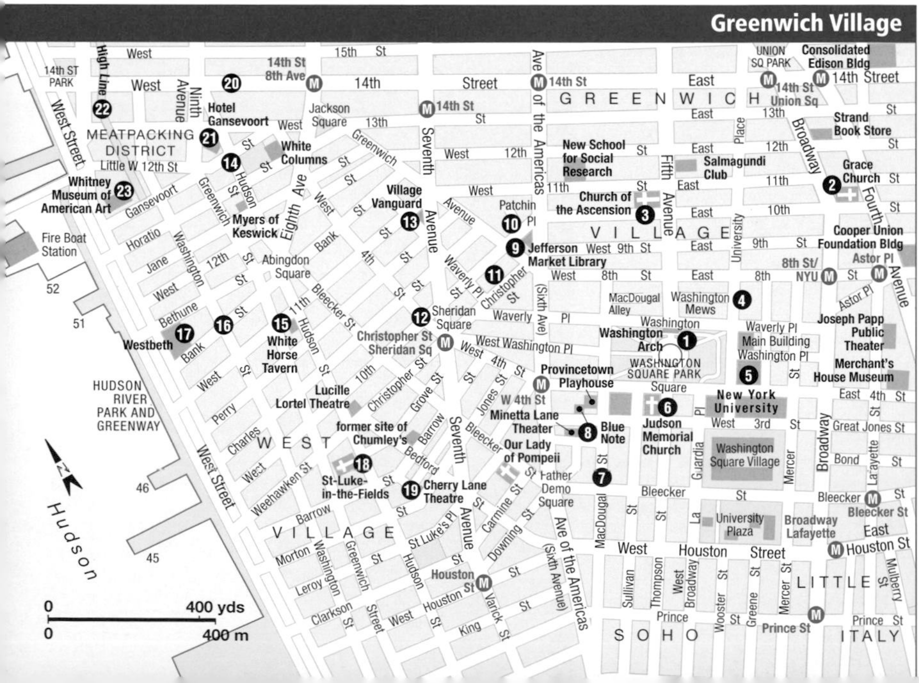

Greenwich Village

The Strand Book Store has 18 miles of new, used and rare books.

facilities are for members only, but there are walk-in classes (www.salmagundi.org; tel: 212-255 7740) should you fancy joining the artistic fraternity for a few hours.

Washington Square sites

Take a stroll along 9th and 10th streets, two of the most picturesque in the city. Lined by stately brick and brownstone houses, they have been home to numerous artists and writers (Mark Twain lived at 14 West 10th). The **Church of the Ascension** ❸ on the corner of Fifth and 10th was designed by Richard Upjohn in 1840, and features a marble altar relief by sculptor Augustus St-Gaudens.

Pretty **Washington Mews** ❹ runs between Fifth and University Place, just above Washington Square. Originally built as stables for the townhouses along Washington Square North, the pretty row houses here and along nearby **MacDougal Alley** were converted to artists' studios after the arrival of the motorcar put stables out of business. The painter Edward Hopper lived and worked at 3 Washington Square North for 54 years, from 1913 until his death in 1967. Washington Mews has retained much brickwork cobbling, and on a winter's day when the snow settles between the bricks in the road, the setting is particularly lovely.

Chess players, Washington Square Park.

All this eventually leads to **Washington Square** itself. Originally a potter's field, where the poor and unknown were buried, it later became a parade ground, and still later a residential park.

Though it's lost the cachet it had in the days of Henry James – who grew up nearby and based his novel *Washington Square* on his childhood memories – on weekend afternoons the park fills with musicians and street performers playing to appreciative crowds of Japanese camera crews, students, tourists, chess hustlers, and pot dealers. During the school term, NYU students congregate on the grass, and the atmosphere is generally less frantic.

With two blocks of Greek Revival townhouses, **Washington Square North** retains a 19th-century elegance, at odds with the monolithic **New York University** ❺ (NYU) buildings across the park. You won't be able to access the resources at Bobst Library unless you request a special pass, but you can still peek inside the lobby at the soaring 12-story atrium. Past NYU's busy Kimmel Student Center and Catholic Center (both on Washington Square South), is **Judson Memorial Church** ❻. Designed in 1890 by Stanford White in Romanesque Revival style, the church has been a cultural and religious center in the Greenwich community for decades.

Village café.

VILLAGE VOICES: BOB DYLAN

In the 1950s and 60s, the café scene of Greenwich Village drew poetic, artistic, and politically inquisitive newcomers to New York. Low rents may well have been a factor, together with a boho-artistic aura that had been gaining strength since the 1920s. Deep in the Village, major musical moments of the mid-20th century took place on MacDougal Street, many at an unpromising little coffee bar called the Café Wha? David Barry, a musician who frequented and played at the café, said, 'It was a grubby, awful scene there.'

In spite of this, a number of careers in the American folk revival began and grew. On first reaching New York on January 24, 1961, 19-year-old Bob Dylan took a subway straight to Greenwich Village and blew into the Café Wha? in a flurry of snowflakes. Barry remembered those times well. 'Although Dylan could neither sing or play the guitar, he clearly had something on stage that none of the rest of us did.'

Joan Baez and Dave Van Ronk were among 'the rest of us' in the exploding Village folk scene. The media also took notice of Dylan, with a laudatory review of one of his performances appearing in the New York Times in September 1961. He came to the attention of Columbia Records after playing harmonica on Carolyn Hester's third album, signed with an agent and changed his last name (it was originally Zimmerman). The famous cover of his second album, The Freewheelin' Bob Dylan, was shot along Jones Street (between West 4th and Bleecker), as Dylan and his girlfriend, Suze Rotolo, walked along huddled together against the cold; at that time the couple were living in Dylan's apartment on West 4th Street. Shortly after the record came out, Dylan's popularity reached a new high and he and Rotolo broke up. He left the Village, but forever left his mark on it. Café Wha? (http://cafewha.com) and the Bitter End (www.bitterend.com) in Bleecker Street, where Dylan also played, are still there today.

Beat streets

Turn off Washington Square South onto **MacDougal Street** ❼, into the heart of what was once a beatnik haven, where world-weary poets wore black, sipped coffee, and discoursed on the meaning of life late into the night. These days, the area is a magnet for out-of-towners, drawn by ersatz craft shops and 'authentic' ethnic restaurants. Only a handful of Beat-era establishments remain, however, including **Café Wha?** on MacDougal between Bleecker and West 3rd, once a hangout of Allen Ginsberg.

Nevertheless, a stroll around these streets offers the pleasure of a pilgrimage down passageways of past grooviness and cloisters of cool. Some nights, echoes of the young Bob Dylan or Jimi Hendrix seem to drift around the intersection of Bleecker and MacDougal streets. And there's still plenty of entertainment, from performances by jazz greats to contemporary drama at the **Minetta Lane Theatre** (http://minettalanenyc.com), toward Sixth Avenue.

West Village street.

Blue Note ❽

Address: 131 W. 3rd Street (between MacDougal Street and Sixth Avenue), www.bluenote.net
Telephone: 212-475 8592

TIP

Note the Playwrights Sidewalk in front of the Lucille Lortel Theater, replete with names like Eugene O'Neill and Sam Shepard, whose celebrated work has been performed here.

Stores on Perry Street.

Opening Hours: music nightly 8pm and 10.30pm with an occasional extra set at 12.30am, also jazz brunch Sun 12.30pm
Entrance Fee: charge
Subway: W. 4th Street

This club has been drawing jazz fans to Greenwich Village for over 25 years. It's comforting to think that no matter what transformations take place on the surrounding streets, inside the Blue Note the beat goes on.

The Village's very own Italian-Gothic fantasy, Jefferson Market Library.

THE WEST VILLAGE

In the area west of the Sixth Avenue (Avenue of the Americas) and a few blocks north, attractive, quiet knots of streets wind around confusingly between the major avenues. This is where the Village hosts the annual Halloween Parade. The area also witnessed the gay-rights riots at the Stonewall Inn in the late 1960s.

A good place to start is the striking **Jefferson Market Library** ❾ at 10th Street and Sixth Avenue. Part of a complex that included the old Women's House of Detention, it was built as a courthouse in 1877. This is where Harry Thaw went on trial in 1906 for shooting America's then most famous architect, Stanford White, after White had an affair with Thaw's wife, in one of New York's most celebrated scandals. The upstairs rooms still have a court-like feel, with dark wood and stained-glass windows. Next door is a pretty community garden, open to all.

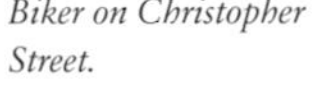

Biker on Christopher Street.

Walk west on 10th Street to **Patchin Place** ❿ – a mews where Eugene O'Neill, journalist John Reed, and poet E.E. Cummings all lived. Continue on **Christopher Street** ⓫, symbolic center of the gay community and a main cross-street that slants across the West Village to a renovated pier, walkway, and bike path that, on a sunny day, make New York seem like a brand-new city. (At night, however, it's still the haunt of hustlers, so be alert.)

Just past **Waverly Place**, with its curved row of small Federal-style houses, is the **Northern Dispensary**. A non-profit health clinic from 1831 until the 1990s, it's one of the oldest public buildings in the city. A few doors up, and nearly four decades ago, the modern gay-rights movement got its spontaneous start one night in 1969 at the **Stonewall Inn** (53 Christopher Street; www.thestonewallinnnyc.com), a gay bar whose habitués got tired of being rousted by police. Today, there's a bar with the same name waving a gay-pride flag and operating next door.

Just across the street, tiny fenced-in **Christopher Park** has a statue of Civil War general Philip Sheridan. **Sheridan**

The Village Vanguard helped to launch the careers of jazz greats Miles Davis and John Coltrane.

Square ⓬ itself isn't a square at all; it's actually at the triangular junction where Grove, Christopher, and West 4th streets meet.

At 121 Christopher Street is the **Lucille Lortel Theatre** (tel: 212-924 2817; www.lortel.org), a theater that for many years has been the friend and supporter of new writers.

Village Vanguard ⓭

Address: 178 Seventh Avenue S. (at W. 11th Street), www.villagevanguard.com
Telephone: 212-255 4037

West 14th Street and 9th Avenue.

TIP

The basketball court on the corner of West 3rd Street and 6th Avenue (aka The Cage) used to be home to some of the city's best pick-up games. It's now primarily reserved for league play, but spectators still come to see the high-flying talent.

Opening Hours: music nightly at 8.30pm and 10.30pm
Entrance Fee: charge
Subway: 14th Street

If it's music that gives a cultural *frisson*, this is the right neighborhood: the tiny Vanguard has been in business over 75 years, and pictures of its musical alumni line its walls. With a capacity of just 123, the historic basement venue has kept the sort of intimacy most jazz clubs – and musicians – only dream of. If you are lucky enough to get tickets, be warned that it's meant for jazz and jazz alone – conversation or, heaven forbid, cell ringtones during a performance are a throw-out-able offence. On Mondays, the house jazz orchestra plays.

West of 4th Street

The nearer to the river you head, the deeper you go into the oldest part of Greenwich Village, which makes up for any lack of the chic and glitz found in nearby districts with a nicely low-key neighborliness.

Flowing north–south is **Hudson Street** ⓮, its main artery. Over the past few years, this area has acquired curious British connections, with a clutch of British businesses on Greenwich Avenue.

A favorite is **Myers of Keswick** (634 Hudson St; www.myersofkeswick.com; tel: 212-691 4194), a British specialty shop where Keith Richards and Elton John have stocked up on pork pies and bags of Walkers crisps. Their sausage rolls are spectacular and, although there isn't any seating, they'll heat them up for you.

White Horse Tavern ⓯

Address: 567 Hudson Street (at W. 11th Street)
Telephone: 212-989 3956, www.whitehorsetavern1880.com
Opening Hours: daily 11am–3am
Subway: Christopher Street

The White Horse has been serving drinks at the corner of 11th Street since 1880, and is one of the last remaining wood-paneled bars in New York. The Horse was a haunt of Dylan Thomas, where he had several too many (some say 18) whiskies, before dragging himself back to the Chelsea Hotel. The next day, he died. Although

The Cherry Lane Theatre.

on the tourist route, the White Horse retains much charm. Weekends are manic, so try to visit during the week.

Pretty thoroughfares

Near the White Horse, cute little **Abingdon Square** leads to the start of **Bleecker Street**. This end of the street has fallen hard to the onslaught of high-fashion stores (Marc Jacobs, Michael Kors, luxury leather specialists Mulberry), and many locally owned businesses have been forced out by escalating rents.

Nevertheless, Bleecker is bisected by some of the Village's prettiest thoroughfares. **Bank Street** ⓰ is particularly scenic, with its cobblestones and pastel houses, and lies in the center of the **Greenwich Village Historic District**'s finest 19th-century architecture.

Toward the west end of Bank Street, **Westbeth** ⓱ is a sprawling, government-funded artists' enclave (sometimes open for performances), that looks out over the Hudson. It's only a short walk from the church of **St-Luke-in-the-Fields** ⓲, built in 1821. **17 Grove Street**, built in 1822, is a wooden home that brims with character, as does **Grove Court**, a gated alleyway with a cluster of attractive brick houses. Grove Street intersects **Bedford Street**, one of the oldest Village byways. At No. 102 is the original 'Twin Peaks,' built in 1830 as an artists' residence, with two peaks in its gabled roof.

Byways and speakeasies

A left turn leads to the former site of **Chumley's**, a speakeasy turned bar and restaurant, where novelist John Steinbeck and playwright Eugene O'Neill were regulars. A leftover from Prohibition, it had an unmarked entrance around the corner on Barrow Street – until it closed in 2008 (word on the street is that it will make a return, although no one's sure when).

Tiny poet Edna St Vincent Millay was a tenant at **75 Bedford Street**, Manhattan's narrowest house at just over 9ft (3 meters) wide. A bigger tenant was John Barrymore, of the theatrical dynasty. And before her break into stardom, Barbra Streisand worked as an usher at the **Cherry Lane Theatre** ⓳ (38 Commerce Street; www.cherrylanetheatre.org; tel: 212-989 2020), a nurturing space for American playwrights since 1924.

St Luke's Place is lined by gracious Italianate row houses. New York's Jazz Age mayor Jimmy Walker lived at No. 6, and two lamps – a sign of mayoral honor – are at the foot of the steps.

MEATPACKING DISTRICT

Until a decade or so ago, the **Meatpacking District** ⓴ was just what it sounded like – a warehousing, wholesale meat market, and distribution area for butchered goods making their way into the city's restaurants and grocery stores. Located on Manhattan's west side, to the west of the West Village and just south of Chelsea, it's bordered on the north

DRINK

Can't finish it? A law in New York permits taking that expensive, half-empty bottle of wine home from restaurants. The law requires the bottle be 'securely sealed' before being bagged.

Dining in the Meatpacking District.

Washington Square Park

Some parks have playgrounds or ponds, art installations or annual festivals and events. More than any other park in New York, Washington Square has personality.

Walking down Fifth Avenue, you spot the Washington Arch from blocks away. Inspired by the Arc de Triomphe, it is a truly grand entrance to Downtown's liveliest patch of green. In Henry James's day, the park contained 'a considerable quantity of inexpensive vegetation, enclosed by a wooden paling, which increased its rural and accessible appearance...' Vegetation remains in the form of trees and flowerbeds, but step through the gate on a weekend afternoon and any thoughts of the rural will be dispelled by the pulsing energy of the place.

Skateboarders zip past as a student from New York University's Tisch School of Arts secures a movie camera to a tripod with dreams of being the next Spike Lee or Martin Scorsese. A breakdance troupe sets up shop near the fountain, turns on a boombox, and tries to entice a crowd of sightseers to drop dollars into their hat. A hungry barista grabs a crepe from one of the city's only vegan pushcarts, while in a shaded corner on the south end, fierce matches rage on concrete chessboards.

The Washington Arch.

Evolution

A colorful history is buried beneath the layers of concrete – at one time it served as a graveyard for the indigent and unknown. In 1888, Mark Twain took a train from Connecticut to meet Robert Louis Stevenson and they sat on the park benches discussing the writer's life, a moment immortalized by artist Francis Luis Mora. On the same benches, Marlon Brando, according to his autobiography, first got drunk and passed out. A group of concerned citizens including Eleanor Roosevelt, who lived on Washington Square West, successfully campaigned to have car traffic removed from the park.

The future and meaning of the park has constantly been debated. Henry James famously hated the Arch, as it represented a bohemian shift in the neighborhood from the refined enclave of his youth. Spring of 1961 saw the Beatnik Riot, where those now-firmly-entrenched bohemians protested against the arcane law that required musicians to obtain permits to perform in the park. The beatniks won, but flash-forward another fifty years, and that freewheeling spirit is once again under fire. A private conservancy has been angling to take over, a move that is sure to sterilize the grittier elements that define the park. Understandably, not all locals are on board.

On the flip side, the place has never looked better. The Arch received a facelift in the late 1990s, while the entire park underwent a massive renovation ending in 2013, a daunting (and, you guessed it, controversial) project that involved realigning the fountain that has been the centerpiece for more than 150 years. With work complete, there is an extra sheen on the soul of Greenwich Village that is, among other things, a campus quad for NYU students, a stage for buskers, and a shady place to rest and play.

by **West 14th Street** ㉑ (or even a couple blocks farther north, depending on who you ask), on the south by **Gansevoort Street**, and from Hudson Street on the east to the Hudson River on the west. In fact, it is so well located (with decent subway and bus access) that it should have seemed inevitable that such prime real estate would eventually be developed for more fashionable pursuits. But, back when this was a red-light district (and the streets were literally stained red from the cow carcasses in the slaughterhouses) there was nothing cool about this stretch of Manhattan.

First came the lounge-style nightclubs, in the late 1990s, lured by the promise of large warehouse spaces – then came the crowds of Manolo- and Jimmy Choo-clad fashionistas, making their way to Pastis restaurant at night and high-end boutiques by day. At its peak, the neighborhood became a symbol of *Sex and the City*-style trendiness, with late-night crowds of fabulous people posing on the cobblestone street – right next to the last remaining meatpacking plants.

Over the next few years, the Meatpacking District went mainstream, trading in the 'insider's secret' pedigree for a more broad popularity. You're as likely to see bachelorette parties and bridge-and-tunnel (Manhattan speak for those from New Jersey and the outer boroughs) club kids in for a night of dancing as you are to glimpse the Manhattan elite at night.

That said, during the day the exclusive boutiques remain a draw for everyone who loves to be current and fashionable. These include storefronts for Diane von Furstenberg (874 Washington Street; www.dvf.com), as well as the New York outpost of Jeffrey (449 West 14th Street; www.jeffreynewyork.com), not to mention a gorgeous glass-encased Apple store (401 West 14th Street; www.apple.com/retail/west14thstreet).

It's no wonder that this is the corner of New York where Google chose to place its East Coast headquarters. Their name, perched on the front of their building at 76 Ninth Avenue, is unmistakable.

Sleeping and eating

Two major hotels – the **Hotel Gansevoort**, with its rooftop pool, and **The Standard** hotel – bring crowds of visitors, and the exclusive **Soho House** (a private club of British

Meatpacking District.

origins, with an even harder-to-access rooftop pool; www.sohohouseny.com) continues to add cachet to the district.

And the restaurant scene here continues to grow. Celebrity chef Jean-Georges Vongerichten kicked things off with **Spice Market**. Mario Batali followed with the gigantic **Del Posto**. Tom Colicchio kept pace by converting his Craftsteak into the farm-to-table Colicchio & Sons. And, because of the club scene, many restaurants keep their kitchens open late into the night.

The **High Line** 22 (see page 150), a public park built on a disused, elevated railroad track, has brought a lot of attention to the area. Now, you can sit on this path-in-the-sky and watch the sunset over the river, without having to buy a loft space – something unimaginable before. Saved from demolition by two friends living in the neighborhood, the High Line (www.thehighline.org) now stretches from Gansevoort Street north to West 34th Street (between 10th and 12 avenues). The park is a masterpiece of horticulture, with vegetable gardens, miniature forests, hidden passages, outdoor art galleries, balconies, and picnic areas, with astonishing views over the Hudson River.

Things change quickly around the Meatpacking District, so there's little point in picking out more specific highlights. However, a growing number of galleries signal the movement of Chelsea's art scene farther south. This trend has been strengthened by the relocation of the Whitney Museum of American Art (see below) from the Museum Mile to a new site at 99 Gansevoort Street. Don't miss the (daily 8am–8pm; www.gansmarket.com), a foodies' paradise offering freshly made tacos, crêpes, healthy juices, pizzas, barbecue, sushi, and many more delicacies.

Whitney Museum of American Art 23

Address: 99 Gansevoort Street, www.whitney.org
Telephone: 212-570 3600
Opening Hours: Wed–Mon 10.30am–6pm, Fri–Sat until 10pm
Entrance Fee: charge
Subway: 8th Avenue, 14th Street

Housed in an amazing building designed by Renzo Piano, the Whitney collection was founded in 1930 by Gertrude Vanderbilt Whitney, whose tastes were for American Realists like Edward Hopper and George Bellows. Since then the museum's policy has been to acquire pieces that represent the full range of 20th-century American art, with works by Georgia O'Keeffe, Willem de Kooning, Jackson Pollock, and Jasper Johns. Every other year it mounts the Whitney Biennial (the next one is scheduled for spring 2017), a survey of provocative new American art.

The White Horse Tavern.

The Meatpacking District at night.

The High Line Elevated Park in Chelsea.

UNION SQUARE AND CHELSEA

The blocks between 14th and 34th streets are buzzing with flowers and fresh produce, art galleries, and a wide variety of restaurants.

Main Attractions

- Gramercy Park
- Madison Square Park
- Flatiron Building
- SoFi
- Theodore Roosevelt Birthplace
- Union Square
- Chelsea Market
- General Theological Seminary
- Rubin Museum of Art

Map

Page 144

The area from Madison Park to Union Square – loosely referred to as the Flatiron District – is home to ad agencies, publishers, restaurants, and new media firms. Chelsea used to have a thriving art gallery scene, now it offers a riverside sports and entertainment development. Even the neighborhood surrounding Gramercy Park has shed its usual well-heeled reserve.

GRAMERCY PARK ❶

On the East Side between 20th and 21st streets, Gramercy Park is a genteel square that punctuates Lexington Avenue and Irving Place with welcome leafy greenery. This is Manhattan's sole private park, established in the 1830s, a place where immaculately kept flower beds and gravel paths sit just out of reach behind an ornate fence. Only residents of the surrounding townhouses have keys, although there are a limited number for guests of the Ian Schrager-led **Gramercy Park Hotel** (www.gramercyparkhotel.com).

Once a faded relic from the Jazz Age, the building has been gutted and redesigned as a lavish, idiosyncratic hotel draped in rich velvets, deep reds and azures, and decorated with antique-framed modern art and glittering chandeliers. The Gramercy's '21st-century bohemia' has scored well with the reviewers that matter, and if celebrity spotting is your thing, head for the resident Rose or Jade bars. Part of the previous building has been put aside as condos, the popularity of which will soon bring a new generation of monied residents to Gramercy Park.

On the park's southern perimeter, look at the elaborate 19th-century facades of the **National Arts Club**, home to the Poetry Society of America, and the **Players Club** next

The lobby of the Gramercy Park Hotel.

The Flatiron Building was once described as 'looking like a monster steamer.'

door, where members have included leading American theater actors, as well as Mark Twain, Winston Churchill, and Frank Sinatra.

Change is afoot on the other side of the Arts Club, at the former Parkside Evangeline Residence for Young Women. Until recently this attractive corner building provided inexpensive, dorm-style accommodation to women attempting to find their feet in New York. Unfortunately its owners, the Salvation Army, sold it to luxury condo developers (though they still run a similar facility, known as the Markle, in the West Village).

Irving Place, which Samuel Ruggles named for his friend Washington Irving, runs south from Gramercy Park to 14th Street, and is lined by pretty brownstones that continue with particular charm along East 19th Street.

At 18th Street, **Pete's Tavern** (www.petestavern.com) is a dark, historic bar where the atmosphere reeks of speakeasies and spilled beer. Its interior has featured in several beer commercials, as well as in episodes of *Seinfeld* and *Sex and the City*. Short-story scribe O. Henry is said to have written *The Gift of the Magi* here. Down at 15th Street,

Union Square and Chelsea

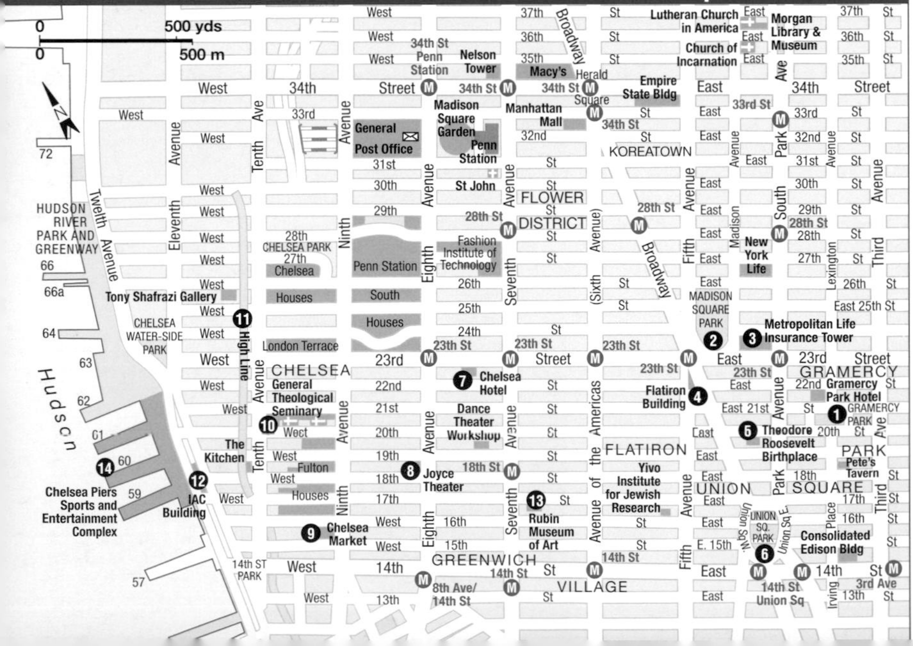

Irving Plaza (tel: 212-777 6800; www.irvingplaza.com) is one of the city's best rock music venues. Drifting northward, the often-overlooked green space between Madison Avenue and Broadway from 23rd to 26th streets is **Madison Square Park** ❷ (www.madisonsquarepark.org). There are often art installations sharing space with the original Shake Shack, which sells arguably the city's best burgers and hot dogs. A block south, the **Metropolitan Life Insurance Tower** ❸, completed in 1909, was briefly considered the world's tallest building at 54 stories. The building, sold several times between 2005 and 2013, is now a property of the Abu Dhabi Investment Authority, which converted it into the **New York EDITION Hotel** (www.editionhotels.com/new-york). The hotel was opened in September 2015 and is managed by Marriott.

Until its recent incarnation as a place to meet and greet like-minded fashion and media types in a number of watering holes, however, the Madison Park area was noted mainly for its proximity to one of Manhattan's favorite architectural whimsies, which rises from the corner where Broadway crosses Fifth Avenue below 23rd Street.

FLATIRON DISTRICT

The triangular Fuller Building raised eyebrows and hopes for a bright future when it was erected in 1902. It soon became known as the **Flatiron Building** ❹ because of its distinctive shape, and is considered by most to be the oldest skyscraper in New York City. Rising 285ft (87 meters) into the air, the Fuller was immortalized in 1903 with a classic black-and-white shot by photographer Alfred Stieglitz, who described the building as 'looking like a monster steamer.' The architect was Daniel Burnham, of the influential Chicago firm of the same name that specialized in early skyscrapers.

Word got around the offices and bars of New York that the building produced particular eddies in the wind that caused women's skirts to fly around as they walked along 23rd Street. Large groups of young men were interested enough to gather in the area to find out. To disperse them, the story goes, cops would chase them away with the words '23, skidoo.'

EAT

One restaurant in Flatiron district not to be missed is Cosme (www.cosmenyc.com), run by the world-famous Mexico City chef Enrique Olvera, who serves up a contemporary take on Mexican dishes.

A statue in Madison Square Park.

FACT

Theodore Roosevelt was the first US president to own a car, fly in an airplane, go underwater in a submarine, and entertain an African-American in the White House (Booker T. Washington, in 1901).

The neighborhood immediately south has been dubbed **SoFi** by realtors, which stands, not surprisingly, for **So**uth of **Fl**at**i**ron, but the nickname hasn't caught on with many others. From here, Broadway follows the old 'Ladies' Mile,' a shopping route that, during the latter part of the 19th century, ranged along Broadway and Sixth Avenue, from 23rd Street down to 9th Street. Lord & Taylor, which began as a small shop downtown on Catherine Street and opened on the southwest corner of Broadway and 20th Street in 1872, moved uptown to 38th and Fifth in 1914, where it is still open for business.

Roosevelt Birthplace ❺

Address: 28 E. 20th Street (at Park Avenue South and Broadway), www.nps.gov/thrb
Telephone: 212-260 1616
Opening Hours: Tue–Sat 9am–5pm
Entrance Fee: charge
Subway: 23rd Street

Just east of Broadway is the place where Theodore Roosevelt, 26th President of the United States (1901–9) was born in 1858. Theodore Roosevelt came from one of the East Coast's wealthiest families, and in the 1850s the house at 28 East 20th Street was a fashionable residence. The current building is actually a 1920s replica of the house in which 'Teddy' spent his childhood: the original was knocked down in 1916, but after his death in 1919 it was faithfully recreated as a memorial. About 40 percent of the furnishings come from the original home; the rest was either donated by family members or are authentic period pieces. The living quarters are only accessible as part of the tour, which is worth taking simply to see how a rich family like the Roosevelts would have lived in the mid-19th century, when this part of New York was considered the wealthy suburbs.

UNION SQUARE ❻

Named for the busy convergence of Broadway and Fourth Avenue, Union Square sits comfortably between 17th and 14th streets. A stylish prospect in the mid-1850s, later it was more or less deserted by genteel residents and became a thriving theater center. Eventually the theaters moved to

Flower District, Chelsea.

Midtown, and the square became known for political meetings – in the years before World War I, anarchists and socialists regularly addressed sympathizers here.

Rallies continued to draw crowds throughout the 1930s, but finally even radicalism dwindled, and the area went into a decline that lasted until the 1980s.

Today, Union Square brims with life, a resurgence that might be attributed to the **Greenmarket** (www.grownyc.org/greenmarket), which brings farmers and their produce to the northern edge of the square on Saturdays (8am–6pm). While there are other fruit and vegetable markets in other parts of the city, this is the biggest and the best. *Union Square Partnership* sponsors free Wi-Fi in the park, and Manhattanites settle in with their tablets and laptops on the benches near the vendors.

Food for the soul can be found at the **Union Square Theatre**, 100 East 17th Street, a historically appropriate locale in light of Union Square's 19th-century theatrical past.

A huge Barnes & Noble and Whole Foods dominate the outer edges of

Union Square's Greenmarket.

Union Square. In the evening, young tourists and skateboarders congregate around their doors.

CHELSEA

West of Fifth Avenue to the Hudson River, from 14th up to about 30th Street, Chelsea borders the Midtown Garment District and includes the ever-shrinking **Flower District**. In the spring and summer, the blocks surrounding West 28th Street are

FACT

The land that makes up the Chelsea Historic District was inherited in 1813 by Clement Clarke Moore. He sold the land but imposed restrictions that kept its elegance intact.

A Sumin ballet performance at the Joyce Theater.

SHOP

Many of the stores in the Chelsea Market have glass walls that back onto a walkway. Too tempting to resist is Amy's Bread. Watch as the loaves are kneaded, shaped, and then placed in an oven, and chances are you'll leave with one under your arm.

crowded with leafy vegetation and bathed in a sweet, loamy odor.

Fifth Avenue between 14th and 23rd streets has stores like Coach and Paul Smith, while **Sixth Avenue** (Avenue of the Americas) is lined by national chains that have taken over the historic Ladies' Mile buildings where fashionable department stores used to reign.

Chelsea Hotel

Walking west on long, busy 23rd Street (or better yet, a ride on the M23 crosstown bus) will take you past the **Chelsea Hotel** ❼ (www.chelseahotels.com). One of the city's most famous residential hotels, this 12-story, red-brick building is where Dylan Thomas died in 1953, Andy Warhol filmed *Chelsea Girls* in 1967, and punk rocker Sid Vicious allegedly murdered his girlfriend Nancy Spungen (he died of a drug overdose before he could be convicted).

The time has passed when you could join the hotel's eclectic collection of residents for a night, or even in the lobby to have a look at the unusual artwork (done by guests and changed at a whim). For the last few years, the fate of the hotel was a mystery, but now it's all clear: it has been sold to a real estate developer and is undergoing a complete renovation, due to be back in operation as a hotel from 2016. As Chelsea itself becomes more and more gentrified, and property prices and desirability soar, the unique character of the hotel will probably change. At the ground level is the El Quijote Spanish restaurant (www.elquijoterestaurant.com), a relic of the days when waiters wore red jackets and paella was served in enormous portions. Grab a bite before it too disappears.

The entrance to the Chelsea Hotel.

Chelsea Market.

Art Deco and dance

The Art Deco sign to the **Joyce Theater** ❽ (175 Eighth Avenue at 19th Street; www.joyce.org) is easily spotted from the street. The Joyce presents some of the city's most innovative dance performances, from Spanish Gypsy flamenco to classical ballet, and Native American troupes.

Other original work is staged at the New York Live Arts (219 West 19th Street; www.newyorklivearts.org). The lobby has a welcoming coffee shop where you can kick back with specialty hot chocolate and a big cookie.

You'll notice many gay-friendly bars and businesses throughout the area, though even parts of that scene are decamping to more affordable areas in the outer boroughs. The Chelsea Cinemas on 23rd Street at Eighth Avenue prides itself in offering the latest films with LGBT themes, as well as a few blockbusters and art house hits.

The striking architecture of the **Chelsea Market** ❾, (www.chelseamarket.com; Mon–Sat 7am–9pm, Sun 8am–8pm), at 75 Ninth Avenue between 15th and 16th streets, was preserved thanks to an ambitious renovation that transformed what were once 18 buildings erected between 1883 and 1930 into a hugely popular indoor food market. Much of the original brickwork and steel has been left bare, giving the food court an artsy, industrial feel.

The interior of the Chelsea Market has a waterfall and sculptured seating, around which are scattered more than 20 locally owned stores selling specialty foods and home design items, as well as plenty of tempting places to eat.

The area is trendy and stylish, so much so that this neighborhood is almost indistinguishable from the cool and gritty Meatpacking District, which stretches west along 14th Street to the Hudson in the West Village.

Fans of architecture will also love the blocks between Eighth and Tenth avenues, from 19th to 23rd streets. This is the **Chelsea Historic District**.

General Theological Seminary ❿

Address: Entrance is at 440 21st Street (between Ninth and Tenth avenues); www.gts.edu
Telephone: 212-243 5150
Opening Hours: check website for daily prayers sessions
Entrance Fee: free
Subway: 23rd Street/Eighth Avenue

This lovely seminary was established in 1817, and prepares students for ordination into the Episcopal Church. Among its best buildings are the Chapel of the Good Shepherd and St Mark's Library. The seminary's tree-lined quadrangle is one of New York's best-kept secrets: a calm oasis amid the busy urban streets all around, where visitors can sit under a tree and listen to the sound of birds.

Walking east on 20th and 21st streets from Tenth Avenue brings you to one of the Chelsea Historic District's most scenic stretches of Greek Revival and Anglo-Italianate townhouses, the tree-lined streets a reminder of Chelsea's desirability as a residential area. A block farther south, between Tenth and Eleventh avenues, **The Kitchen** (512 West 19th Street; http://thekitchen.org) is a long-standing center where video, dance, and performance art are staple fare.

Parallel to Tenth Avenue and stretching to the West Village is the **High Line** ⓫ , a disused railroad line

DRINK

If you like a little competition with your cocktails, consider some ping-pong at SPiN (48 East 23rd Street, http://newyork.wearespin.com) or pool at Slate (54 West 21st Street, www.slate-ny.com), two upscale clubs with music and games.

Detail from a mandala painted on cotton at the Rubin Museum.

The High Line

It's only fitting in a city where most new development is of the vertical variety that one of its newest parks is an elevated one – and it's as lovely as it is unique.

The city's most famous green space is easily Central Park – but its coolest is the High Line. Opened in 2009, this innovative stretch of walkways and flora is located on an elevated train track that was used between the 1930s and 1980 to ship meat to Chelsea's refrigerated warehouses from the Meatpacking District (see page 137).

Climb up to the High Line and you will be instantly transported away from the taxis and buses to a walking path that has been landscaped and lined with the type of plant life that grew here naturally after the rail was abandoned – tall grasses, wild flowers, and low bushes. Space can be tight in summer and on weekends, so bikes and dogs are not allowed, but in winter it feels eerily hushed and removed from the noise of the city.

The High Line and the Standard Hotel.

The first section of the park to open runs from Gansevoort Street, in the West Village, to 20th Street in Chelsea; the second stretch, which covers 20th to 30th streets, opened a little over a year later; the final leg, skirting the Hudson River all the way to the 34th Street was completed in 2014.

Fresh Perspectives

No matter where you start, your walk will offer an entirely new vantage point on the metropolis. You may pass so close to certain condos that you can almost reach out and knock on a living room window (resist the temptation). You will, quite literally, pass under the Standard Hotel. As Robert Hammond, cofounder of the Friends of the High Line, said, 'There's a spot around 17th Street where you can stand and see buildings by Frank Gehry, Jean Nouvel, and Shigeru Ban." Gentle fountains and miniscule gardens are scattered throughout, not to mention carts tempting with ice cream. This is one corner of the city where you are encouraged to linger.

You'll quickly become aware that the High Line is, in fact, not a straight line – it is a meandering, winding path. In areas where it widens, there are benches, and an amphitheater used for lectures, discussions, and as outdoor classroom for the High Line's programs for schoolchildren.

It's no surprise that the city's newest park hosts some of the city's newest food. Well-chosen vendors keep idlers fed along the walkways between Little West 12th ánd West 18th street. While at the West 30th Street entrance, there's a lot (aptly, if not creatively, named The Lot) with a mobile beer garden and welcoming attitude to local food trucks. Success here sometimes encourages truck owners to take the dive and open storefronts.

For more information on visiting, go to www.thehighline.org or tel: 212-500 6035. There is no charge, and park hours change seasonally.

Relaxing on the High Line.

that has been transformed into a sky-high green promenade for walkers (see page 150).

Dominating the space between West 18th and 19th streets at Eleventh Avenue is the Frank Gehry-designed **IAC Building** ⓬. This is the acclaimed architect's first NYC office building. Not everyone is pleased with the enormity of the edifice, which is way out of scale for low-key Chelsea, but few can fault its impressive facade.

Galleries on the move

Once SoHo became overrun with boutiques and restaurants, gallery owners moved north to Chelsea, but now the rising prices of the properties are making them change neighborhood yet again. Even one of the best, the **Tony Shafrazi Gallery** (www.tonyshafrazigallery.com; tel: 212-274 9300) – with past exhibits focused on names as famous as Andy Warhol, Picasso, and Keith Haring – had to relocate, and is most likely to re-open in Brooklyn.

Rubin Museum of Art ⓭

Address: 150 W. 17th Street (at Seventh Avenue), http://rubinmuseum.3org
Telephone: 212-620 5000
Opening Hours: Mon and Thu 11am–5pm, Wed 11am–9pm, Fri 11am–10pm, Sat–Sun 11am–6pm
Entrance Fee: charge
Subway: 18th Street

On any adventure into Chelsea, consider a visit to one of the city's under-the-radar set of galleries. The Rubin is the first museum in the Western world dedicated to the art of the Himalayas and surrounding regions. The emphasis is on educating visitors about the religion and culture of southern Asia, with displays of jewelry, textiles, photography, statuary, and paintings, which are paired with fascinating wall notes and interactive displays. As a surprising and welcome bonus, the museum hosts a variety of concerts, including many jazz and singer-songwriters, in its intimate, cherrywood-lined performance space.

Gallery-hopping

This activity is particularly popular on Thursday nights, when most venues keep later hours, but note that most galleries tend to close on Mondays. Despite the avant-garde nature of some of the work, the galleries

TIP

Not only do the exhibitions change periodically, but the galleries in Chelsea come and go with little warning. For up-to-date locations and offerings, check http://chelseagallerymap.com. NB. Most are closed on Mondays.

Hailing a taxi.

TIP

When visiting Chelsea Piers, ask someone to tell you about the site's history. One fascinating fact is that the *Titanic* was scheduled to dock at the piers on April 16, 1912. Of the 2,000 passengers onboard the doomed liner, only 675 were rescued. The survivors arrived at Chelsea Piers four days later.

themselves are mainly unintimidating places, and inquiries are met with friendly, informed responses.

The **Pace Galleries** (508, 510 and 534 West 25th Street; www.pacegallery.com) are worth seeing, the size of the spaces allowing for some impressive works. The appearance of Comme des Garçons on 22nd Street and Pink Tartan at 25th Street has been the first sign that change might be afoot in the neighborhood, as art turns into retail.

In the early days of moving pictures, the Famous Players Film Studio was located on West 26th Street; today, the **Silver Screen Studios** at Chelsea Piers are where such popular TV shows as *Law and Order* were produced.

Chelsea Piers ⓮

Address: W. 23rd Street (at Twelfth Avenue and Hudson River), www.chelseapiers.com
Telephone: 212-336 6666
Opening Hours: daily, various opening hours
Entrance Fee: charge
Subway: 23rd Street/Eighth Avenue

The last stop on the crosstown M23 bus is **Pier 62**, the hub of this huge sports and entertainment complex, which sprawls south along the Hudson

The view over Chelsea Piers.

from 23rd to 17th streets, and which has brought a wealth of leisure opportunities to the city.

A Fitness Club is open to members only, but there are other facilities the public can use for a fee. The development includes **Pier 61**, with the double Sky Rink, **Pier 60**, which has a fabulous spa with a range of treatments including facials and massages, and **Pier 59**, which offers a golf-driving range. Other activities include bowling, indoor soccer, dance classes, and basketball.

The Chelsea cruise

The transformation of Chelsea's dilapidated piers has given new access to the Hudson River. Passenger yachts and schooners (Classic Harbor Line, tel: 212-627 1825, www.sail-nyc.com; and Spirit Cruises, tel: 866-483 3866, www.spiritcruises.com) offer day and evening cruises, with wine tastings, music, and dinner often included. For landlubbers, the walkway by the piers weaves around for more than a mile, providing great riverside views and fine sunsets.

GREEN AND FRESH

If you were to ask celebrity chefs with restaurants near Union Square Park where they buy their ingredients, many could simply point out the window to the patches of concrete and the farm stands that are set up every Saturday 8am–6pm. The Union Square Greenmarket is more than a place to find apples in the fall and peaches in the summer. It is a community meeting place and essential source of produce for many New Yorkers, including those who make a living out of making meals.

Organic, and often exotic, meats are available alongside hand-tied pretzels, locally grown vegetables, and goat's cheese. The Lower East Side Ecology Center runs a composting program, so locals can dispose food scraps, while GrowNYC offers a textile recycling drop-off. At peak seasons, as many as 140 vendors will be hawking their products to 60,000 shoppers, and the variety is astounding. You can easily find supplies for a gourmet picnic, including wine, artisan bread, and homemade jams. And those celebrity chefs who shop there also do cooking demonstrations there, often concentrating on specific ingredients. For more information visit www.grownyc.org.

Frank Gehry's IAC Building.

TIMES SQUARE

Revitalization marches on at the Crossroads of the World, where these days most of the traffic is either on foot or by bike.

Times Square has long shaken off the seedy image it acquired during the 1960s. The introduction of pedestrian-only areas between 42nd and 47th streets have made it a more attractive place for visitors.

Times Square, named for the *New York Times* offices that formerly anchored it, has a history as lively as its street life. Theaters, hotels, and restaurants sprang up in the 1920s, when impresarios like the Shubert Brothers staged 250 shows a year. Prohibition brought speakeasies, gangsters, and the characters of Damon Runyon's earthy tales. At the end of World War II, more than 2 million people crowded into the area to celebrate V-J Day. But by the 1960s, Times Square was known mainly for its sleaze, crime, and pornography. In the 1990s, the square was transformed back into a tourist magnet for the more than 20 million visitors who come here each year. Of course, with the tourists came traffic jams and the less-than-gracious crowds. In recent years, the renovation of Father Duffy Square and the conversion of Broadway from 42nd to 47th streets into a pedestrian-only zone have done wonders to alleviate these problems. The square is far from a calm harbor, but it has been a long time since it has been this inviting.

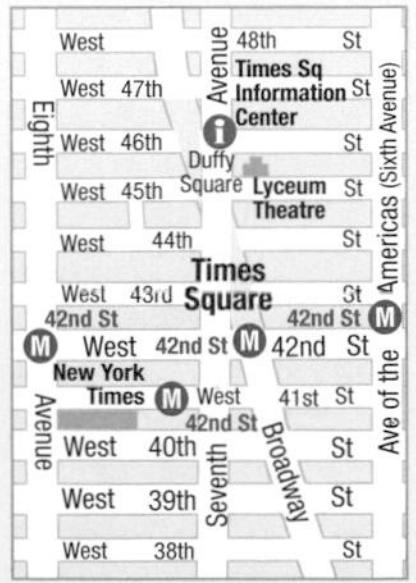

The Essentials

Address: Broadway between 42nd and 48th streets; www.timessquarenyc.org

Opening Hours: Walking tours multiple times daily. More information at http://walkinbroadway.com

Subway: 42nd Street/Times Square

Musical theater has a long tradition on Broadway, beginning as early as the 17th century. Theaters were originally located in Lower Manhattan, but over time moved farther north to Midtown.

The musical Guys and Dolls first premiered on Broadway in 1951 and has had numerous revivals since.

The Great White Way: tickets for walking tours of Broadway can be purchased in the TKTS Booth at Times Square, located under the red steps.

THE NEW YORK TIMES

A mosaic tile advertisement for the newspaper that gave the square its name.

Times Square took its name from the *New York Times*, formerly headquartered at the Times Tower, where 42nd Street intersects Seventh Avenue, and now called One Times Square. The *New York Daily Times*, founded in 1851 (the *Daily* was dropped in 1857), was bought in 1896 by ambitious Tennessee newspaperman Adolph S. Ochs.

The paper moved to 229 West 43rd Street in 1913, where Ochs's great-grandson, chairman Arthur Sulzberger Jr, continued the mission to produce 'an independent newspaper... devoted to the public welfare' under the well-known slogan: 'All the News That's Fit to Print.'

In a decision that has delighted Manhattanites, the company commissioned architect Renzo Piano to create a new addition to the New York skyline at Eighth Avenue between 40th and 41st streets. This landmark *Times* building changes color with the light.

The *New York Times* has won 95 Pulitzer Prizes, and has a circulation of over 1 million readers.

Breadlines on Broadway: during the Great Depression in the 1930s, a city newspaper opened a relief kitchen in Times Square to feed the poor.

The eye-catching red steps of the TKTS Pavillion, Times Square.

MIDTOWN WEST

The lights shine most brightly here, glittering off tourist-friendly Times Square, the masterpieces at the Museum of Modern Art, and the kick lines at Radio City.

Main Attractions

Macy's
Times Square
Broadway
Bryant Park
Radio City Music Hall
Museum of Modern Art
Carnegie Hall

Map

Page 158

The West Side shines more brightly than the East, at least in terms of sheer neon wattage, and what Midtown West lacks in finesse it makes up for tenacity. This is where billboards vie with world-class art, and where, as the old saying goes, there's a broken heart for every light on Broadway.

At the center of it all, Times Square has donned new neon baubles like an aging beauty queen with a facelift. Flash and frenzy dazzle the eye. The physical home of NASDAQ at 4 Times Square (the tower with the H&M logo on) dominates, with a huge LED display teeming with the latest stock-market quotes. And Broadway – the glamorous Great White Way – scrambles for that next big hit.

But then, that's the story of Midtown West. It's been bruised, but it's never gone down for the count. The lights that burn on Broadway, and a bevy of new hotels, restaurants, stores, and other businesses, make sure the West Side is alive and booming.

AROUND HERALD SQUARE

Starting at 34th Street, the transition from East to West Midtown begins at **Herald Square ❶**, where Broadway intersects Sixth Avenue. Named for the *New York Herald* newspaper, whose headquarters once stood here, today this chaotic intersection is best known for its retail temples.

Just south of Herald Square is the slightly faded **Manhattan Mall** (www.manhattanmallny.com), where four of the building's nine floors are occupied by nearly a dozen eateries and a variety of retailers aimed at teenage tastes and corresponding slim-line wallets. The big draw in this area, however, is New

The Rockettes perform at the opening night of the Radio City Christmas Spectacular at Radio City Music Hall.

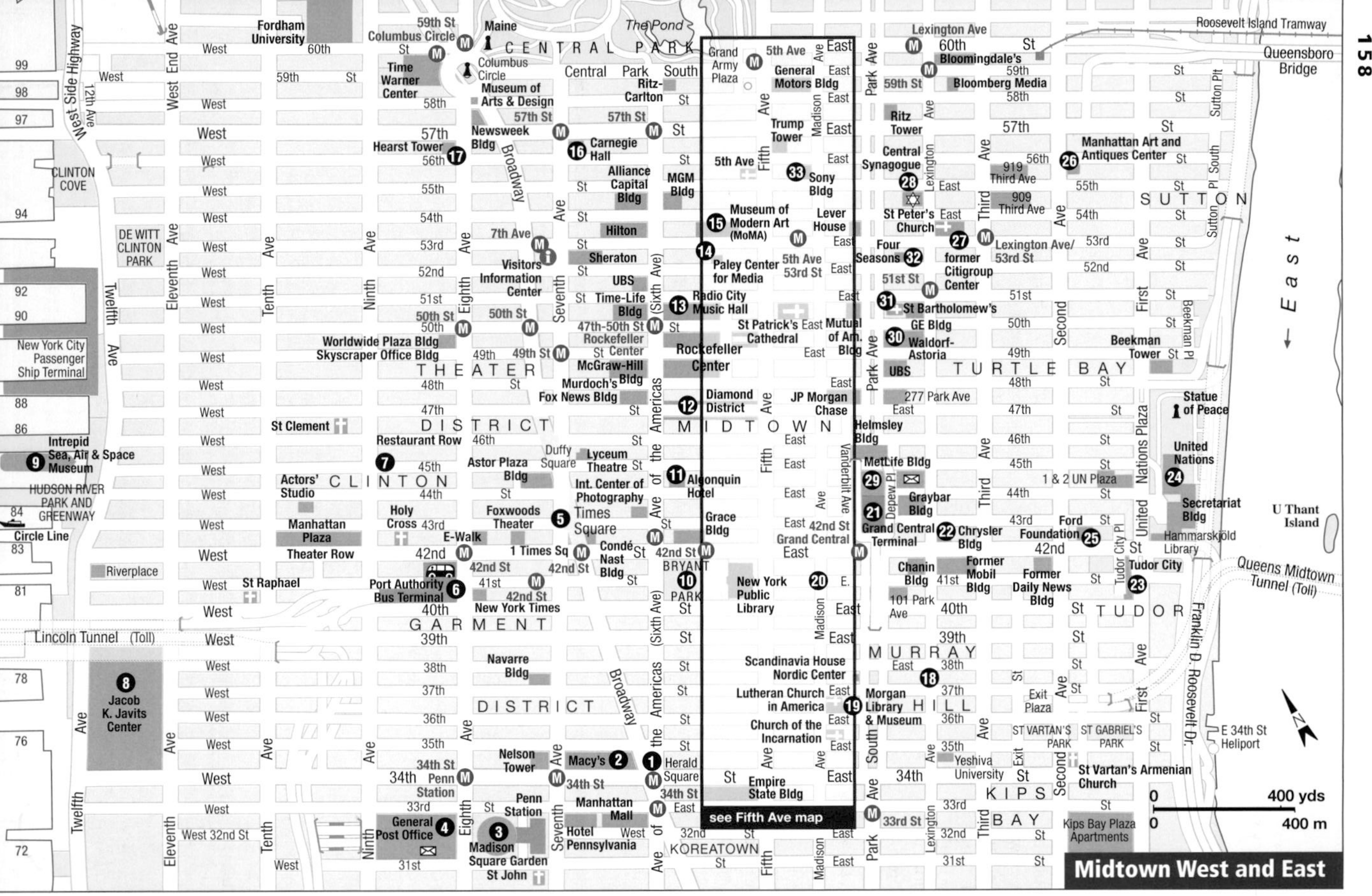

Midtown West and East
400 yds
400 m
see Fifth Ave map
East
Roosevelt Island Tramway
Queensboro Bridge
U Thant Island
Queens Midtown Tunnel (Toll)
Franklin D. Roosevelt Dr.
E 34th St Heliport
SUTTON
TURTLE BAY
TUDOR
MURRAY HILL
KIPS BAY
MIDTOWN
KOREATOWN
BRYANT PARK
GARMENT DISTRICT
THEATER DISTRICT
CLINTON
CENTRAL PARK
The Pond
DE WITT CLINTON PARK
CLINTON COVE
HUDSON RIVER PARK AND GREENWAY
ST VARTAN'S PARK
ST GABRIEL'S PARK
Lincoln Tunnel (Toll)
West Side Highway
Twelfth Ave
Eleventh Ave
West End Ave
Tenth Ave
Ninth Ave
Eighth Ave
Seventh Ave
Broadway
Sixth Ave
Avenue of the Americas
Fifth Ave
Madison Ave
Park Ave
Park Ave South
Vanderbilt Ave
Lexington Ave
Third Ave
Second Ave
First Ave
United Nations Plaza
Beekman Pl
Sutton Pl
Sutton Pl South
Tudor City Pl
Depew Pl
Central Park South
Grand Army Plaza
Columbus Circle
Times Square
Duffy Square
Herald Square
1
2 Macy's
3 Madison Square Garden
4 General Post Office
5 Times Square
6 Port Authority Bus Terminal
7 Restaurant Row
8 Jacob K. Javits Center
9 Intrepid Sea, Air & Space Museum
10 Bryant Park
11 Algonquin Hotel
12 Diamond District
13 Radio City Music Hall
14 Paley Center for Media
15 Museum of Modern Art (MoMA)
16 Carnegie Hall
17 Hearst Tower
18
19 Morgan Library & Museum
20 New York Public Library
21 Grand Central Terminal
22 Chrysler Bldg
23 Tudor City
24 United Nations
25 Ford Foundation
26 Manhattan Art and Antiques Center
27 former Citigroup Center
28 Central Synagogue
29 MetLife Bldg
30 Waldorf-Astoria
31 St Bartholomew's
32 Four Seasons
33 Sony Bldg
Statue of Peace
Secretariat Bldg
Hammarskjöld Library
Beekman Tower
Bloomingdale's
Bloomberg Media
919 Third Ave
909 Third Ave
St Peter's Church
Ritz Tower
GE Bldg
UBS
277 Park Ave
Helmsley Bldg
Graybar Bldg
Chanin Bldg
101 Park Ave
Former Mobil Bldg
Former Daily News Bldg
1 & 2 UN Plaza
Yeshiva University
St Vartan's Armenian Church
Kips Bay Plaza Apartments
Exit Plaza
General Motors Bldg
Trump Tower
Lever House
Mutual of Am. Bldg
JP Morgan Chase
St Patrick's Cathedral
Rockefeller Center
Scandinavia House Nordic Center
Lutheran Church in America
Church of the Incarnation
Empire State Bldg
Grace Bldg
MGM Bldg
Ritz-Carlton
Alliance Capital Bldg
Hilton
Sheraton
Time-Life Bldg
McGraw-Hill Bldg
Murdoch's Bldg
Fox News Bldg
Lyceum Theatre
Int. Center of Photography
Condé Nast Bldg
Manhattan Mall
Hotel Pennsylvania
Penn Station
St John
Nelson Tower
Navarre Bldg
New York Times
Foxwoods Theater
Astor Plaza Bldg
E-Walk
Visitors Information Center
Newsweek Bldg
Museum of Arts & Design
Maine
Time Warner Center
Worldwide Plaza Bldg
Skyscraper Office Bldg
Holy Cross
Fordham University
St Clement
Actors' Studio
Manhattan Plaza
Theater Row
St Raphael
Riverplace
New York City Passenger Ship Terminal
Circle Line
59th St Columbus Circle
57th St
50th St
49th St
47th-50th St Rockefeller Center
42nd St
1 Times Sq 42nd St
Grand Central 42nd St
5th Ave 53rd St
Lexington Ave/53rd St
51st St
59th St
Lexington Ave
5th Ave
33rd St
34th St Herald Square
34th St
34th St Penn Station
7th Ave
99
98
97
94
92
90
88
86
84
83
81
78
76
72

York's very definition of a 'big store' – Macy's.

Macy's ❷

Address: 151 W. 34th Street (at Broadway), www.visitmacysusa.com
Telephone: 212-695 4400
Opening Hours: Mon–Tue 9.30am–10pm, Wed–Fri 9am–11pm, Sat 8am–11pm, Sun 10am–10pm
Subway: 34th Street/Herald Square

A New York institution for more than a century, Macy's is, like the sign says, the biggest department store in the world, and worth seeing for its size alone. The giant building is divided into a men's and a women's store, which can be a little confusing if you get stuck in one but want the other, but staff are always on hand to point you in the right direction. Don't leave without visiting the 'Cellar,' a gourmet kitchenware emporium with gadgets and accessories that even the most creative chef would covet.

The Garment District

Exiting Macy's on Seventh Avenue puts you right in the middle of the Garment District, a jangly, soot-covered workhorse that still turns out its share of America's fashion. There's not much to do or see here, except take in the ambience, but dedicated bargain-hunters have been known to walk away with first-class deals from the factory floor or sample sales.

Showrooms also remain in the area, where you can find the latest, if not always the greatest, fashions, although you may have to shop around a little, both for the bargains and the showrooms themselves. That said, you are much less likely to see young men pushing clothing racks through the streets than you would in the past. These days, high-rise condos and hotels are going up and small offices are taking over the buildings that used to house manufacturers.

The structure at Seventh Avenue and 33rd Street is Madison Square Garden, disliked by purists not only for its functional design but also for replacing McKim, Mead, & White's magnificent Pennsylvania Station, demolished in 1963. The 'new' **Penn Station** is now 50ft (15 meters) beneath it, where it shuttles a quarter-million commuters daily to Long Island and New Jersey, as well as Amtrak destinations. Soon, on 33rd

Macy's Thanksgiving Day Parade.

TIP

For those arriving in Penn Station, skip the cabstand at 32nd Street and Seventh Avenue. The wait there can be interminable. Go to the lesser-used exits at Eighth Avenue and flag down a cab yourself. It's more work, but it's much quicker.

Street between Seventh Avenue and the Madison Square Garden, there will be the pedestrianized Plaza33, decorated with sculptures by Keith Haring and Roy Lichtenstein.

Madison Square Garden ❸

Address: Seventh Avenue (at 31st and 33rd streets), www.thegarden.com
Telephone: 212-465 6741
Opening Hours: schedule of events change daily; tours daily 10am–3pm
Entrance Fee: charge
Subway: 34th Street/Penn Station

The latest iteration of the venue once located between Madison and Fifth avenues – that is, in Madison Square itself – this is one of America's biggest entertainment arenas, where rock and pop shows, ice hockey, basketball games, tennis matches, and even circuses are held. Whatever your feelings about the building, there's no denying it fulfills its function.

The best way to appreciate this building is to attend one of the Garden's events. Last-minute tickets for sports events are often available on the day (don't expect to sit together if there's more than one of you), or you can book ahead online or through Ticketmaster (www.ticketmaster.com).

The New York Knicks vs. the Charlotte Bobcats at Madison Square Garden.

There are few New York experiences more authentic than watching a home team play at home. Just don't expect a quiet game.

If you're a Glenn Miller fan, you may want to check out the venerable **Hotel Pennsylvania** (www.hotelpenn.com), across Seventh Avenue at 33rd Street. This used to be the Big Band era's hottest ticket, immortalized by Miller's hit *Pennsylvania 6-5000* – still the hotel's phone number. Sadly, the busy terminus-style lobby has replaced glamour with function, but at least it's easy for guests to purchase theater tickets and newspapers from the various stands in reception.

Behind Madison Square Garden, the **General Post Office** ❹ is hardly an attraction, but it *is* impressive, with a monumental Corinthian design that makes your average Greek temple look like a tiki hut. There's also the oft-quoted slogan on the frieze: 'Neither snow nor rain nor heat nor gloom of night stays these couriers from the swift completion of their appointed rounds.' The motto was stolen from Herodotus, who obviously never mailed a letter in Manhattan.

Heading back to Herald Square, Broadway slices through the Midtown grid up to 42nd Street. This is the Downtown end of Times Square, the garish heart of Midtown West, and one of the city's most dramatic success stories.

TIMES SQUARE ❺

Address: Broadway (at 42nd to 48th streets), www.timessquarenyc.org
Subway: 42nd Street/Times Square

Stretching along **Broadway** to 48th Street, with the **Theater District** sprawled loosely on either side, Times Square has had long-awaited renovations that have once again made it the 'Crossroads of the World.' The most exciting development is the conversion of Broadway from 42nd to 47th Street into a pedestrian-only mall. The whole of Times Square is a non-smoking area.

Whether you're here for a show or not, be sure to take a stroll down **Shubert Alley**, a busy walkway that runs behind the Booth and Shubert theaters, from 45th to 44th Street. **Sardi's** restaurant (234 West 44th Street; www.sardis.com), is a venerable Broadway landmark. In addition to its fabled dining rooms with star caricatures galore, there's a great bar, abuzz with show talk before or after the theater. Sadly, Vincent Sardi Jr, son of the founder, died in 2007, but the show, as they say, goes on.

Theatrical nostalgia buffs should head for the **Lyceum Theatre**, a block east on 45th Street. Open since 1903, it is the oldest continually operating theater on Broadway and – with its elaborate Baroque facade and dramatic mansard roof – probably the most beautiful.

The Times Square Visitor Center is now closed permanently, but all the information needed can be found at the official website (see above) or you can ask any of the Public Safety Officers. The Broadway Walking Tours now start from The Actor's Chapel, at 239 West 49th Street three times a day at 9.30am, 11.30am, and 2pm. More information on these can be found at http://walkinbroadway.com.

Madison Square Garden.

Times Square is changing all the time, and over the past few years or so has started to attract the sort of big-name businesses that first put it on the map: Reuters, and Ernst & Young have office space there; Condé Nast, who gave their name to the tower at 4 Times Square, has recently moved to One World Trade Center. Now, one of the tower's principal tenants is H&M.

The pedestrianized section of Times Square.

EAT

For Korean food, head over to West 32th Street between Broadway and Fifth Avenue, aka Koreatown. There are a few other notable Korean eateries in the blocks north and south of here, but this is the heart of the Seoul-ful action. There's karaoke to boot.

One cultural attraction is the **Lyric Theatre**, a relatively new theater with wide aisles and good views of the stage from most seats. Formerly known as the Hilton Theatre, the Ford Center for Performing Arts, and Foxwoods Theatre, it has now reverted to its original name after a thorough renovation. Built on the site of the old Lyric Theater (1903), the building has retained some of its elegant facade.

The theater also occupies the site next door, the former premises of the Apollo Theater (1920), and the design has incorporated into its internal decor some of the Apollo Theater's embellishments. Appropriately, for several years, the theater was the Broadway home of the most recent revival of that perennial musical, *42nd Street*. Its most famous latest production was also Broadway's most expensive: *Spider-Man Turn off the Dark*.

Also on 42nd Street are New York's outlet of the world-famous **Madame Tussauds** wax museum (www.madametussauds.com), the **E-Walk** entertainment complex (with 13 movie theaters) and the AMC Empire (www.amctheatres.com), which has 25 movie screens. Most of the dining choices are from chain restaurants.

I want my MTV

At the corner of 44th Street is the **Viacom** building (One Astor Plaza), where the **Times Square Studio** and headquarters of **MTV** are located. Joining the retail roster on the square and keeping with the MTV vibe are **Forever 21** and **Aeropostale**, two low-cost, youth-oriented fashion outlets.

Despite the square's transformation, there's still a perceptible sleaze factor seeping over from the few remaining sex shops that are peppered between the discount clothing and cheap food joints on Eighth Avenue, where the **Port Authority Bus Terminal** ❻ (between 40th and 42nd and now cleaned up) is a major commuter hub.

This sleazy atmosphere continues to change, however, a fact exemplified by the new **New York Times Building**, opposite the bus terminal on Eighth Avenue, between 40th and 41st. This gleaming addition to the NY skyline has been designed by Renzo Piano using ceramic tubes to create a curtain-wall effect that acts

The New York Times Building

as a sunscreen, and changes color throughout the day.

WEST OF TIMES SQUARE

Heading west and a little to the north on Eighth or Ninth avenues, things get interesting in the old **Hell's Kitchen** neighborhood, now known as **Clinton** ❼. At the start of the 20th century, Hell's Kitchen was one of the most notorious slums in the country. Immigrants were crammed into unsafe and unsanitary tenements, and Irish gangs governed the streets like petty overlords. The police were afraid to venture into the neighborhood alone.

There's still a certain gut-level edginess to the area, and a new generation of immigrants, but there are also artists and actors, as well as culinary discoveries to be made. Ninth Avenue from 57th Street to 42nd Street is a globetrot for diners, with reasonably priced restaurants offering an atlas of international cuisines.

A stretch of West 46th Street from Eighth to Ninth avenues – known as **Restaurant Row** – is a solid block of brightly colored eateries popular among the pre-theater crowd. During the annual **Ninth Avenue International Food Festival** (May; www.ninthavenuefoodfestival.com), thousands of New Yorkers flock to gorge themselves on a huge variety of delicacies available from street vendors and the restaurants themselves. If you love to eat, this is an event that you should go out of your way to attend.

Off-Broadway

There's also an active Off-Broadway theater scene on 42nd Street between Ninth and Tenth avenues, where the block of small, experimental, or low-budget venues here are known collectively as **Theater Row**. This makes an attractive pairing with Restaurant Row for an evening out.

On the way between Restaurant Row and Theater Row, theater-lovers might consider a quick detour down West 44th Street. Between Ninth and Tenth avenues is the headquarters of New York's most famous acting school – the legendary **Actors' Studio** (http://theactorsstudio.org).

Though there's not much to look at, this small building on an otherwise residential street spawned such greats as Marlon Brando, James Dean, Paul Newman, and Robert De Niro – all practitioners of the school's 'Method' style of acting.

Harborside

There's little of note to see west of here, except for the **Jacob K. Javits Center** ❽, (www.javitscenter.com) at Twelfth Avenue and 34th Street. This is one of the country's largest convention and exhibition spaces – home to the National Boat Show and other events – and it keeps getting larger. In 2010 a new hall, Javits Center North, was completed, and later, the second largest green roof in the US, with its gardens inhabited by 11 species of birds. Conventioneers love being here, but unless you have an interest in one of the visiting exhibitions, it's not worth going out of your way to the Javits.

TIP

Circle Line cruises (www.circleline42.com, tel: 212-563 3200), on West 42nd Street, have been offering tours since 1945 – a three-hour boat trip around Manhattan, with entertaining commentary. Night-time tours are also available, and from May through September you can try The Beast, a hair-raising ride by speedboat.

The bright lights of Times Square.

The Jacob K. Javits Center is growing bigger and better than ever, thanks to state funds granted for expansion.

Non-delegates might like to consider a little sightseeing. A bit farther uptown, at Pier 83 on 42nd Street, **Circle Line** boats depart for delightful cruises around Manhattan.

Intrepid Sea, Air, and Space Museum ❾

Address: Pier 86 (at W. 46th Street and 12th Avenue), www.intrepidmuseum.org
Telephone: 212-245 0072
Opening Hours: daily 10am–5pm, until 6pm Sat–Sun Apr–Oct
Entrance Fee: charge
Subway: 42nd Street/Port Authority

The museum is centered on one giant exhibit, the USS *Intrepid*, a decommissioned World War II aircraft carrier with a deck the size of a few football fields. It's strewn with aircraft, from fighter jets to a Concorde and a retired submarine, the USS *Growler*. The *Intrepid* recently underwent a $58 million refurbishment, and acquired its highest-flying attraction, the decommissioned Space Shuttle *Enterprise*, which resides in its own pavilion with 17 accompanying exhibits from NASA's space program.

The Intrepid Sea, Air, and Space Museum.

STROLLING SIXTH AVENUE

For an alternative route, walk east instead of west from Times Square to **Sixth Avenue**. Signs announce the **Avenue of the Americas**, but don't be fooled: to New Yorkers, Sixth Avenue is Sixth Avenue, no matter how many flags hang from the lampposts. At the corner of 42nd Street is pretty **Bryant Park** ❿, (www.bryantpark.org) a leafy venue for fashion shows, summer concerts, and outdoor movies. In winter there's skating on the pond, a pretty sight, especially when the snow is piled high around the **Bryant Park Grill** (http://arkrestaurants.com/bryant_park), which looks out over the park from behind the New York Public Library. The Art Deco **Radiator Building** at 40th Street is now the fashionable **Bryant Park Hotel** (http://bryantparkhotel.com) and bar, and is helping to perk up the square around the park.

Clubs and diamonds

Turning right at 44th Street leads to the neighborhood of the **Algonquin Hotel** ⓫ (www.algonquinhotel.com), where Dorothy Parker, Robert

The Art Deco Radiator Building.

Benchley, and other distinguished literati traded wit at the famous Round Table. Although the hotel has undergone a $5 million renovation in 2012, much has been done to preserve the appearance and atmosphere of this historic hotel.

If you are rich or well connected, West 44th Street has several opportunities for genteel rest and relaxation. No. 27 is the premises of the **Harvard Club**, whose interior can more easily be observed by peering into a back window, rather than shelling out for four years' education; No. 37 houses the distinguished **New York Yacht Club**, with an 1899 nautically themed Beaux Arts facade.

Another right turn off Sixth Avenue leads to the **Diamond District** ⓬, a block-long enclave along 47th Street where close to $500 million's worth in gems is traded every day. Most of the diamond merchants are Hasidic Jews, distinguished by black suits, wide-brimmed hats, and long beards. From 47th Street north, corporate monoliths march up Sixth Avenue. Names change, but the structures stay the same. This stretch of Sixth is really the backyard of the Rockefeller Center and its famous performance space.

Radio City Music Hall ⓭

Address: 1260 Sixth Avenue (at 50th and 51st streets), www.radiocity.com
Telephone: 212-247 4777
Opening Hours: box office daily 11.30am–8pm; tours daily 10am–5pm
Entrance Fee: charge
Subway: 47th–50th Street/ Rockefeller Center

The world's largest indoor theater graces the west side of the Rockefeller Center. Built in 1932 as a palace for the people, both the exterior and interior are magnificent, and a guided tour is highly recommended. From the massive chandeliers in the Grand Lobby to the plush, scalloped auditorium, Radio City was built to impress; it's the last word in Art Deco extravagance. The acoustics are excellent, and even the restrooms were custom-designed. The Stuart Davis mural that graced the men's smoking lounge was

TIP

The PATH train is a subway that runs from 33rd Street, along Sixth Avenue with stops at 23rd, 14th, and 9th streets, then over to Christopher Street before tunneling under the Hudson into the wilds of New Jersey. Fares can be paid by MetroCards, making this a useful local alternative to the 1, F, and V trains.

Bryant Park.

The Show Goes On

Even in the darkest days of financial crisis, the Broadway lights have continued to shine and make visitors forget their troubles.

Broadway's 40 theaters sell more than 12 million tickets annually, earning upward of $1 billion. Andrew Lloyd Webber's imported musical megahits – *Phantom of the Opera*, *Cats* – used to dominate the box office, but American dramas and comedies (often lumped together as 'straight plays') have a stronger foothold these days, vying for eyes along with musicals based on popular films and always-reliable revivals. In an average season of 35 new productions, roughly half will be new plays. Recent hits like *The Book of Mormon* have been selling tickets over a year in advance, and mainstays like *The Lion King* and *Wicked* continue to play to packed houses. Even the critically dismissed *Spider-Man* musical pulled in nearly $1 million a week.

Lyceum Theater.

In the early 20th century over 100 new plays were staged each season. Playwrights and composers like Eugene O'Neill, Lillian Hellman, Cole Porter, Irving Berlin, Rodgers and Hart, Arthur Miller, and Tennessee Williams all made their names in New York, and their work is often revived.

Of the 40 theaters known as 'Broadway,' only a handful are on the Great White Way itself, including the Broadway Theatre, the Palace, and the Winter Garden. The rest are on side streets from 41st to 54th Street, not counting the Vivian Beaumont Theater at Lincoln Center, home to a recent celebrated run of *The King and I*.

One of the oldest and most splendid theaters, the Lyceum (1903), is a neo-Baroque beauty on West 45th Street, just east of Times Square. The New Victory on 42nd Street is even older, but has had a more troublesome history. Built by Oscar Hammerstein in 1900 as the Theatre Republic, its name was given a patriotic boost during the 1940s. Thirty years later it was reduced to showing porno movies, but now the New Victory presents colorful, fresh productions, often aimed at children.

Starting Small

Broadway may make the headlines, but Off-Broadway is considered by many to be the true soul of New York theater. Some playwrights bypass Broadway altogether in favor of smaller venues. Off-Broadway is also where plays are staged that are unsuitable for the mainstream, whether for their content or for cost reasons. A hit in an Off-Broadway theater like Playwrights Horizons or the Public Theater provides the confidence backers need to move uptown. *Rent*; *Bring In 'Da Noise, Bring In 'Da Funk;* and *A Chorus Line* started this way.

With limited time on a New York visit, it can be better not to fixate on a particular show, but to have a number of options, and choose the one that offers the best ticket deal. It can also be rewarding to play a hunch and try something relatively unheard of. This may offer the most memorable kind of New York theater experience, as well as giving the chance to see something spectacular before the critics make ticket prices soar.

thought so important, it was acquired by the Museum of Modern Art.

The **Paley Center for Media** ⓮ (25 West 52nd Street; http://media.paleycenter.org; tel: 212-621 6600; Wed–Sun noon–6pm, Thu until 8pm; charge), formerly the Museum of Television and Radio, is a feast for committed couch potatoes. The vast archive of vintage radio and TV shows can be accessed at viewing consoles, and is the perfect rainy-day activity. There are daily screenings, too.

Everyone's favorite slogan.

Museum of Modern Art ⓯

Address: 11 W. 53rd Street (at Fifth and Sixth avenues), www.moma.org
Telephone: 212-708 9400
Opening Hours: daily 10.30am–5.30pm, until 8pm on Fri
Entrance Fee: charge, free on Fri 4–8pm
Subway: 53rd Street/Fifth Avenue

The Museum of Modern Art, known to culture vultures as MoMA, offers one of the world's most exciting and provocative art collections (see page 170). Even if the thought of modern art leaves you cold, the building alone is worth visiting. The ingenious use of light and space means you can be walking along a corridor and suddenly find yourself looking out over a sculpture, or through to the city outside.

Perhaps the most accessible section is the Architecture and Design floor, with groundbreaking objects on display. It is these imaginative inclusions that, combined with some of modern art's most famous paintings, give MoMA the edge. Be prepared for crowds of fellow art-lovers.

RADIO CITY ROCKETTES

Four times every day during the Christmas season, the Radio City Rockettes perform in their Art Deco palace in Rockefeller Center. The Rockettes began in St Louis as the 'Missouri Rockets,' and were brought to New York by S.L. (Roxy) Rothafel, who adjusted their name to the 'Roxyettes' and debuted their high-precision, all-American show at his own Roxy theater. They danced at the opening of Radio City Music Hall on December 27, 1932, and have been resident ever since. The Christmas show is an American institution and draws an audience of over 1 million people. Proficiency in jazz and tap dancing, and a height between 5'6" and 5'11" (1.68–1.8 meters) are requirements for ensemble dancers; principals also need strong ballet skills.

Radio City Music Hall.

EAT

For a touch of elegance after the neon wattage of Times Square, head north to 57th Street, and the opulent, indefatigable Russian Tea Room (www.russiantearoomnyc.com).

Carnegie Hall 16

Address: 57th Street and Seventh Avenue, www.carnegiehall.org
Telephone: 212-903 9765
Opening Hours: box office Mon–Sat 11am–6pm, Sun noon–6pm (box office closed Sat–Sun June–mid-Aug); tours Mon–Fri 11.30am, 12.30pm, 2pm, and 3pm, Sat 11.30am and 12.30pm, Sun 12.30pm
Entrance Fee: charge
Subway: 57th Street

As every American knows, there's only one way to get to Carnegie Hall – practice, practice. The joke is about as old as the hall itself, which was built in 1891 by super-industrialist Andrew Carnegie. Ever since Tchaikovsky conducted at the opening gala, Carnegie Hall has attracted the world's finest performers, including Rachmaninov, Toscanini, and Sinatra. It's a shame that the hall's exterior isn't quite as inspiring as its history or acoustics.

Carnegie Hall is, in fact, the umbrella title for three separate halls. The Issac Stearn Auditorium/ Ronald O. Perelman Stage is the hall's original space. The auditorium seats nearly 3,000 people and was described by Isaac Stearn as 'larger than life.' Two smaller stages complete the complex, one with 600 seats, and one half that size.

Midtown goes green

Two blocks west is another of the city's spectacular recent constructions, the **Hearst Tower 17**, soaring up like a giant, glass origami-model, with walls of glass facets that catch the light in ever-changing colors. This is also New York's first recognized 'green' skyscraper; low-impact technologies and recyclable materials having been used throughout.

Midtown West wraps up with a flourish on **Central Park South**, famed for luxury hotels and lines of limousines. It's a good place to catch a **horse-drawn carriage** and clip-clop around the park – especially in December, when Midtown glistens with holiday lights.

The Mariinsky Orchestra, conducted by Valery Gergiev, performs in Carnegie Hall.

Hearst Tower.

MUSEUM OF MODERN ART

Attention and praise is lavished on MoMA's building almost as much as on its world-class collection.

The Starry Night, 1889, Vincent Van Gogh. 'Looking at the stars,' he said, 'always makes me dream.'

'One of the most exquisite works of architecture to rise in this city in at least a generation' was the New York Times's welcome to MoMA's Midtown home, when it reopened at the end of 2004 after an extensive refit.

Yoshio Taniguchi, the Japanese architect chosen for the project, said his aim was 'the imaginative and disciplined use of light, materials, and space.' The facility offers almost twice the floor space of the former building, with airy galleries on the second floor and more intimate exhibition areas on the levels above. The top floor provides expansive, sky-lit space for temporary exhibitions. The much-admired Sculpture Garden follows the original 1953 design, setting Rodin, Picasso and Tony Smith pieces among trees and calm reflecting pools.

The museum has since purchased the building next door and plans further expansions. After protests, the former home of the American Folk Art Museum will now not be demolished, but the reconstruction is due to finish by 2018.

Innovative furniture designs.

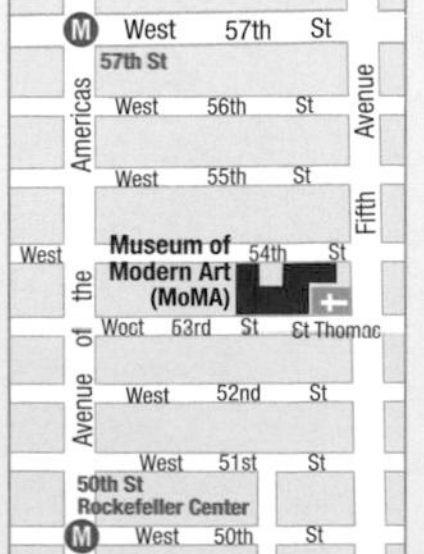

The Essentials

Address: 11 West 53rd Street, between Fifth and Sixth avenues; www.moma.org
Tel: 212-708 9400
Opening Hours: daily 10.30am–5.30pm, until 8pm on Fri
Entrance Fee: charge, free on Fri 4–8pm
Subway: 53rd Street/ Fifth Avenue

MoMA was a daring pioneer when it opened in 1928 and has been hugely influential in the development of modern art.

MOMA IN THE MAKING

MoMA's dazzling extension was designed by Japanese architect Yoshio Taniguchi.

The Museum of Modern Art's collection was started by Abby Aldrich Rockefeller, Mary Quinn Sullivan, and Lillie P. Bliss in 1929, with just eight prints and a single drawing. Abby's enthusiasm for the works of modern artists like Matisse, Van Gogh, and Chagall was not shared by her husband, John D. Rockefeller, who decried the work as 'unintelligible,' and unfit for public viewing. The opening show of works by Cézanne, Gauguin, Van Gogh, and Seurat was held on the 12th floor of a building on 57th Street and Fifth Avenue. After three transfers to larger premises, MoMA moved to its present location in 1939.

The museum's collection, which began so modestly, now includes almost 200,000 works, among them paintings, sculptures, drawings, prints, photographs, architectural models and drawings, furniture, and design objects. MoMA also has around 22,000 films and 4 million film stills. The library and archives are among the premier facilities of their kind in the world.

La Clownesse assise (The Seated Clowness), 1896, Henri de Toulouse-Lautrec. Diminutive Lautrec is best known as a postermaker and chronicler of the Belle Epoque, and the girls of Paris's fin de siècle Moulin Rouge nightclub in particular.

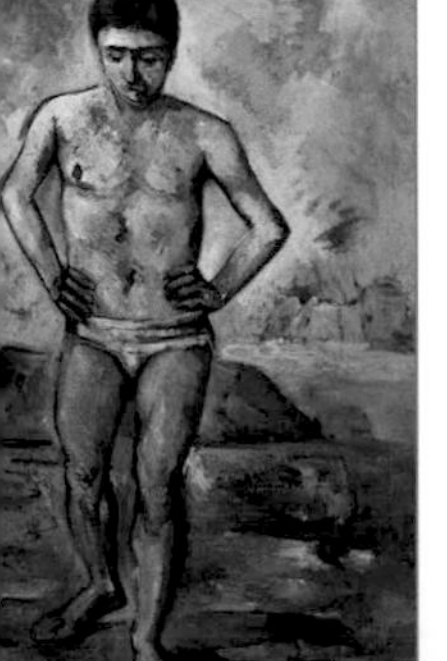

The Bather, c.1885, by Paul Cézanne, one of the great Post Impressionists and the painter whom Henri Matisse described as 'the father of us all.'

Yoko Ono's Wishing Tree.

View of Fifth Avenue, towards the Empire State Building.

FIFTH AVENUE

Paris has the Champs-Elysées, London has Bond Street, Rome has the Via Veneto, but only New York has Fifth Avenue.

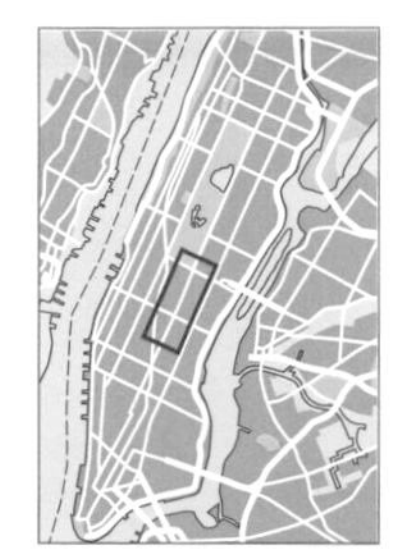

There are few streets that evoke the essence of the city as powerfully as Fifth Avenue. It's all here – the audacity of the Empire State Building, the ambition of the Rockefeller Center, and the old-world elegance of the Plaza Hotel.

Fifth Avenue begins at Washington Square, near the crooked streets of Greenwich Village. Rolling up past the Flatiron Building to Madison Square Park – the site of the original Madison Square Garden – the avenue marches past the Empire State Building and Rockefeller Center, hugs Central Park for 26 scenic blocks, before plunging into 'Museum Mile' (see page 210), and some of the city's most important art collections.

Timeline of the city

Continuing past the mansions and embassies of the Upper East Side, Fifth runs a sketchy course through Harlem, bisecting Marcus Garvey Park, before coming to a halt just before the Harlem River. South to north, culturally, socially, and economically, few streets in the world can provide a more varied tour of extremes. It's a timeline of the city.

EMPIRE STATE BUILDING A

Address: 350 Fifth Avenue (at 33rd and 34th streets), www.empirestatebuilding.com
Telephone: 212-736 3100
Opening Hours: daily 8am–2am
Entrance Fee: charge
Subway: 34th Street/Herald Square

The world's most famous skyscraper rises like a rocket from the corner of 33rd Street. When it was completed in 1931, this was the tallest structure in the world. Currently the city's third tallest building, now that One

Main Attractions
Empire State Building
New York Public Library
Rockefeller Center
Saks Fifth Avenue
St Patrick's Cathedral
Grand Army Plaza
Plaza Hotel
Central Park

Map
Page 174

The imposing lobby of the Empire State Building.

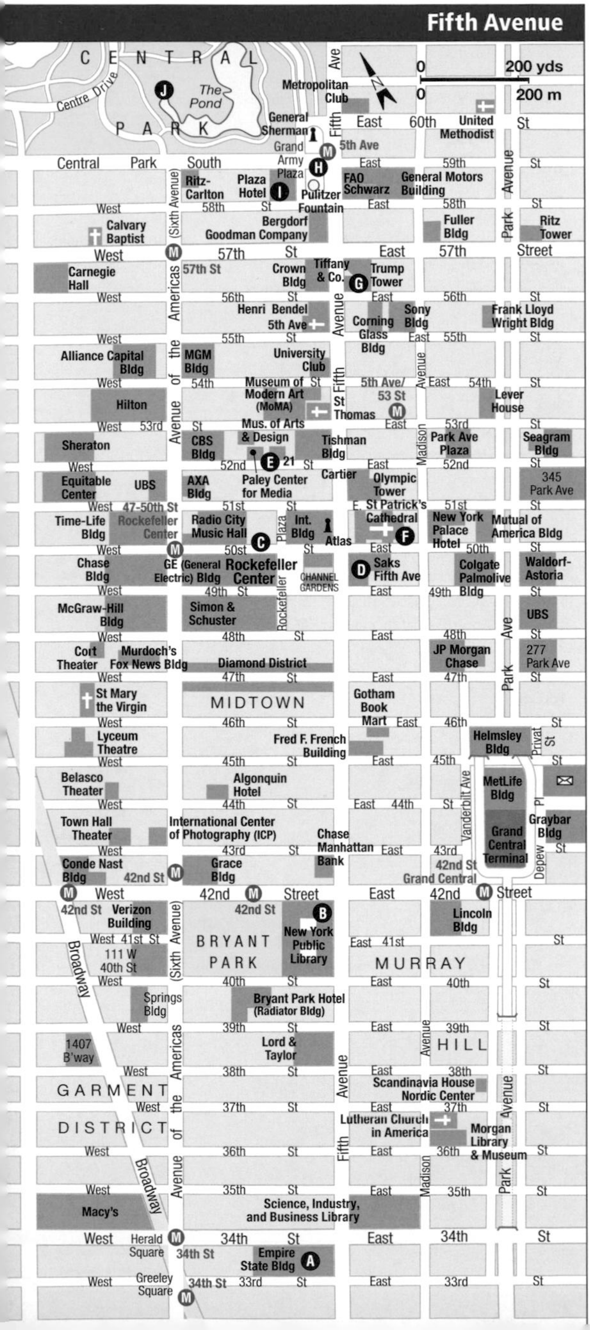

Fifth Avenue

World Trade Center is complete, it doesn't even crack the top thirty worldwide. When it comes to the view, however, the Empire State can't be beat. On a clear day you can see for as far as 80 miles (130km), while at night, Manhattan spreads out far below, a floating sea of winking, twinkling lights.

If you plan to visit during the day, try to get here as early as possible, as the long lines can take something away from the experience. At the concourse level, enter the marble Art Deco lobby, where you are directed to the high-speed elevator that zips straight up to the 86th-floor observation deck. Outside, there are powerful binoculars to peer through, and a couple of souvenir stands in the covered viewing area.

If this is your first visit to New York, it's a good idea to rent the audio tour – an entertaining and informative overview of the city as it spreads out in front of you. Expect a security check on arrival, which involves a lot of waiting around.

Kong and Fay Wray climb to the 102nd floor in the 1933 movie King Kong.

View from the Empire State Building.

Observation deck

For an additional fee, you can ascend to the smaller observatory way up on the 102nd floor, which is just about the spot where in 1933 Fay Wray (and, more recently, Naomi Watts in the 2005 remake) made her tearful final farewells to the 'tallest, darkest leading man in Hollywood,' a giant ape by the name of King Kong. Movie posters, photos, and other memorabilia from Wray's private collection are on permanent display in the lobby downstairs.

Kong isn't the only one who met his fate up here. Of the more than 30 people who have jumped off the building, only two were wearing parachutes, and they were both arrested as soon as they landed. On a happier note, a handful of lucky couples are given permission to plight their troth at the top of the building every Valentine's Day.

The **New York Skyride** (www.skyride.com; charge), inside the building, offers a simulated flight above the city (this is not recommended for those who suffer from motion sickness).

Optimistic design

The Empire State was planned in the optimistic 1920s, but by the time it was completed the United States was in the depths of the Great Depression, and office space was not fetching a premium. In its first year of operation until March 1932, the

QUOTE

'I believe in the sacredness of a promise, that a man's word should be as good as his bond; that character – not wealth or power or position – is of supreme worth.'

John D. Rockefeller

The Beaux Arts New York Public Library.

TIP

The lighting of the Rockefeller Center Christmas Tree in November is best watched on television. Crowds are always far too thick, views are often obstructed, and you're much more likely to see rain than snow this time of year.

observation deck took as much as the rent collected on the whole of the rest of the building put together.

The Empire State Building's upper floors are illuminated at night, and special light displays are put on for commemorations, festivals and holidays, including the Fourth of July, Christmas, and Hanukkah (see the website for a complete schedule).

Illuminated display

The building was first opened on May 1, 1931, with a dazzling display switched on from Washington DC by President Herbert Hoover, and the illuminations have been a feature ever since. The colored floodlights were installed in 1964, and have traditionally signaled events such as Frank Sinatra's 80th birthday (the singer's death was also marked by the crown of the building being bathed in blue light, for Frank's nickname 'Ol' Blue Eyes.') After the death of *King Kong* actress Fay Wray, the Empire State stood for 15 minutes in complete darkness.

On Queen Elizabeth II's Golden Jubilee in 2002, the Empire State paid tribute with a display of purple and gold. Mayor Bloomberg said this was also a way of saying thank you for the support Great Britain gave after the September 11, 2001, attacks. In 2011, the Green Building Council granted the building LEED Gold Status after an extensive, environmentally friendly series of renovations.

Around the Empire State

A block east, the less glamorous **Science, Industry, and Business Library** (188 Madison Avenue at 34th Street; tel: 917-275 6975; www.nypl.org) is a valuable addition to the city's library facilities, with a huge stock of research materials including business and science journals, CD-ROMs, and handbooks for personal or professional study. It's a good place to get online if you've left your laptop behind, with computers for public use.

Five blocks north at Fifth and 39th Street, **Lord & Taylor** (www.lordandtaylor.com) is one of New York's best-known department stores; people have been known to line up just to peer into its windows.

Skating at Rockefeller Center.

New York Public Library B

Address: Fifth Avenue (at 42nd Street), www.nypl.org
Telephone: 917-275 6975
Opening Hours: Mon and Thu–Sat 10am–6pm, Tue–Wed 10am–8pm, Sun 1pm–5pm
Entrance Fee: free
Subway: 42nd Street/Bryant Park

Directly across the street, in warm weather, office workers and tourists can be found lounging in front of New York's coolest library, under the watchful gaze of two stone lions that flank the marble steps.

Stretching between 40th and 42nd streets, this glorious 1911 Beaux Arts monument is one of the world's finest research facilities, with a vast collection that includes 15 million items and the first book printed in the United States – the *Bay Psalm Book* from 1640 – and the original diaries of Virginia Woolf.

In addition to a fine collection of paintings, there is a third space for exhibitions. Topics are varied and have covered everything from Japanese picture books to New York City garbage.

The biggest treasure of all, however, may be the main Reading Room, a vast, gilded gem with windows that overlook **Bryant Park**. Ask inside about joining one of the free tours of the library (now known as the Stephen A. Schwarzman Building thanks to a sizable donation by the billionaire investor); they take place two times a day (at 11am and 2pm, once a day, at 2pm, on Sunday).

ROCKEFELLER CENTER C

Address: Fifth Avenue (at 48th to 51st streets), www.rockefellercenter.com
Telephone: 212-588 8601
Opening Hours: plaza and concourse daily 7am–midnight, Top of the Rock from 8am, other attractions close earlier
Entrance Fee: charge for tours and Top of the Rock; otherwise free
Subway: 47th–50th Street/ Rockefeller Center

Tours of the NBC studios depart every 30 minutes

At 49th Street, Fifth Avenue lives up to its legend, thanks in large part to **Rockefeller Center**, one of the world's biggest business and entertainment complexes, and a triumph of Art Deco architecture. Rockefeller Center has been called a 'city within a city,' and it's got the numbers to prove it. The center's daily population (including visitors) is more than 200,000. If it were a city, that number would place it in the top 100 biggest in the country. It would certainly be the most crowded. It has more than

The stone lions in front of the New York Public Library are called Patience and Fortitude.

EAT

Chocolate fans' eyes pop out when they see La Maison du Chocolat (www.lamaisonduchocolat.us), the exquisite French chocolatiers at the foot of the GE Building in Rockefeller Plaza. In the summer months, there's also freshly made ice cream to savor.

100,000 telephones, almost 50,000 windows, and nearly 400 elevators.

Add to this a 2-mile (3km) underground concourse, numerous stores and dozens of places to eat, four subway lines, a post office, foreign consulates, and the world's most famous auction house, Christie's, and you've got quite a little metropolis. Indeed, when Rockefeller first envisaged the complex – as a development to house the city's burgeoning TV and radio industry – he called it 'Radio City.'

The **Channel Gardens** – so named because they separate La Maison Française on the left and the British Building on the right, just as these countries flank the English Channel – draw visitors into the center of the plaza. This is where the famous Christmas tree, lit with countless bulbs, captivates holiday visitors. The *Today* show (www.today.com) is broadcast from a glassed-in studio here, too.

Tours of **NBC Studios** (www.nbcstudiotour.com; charge) depart every 30 minutes; tours of the Rockefeller Center (charge) depart hourly (Mon–Fri 8.30am–2pm, Sat–Sun 8.30am–5pm).

Rockefeller Center was completed in 1933.

In summer, there are concerts in the sunken courtyard, while in the winter there's a hugely popular ice-skating rink.

30 Rock

Rockefeller Plaza is dominated by the 70 floors of the soaring 850ft

Saks Fifth Avenue.

(259-meter) **30 Rockefeller Center** or **the Comcast Building**, renamed in July 2015 after its newest owner. Formerly known as the RCA Building and the GE Building, it is also known locally as '30 Rock.' The Rockefeller family retain offices on the 54th and 56th floors. In 2011, the Federal Communications Commission approved a merger between NBC and the Comcast cable company, ushering in a new era for 30 Rock. It was inevitable that the Tina Fey and Alec Baldwin sitcom that bore the same name as the building would lampoon the move, referring to its new parent company as 'Kabletown... with a K.'

As the headquarters of NBC, 30 Rock is the home of the comedy show *Saturday Night Live* and many of the network's New York facilities. The building was also the setting for a famous photograph taken in 1932 during the construction of the center by Charles C. Ebbets called *Lunchtime atop a Skyscraper*. Sitting astride a steel girder with no harnesses, 11 workers casually lunch and chat, 850ft (260 meters) above the city.

Top of the Rock

Rockefeller Center's best tourist attraction is the **Top of the Rock** (www.topoftherocknyc.com; daily 8am–midnight; charge). Situated 70 floors above ground, the observation deck offers a different perspective of the city from the Empire State, including terrific sightings of Central Park, and has one major advantage – a clear view of the iconic building itself. The lines for the deck are often shorter, though purists may argue that the experience lacks the class of visiting the Empire State.

Saks, St Pat's, and 21

Back on Fifth Avenue, **Saks Fifth Avenue** **D** (611 Fifth Avenue; www.saksfifthavenue.com; tel: 212-753 4000; Mon–Sat 10am–8.30pm, Sun 11am–7pm) is the supremely elegant flagship department store for Saks shops across America, from Dallas to San Diego. There are numerous great shopping opportunities here, including an enormous women's shoe department that they say has its own zip code, 10022 (not really). On the next corner up is the **International Building**, with Lee

Paul Manship's gilded statue, Prometheus Bringing Fire to the World, is the centerpiece of Rockefeller Plaza.

FOLLOW THAT CAB

There are few more recognizable New York icons than the taxicab, and that's no surprise. They've been here for more than 100 years. Hansom cabs charging exorbitant fares ruled the streets for a time. That was until 1907, when an enterprising businessman named Harry N. Allen released a fleet of 65 French-made gasoline-powered vehicles into the city. The honeymoon period was short, and Allen soon faced the wrath of his drivers, who unionized and argued for better pay – a story that would be repeated many times and an appropriate beginning to the age of the yellow cab.

Checker Cabs were the dominant vehicles for the first half of the 20th century, their bright colors and signature checkered stripes easy to spot on a rainy city street. To regulate the industry, the city established a medallion system in 1930s, which limited the number of official cabs. By 1970, all official cabs had to be painted yellow.

As automotive trends changed, so too did the design of taxis. Checker Cabs made way for Ford Crown Victorias and the somewhat recent addition of mini vans. In late 2013, the city introduced a completely redesigned Taxi of Tomorrow, the result of a controversial contest where Nissan was named the victor.

Lawrie's monumental bronze figure of Atlas crouching under the weight of the world, over 25ft (8 meters) tall, at its entrance.

Two streets up is another classic dining venue, **21** Ⓔ (21 West 52 Street; www.21club.com; tel: 212-582 7200), where every president since FDR has been elegantly entertained. The atmosphere is hushed, the lighting low – and the steak tartare still sets the standard.

St Patrick's Cathedral Ⓕ

Address: Fifth Avenue (at 50th and 51st streets), http://saintpatrickscathedral.org
Telephone: 212-753 2261
Opening Hours: daily 6.30am–8.45pm, first Mass at 7am daily (8am on Sat)
Entrance Fee: free
Subway: 50th Street/Rockefeller Center

Taxi SUV.

The site of St Patrick's was purchased in 1810 to build a Jesuit school, and the cornerstone of the church was laid on August 15 – the Feast of the Assumption – 48 years later. Work was suspended during the Civil War, but the first American cardinal, John McCloskey, got construction back underway in 1865, opening the doors in May, 1879. Extensive renovation in 1927–31 included installation of the great organ.

The cathedral is a formidable Midtown landmark, its Gothic facade an intriguing counterpoint to the angular lines and smooth surfaces of

Upscale shopping on 57th Street.

the skyscrapers around it. And yet St Pat's is unmistakably New York: where else would one need tickets to attend midnight Mass? Look around the interior, where F. Scott Fitzgerald married his Southern belle, Zelda, before going on to literary fame and domestic hell. Alternatively, take a seat and breathe in the sweet smell of incense – the twinkle of candles and gentle hum of voices makes St Pat's a calming spot in the middle of the hustle of the city. There are free, guided walk-in tours of the cathedral (although contributions are appreciated) on various days between Mon and Fri at 10am (see details on the website).

Serious shopping

Beyond St Patrick's, Fifth Avenue returns to more worldly concerns, namely, upscale shopping. **Tiffany & Co., Cartier**, **Gucci,** and **Armani** are a few that feed into the avenue's élan.

At 57th Street, ladies who lunch totter on stilettos between **Prada** and the expensive emporia inside the **Trump Tower** G (www.trumptowerny.com). Now mainly ultra-luxurious condominiums, the tower is worth stopping by for a glimpse of the big-spending opulence synonymous with Manhattan in the 1980s. Viewers of Donald Trump's TV show *The Apprentice* will recognize its marble atrium and waterfall.

While part of Fifth Avenue has been colonized by chain stores, retail is still a leisurely pursuit at **Henri Bendel** and **Bergdorf Goodman**. Built on the former site of a Cornelius Vanderbilt mansion, Bergdorf is more like a collection of small boutiques than a department store. Exquisite, and expensive.

Grand Army Plaza H on 59th Street punctuates Fifth Avenue and marks the boundary between Midtown and the Upper East Side. It borders the **Plaza Hotel** I (www.theplazany.com), a home-away-from-home for Mark Twain. The Plaza has undergone major renovation, with some rooms now condominiums or retail spaces, and the Oak Room now relegated to legend. There are still plenty of accommodations for visitors, however, and the dining options have become more diverse.

The views of **Central Park** J (see page 182) are worth the price of a cocktail in the Plaza's Champagne Bar.

Christmas at the Rockefeller Center.

THE CORNER OF FIFTH AND CHRISTMAS

Most New Yorkers have a 'seen it once, don't have to see it again' attitude when it comes to Christmas window displays, but even the biggest Scrooge is bound to crack a smile during a snowy December evening walk down Fifth Avenue. It has been a game of one-upmanship for decades, where retailers like Fendi and Louis Vuitton try to outdo the masters of lights and dioramas, Saks Fifth Avenue. There's still a place for animatronic angels and elves and that place would be Lord & Taylor, where the displays retain the quaint handmade qualities of yesteryear. At other stores technology has yielded some fantastic new amusements in the form of lasers and LED screens. Traditionalists point to the Rockefeller Center Christmas Tree as the peak of holiday ornamentation, but the UNICEF Snowflake, a glittering crystal marvel that hangs at 57th Street and Fifth Avenue, also has its fans. A Fifth Avenue window walk should actually take you as far east as Lexington Avenue and as far west as Sixth Avenue, because it wouldn't be the same without a peek through the glass at Bloomingdale's and Macy's. All in all it encompasses more than 20 blocks of entertainment and you don't ever have to open your wallet or purse.

CENTRAL PARK

Stretching from Grand Army Plaza to Harlem, Central Park is the playground and meeting place of the metropolis.

Central Park is a recreational and cultural space, as well as an oxygenating green area in the middle of this crowded, towering city. Frederick Law Olmsted and Calvert Vaux designed the 843-acre (340-hectare) park in 1858. Olmsted's aim was, in his words, to 'supply hundreds of thousands of tired workers who have no opportunity to spend summers in the country with a specimen of God's handiwork.' The project was known as 'Greensward.'

It's amazing how natural the rolling hills and tranquil ponds seem, because the entire landscape of the park is manufactured, just like the skyscrapers that skirt the edges. Before construction of the park, it was swampy land, inhabited by poor Irish and German immigrants and a well-established African-American community known as Seneca Village. All were displaced, a cruel irony after Olmsted's pledge of designing it for 'tired workers.'

Recently, city officials established eight 'Quiet Zones,' clearing certain areas of the buskers that used to fill the park with music. Still, there is a good deal of other no-cost entertainment to be found. In summertime, the New York Public Theater stages *Shakespeare in the Park* at the Delacorte Theater. Tickets are

Cherry blossom in springtime.

Approximately 230 species of bird can be found in the park, including American Robins.

Popular prints and posters for sale.

View of Central Park from Midtown.

Despite the introduction of 'Quiet Zones,' performers of all varieties can still be found in the park.

Central Park

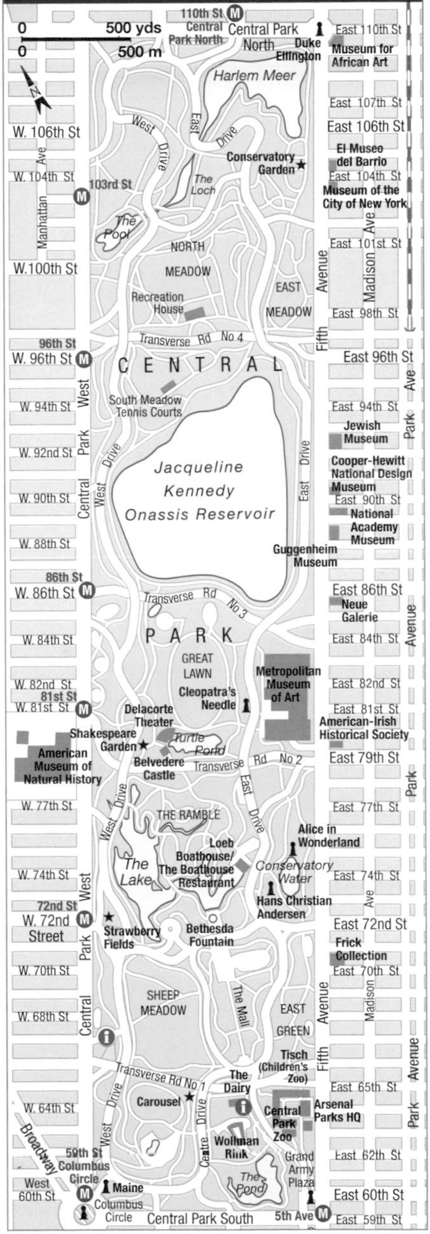

free, but getting a pair requires showing up early in the morning and waiting in line at the box office. The New York Philharmonic and the New York City Opera give outdoor performances on the Great Lawn, and SummerStage festival brings contemporary acts to an open-air venue at Rumsey Playfield for concerts, many with free admission. In wintertime, Wollman Rink provides classes and a picturesque venue for ice skating. For details, visit www.centralparknyc.org.

The Henry Luce Nature Observatory is housed in Belvedere Castle, which was designed by the park's architect, Frederick Law Olmsted, and constructed in 1872.

Classic horse-drawn carriages line up along Central Park South between Fifth and Sixth avenues. The vintage buggy rides are available year-round.

Squirrels were introduced to Central Park in 1877.

The Imagine mosaic, commemorating John Lennon.

Walkers stroll down an avenue of trees following a snowstorm.

CENTRAL PARK WILDLIFE

The first place many visitors go to see wildlife in Manhattan is the Central Park Zoo, which accommodates scores of exotic creatures in different habitats. The Polar Circle is home to penguins and eider ducks. The Tropical Zone houses tropical birds as well as lemurs, coatis, and innumerable frogs, lizards, snakes, and toads. The Temperate Territory is where red pandas and Japanese macaques live. And there are special exhibits dedicated to sea lions and the rare snow leopard. Although the present zoo dates only from 1988, the first menagerie was established in 1864. Seventy years later, a 'storybook' zoo was created by the Depression-era Works Progress Administration.

It takes a bit more effort, but there's plenty of wildlife to see outside of the walls of the zoo as well. The park is home to fish, reptiles, amphibians, and a handful of mammals including squirrels, raccoons, and woodchucks – not to mention the occasional wayward coyote. There are approximately 230 species of birds that live among the 25,000 trees. If that number seems impressive, consider that from 2009 to 2011, two men took on the task of mapping all those trees. They mapped 19,933 in total.

Wollman ice rink.

Hans Christian Andersen takes a seat and prepares to tell a story. Among the statues to delight children are Mother Goose, Humpty Dumpty, Little Jack Horner, and Little Bo Peep.

The Midtown Manhattan skyline.

MIDTOWN EAST

In the mornings, watch the well-dressed masses emerge from Grand Central Terminal and hurry into the shining skyscrapers that surround it, and you might catch a glimpse of the glamorous sheen that still exists well past the Mad Men era.

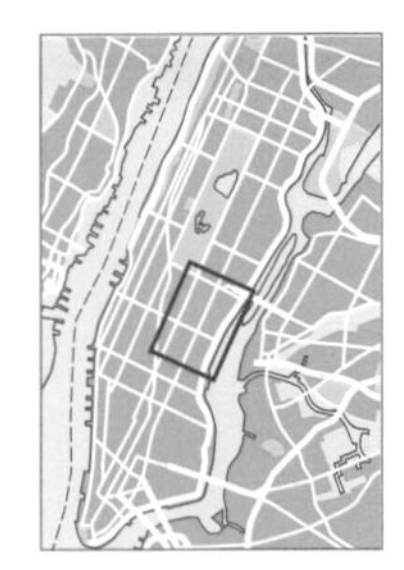

Main Attractions
Morgan Library & Museum
Madison Avenue
Grand Central Terminal
Chrysler Building
United Nations
Waldorf-Astoria
Sony Building

Map
Page 158

Midtown East covers many of the images Manhattan conjures up when people think of New York. This is where the city's corporate heart beats loudest, where power-lunching, power-shopping, and sidewalk power-phoning is a daily way of life.

Like its counterpart to the west, Midtown East begins above 34th Street, and rises to a bustling climax between 42nd Street and the Queensboro (59th Street) Bridge, beyond which lies the calmer Upper East Side. Stretching from Fifth Avenue to the East River, it's a compact, energetic microcosm of Manhattan, encompassing steel-and-glass office towers, historic hotels, and familiar landmarks like the Chrysler Building, Grand Central Terminal, and the United Nations, not to mention some very exclusive neighborhoods.

HILLS AND BAYS

Along 35th Street is the southern border of **Murray Hill** ⓲, a classy residential area in the shadow of sleek Midtown office buildings, its cross-streets lined by brownstone relics of a more genteel era. A plaque on the south side of 35th Street and Park Avenue marks the center of an 18th-century farm owned by Robert Murray, 'whose wife, Mary Lindley Murray (1726–82), rendered signal service in the Revolutionary War.' It was said she cleverly delayed a British advance by inviting the officers to tea, but later, doubt was cast on this story. Close by, on Madison Avenue, the lovely **Church of the Incarnation**, built in 1864, has beautiful stained-glass windows by Tiffany, LaFarge, and Burne-Jones, among others.

The Art Deco facade of the Waldorf-Astoria, one of New York's grandest hotels.

Morgan Library & Museum ⓳

Address: 225 Madison Avenue (at 36th Street), www.themorgan.org
Telephone: 212-685 0008
Operating Hours: Tue–Thu 10.30am–5pm, Fri 10.30am–9pm, Sat 10am–6pm, Sun 11am–6pm
Entrance Fee: charge (free Fri 7–9pm)
Subway: 33rd Street

Also called the Pierpont Morgan Library, this private collection was opened to the public by J.P. Morgan Jr in 1924. It was amassed by his father, Pierpont Morgan, the most powerful banker of his time and an avid collector, whose interests ranged from Egyptian to Renaissance art and Chinese porcelain.

The Morgan has been comprehensively renovated and given a new 'campus' by brilliant Italian architect Renzo Piano, which incorporates the original historic buildings while doubling the exhibition space. There are artistic, literary, musical, and historical works, including drawings by Rembrandt and Rubens and original scores from Mozart and Beethoven. The history of writing and printing was one of Morgan's passions, so the library is strong in this area, with 5,000-year-old carved tablets, three Gutenberg Bibles and manuscripts by Charles Dickens, Mark Twain, and other writers.

The East Room of the Morgan Library.

The new building on Madison Avenue is 'crowned' by a beautiful, naturally lit Reading Room, with excellent facilities for 21st-century researchers. You can see the original pillared entrance on 36th Street.

The West Room of the J.P. Morgan Library.

Sniffen Court

From the Morgan, walk east across Park and Lexington avenues, to reach one of the city's tiniest and most charming historic districts. Behind iron gates and opposite a Yeshiva University building, the red-brick row houses of **Sniffen Court** were constructed in Romanesque Revival style at the time of the American Civil War, and were originally stables for Murray Hill's grander residences (now, of course, very expensive and highly desirable real estate). If you peer through the gates you can make out the horse-relief on the back wall that marks out the former studio of sculptor Malvina Hoffman.

AROUND GRAND CENTRAL

Along the west side of Murray Hill is **Madison Avenue** ⓴. Historically, this has been the spiritual home of the advertising industry, especially the blocks between 42nd and 57th streets. Madison Avenue is one of the city's commercial nerves, where sharp-suited men and women buy their clothes at Brooks Brothers on 44th Street and stop off for cocktails at the Yale Club one block east on Vanderbilt, before running to catch their trains home to leafy suburbs.

Grand Central Terminal ㉑

Address: 42nd Street and Lexington Avenue, www.grandcentralterminal.com
Telephone: 212-340 2583
Operating Hours: daily 5.30am–2am
Subway: 42nd Street/Grand Central

Often incorrectly referred to as 'Grand Central Station,' the terminal greeted 150,000 people when it opened at 12.01 on the first Sunday in February, 1913. Today, 750,000 people cross the concourse of the opulent building every day – over 1 million pass through daily during the Christmas holidays.

Grand Central houses bars, a food court, excellent restaurants, shops, and a branch of the New York Transit Museum to entertain those waiting for a train, as well as the iconic clock that everyone uses as a meeting point.

With entrances at Vanderbilt and 42nd Street, and at Park and Lexington avenues, Grand Central is the hub for Metro-North commuter lines reaching deep into the suburbs of Westchester County and neighboring Connecticut. More than 550 trains depart from here. Grand Central was saved from demolition by the Landmarks Preservation Commission in the 1960s, and so this 1913 Beaux Arts masterpiece stands as a reminder of days when travel was a gracious experience.

Vaulted ceilings

To retain its grandeur, the terminal underwent a $200 million restoration. Advertising signs were removed, new restaurants and stores opened, including an indoor food hall for last-minute purchases, and the glorious illuminated zodiac on the

KIDS

The Morgan Library has the original manuscript of Charles Dickens's *A Christmas Carol.* On the first Sunday in December each year the library hosts an all-day celebration of the book, with family activities that include storytelling, readings, and dancing.

Grand Central Terminal prepares for Christmas.

KIDS

Grand Central has become a destination for food as well as for transportation. Besides upscale places like the Oyster Bar and the Campbell Apartment cocktail lounge, there's a market (www.grandcentralterminal.com/market) that sells fresh gourmet produce and a food court with a dizzying array of cuisines, from Japanese to Indian, Turkish and French.

vaulted ceiling of the main concourse – one of the world's largest spaces – gleams like new.

All except, that is, for a dark patch above Michael Jordan's The Steak House. This was left untouched, to give an understanding of the extent of the restoration effort.

The magnificent astronomical zodiac ceiling was commissioned by the Vanderbilt family from French artist Paul César Helleu in 1912. The constellations were painted back to front, and the Vanderbilts hastily improvised the explanation that it represents a 'God's-eye view.'

The four faces of the clock over the information desks are said to be made from opal (really, they're made from colorful Tiffany glass); the clock has a value estimated by Sotheby's and Christie's at between $10 and $20 million. The flag that hangs above it commemorates the terrorist attacks of September 11, 2001.

Grand tours

Grand Central is the rare commuter hub that's also a tourist destination, and you can spot the out-of-towners pretty easily – they're the ones looking up. Tours are given by the Municipal Art Society every day at 12.30pm (http://docentour.com/gct; tel: 212-464 8255; charge). Self-guided audio tours are also available in the terminal from booths marked 'GCT Tour.' Alternatively, download an application for iPhone and Android phones at http://myorpheo.com/tour-apps-portfolio/official-grand-central-tour. Before leaving, be sure to see the **Oyster Bar** on the lower level, an architectural and culinary landmark.

Chrysler Building ㉒

Address: 42nd Street and Lexington Avenue

Subway: 42nd Street/Grand Central

One block east on Lexington Avenue, the famed Chrysler Building is one of the jewels of the Manhattan skyline. Erected by William Van Alen for auto tsar Walter Chrysler in 1930, its Art Deco spire rises 1,046ft (319 meters) into the city air like a stainless-steel rocket ship powered by gargoyles.

The building was designated a New York City landmark on September 12, 1979. Three years later, the stainless-steel arches and triangular windows were illuminated by bright

View of the Chrysler Building in the 1930s.

BUILDING THE CHRYSLER

In a fantastically theatrical gesture, all seven stories of the steel-clad pinnacle were assembled inside the building, then hoisted into place in an hour and a half. Walter Chrysler's automobile business provided inspiration for much of the spectacular detail, but Van Alen may have regretted his choice of client, since his fee was never paid. The Chrysler was the first building to reach above 1,000ft (305 meters), and was the tallest in the world, until the Empire State Building snatched that title the following year.

Unfortunately, visitors are not allowed past the lobby, but stop in to admire the marble, bronze, and hardwoods as well as the epic murals on urban transportation and human endeavor.

The Grand Concourse of Grand Central Terminal.

white lights for the first time. This glorious lighting scheme was specified in Van Alen's original plan, but it took the city more than 50 years to implement the scheme.

The Chrysler Building is not open to the public, but visitors are allowed into the lobby. The steel-clad street-level facade is worth seeing up close, while the tower provides classic Manhattan views from any approach in the city.

TOWARD THE UNITED NATIONS AND THE EAST RIVER

Continuing east on 42nd Street, walk on past the crowds and the **Grand Hyatt Hotel** (which adjoins Grand Central, and was built over the old Commodore Hotel), to the former Daily News building, between Third and Second avenues. This Art Deco structure, though no longer home to the newspaper, looks so much like the headquarters of the fictional *Daily Planet* that they used it in the *Superman* movies from the 1970s and 80s. Check out the gigantic globe in the lobby before continuing east toward First Avenue, past the steps leading up to **Tudor City** ㉓, a private compound of Gothic brick high-rises that is positioned at a different street level, and has its own tiny park and play area. The development dates from the 1920s, and was designed to attract middle-class buyers out of the suburbs and back into the city. At the time,

Le Corbusier designed the UN's Secretariat building.

land along the East River was filled with slums and slaughterhouses, one reason why all the windows face west, toward the Hudson River.

United Nations 24

Address: First Avenue and 46th Street, http://visit.un.org
Telephone: 212-963 4475
Operating Hours: guided tours Mon–Fri 9am–4.30pm
Entrance Fee: charge
Subway: 42nd Street/Grand Central

The busy flag-lined entrance of the United Nations is opposite 46th Street. Once inside, the gentle patter of unfamiliar languages reminds you that you are now in international territory. Guided tours last 45 minutes and depart every 30 minutes from the visitor's center. Audio tours are available in 20 languages. There's not a lot to see unless you take the tour, but don't miss the Chagall stained-glass windows or the lower-level gift shop, which sells inexpensive handicrafts from all over the world, and the Permanent Memorial to the Victims of Slavery and the Transatlantic Slave Trade (access is free) opened in 2015.

The Chrysler Building.

Every Wednesday at 10.30am there is a weekly briefing organized by the Remember Slavery Programme.

When major delegations are in the town, the neighborhood, particularly the FDR Drive, is snarled with traffic.

The ornate clock above the entrance to Grand Central Terminal.

THE UNITED NATIONS

The name 'United Nations' was devised by President Franklin D. Roosevelt and first used in the 'Declaration by the United Nations' of January 1, 1942, during World War II, when representatives of 26 nations pledged their governments to continue fighting together. The UN charter was drawn up in 1945 and signed by delegates from 50 countries; in the new millennium, membership had risen to over 190 countries.

Just like a foreign embassy, the United Nations' grounds, which cover 18 acres (7 hectares) along the East River, are not considered a part of the United States, and are outside the jurisdiction of city, state, and federal laws. The UN maintains its own independent police force, fire department, and post office.

Forgo a cab and walk the few extra blocks to the subway.

Historic districts

Back on 42nd Street, the lobby garden of the **Ford Foundation** ㉕ – glass-enclosed, all lush trees and flowers – is considered one of the city's most beautiful institutional environments. The building's interior offices look over the small oasis, a clever utilization of a usually uninspiring space. This part of town is also home to three of the city's classiest addresses. **Turtle Bay** – once home to privacy-loving celebrities such as Katharine Hepburn, the conductor Leopold Stokowsky, and author Kurt Vonnegut – is a historic district between 48th and 49th streets where 19th-century brownstones share a garden hidden from the public.

Beekman Place, between First Avenue and the East River, is a two-block enclave of elegant townhouses and apartments set along the river. One of its houses was once the home of famed songwriter Irving Berlin.

Sutton Place is an oft-used synonym for luxury, in books and movies. Starting above 54th Street and stretching north for five blocks, its high-rises are filled with dowagers and poodles. Visual relief is provided by a few still-surviving cul-de-sacs of townhouses, gardens, and promontories offering tantalizing views of the East River.

Nearby is the eclectic **Manhattan Art and Antiques Center** ㉖ on Second Avenue between 55th and 56th streets (www.the-maac.com; tel: 212-355 4400). It's a strange cross between a museum of curios and a shopping arcade. Over 100 small stores are housed here in glass-fronted rooms, selling everything from antique clocks and furniture to carved tusks. It's really a place to wander around rather than to shop, unless you have a big budget and an even bigger suitcase. On the lower level, you'll find that increasingly rare big-city amenity, public restrooms.

On the way back toward Midtown, another interesting place to call is **601 Lexington** ㉗, on 54th Street between Third and Lexington avenues. Formerly the Citigroup Center, its slanted roof makes this a skyline standout, while the indoor atrium

The distinctive slanted roof of 601 Lexington (formerly known as the Citigroup Center).

DRINK

Mixological lore has it that the Bloody Mary was invented at the King Cole Bar (www.kingcolebar.com) in the St Regis Hotel on East 55th and Madison. We think it originated at Harry's Bar in Paris, but this is still a peach of a place, with a Maxfield Parrish mural, killer cocktails, and lighting that continues to flatter after too many drinks.

lined by shops and cafés makes a pleasant pit stop. Before exiting onto Lexington Avenue, drop by **St Peter's Church**, a modern, angular building, which includes a light and airy chapel. St Peter's is renowned for its weekly jazz Eucharist (http://saintpeters.org/jazz); it also hosts frequent concerts.

The **York Theatre** (www.yorktheatre.org), where plays by authors both known and unknown are presented, takes the stage on the church's lower level, and operates a program of community-focused events, such as afternoon films for the elderly.

Walking north, note the landmark **Central Synagogue** 28 (www.centralsynagogue.org), at the corner of 55th Street. Built in 1872, it adds a note of exotic, Moorish-style grace to an otherwise ordinary block. The synagogue was rebuilt and reopened in September 2001, after being severely damaged by a fire.

Boutiques and galleries

There are boutiques and galleries in both directions on **57th Street**, where the prices on both clothes and paintings get more expensive the closer

Tudor City.

you walk to Fifth Avenue. Toward Third, expensive gadgets galore are on sale at **Hammacher Schlemmer** (www.hammacher.com), while continuing west on 57th you'll find such fashion fortresses as Turnbull & Asser, Chanel, and Burberry.

Along the way to these stores, be sure to notice the **Fuller Building**

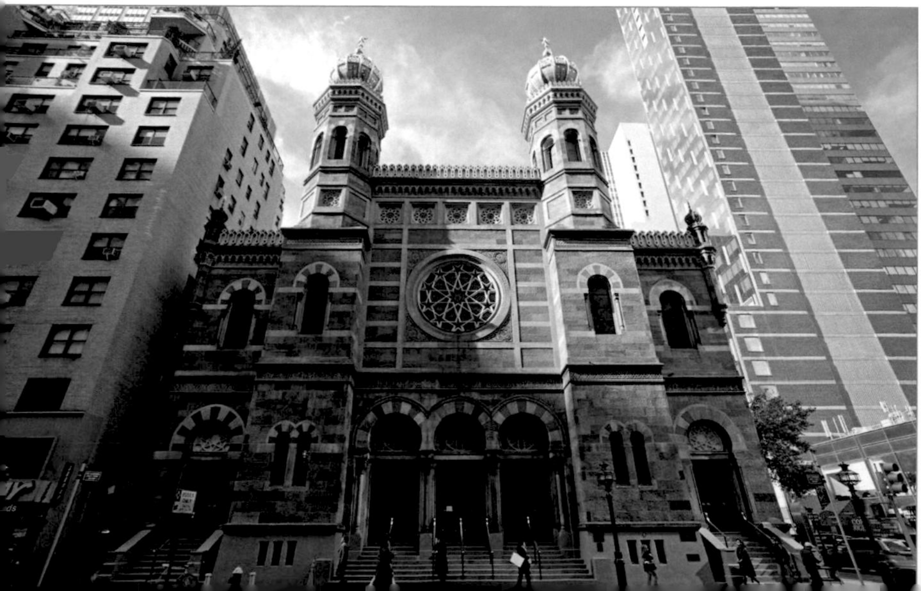

Central Synagogue.

(41 East 57th Street, at Madison Avenue), which was built in 1929. The building's (separate) main entrance is embellished by a city skyline motif. The lobby is another glorious example of Art Deco splendor. The floor mosaics depict the Fuller company's original headquarters when it was located in the Flatiron Building. The Fuller's midsection is home to numerous art galleries; the frequent exhibitions are open to the public. A directory is available from reception.

ABOVE GRAND CENTRAL

The view down Park Avenue stops abruptly at the **MetLife Building** ㉙ (originally known as the Pan-Am Building), which was plonked on top of Grand Central Terminal in the early 1960s. Fortunately, beyond it this part of the avenue still retains some of its original glamour.

The **Waldorf-Astoria** ㉚ (www.waldorfastoria.com), between 49th and 50th, is one of the city's grand hotels and one of its most famous, having attracted guests of the royal and presidential variety ever since it opened on this site in 1931. The Duke and Duchess of Windsor and Cole Porter were only some of the 'permanent residents' who lived in the hotel's exclusive towers. The original Waldorf-Astoria on Fifth Avenue, which had brought a new level of luxury to New York's hotel world in the 1890s, had been torn down to make way for the Empire State Building. The hotel retains its air of opulent exclusivity, and the high-ceilinged reception area is populated by wealthy guests lounging in overstuffed armchairs. However, in 2014 it was bought by the Chinese Anbang Insurance Group for $1.9 billion, which plans to convert some top floor rooms into luxury residential apartments.

The domed **St Bartholomew's Church** ㉛ opened its doors on Park Avenue and 50th Street in 1919, and is a fine example of neo-Byzantine architecture. The church has an evocative program of lighting that changes depending on the religious calendar, meaning that a visit around Christmas will reveal a bright, well-lit interior, while during Lent the church is shrouded in darkness.

One block west, on Madison, the fancy **Lotte New York Palace Hotel** incorporates as part of its public rooms two of the **Villard Houses**, 19th-century mansions once used as offices by the Archdiocese of New York. Built in 1884 by the architectural firm McKim, Mead, & White, these half-dozen houses were designed to look like one large Italian palazzo. The owner was the journalist and railway magnate Henry Villard, for whom the houses are named.

Almost 100 years later, when two of the mansions were sold to provide a lavish interior for the Palace, New York historians took exception to the sale. Today, the hotel serves afternoon tea beneath a vaulted ceiling designed by Stanford White.

The MetLife Building was constructed in 1963, 50 years later than Grand Central, seen in the foreground.

A stained-glass window by Marc Chagall graces the United Nations building.

TIP

There's a feast for the eyes as well as the palate at the fabulous Four Seasons restaurant. The most famous piece is the Picasso tapestry, but other artists have included Miró, Jackson Pollock, and Roy Lichtenstein.

Picasso for a season

There are lines of limos waiting in front of the **Four Seasons** ㉜ (www.fourseasonsrestaurant.com), on East 52nd Street between Park and Lexington, a restaurant so important that its interior has been declared a historic landmark. Picasso's 22ft (6.7-meter) painted curtain from a 1920 Diaghilev ballet, *Le Tricorne*, hangs inside, and luminaries from the worlds of politics and publishing do likewise. Unfortunately, the Four Seasons will be moving out in July 2016 when its lease expires, as the current owner of the Seagram Building, Aby Rosen, is planning to replace it with another restaurant.

Nevertheless, it is still worth seeing the distinctive **Seagram Building itself**. The tycoon Samuel Bronfman, head of Seagram Distillers, had planned to erect an ordinary office block until his architect daughter introduced him to Mies van der Rohe. The result is one of the most emblematic and influential Modernist constructions of the 1950s.

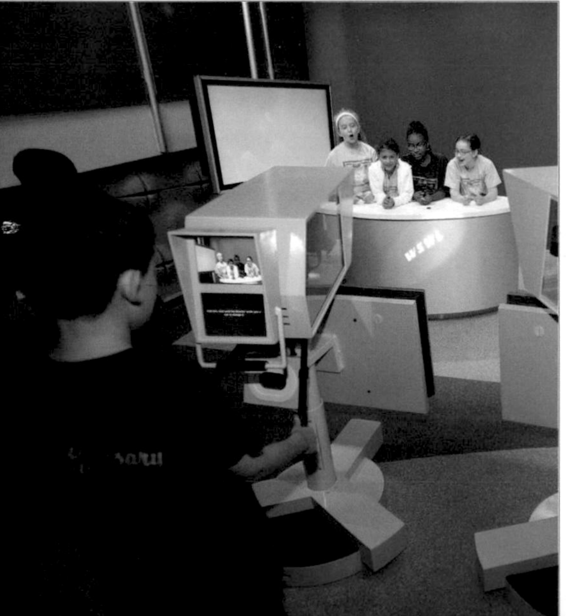

In the production studio at Sony Wonder Technology Lab.

In the 1980s, some of New York's biggest corporations created public spaces, and contributed significantly to the quality of crowded Midtown life. One of the first was tiny little **Paley Park**, on East 53rd Street between Madison and Fifth avenues, built on the site where the glamorous Stork Club once resided. Slightly raised above street level, the park is an excellent place to stop off and rest from the outside world. Tables and chairs provide ample seating space, and a water feature provides a calming background noise.

Tech wonders

A short walk away, Philip Johnson's mammoth **Sony Building** ㉝ (originally built for AT&T), on Madison Avenue between 55th and 56th streets, includes a public arcade squeezed between shops displaying the latest Sony equipment. Drop into the **Sony Wonder Technology Lab** for interactive exhibits and demonstrations of how all this stuff works (www.sonywondertechlab.com; tel: 212-833 8100; Tue–Sat; free, advance booking essential).

At 56th Street and Madison is the former **IBM Building** (now 590 Madison Avenue), a sharply angled tower designed in 1983 by Bauhaus-inspired architect Edward Larrabee Barnes. Its entrance is set back away from the street in a hollowed, cut-out part of the building, the empty space seeming to defy the rest of the structure's enormous height and massive weight. The underground concourse often hosts exhibitions of interest to the public.

Alternatively, head for the atrium, previously a bamboo-filled garden but now stripped of much of its greenery to make way for extra seating or artistic and contemplative sculpture. There's casual dining on the mezzanine, where you can kick back and relax before heading back into the adrenaline-pumping Midtown madness outside.

Skyscrapers

New York has always aimed high, and with landmark new buildings from Norman Foster, Renzo Piano, and Frank Gehry, the city is still reaching for the sky.

New York is a vertical city. The first skyscraper was Daniel Burnham's 1902 Flatiron Building, which is 285ft (87 meters) high. On a knife-edge lot at Broadway and Fifth Avenue, the Flatiron gained instant élan from its height and classical styling, and romance from its look of sailing up Broadway.

Traditional styles often inspired the tallest buildings, however. Napoleon LeBrun designed the 700ft (210-meter) Metropolitan Life Insurance tower (Madison Avenue at East 23rd Street) after St Mark's Campanile in Venice. Architect Cass Gilbert built the Woolworth Building, which soars for 792ft (241 meters), but harks back to Gothic styles.

New York's iconic 20th-century skyline was wrought more by politics than art. As buildings rose ever higher, planners feared that city streets were becoming lightless canyons. A 1916 zoning formula capped street-level facades by the width of the street, so towers of unlimited height rose only over a quarter of a building plot. This led to the 'setback' feature, which is now a New York icon.

The boom and confidence of the 1920s led to the classic era, exemplified by William Van Alen's Chrysler Building. The gleaming spire of the 1,046ft (319-meter) 1930 Art Deco masterpiece tops a pinnacle of stainless-steel automotive motifs and gargoyles. The 1,454ft (443-meter) Empire State Building (Shreve, Lamb, & Harmon) took the 'world's tallest' title from the Chrysler in 1931. Raymond Hood's 1934 RCA Building in the Rockefeller Center is more muted Art Deco, softer than the monolithic skyscrapers.

Postwar

The International style arrived in Mies van der Rohe's 1958 Seagram Building (375 Park Avenue), graceful glass curtain walls rising from an open plaza. Many anonymous 1950s and 60s glass boxes showed the same style with less aplomb. Far above the crowd, the 1,368ft (417-meter) Twin Towers of the World Trade Center (1976) were a New York icon on a par with the Empire State – a status tragically confirmed by the towers' destruction during the terrorist attacks on September 11, 2001.

Recent architectural efforts have again brought imaginative elements to the skyscraper. The triangular panels of the 2006 Hearst Tower, by English architect Norman Foster, are integral to the heat, light, and air management system, while Renzo Piano's new tower for *the New York Times* has sun-screen-walls of ceramic tubes. Frank Gehry's 8 Spruce Street has become the city's newest avant-garde wonder, while One World Trade Center scrapes the highest bit of sky. Another recent trend is for pencil-thin, ultra-luxurious residential towers such as the 1,396ft (426-meter) 432 Park Avenue designed by Rafael Viñoly. It became the tallest residential building in the world when it was completed in 2014.

You can find out more about this distinctive aspect of New York's architectural heritage at the Skyscraper Museum in Battery Park City (see page 77).

8 Spruce Street by designed by Frank Gehry.

The Metropolitan Museum of Art.

UPPER EAST SIDE

Opulence is in the air here. Old-money New Yorkers glide from Millionaires' Row to Museum Mile before a session of retail therapy at Barneys or Bloomies.

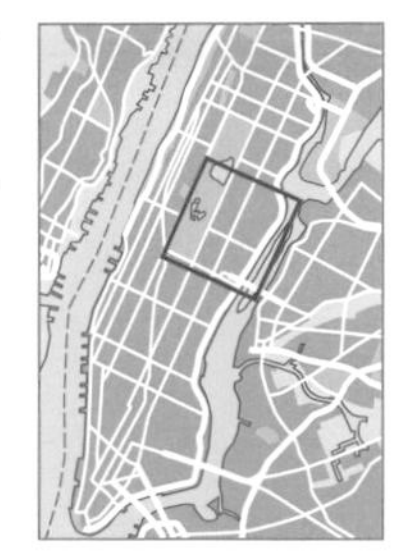

Main Attractions

Frick Collection
Metropolitan Museum of Art
Guggenheim Museum
Cooper-Hewitt National Design Museum
Jewish Museum
Park Avenue
Roosevelt Island

Map

Page 200

The Upper East Side's romance with wealth began in the late 1800s, when the Four Hundred – so called because a social arbiter decreed that in all of New York there were only 400 families that mattered – moved into Fifth Avenue, in order to cultivate roots alongside Central Park.

The homes they built were the most luxurious the city had seen – mansions and townhouses furnished like European palaces and filled with priceless art. Since then, the Carnegies, the Fricks, and the Astors have moved to greener pastures, but the Upper East Side has never lost its taste for the good life, and even the areas east of Lexington Avenue, formerly fairly affordable, are now highly desirable.

An air of wealth

The scent of wealth is, unsurprisingly, most intoxicating on the stretch of **Fifth Avenue** ❶ facing the park, known to old-time New Yorkers as **Millionaires' Row**. At the corner of 60th Street is J.P. Morgan's stately **Metropolitan Club** ❷, founded in 1892 after one of the financier's nouveau riche buddies was denied membership at the Union Club. The enormous **Temple Emanu-El** ❸ (www.emanuelnyc.org) cuts a brooding figure at the corner of 65th Street, where 2,500 worshipers can gather under its soaring roof, making this cavernous, echoing temple one of the largest reform synagogues in the world.

In the East 70s are a number of splendid old style mansions. These include the **Harkness House** (1 East 75th Street), home to the Commonwealth Fund; the chateau-style **James B. Duke House** (1 East 78th Street), which houses the New York University Institute of Fine Arts; and

The view over the Upper East Side and Central Park.

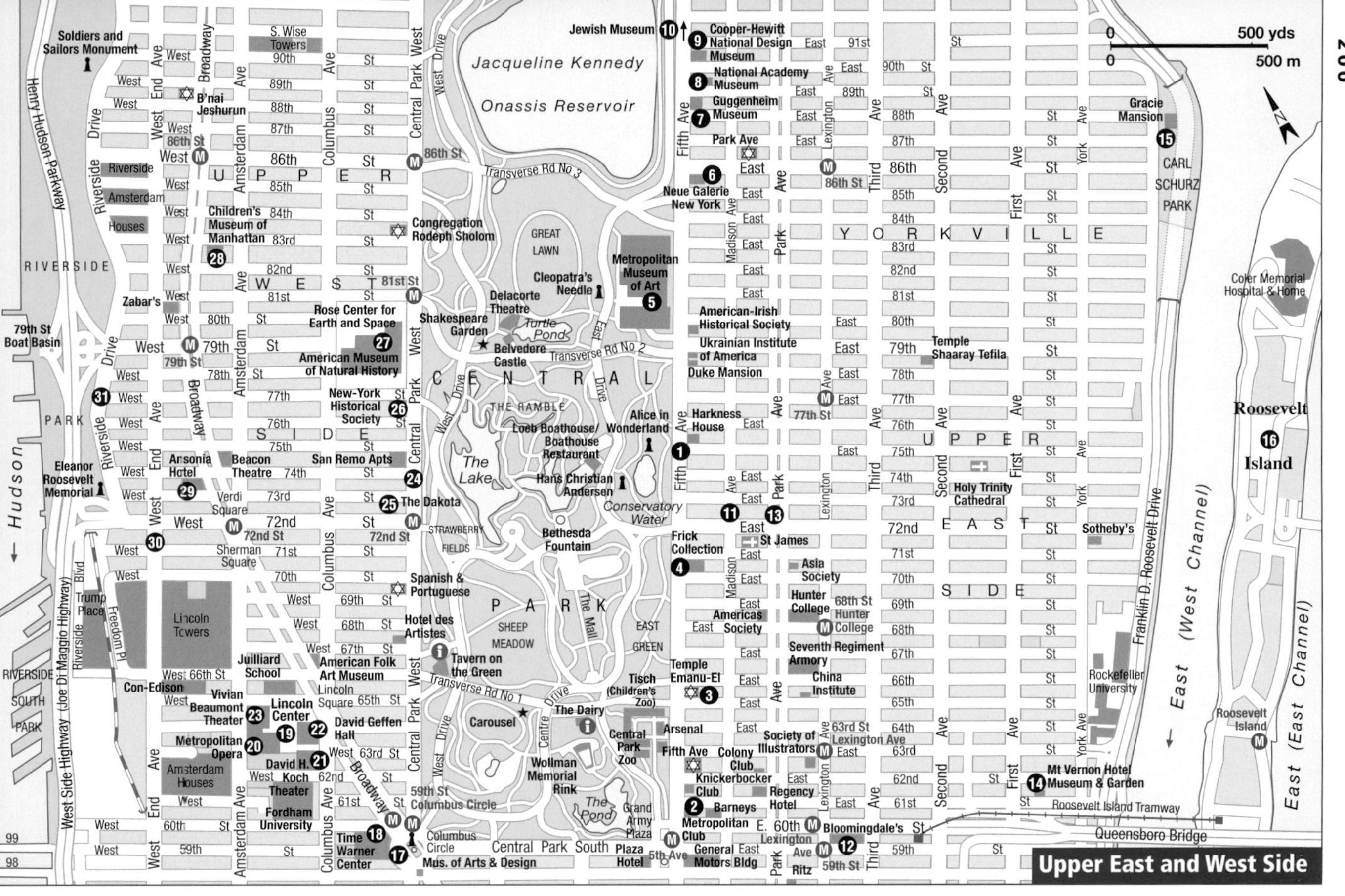

Upper East and West Side
500 yds
500 m
0
0
East (East Channel)
East (West Channel)
Roosevelt Island
Roosevelt Island
Coler Memorial Hospital & Home
CARL SCHURZ PARK
Gracie Mansion
Franklin D. Roosevelt Drive
Rockefeller University
Queensboro Bridge
Roosevelt Island Tramway
Mt Vernon Hotel Museum & Garden
Sotheby's
YORKVILLE
UPPER EAST SIDE
Holy Trinity Cathedral
Temple Shaaray Tefila
York Ave
First Ave
Second Ave
Third Ave
Lexington Ave
Park Ave
Madison Ave
Fifth Ave
Bloomingdale's
59th St
Lexington Ave
Ritz
Regency Hotel
Society of Illustrators
China Institute
Seventh Regiment Armory
Hunter College
68th St Hunter College
Asia Society
St James
Americas Society
Temple Emanu-El
Colony Club
Knickerbocker Club
Barneys
Metropolitan Club
General Motors Bldg
Frick Collection
Harkness House
Duke Mansion
Ukrainian Institute of America
American-Irish Historical Society
Neue Galerie New York
Park Ave
Guggenheim Museum
National Academy Museum
Cooper-Hewitt National Design Museum
Jewish Museum
86th St
77th St
Jacqueline Kennedy Onassis Reservoir
Transverse Rd No 3
Transverse Rd No 2
Transverse Rd No 1
GREAT LAWN
Cleopatra's Needle
Metropolitan Museum of Art
Turtle Pond
Delacorte Theatre
Belvedere Castle
Shakespeare Garden
THE RAMBLE
The Lake
Loeb Boathouse/ Boathouse Restaurant
Hans Christian Andersen
Alice in Wonderland
Conservatory Water
Bethesda Fountain
The Mall
EAST GREEN
SHEEP MEADOW
STRAWBERRY FIELDS
Tavern on the Green
Carousel
The Dairy
Wollman Memorial Rink
The Pond
Central Park Zoo
Tisch (Children's Zoo)
Arsenal
Grand Army Plaza
Plaza Hotel
Central Park South
Mus. of Arts & Design
Columbus Circle
CENTRAL PARK
East Drive
West Drive
Centre Drive
Central Park West
Columbus Ave
Amsterdam Ave
Broadway
West End Ave
Riverside Drive
Henry Hudson Parkway
West Side Highway (Joe Di Maggio Highway)
Hudson
79th St Boat Basin
RIVERSIDE PARK
RIVERSIDE SOUTH PARK
Soldiers and Sailors Monument
Eleanor Roosevelt Memorial
Riverside Amsterdam Houses
Zabar's
B'nai Jeshurun
S. Wise Towers
Children's Museum of Manhattan
Congregation Rodeph Sholom
Rose Center for Earth and Space
American Museum of Natural History
New-York Historical Society
San Remo Apts
The Dakota
Spanish & Portuguese
Hotel des Artistes
American Folk Art Museum
David Geffen Hall
Lincoln Center
David H. Koch Theater
Fordham University
Juilliard School
Vivian Beaumont Theater
Metropolitan Opera
Amsterdam Houses
Lincoln Towers
Con-Edison
Trump Place
Freedom Pl
Riverside Blvd
Time Warner Center
Beacon Theatre
Verdi Square
Sherman Square
Arsonia Hotel
72nd St
79th St
81st St
86th St
66th St
59th St Columbus Circle
UPPER WEST SIDE

The Garden Court at the heart of the Frick mansion.

the **Payne Whitney House** (972 Fifth Avenue), a fabulous Renaissance-style palazzo that now serves as the cultural center of the French Embassy.

The Carlyle on East 76th Street stakes its claim as one of the city's most luxurious hotels. A favorite with royalty, it's also home to the Café Carlyle (Woody Allen plays clarinet here on occasion) and Bemelmans Bar, two of the city's most enduring and upscale evening spots.

International relations are the order of the day on the Upper East Side: the Fletcher-Sinclair mansion at 79th and Fifth is the **Ukrainian Institute**, with the **American-Irish Historical Society** farther up at No. 991 (the corner of 80th Street). Between 68th and 69th streets, the classic McKim, Mead, & White building at 680 Park Avenue is now home to the **Americas Society**, while the Georgian-style house at No. 686 is the **Italian Cultural Institute**.

Frick Collection ❹

Address: 1 E. 70th Street (at Fifth and Madison avenues), www.frick.org
Telephone: 212-288 0700
Opening Hours: Tue–Sat 10am–6pm, Sun 11am–5pm
Entrance Fee: charge
Subway: 68th Street/Hunter College

At the corner of Fifth Avenue and 70th Street, this grand art collection is

TIP

The Upper East Side is primarily a residential neighborhood. While there are a number of places to find a bite, don't count on stumbling upon a classic New York eatery on every corner. If you're looking for a special meal, plan ahead, or you'll be wandering hungry amid the museums and apartment buildings.

The Frick mansion.

showcased in the former home of steel magnate Henry Clay Frick, whose passion for art was surpassed only by his ruthlessness in business. It consists mostly of works by great European masters from the 16th to the 19th century – Vermeer, Velázquez, Goya, Constable, and more. The gallery is also one of the city's more successful marriages between art and setting, with a tranquil garden court, and soft furnishings to luxuriate in when art-lovers' feet are tired from standing in front of the paintings. The Frick's annual concert season showcases young classical musicians (tickets must be booked in advance).

The Comtesse d'Haussonville by Ingres, from the Frick.

MUSEUM MILE

Between 82nd and 104th streets are nine cultural treasures so lavish that this stretch of Fifth Avenue has become known as **Museum Mile** (see page 210).

Metropolitan Museum of Art ❺

Address: 1000 Fifth Avenue (at 81st and 82nd streets), www.metmuseum.org
Telephone: 212-535 7710
Opening Hours: Sun–Thu 10am–5.30pm, Fri–Sat 10am–9pm
Entrance Fee: charge (recommended donation)
Subway: 86th Street

Opened on its present site in 1880, the Met is a sprawling Gothic behemoth with the largest art collection in the US. The permanent collection is truly impressive, and the newer

HENRY CLAY FRICK

Henry Clay Frick (1849–1919) invested his savings in a coalmine while working in his uncle's store, and by the age of 30 was a millionaire and 'the Coke King of Pennsylvania.' With his associate (and later bitter rival) Andrew Carnegie, he dominated the US coal and steel businesses for decades. After he turned 50, he devoted a little less time to business and more to his other passion – art collecting. In 1905 Frick moved from Pittsburgh to New York, after he was told the steel city's air was bad for his paintings, and built a neoclassical mansion for himself and his Old Masters.

At his death, Frick was estimated to be worth $75–100 million, and the mansion worth $5 million, both astounding sums for the time. In his eulogy, it was announced that his entire art collection and mansion would be 'turned over to the public use and enjoyment.' Upon the passing of Frick's wife Adelaide in 1931, the terms of his will were set into motion. After major renovations by legendary architect John Russell Pope, the mansion opened its doors as a museum in late 1935 at a ceremony attended by Charles Lindbergh and a laundry list of the New York elite: Astors, Rockefellers, Vanderbilts, and others.

galleries carry on the legacy of diversity and excellence (see page 208).

At 86th Street is the **Neue Galerie New York** ❻ (1048 Fifth Avenue; www.neuegalerie.org; tel: 212-628 6200; Thu–Mon 11am–6pm; charge), with Austrian and German art, including pieces by Gustav Klimt. The museum offers a popular First Fridays program – they are open with free admission on the first Friday of each month from 6–8pm. They also have a fantastic bookstore and a design shop with jewelry, flatware, and stunning items for the home.

Guggenheim Museum ❼

Address: 1071 Fifth Avenue (at 89th Street), www.guggenheim.org
Telephone: 212-423 3500
Opening Hours: Fri and Sun–Wed 10am–5.45pm, Sat until 7.45pm
Entrance Fee: charge, pay what you wish Sat 5.45–7.45pm
Subway: 86th Street

Founded in 1937, the Solomon R. Guggenheim Museum – its full name – was relatively new among the city's leading art repositories, but this was no disadvantage. Newcomer though it was, the Guggenheim shared top billing on the cultural marquee thanks largely to Frank Lloyd Wright's fabulous building, which opened in 1959 to mixed critical reviews, but much New York buzz.

The treasures inside are based on Solomon and Peggy Guggenheim's personal collections, showcasing Expressionism, Cubism, and the general trend toward abstraction. Artists given due attention include Klee and Kandinsky, Mondrian and Modigliani, Picasso of course, and later painters like Jackson Pollock and Roy Lichtenstein. Visiting exhibits have run the gamut from the Spanish masters to 20th-century motorcycle design. The Guggenheim really is a New York masterpiece, and one museum not to miss.

Also on Museum Mile at 89th Street is the **National Academy Museum and School of Fine Arts** ❽ (1083 Fifth Avenue; www.nationalacademy.org; tel: 212-369 4880; Wed–Sun 11am–6pm; charge), with a collection of over 5,000 19th- to 21st-century American artworks. Next comes the **Cooper-Hewitt National Design Museum** ❾ (2 East 91st Street at Fifth Avenue; www.cooperhewitt.org; tel: 212-849 8400; Sun–Fri

The Guggenheim.

EAT

A special place to stop for coffee and a snack on Museum Mile is the Neue Galerie's Café Sabarsky (http://kg-ny.com) – an evocation of the great cafés of pre-1914 Vienna, with Art Nouveau decor and sinful pastries.

The Cooper-Hewitt National Design Museum.

10am–6pm, Sat till 9pm; charge) in the landmark Andrew Carnegie mansion. The exhibits, with displays on the history and process of design and an onsite master's program for students, look especially impressive after an extensive renovation completed in 2014. There are free tours: weekdays at 11.30am and 1.30pm, weekends at 1pm and 3pm. Be sure to also visit the mansion's marvelous garden (Mon–Fri from 8am; free).

Jewish Museum ❿

Address: 1109 Fifth Avenue (at 92nd Street), http://thejewishmuseum.org
Telephone: 212-423 3200
Opening Hours: Fri–Tue 11am–5.45pm, Thu 11am–8pm, closes Fri at 4pm in winter
Entrance Fee: charge; free on Sat
Subway: 96th Street

One of the world's largest centers of Jewish culture contains a vast collection of historical and contemporary Jewish art, as well as the National Jewish Archive of Broadcasting. In observance of the Sabbath the museum is free on Saturdays, and all electronic exhibits are closed.

The very top of the 'Mile' includes the **Museum of the City of New York** (www.mcny.org) at 103rd Street and the **El Museo del Barrio** (www.elmuseo.org) at 104th Street.

EAST SIDE AMBIENCE

Geographically, Fifth Avenue is only one block away from **Madison Avenue ⓫**, but in spirit they're

The National Academy Museum and School of Fine Arts.

worlds apart. Wave goodbye to the prim and proper salons of the Four Hundred, because Madison Avenue is the land of ritz and glitz – a slick marketplace custom-crafted for the hyperactive, top-of-the-line discriminating consumer. It's a little bit mellower in the pleasant low-90s neighborhood of **Carnegie Hill** than it is in the 60s, but if you cross over from the top of Museum Mile you'll still find plenty of upscale boutiques, gourmet delicatessens, little chi-chi stores, and art galleries worth exploring.

At the corner of Madison Avenue and 75th Street stands the **Met Breuer** (www.metmuseum.org/visit/the-met-breuer), located in the former home of the Whitney Museum of American Art, designed by Marcel Breuer. Dedicated to contemporary art, it opened in 2016 as an offshoot of the Metropolitan Museum of Art (see page 208). The cantilevered structure is a work of art in its own right, second only to the Guggenheim among the Upper East Side's most striking architectural expressions.

Exhibition at the Met Breuer.

Barneys and Bloomies

From 75th to 59th Street, Madison is a bacchanalian feast of conspicuous consumption. The names on the storefronts are a roster of the fashion elite: Ralph Lauren, Giorgio Armani, Prada, Calvin Klein.

Most of these megastar stores are more for browsing than serious buying, except for those accompanied by a huge bankroll. A quintessentially New York shopping scene is **Barneys New York** (www.barneys.com) on 61st Street, one of the movers and shakers of Manhattan's retail world. In

ROAD RUNNERS

The city's biggest running club, with more than 40,000 members, has its office just off Fifth Avenue. Its signature event is the New York Marathon on the first Sunday in November, but that's just one of dozens of races it organizes throughout the year. Among the most unusual races is September's 'Fifth Avenue Mile,' a mad dash that starts outside the Met Museum. Some of the world's best runners use the events for training, but they're also open to the public. Even if your jogging speed isn't much faster than a waddle, you can still sign up for a race at www.nyrr.org. It's a fantastic way to meet New Yorkers, see Central Park, and tour some of the boroughs.

Runners crossing the 59th Street Queensboro Bridge during the New York City Marathon.

addition to the best designs, there's a chic lower-level restaurant in which weary wallet-wielders can refresh and revive. It has two other branches in New York at 2151 Broadway and 194 Atlantic Avenue in Brooklyn.

Serious shoppers may head straight for one of the city's retail queens: **Bloomingdale's** ⓬ (www1.bloomingdales.com) on 59th Street – an institution that dyed-in-the-wool New Yorkers could not live without. Bloomies is almost always crowded – oppressively so at holiday or sale times – but if you only go to one big store, this should be it. Bloomingdale's is so popular, there are branches in SoHo and other locations. As a reward for the kids afterwards, make a stop at **Dylan's Candy Bar** (www.dylanscandybar.com), a sweet dream come true just behind Bloomie's, owned by Ralph Lauren's daughter, Dylan.

The distinctive Seventh Regiment Armory.

Park Avenue style

Skipping east to **Park Avenue** ⓭, the scene changes dramatically. Compared to the flashy indulgence of Madison Avenue, Park seems like a highly trafficked Parisian boulevard. A highlight is the **Regency Hotel**, (www.loewshotels.com) a favorite for power breakfasts among big-wheel media types, and where the elegant library bar serves small bites and big cocktails. Another is the **Colony Club** at 62nd Street, which has a stately red-brick facade, appropriate to the stately society women who make up its members' list.

There are several cultural sites, among them the museum at the **Society of Illustrators** (128 East 63rd Street between Park and Lexington avenues; www.societyillustrators.org; tel: 212-838 2560; Tue 10am–8pm, Wed–Fri 10am–5pm, Sat noon–4pm; charge, free Tue 5–8pm).

Continuing north, it's near-impossible to miss the **Seventh Regiment Armory** at Park and 66th. Built in the 1870s to resemble a medieval castle, the recently renovated building now serves as an exhibition hall for alternative art shows organized by the non-profit institution Park Avenue Armory (www.armoryonpark.org).

At 70th Street, the **Asia Society Museum** (725 Park Avenue; http://asiasociety.org; tel: 212-288 6400; Tue–Sun 11am–6pm, until 9pm Fri, except in summer; charge, free on Fri 6–9pm) houses the Rockefellers' collection of Asian art and the contemporary Asian art collection. There are also performances, movies, and other events related to Asian culture.

Yorkville and farther east

East of Park Avenue, the Upper East Side slips in the prestige department, but makes up for it with a dash of self-indulgence. Once dominated

Bloomingdale's.

by Eastern European immigrants, much of the area is now gentrified, but remnants of the old German and Czech quarters survive in **Yorkville**, between 79th and 98th streets.

Between First and York avenues, the **Mount Vernon Hotel Museum and Garden** ⓮ (421 East 61st Street; www.mvhm.org; tel: 212-838 6878; Tue–Sun 11am–4pm; charge) is one of the few 18th-century buildings still standing proud in Manhattan. Furnished with period antiques, it's a marvel of survival, as it nestles under the Queensboro Bridge. **Sotheby's**, the high-stakes auction house, is 10 blocks away, at York Avenue and 72nd Street.

At 88th Street and East End Avenue, within **Carl Schurz Park**, is **Gracie Mansion** ⓯, another survivor from the 18th century and the official residence of the mayor of New York. Currently the home of Mayor Bill de Blasio and his family, the house was built by Scots-born Archibald Gracie as a summer home, and was first used in 1942 by Mayor Fiorello LaGuardia. Weekly tours take place on Tuesdays (www1.nyc.gov/site/gracie/index.page; free, booking requested).

Hitch a ride on the **Roosevelt Island Tramway** at Second Avenue and 60th Street: the views are unique and lovely, especially at sunset.

ROOSEVELT ISLAND ⓰

Across the water by cable-supported tram, Roosevelt Island is a 147-acre (60-hectare) respite from urban living. This tiny (2-mile/3km), tranquil, cigar-shaped island contains one main street, one church, one supermarket, a few restaurants, and one of the city's more recent subway extensions.

This 'annexation' made Roosevelt a highly desirable residential neighborhood – witness the sleek apartments of **Manhattan Park**. Amenities include an indoor pool, playgrounds, and five small parks. From the walkways edging the shoreline there are panoramic views of the East Side, and at the north end you can admire a stone lighthouse from 1872. Madison Avenue seems a long way away.

TIP

Roosevelt Island's subway station is preferred by commuters, but the most enjoyable way to get there is on the Roosevelt Island Tramway, which leaves from the corner of Second Avenue and 60th Street (more at http://rioc.ny.gov/transportation.htm). On the way, you get a wonderful view of all the great towers of the Upper East Side.

The Roosevelt Island Tram crosses over the East River.

THE METROPOLITAN MUSEUM

The *grande dame* of American museums displays many of the oldest treasures and most important moments in the history of art.

The Metropolitan Museum of Art is a palatial gallery with a collection of paintings, sculpture, drawings, furnishings, and decorative arts spanning 10,000 years of human creativity. With exemplary works from major European artists such as Bruegel the Elder to Botticelli and from Van Gogh to Velázquez and Vermeer, nearly every civilization is represented. Exhibits feature art objects from Archeulian flints found in Egypt dating to the Lower Paleolithic period (300,000–75,000 BC), right up to 21st-century designs from couturier Alexander McQueen.

The Met has six cafes and bars, ranging from the airy cafeteria to the more formal Petrie Court Café. In the summer and fall, the views of Central Park from the roof garden are unsurpassed, and the newly redesigned outdoor space along Fifth Avenue is a great place to rest. The museum's online gallery has excellent study resources, an art timeline, and podcasts.

The Essentials

Address: 1000 Fifth Avenue at 82nd Street; www.metmuseum.org
Tel: 212-535 7710
Opening Hours: Sun–Thu 10am–5.30pm, Fri–Sat 10am–9pm
Entrance Fee: charge (recommended); audio guides also available for a fee
Subway: 86th Street

The Metropolitan moved to its Fifth Avenue location in 1880, although the facade was remodeled in 1926. In total, the Met houses a collection of more than 2 million pieces.

A gold Inca funerary mask (9th–11th century) from Peru.

The 18th-century bedroom from the Palazzo Sagredo, Venice, complete with elaborate stuccowork and cherubs in relief upon the ceiling.

The Great Wave at Kanagawa, by Katsushika Hokusai, is a woodblock print made between 1830 and 1832. The artist said of this period in his life, 'Nothing I did before the age of 70 was worthy of attention.'

GREEK AND ROMAN GALLERIES

Even a museum this big has room to grow. The Greek and Roman galleries opened in 2007 and were built specifically to house and display the Metropolitan's art c.900 BC to the early 4th century AD. The collection is a monumental showcase that describes the parallel developments of Greek art in the Hellenistic period and the arts of southern Italy and Etruria, culminating in the rich and varied world of the Roman Empire. Many of the thousands of works in the spacious galleries had not been on view to the public since their creation, which was up to 3,000 years ago.

Then 2011 saw the opening of another years-in-the-making endeavor. The Arts of the Arab Lands galleries are located directly above the Greek and Roman ones and continue the story of ancient and medieval art to the east, depicting Islamic painting, textiles, sculpture, woodworking, earthenware, and arms from Turkey to South Asia. If you see one thing there, make it the ornate 16th-century carved wooden ceiling in the Koç Family Galleries.

The museum has a large collection of Cycladic art, from the ancient peoples of the Aegean Islands. Pieces include this female marble figure, which dates from c.2500 BC and is attributed to the Bastis Master.

The Met's collection of Islamic arts includes Anatolian, Ottoman, and Turkoman rugs, with decorative as well as devotional pieces on display. After eight years of construction, the museum opened a 19,000-sq-ft (1,765-sq-meter) gallery for the collection.

MUSEUM MILE

Some of America's finest cultural treasures are housed in fabulous museums that line the east side of Central Park.

Frank Lloyd Wright's architectural showpiece is the Solomon R. Guggenheim Museum on Fifth Avenue.

Museum Mile is a cultural parade of some of the US's finest examples of art, culture, and history, housed in eight to ten (depending on your definition), mainly opulent, galleries along Fifth Avenue, from 82nd Street and the Metropolitan Museum of Art, all the way north past the Latin American cultural museum, El Museo del Barrio, at 104th Street to the northeast corner of Central Park.

A newcomer to the auspicious mile (which is now, technically, more than a mile), the Africa Center, is due to open its latest incarnation sometime in the near future (delays have plagued it for years) between 109th and 110th streets, the first museum to be built on the mile since 1959. The Neue Galerie features German art and cultural exhibits. The Solomon R. Guggenheim Museum, housed in the remarkable spiral Frank Lloyd Wright building, hosts exhibitions on a grand scale. The Jewish Museum has art and culture from its own perspective at 92nd Street.

The National Academy Museum and School of Fine Arts tutored John Singer Sargent and Thomas Eakins, among other talents, while a branch of the Smithsonian, the Cooper-Hewitt National Design Museum, showcases highly decorative arts in a Beaux Arts mansion.

The Metropolitan Museum is the largest museum in the United States.

Some of America's finest cultural treasures are housed in galleries on the stretch of Fifth Avenue between 82nd and 110th streets.

MUSEUM MILE FESTIVAL

The National Academy Museum and School of Fine Arts is the country's oldest artist-run organization, founded in 1825 to train artists and show their work.

From 6 to 9pm on the second Tuesday in June each year, the Museum Mile Festival (http://museummilefestival.org) signals that Fifth Avenue is closed to road traffic from the Metropolitan Museum at 82nd Street, all the way to 105th Street.

Musicians, street performers, and food stalls line the length of the route, and all of the museums are open to the public for free in what is the city's biggest and most culturally diverse block party.

Special temporary exhibits are often mounted to coincide with the festival, and art activities with kids in mind are held in the street. Live music is performed, some for dancing, some for background listening, and some for contemplation, ranging from jazz to string quartets to Broadway show tunes.

The event has been a highly popular fixture in the New York cultural calendar since the festival's inception in the late 1970s, and regularly attracts a high-spirited crowd of more than 50,000 art aficionados, fun-seekers, and unwitting travelers who stumble upon it.

The Jewish Museum has an excellent collection of Judaica: art artifacts, photographs, and antiques that tell the story of Jewish persistence in an age-old struggle.

The Cooper-Hewitt National Design Museum's international collection includes decorative arts, product design, textiles, and wallpapers. The library has more than 70,000 books, and there is an archive of drawings and photographs.

The Neue Galerie is housed in a splendid Beaux Arts-style mansion built in 1912–14 by architects Carrère & Hastings.

The Time Warner Center.

UPPER WEST SIDE

More laidback than its counterpart across the park, the land of ballet and dinosaur bones is also an underrated place to dine and shop.

The highlights of the Upper West Side tend to be around Broadway, Columbus and Amsterdam avenues, a sort of 24-hour circus squeezed between the calm of Riverside Drive and Central Park West. The entrance to all this is **Columbus Circle** ⓱, with its hustling bustle of cars, pedestrians, and skateboarders, and the Time Warner Center, whose asymmetric glass towers loom over and almost dwarf the stately statue of Christopher Columbus.

High-flyers

The southern part of the neighborhood has moved up in the world in recent years, due in great part to the Time Warner Center, but also to the growth of residential apartment towers in the far west, home to prosperous young hedge-funders and their starter families.

On the south side of Columbus Circle, look for the striking concrete-and-glass building which is the latest home of the **Museum of Arts and Design** (tel: 212-299 7777; www.madmuseum.org; Tue–Sun 10am–6pm, Thu–Fri until 9pm; charge, pay-what-you wish on Thu 6–9pm). On the north side is the gleaming **Trump International Hotel and Tower**. The hotel is across from the gateway to Central Park, which is usually thronged with people playing music, eating lunch, passing through, or just plain hanging out. Vendors crowd the sidewalks, and pedicab drivers troll for passengers. Feel free to flag one down if your feet are tired, but consider yourself warned: rides aren't cheap.

The **Time Warner Center** ⓲ has made space for dozens of stores aimed squarely at affluent shoppers, and some very pricey restaurants, including an eatery that is currently

Main Attractions

Columbus Circle
Time Warner Center
Lincoln Center
Metropolitan Opera
David Geffen Hall
American Museum of Natural History
Riverside Park

Map

Page 200

The Trump International Hotel and Tower, with its gleaming globe.

TIP

There are a few places in Manhattan where the difference between an express and local train makes a big difference. Hop on a D or A train at Columbus Circle and the next stop will be 125th Street. Choose a B or C and 125th will be your 8th stop.

New York's most expensive, **Masa** ($450 prix-fixe). The center does have less expensive options, including a branch of the organic produce chain Whole Foods, where you can pick up something to eat in the food court or for a picnic in Central Park.

CNN is on the third floor of the Time Warner Center, and you can peek through the windows at the studio. On the north side of the complex at the corner of 60th Street and Broadway is the entrance to the home of **Jazz at Lincoln Center** (tel: 212-258 9800; www.jalc.org), a world-class concert venue (see page 222).

Timesculpture by Philip Johnson, at Lincoln Center.

Following Columbus

After soaking up culture at Lincoln Center, cross **Columbus Avenue** for the **American Folk Art Museum** (2 Lincoln Square; tel: 212-595 9533; www.folkartmuseum.org; Mon–Thu 11.30am–7pm, Fri noon–7.30pm, Sat 11.30am–7pm, Sun noon–6pm; free). This was a secondary branch of the main museum (formerly on West 53rd Street), but due to budgetary issues, it is now the sole branch and home to works by traditional, self-taught and outsider artists from the 18th and 19th centuries. The collection has some beautiful and striking pieces of art and textiles that would be equally at home in a gallery at the MoMA, including a lovely collection of Amish quilts and a more recent addition – a patchwork-quilt memorial to the victims of the attack on the World Trade Center. The museum also has a great little gift shop.

William Matthew Prior's portrait of an unknown child with puppet (1830), American Folk Art Museum.

THE BROADWAY CULTURE TOUR

If culture is high on your list, try this route through the Upper West Side. From Columbus Circle, Broadway swerves west toward Columbus Avenue and nicks the corner of Lincoln Center, flanked on one side by the Juilliard School and on the other by **Fordham University**. Even to be accepted at the **Juilliard School** is an honor, as the highly selective enrollment and small classes draw some of the most talented students in America. Trumpeter Miles Davis was an alumnus, and for a while lived a few blocks north on West 77th Street.

Lincoln Center ⓳

Address: Columbus Avenue (between 62nd and 65th streets), www.lincolncenter.org
Telephone: various box offices (see individual theaters)
Opening Hours: tours depart daily from the David Rubenstein Atrium, March–May: Mon–Fri 11.30am and 1.30pm, Sat 11.30am and 3pm, Sun 3 pm; Jun–Feb: Mon–Sat 11.30am and 1.30pm, Sun 3pm
Entrance Fee: charge
Subway: 66th Street/Lincoln Center

Construction of the **Lincoln Center for the Performing Arts** (see page 222) began in 1959 as part of a massive redevelopment plan to clean up the slums that occupied the site. Now, the center is one of the city's most popular venues, with attendance running at about 5 million people a year.

Around Lincoln Center

The black marble fountain in the middle of the plaza is surrounded by the glass-and-white-marble facades of the center's three main structures. The **Metropolitan Opera** ⓴ (tel: 212-362 6000; www.metopera.org) is directly in front, with two large murals by Marc Chagall behind the glass wall – *Le Triomphe de la Musique* to the left, *Les Sources de la Musique* to the right. The Met is home to the Metropolitan Opera Company from September to April, and the American Ballet Theater from May to July. Although marvelous, its productions and performers carry a hefty price tag, but the tiny **Gallery Met** just off the main foyer has a collection of paintings which you can see free of charge.

To the left of the central fountain, the **David H. Koch Theater** ㉑ (tel: 212-870 5500; http://davidhkochtheater.com) is shared by the New York City Ballet – a bit more adventurous than the Met, and less expensive. The third side of the main plaza is occupied by

EAT

A dinner at Thomas Keller's heavenly Per Se (10 Columbus Circle; tel: 212-823 9335; www.thomaskeller.com/per-se) goes for more than $300 per person, and that's without the wine. Do you dare?

A ballet performance at Lincoln Center.

TIP

If dioramas are not enough, the American Museum of Natural History will try to bring you closer to the real thing. The museum runs a tour division (www.amnh.org/amnh-expeditions), with lecturer-led journeys to see the solar eclipse from Machu Picchu, to explore the geologic wonders of Iceland, or to dig for dinosaur bones in Colorado.

Lincoln Center and the Metropolitan Opera building.

David Geffen Hall ㉒ (tel: 212-721 6500; www.lincolncenter.org/venue/david-geffen-hall), home of the New York Philharmonic and the Mostly Mozart summer concert series.

Two secondary courtyards flank the Metropolitan Opera. On the right, the **Vivian Beaumont Theater** ㉓(tel: 212-501 3100) is fronted by a shady plaza and reflecting pool, around which office workers gather for lunch. The oxidized bronze sculpture in the center of the pool is by Henry Moore. A spindly steel sculpture by Alexander Calder is near the entrance to the **Library of the Performing Arts**. The Bandshell in **Damrosch Park** is used for free concerts in summer. These are usually around lunchtime, but there are occasional performances in the early evenings too. Recently, Lincoln Center complex has gradually transformed, with new street-level entrances for many venues and a major overhaul of **Alice Tully Hall**, used for chamber music. Most visible is the new two-story building at 65th Street that houses the Elinor Bunin Munroe Film Center (www.filmlinc.org). On its roof, an Illumination Lawn invites visitors to relax in a slightly incongruous, but lovely, grassy enclave. The entire complex is more stunning than ever.

CENTRAL PARK WEST

Central Park West ㉔ takes over from Eighth Avenue, branches off Columbus Circle and heads up into the West Side's most affluent residential section. The apartment houses overlooking the park are among the most lavish in the city – like the famous twin towers of the **San Remo Apartments**, built in 1931 – and the cross streets, especially 74th, 75th, and 76th, are lined with equally splendid brownstones. At the corner of West 67th Street, the **Hotel des Artistes** has numbered Valentino, Isadora Duncan, Noel Coward, and Norman Rockwell among its tenants.

The most famous apartment building on this stretch is **The Dakota** ㉕, built in 1884 by Henry Hardenbergh, who also designed the Plaza Hotel. At the time, people joked that it was so far outside the city, 'it might as well be in the Dakota Territory,' which explains the Indian's head above the entrance.

Dinosaurs grace the halls of the American Museum of Natural History.

Imagine

Urban streets caught up with The Dakota soon enough, and over the years the building has attracted tenants like Boris Karloff, Leonard Bernstein, and Lauren Bacall, and was the setting for the 1968 movie *Rosemary's Baby*. Most famously, John Lennon lived at The Dakota and was shot outside it in 1980. **Strawberry Fields**, a touching knoll dedicated to his memory, is across the street a few steps into Central Park (see page 182).

These days, foreign students buy Lennon merchandise from the surrounding stands, and visitors converse on memorial benches bordering Strawberry Fields' *Imagine* mosaic.

From 72nd Street, it's a short walk uptown, past the somber facades of the Universalist Church and the **New-York Historical Society** 26 (170 Central Park West; tel: 212-873 3400; www.nyhistory.org; Tue–Thu and Sat 10am–6pm, Fri until 8pm, Sun 11am–5pm; charge), New York's oldest museum, with permanent exhibitions on the city's history, to the 79th Street entrance of the American Museum of Natural History, the *grande dame* of Manhattan museums, which sprawls over several blocks of the city.

American Museum of Natural History 27

Address: 79th Street (at Central Park West), www.amnh.org
Telephone: 212-769 5100
Opening Hours: daily 10am–5.45pm
Entrance Fee: charge
Subway: 81st Street

Guarded by an equestrian statue of Theodore Roosevelt, the museum's main entrance is one of many additions built around the original structure (see page 226). The original facade – a stately Romanesque arcade with two towers – was built in the late 1800s, and can be seen from 77th Street. The front steps have become a meeting point, where families and school groups study guidebooks and maps.

For children, a visit to the museum is a must, but with nearly

TIP

Periodically throughout the year, the American Museum of Natural History hosts 'Night at the Museum Sleepovers' for children aged 6 to 13 and their parents. They provide cots, snacks and unforgettable, and dimly lit, tours through the most popular exhibits. Call 212-769 5200 to book.

Exhibits from the American Museum of Natural History.

Taking religion to the streets.

50 exhibition halls housed in 25 buildings, there's plenty for grown-ups to see, too. Some of the exhibits are more successful than others, but choice is the main problem here.

Highlights include a 34-ton (31,000kg) meteorite, the largest blue sapphire in the world, and a full-sized model of a blue whale. The world's tallest dinosaur – the 50ft (15-meter) Barosaurus – is in the Theodore Roosevelt Rotunda.

The Hayden Planetarium.

The museum also includes a gigantic screen **Imax Theater**, in addition to the **Rose Center for Earth and Space**, which houses the **Hayden Planetarium**.

From October to May the **Butterfly Conservatory** provides a popular opportunity to see some rare and beautiful tropical butterflies as they flutter around a temporary enclosure erected inside the building.

Don't even think about doing the whole museum in one shot, and expect to spend some of your time trying to find your way around, despite having a floor plan.

Classic and organic

Head back over to Columbus Avenue for some high-grade browsing. Shopping along this Uptown stretch can be a pleasant, almost small-town activity in comparison with the Midtown mayhem of Macy's and other places. Trees line the sidewalks, while dog walkers spilling over from Central Park contribute to a gentler pace.

The Uptown branch of **Kiehl's** (154 Columbus Avenue; www.kiehls.com), a generations-old natural cosmetics and perfume apothecary, is worth visiting. New additions to the classic range include lip glosses and SPF-rated face cream, all in traditionally simple packaging.

There are far too many clothing stores to list by name, but those that deserve special mention are north of 68th Street. There's upscale women's wear at **Eileen Fisher** (10 Columbus Circle), and equally upscale men's wear at **Frank Stella** (440 Columbus).

Columbus's proximity to Central Park – the Uptown dog-walker's playground – is recognized at various pet stores. There's also a wide selection of funky vintage wear (and wares) at a flea market every Sunday between 76th and 77th streets (www.greenfleamarkets.com). Here, locals like to browse before or after brunch with friends or family.

A cycle path.

THE FAR WEST

Skipping west to **Amsterdam Avenue**, the scene is dressed down, but still trendy: restaurants, boutiques, and bars with a twenty-something clientele dominate, though there are a few remaining bodegas and traditional neighborhood shops like **West Side Kids** at 84th Street, with its unusually intelligent toy inventory.

At 80th and Broadway, **Zabar's** (www.zabars.com) is the gourmet store against which gourmet stores are measured. Even if you're not in the mood for buying, it's worth elbowing your way to the counter for a free taste of all the goodies; visiting the store is worthwhile for the smells alone.

At 212 West 83rd Street, the amusing **Children's Museum of Manhattan** ㉘ (tel: 212-721 1223; www.cmom.org; Tue–Sun 10am–5pm, Sat until 7pm; charge) is a brightly colored multilevel kiddy kingdom with interactive exhibits and special events. The noise level is high, so arrive very calm or come equipped with earplugs.

And back on Columbus Avenue, just off 87th Street, give a salute to the noble work being done at the Wild Bird Fund Center (www.wildbirdfund.org), a rehabilitation center for injured birds and an education center for local children.

Off-Off-Broadway

In recent years, new meaning has been added to the term 'Off-Broadway,' with an Upper West Side scene that includes performances and literary readings at **Symphony Space**, on Broadway between 94th and 95th streets, and the **Beacon Theatre** (www.beacontheatre.com), at 2124 Broadway and 74th Street, a popular music venue where you might catch the Allman Brothers one night and a gospel group the next.

KIDS

Kids' stores near Columbus are good value. Kidville at 205 West 88th Street is a 'boutique' and hair salon with fire trucks, airplane, and car-shaped seats to entice the under-5s in for a haircut.

LIFE IN THE BIKE LANE

Organizations like Transportation Alternatives (www.transalt.org), a non-profit seeking to 'reclaim New York's streets from the automobile,' found friends in the Bloomberg Administration. Since 2006, the number of bike lanes in the city has dramatically increased, with more than 1,000 miles (1600km) now available to the hundreds of thousands of urban cyclists. Moreover, cycling in New York has never been safer with new separate bike lanes being constructed every year. No wonder, the number of cyclists rose by 100 percent in years 2007-2014. Now, more than 200,000 of New Yorkers take to the streets on their bikes every day. It is a well-known fact that the quickest way up the West Side is by bicycle on the Waterfront Greenway along the Hudson River. You can easily pedal from Houston Street to 72nd Street in 15 minutes, with the added bonus of spectacular river views. Locals know this, of course, and every morning the Greenway is like a miniature highway of joggers and cyclists – some in business suits racing to meetings.

With the addition of bike lanes on Amsterdam Avenue, not to mention Riverside and Central parks, negotiating the Upper West Side on two wheels has never been easier. Don't worry about bringing your own ride. Many shops, including Toga Bikes at 110 West End Avenue and 64th Street (tel: 212-799 9625; http://togabikes.com), offer rentals for reasonable prices. For cycling maps and up-to-date information on cycling lanes, check www.nyc.gov.

SHOP

Grab a bag of bagels from 72nd Street Bagels, top it off with some white-fish dip from Zabar's, and head off to the park or the river for a real New York-style picnic.

The lavish interior of the Beacon Theatre.

Shopping continues on Broadway with the appearance of **Barneys CO-OP** at 2151, the 'neighborhood-sized' and more laidback relation of the upscale department store that is popping up at desirable locations throughout the city. Thrift-store fans with an aversion to actual thrift stores can find cute and kooky things at **Urban Outfitters** (at both 72nd and 100th streets and Broadway).

Occupying the entire block between 73rd and 74th streets is The **Ansonia** ㉙, and while it's a little worn around the edges, this is still the *grande dame* of West Side apartment buildings, with a resident list that over the years included Enrico Caruso, Igor Stravinsky, Arturo Toscanini, and Theodore Dreiser.

The building was particularly popular with singers and musicians because its thick internal walls allowed them to practice without disturbing the neighbors. Although retailers now dominate the first floor, The Ansonia's mansard roof, towers, and fabulous terracotta detailing still add up to a Beaux Arts fantasy that captures the gaze and won't let go.

Down by the Riverside

A tour of the far west of New York finishes nicely by taking 72nd Street to **West End Avenue** ㉚, then on to Riverside Drive. North of 72nd Street, West End Avenue is affluent and strictly residential; a great place to live, but not a particularly fascinating place for visitors. Humphrey Bogart lived for a while in Pomander Walk, an English-style mews situated between 94th and 95th streets, West End Avenue, and busy Broadway.

South of 72nd Street, a mini-city of high-rise apartments has altered the Hudson River skyline on Riverside Boulevard, not to be confused with **Riverside Drive** ㉛, which winds along the edge of Frederick Law Olmsted's **Riverside Park**. The 72nd Street entrance has a bronze sculpture of Eleanor Roosevelt, one of only four statues of real-life women gracing New York's parks.

This is a picturesque corner of Manhattan, with sweeping views of the Hudson River. In warm weather, Manhattanites come to the **79th Street Boat Basin** for drinks and burgers.

The Ansonia.

LINCOLN CENTER

Lincoln Center for the Performing Arts is a massive cultural village, with companies from opera to jazz and more than 25 performance venues.

A meeting place, an outdoor space in which to relax, a plaza with sculptures, and a mini-metropolis of concert venues: Lincoln Center is all of these and more. New York City's capital of culture covers more than 16 acres (6 hectares) and includes a community of 11 institutes that teach, commission, and showcase almost all forms of musical and theatrical art.

Permanent home to both the New York Philharmonic and the Metropolitan Opera, the center is also a place of study, housing the Juilliard School, the School of American Ballet, and both the Film and Chamber Music societies. On any night of the week, something exciting and innovative will be happening here.

Film fans will want to visit in early October when the New York Film Festival has gala premieres at Alice Tully Hall. In August, David Geffen Hall (formerly Avery Fisher Hall) hosts the Mostly Mozart Festival. And everyone gets to strut their stuff in early July, during the outdoor dance and jazz extravaganza, Midsummer Night Swing.

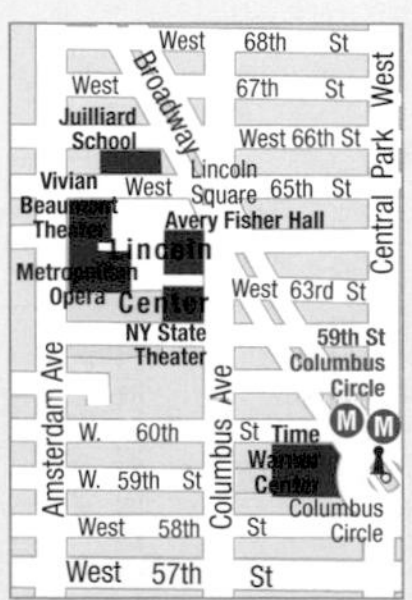

The Essentials

Address: between West 62nd and 65th streets and Columbus and Amsterdam avenues; www.lincolncenter.org
Tel: various box offices; see page 215
Opening Hours: tours daily 10.30am–4.30pm
Entrance Fee: charge for performances
Subway: 66th Street/ Lincoln Center

Dancers perform at the Lincoln Center's Hearst Plaza.

Lincoln Plaza is the epicenter of culture in New York.

Robert McFerrin made history as the first black male soloist in the Metropolitan Opera's history when he sang in the 1995 production of Aida.

THE METROPOLITAN OPERA

Soprano Renée Fleming as Tatiana in Tchaikovsky's opera Eugene Onegin.

The first performance of the Metropolitan Opera was of Charles Gounod's *Faust*, which took place on October 22, 1883. Tenor Enrico Caruso and conductor Arturo Toscanini graced the stage of the opera house's first premises, on 39th Street and Broadway.

The Met's new home opened in 1966 with the world premiere of Samuel Barber's *Antony and Cleopatra*. The company is committed to bringing opera to a wider audience. Initiatives include reduced-price tickets, live high-definition broadcasts to theaters in the US and in Europe, streaming internet transmissions, and satellite radio broadcasts.

For anyone with shaky Italian or German, there are simultaneous translations to individual screens at every seat in the opera house.

Alexander Calder's sculpture Le Guichet (The Ticket Window) stands in front of David Geffen Hall and was presented to the center in 1965.

Under the directorship of Wynton Marsalis, Jazz at Lincoln Center's home is the Frederick P. Rose Hall in the Time Warner Center. The hall encompasses three performance spaces and the Irene Diamond Education Center.

Reclining Figure, a two-piece bronze sculpture, was commissioned for Lincoln Center Plaza in 1962 from English artist Sir Henry Moore, and unveiled in 1965.

Classical and modern architectural styles blend to make the airy plaza a relaxing place to be.

Lincoln Center and the Juilliard School are known for their dance troupes. The New York City Ballet is made up of 92 young dancers who perform mainly contemporary works, most commissioned especially for the company. George Balanchine was the co-founding director.

Dancers and performers can frequently be seen entering and exiting the hall if you're looking for an autograph.

IMPROVEMENTS TO LINCOLN CENTER

American Jazz Musician Bobby Watson leads his band Horizon at Jazz at Lincoln Center.

Since 1959, when President Dwight D. Eisenhower broke ground for the new Lincoln Square Urban Renewal Project, this cultural village within New York has continued to grow and mature. Ongoing improvements occur regularly; the most recent ones include a new book store for Juilliard, modernization to the Alice Tully Hall and Peter J. Sharp Theater, stunning new entrances for most venues, and an extensive renovation of the north and central plazas, where the two-story Elinor Bunin Munroe Film Center was built, complete with a rooftop Illumination Lawn. Many of the plans were completed in time for the center's 50th anniversary in 2009. A major redevelopment of the campus area was completed in 2012 with the construction of the President's Bridge over West 65th Street.

Tickets for Lincoln Center performances go on sale up to a year in advance, and can be booked from the website. The entire outdoor space of Lincoln Plaza is now covered by free Wi-Fi internet access. Be careful if using your laptop by the fountains, though.

A popular public space both day and night, the computer-controlled fountains in the plaza are adjusted according to the wind, in order to prevent visitors sitting nearby from being drenched with water.

THE AMERICAN MUSEUM OF NATURAL HISTORY

From whales in the depths of the oceans to fragments of far-distant worlds, AMNH makes natural history fun. There are sleepovers, too.

The American Museum of Natural History on the Upper West Side has one of the most popular collections in New York City. It's also one of the United States' largest, and takes days to explore. Apart from the 45 permanent exhibition halls, there are monthly lectures (on everything from birds to wine), several traveling exhibitions, an IMAX theater, a state-of-the-art planetarium, music events and the more recent 'Night at the Museum Sleepovers,' where kids and their parents get to explore the halls with flashlights and doze amid the exhibits.

The bones still bring the crowds, though, and they're as awe-inspiring now as they were when paleontologist – and Indiana Jones inspiration – Roy Chapman Andrews was director over 75 years ago. And it's not just dinosaurs. Massive creatures that walked the earth with man – wooly mammoths, giant sloths, saber-toothed cats – inspire almost as many oohs and aahs as the T-Rex.

The museum's dioramas of habitats depict the environs, habits, and behavior of innumerable species of mammals, reptiles, insects, and aquatic life. Kids love the elephants in particular.

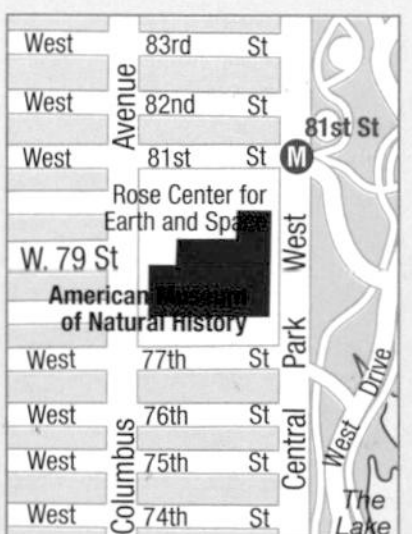

The Essentials

Address: 79th Street and Central Park West; www.amnh.org
Tel: 212-769 5100
Opening Hours: daily 10am–5.45pm
Entrance Fee: charge; audio guides also available
Subway: 81st Street

The Rose Center for Earth and Space includes a spiral walking tour of the growth of the universe, vividly demonstrating the concepts of cosmic scale.

A dramatic, full-size model of a blue whale dominates the Milstein Family Hall of Ocean Life. Marine ecosystems, including coral reefs, are depicted, along with dioramas and exhibits on vertebrates and invertebrates.

The 77th Street entrance to the museum, which consists of 25 buildings and 46 exhibition halls.

HUMAN ORIGINS

Exhibits tell the history of civilization, drawing from cultures all over the world, including these rare sculptures from Asia.

The museum's Anne and Bernard Spitzer Hall of Human Origins exhibits remains and artifacts that tell the story of humanity's progression and the birth of civilization. Using fossil records, carbon dating, and the latest gene technology, mankind's development from a threatened hunter-gatherer to a dexterous toolmaker and gregarious mass communicator is traced and described.

The 93,000-year-old remains of a woman and child buried near Nazareth, in Israel, give clues to the nature of civilization at that time. The very fact that they were buried means that formal rituals had already been established.

The bottom half of the Hayden Sphere houses the Big Bang exhibit, which takes visitors on a multi-sensory re-creation of the Big Bang and recreates the beginnings of the universe.

The world famous Apollo Theater.

HARLEM AND THE HEIGHTS

Harlem is in the wake of a renaissance, with new museums and celebrated dining, while the leafy quiet of Morningside, Hamilton, and Washington Heights are being rediscovered.

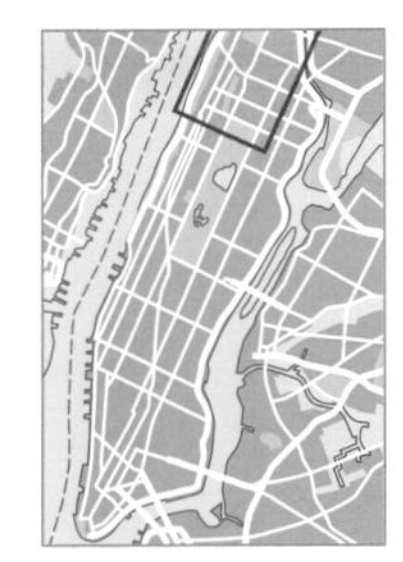

Main Attractions

- Apollo Theater
- Studio Museum
- Schomburg Center
- El Museo del Barrio
- Museum of the City of New York
- Columbia University
- The Cloisters
- Dyckman Farmhouse Museum

Maps

Page 230

An Alabama-born, African-American professor recalled being an 18-year-old in Europe in the late 1950s. He was asked repeatedly about Harlem, a place he'd never been in his life. His inquisitors didn't want to hear this. The man was black; he lived in the United States; therefore he had to be from Harlem. What they didn't know was that the only thing he 'knew' was based on the same stereotypes shared by the Europeans, that Harlem was full of naughty nightlife, devilish dancing, mind-blowing music, dangerous dudes, and wicked women.

Harlem heritage

That heritage is palpable up and down the neighborhood's avenues. But there was, and is, much more to Harlem. As well as the area's well-documented attractions, urban pioneers driven out of the rest of Manhattan by rising prices have discovered Harlem's handsome buildings – even ex-president Bill Clinton has an office on 125th Street. Many have been restored to their former elegance, and real-estate prices continue to climb. Harlem has recaptured some of its mojo.

In the early 1900s, black people began moving into homes on 135th Street, west of Lenox Avenue. From then on, Harlem became a place where Americans of African descent made their presence felt. Poet Langston Hughes (see page 234) and writer Zora Neale Hurston, along with musicians Duke Ellington, Billie Holiday, and Ella Fitzgerald, all launched their careers here in the 1920s and 30s, during what was termed the Harlem Renaissance.

Later, Harlem, or more precisely, a restaurant called Sherman's Barbeque at 151st Street and Amsterdam

Street Art on 125th Street

TIP

Welcome to Harlem (http://welcometoharlem.com) is a website that collects business and event listings. Visit the site to discover what's going on whatever month you're visiting.

Avenue, was where music producer Phil Spector's all-girl singing group the Ronettes brought the Beatles in 1964. More headlines were made in the mid-1970s when Cuba's Fidel Castro took up residence in Harlem's Hotel Teresa, where he brought in live chickens and made his own food for fear he might be poisoned while attending UN functions in Midtown.

New attractions

Two cultural institutions continue Harlem's post-millennium renaissance. **The Gatehouse** (150 Convent Avenue at 135th Street; tel: 212-281 9240; www.harlemstage.org) opened in 2006 in a renovated building, and showcases new theater and dance groups and musicians. And in the near future, a long-anticipated permanent home for **The Africa Center** will open (see page 233).

Geographically, the area is divided into Central Harlem (which includes 125th Street), East Harlem (sometimes called Spanish Harlem), and West Harlem, encompassing Morningside and Hamilton Heights. The most enjoyable way to see this part of the city is to take an organized tour.

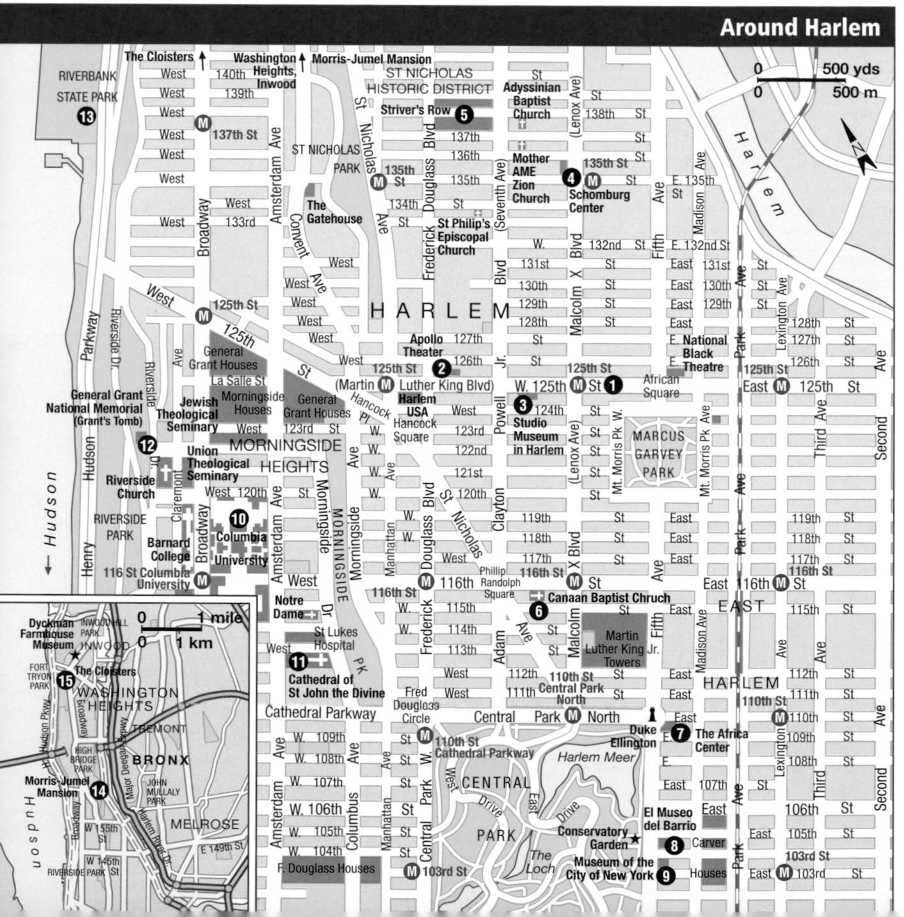

125TH STREET ❶

A good place to begin is Harlem's famous main drag. It's Fifth Avenue and Times Square compressed into one river-to-river street, a street where every north–south Manhattan subway stops and several north–south buses cross over. A prime shopping area, it pulses with throngs of people, street vendors, and music blasting from record stores. Officially, 125th Street is now known as **Martin Luther King Boulevard**, and it's home to many of Harlem's foremost attractions.

Apollo Theater ❷

Address: 253 W. 125th Street (at Frederick Douglass Boulevard), www.apollotheater.org
Telephone: 212-531 5305
Opening Hours: box office Mon–Fri 10am–6pm, Sat noon–5pm
Subway: 125th Street

This is where the presence of singers Billie Holiday, Mahalia Jackson, Dinah Washington, and Ella Fitzgerald can still be felt, especially during the Apollo's weekly Amateur Night (every Wednesday). Other music stars whose careers have been launched at the Apollo include Stevie Wonder and Marvin Gaye.

The experience of seeing rising young talent, while at the same time being a part of the highly responsive, and sometimes harshly critical Apollo audience, is not to be missed. The legendary James Brown lay in state here in December 2006, before his funeral in Georgia. Thousands of fans filed past his onstage coffin, as tracks from the singer's *Live at the Apollo* were broadcast to the crowds outside. For information on Apollo tours, tel: 212-531 5363.

There's more nightlife at the old-style **Showman's Bar** (www.showmansjazzclub.com) at No. 375, a jazz club that still hosts live acts, and at the **Cotton Club** (http://cottonclub-newyork.com), which moved to No. 656.

The Amateur Night Show Off Quarter Finals at the Apollo Theater.

Studio Museum in Harlem ❸

Address: 144 W. 125th Street (near Adam Clayton Powell Jr Boulevard), www.studiomuseum.org
Telephone: 212-864 4500
Opening Hours: Thu–Fri noon–9pm, Sat 10am–6pm, Sun noon–6pm
Entrance Fee: charge, free Sun
Subway: 125th Street

This dynamic museum hosts changing exhibitions in addition to a permanent

TIP

Harlem hasn't been this good in years. Try Shrine at 2271 Adam Clayton Powell Jr Boulevard for Afro-beat, soul, and funk, and Showman's for live jazz and blues concerts as well as the famous tap-dancing show.

RENAISSANCE MEN AND WOMEN

Italy had Michelangelo, da Vinci, and Botticelli. Harlem had Hughes, DuBois, and Garvey. The period from 1910 to 1940 known as the Harlem Renaissance was a movement of the arts, but just like the one in Italy, it was also a movement of the mind. Perception of the African-American experience would change radically thanks to efforts of musicians, writers, artists, entrepreneurs, and intellectuals.

Duke Ellington and Count Basie had them dancing in the Cotton Club, but their contributions to early jazz would soon trickle south, and spread across the country, ushering in a distinct new American musical genre. Zora Neale Hurston's *Their Eyes Were Watching God* was first met with criticism, but went on to become one of the most celebrated novels of the last century. Political leaders were wordsmiths; James Weldon Johnson wrote poems and songs, but also speeches and papers as the leader of the NAACP. Rich philanthropists, such as self-made millionaire Madam C. J. Walker and her daughter A'Lelia, proved that even a black woman could make a fortune in America. Largely unnoticed in his time, artist William Johnson died penniless in a Long Island institution. Yet his legacy grows: His print *Blind Singer* was recently purchased by Washington DC's National Gallery of Art.

TIP

Among the best of all the tours in Harlem are those organized by Harlem Heritage (tel: 212-280 7888; www.harlemheritage.com), led by local residents and with a light-hearted, lightly scholarly approach. Visitors come away with a real feeling for the streets.

collection of contemporary work by artists of the African diaspora. There are extensive archives, including those of James Van Der Zee, who photographed Harlem's jazzy dancing days of the 1920–40s. The Studio Museum also holds workshops and shows films. A short distance away, at 2031 Fifth Avenue, the **National Black Theatre** (www.nationalblacktheatre.org) is an innovative performing arts complex that hosts music, dance, and drama performances.

From 125th Street, walk up one of the neighborhood's north-south streets, like **Malcolm X Boulevard** (also called Lenox Avenue) or **Adam Clayton Powell Jr Boulevard** (also Seventh Avenue). Malcolm X Boulevard is probably Central Harlem's best-known street after 125th Street.

Schomburg Center ❹

Address: 515 Malcolm X Boulevard (at 135th St), www.nypl.org/research/sc
Telephone: 917-275 6975
Opening Hours: Mon–Sat 10am–6pm, until 8pm on Tue–Wed
Entrance Fee: free
Subway: 135th Street

The landmarks along Malcolm X Boulevard include this Center for Research in Black Culture. Here lie, interred beneath the foyer, the ashes of the acclaimed poet Langston Hughes. There is no more fitting spot than this library, a goldmine of books, records, films, and photos about black Americans in general and Harlem in particular. It's also where Alex Haley did much of the research for his book, later a TV epic, *Roots*.

From the Schomburg it's a short distance to the **St Nicholas Historic District**, rows of 19th-century townhouses situated between 137th and 139th streets, known as **Striver's Row** ❺ in honor of the professionals who moved here in the 1920s.

Along the side streets are evidence of the regeneration achieved by this new era of Harlem professionals.

The Abyssinian Baptist Church.

On a Sunday morning in Central Harlem, don't miss the opportunity to attend services at a local church. The fervor of the singing and the response of the congregations are stirring; it's a spiritual experience that is hard to replicate elsewhere.

Sunday gospel

To judge by the diversity of the congregation at **Canaan Baptist Church** ❻ on 116th Street every Sunday, visitors from all over the world have discovered the appeal of the local gospel music, as non-New Yorkers are as much in evidence as Harlemites.

Harlem's churches have long played a significant role in its political, economic, and cultural life. In addition to the Canaan, the **Abyssinian Baptist Church**, the **St Philip's Episcopal Church**, and the **Mother AME Zion Church** have all been influential since the early 1900s.

Gospel tours are conducted by **Harlem Spirituals-New York Visions** (tel: 212-391 0900/800-660 2166; www.harlemspirituals.com). Evening jazz tours can be arranged, too.

EAST HARLEM

Traditionally, this was considered Spanish Harlem, its residents having close ties with Puerto Rico. But East Harlem also includes a strong Haitian presence, as well as the remnants of an old Italian section along First and Pleasant avenues, above 114th Street. Frank Sinatra enjoyed the pizzas at **Patsy's**, 2287 First Avenue (between 117th and 118th streets, www.thepatsyspizza.com) so much that it's said he used to have stacks of them flown across the country to his mansion in California. Patsy's still does a mean pizza today; the secret is a coal-fired oven.

Three other East Harlem attractions are part of the famous 'Museum Mile' (see page 210) that begins on the Upper East Side and, with a stately march of cultural awareness, continues north into Harlem.

The Africa Center ❼ (www.theafricacenter.org), which has had a nomadic existence since it opened in 1984, has found a permanent home on Fifth Avenue between 109th and 110th Street. It is the first new museum to be built along Museum Mile since the Guggenheim, in 1959. Celebrating and showcasing the cultural life and heritage of Africa, there is a tower of luxury condos built above, facing Central Park, while the museum itself has a shimmering glass wall on one side, and a soaring wall of wood from Ghana on the other. At the time of writing, it was due to be open from summer 2016, although previous launch dates have been and gone!

El Museo del Barrio ❽

Address: 1230 Fifth Avenue (at 104th Street), www.elmuseo.org
Telephone: 212-831 7272

SHOP

One-stop shopping awaits at Harlem USA (www.harlem-usa.com), a huge complex at 300 125th Street. As well as several chain stores, there's a gym and the multi-screen Magic Johnson movie theater.

Poet Langston Hughes, whose ashes are interred at the Schomburg Center.

FACT

Jazz poet Langston Hughes's works made him a light of the Harlem Renaissance of the 1920s and 30s. His earthy sketches of black life were controversial: 'I knew only the people I had grown up with,' he wrote, 'and they weren't people whose shoes were always shined, who had been to Harvard, or who had heard Bach.'

Opening Hours: Tue–Sat 11am–6pm
Entrance Fee: charge; free every third Sat of the month
Subway: 103rd Street

New York's leading Latino cultural institute was originally founded by Puerto Rican educators and artists, but now covers the artistic impact of the Caribbean too. Festivals and workshops held throughout the year are designed to involve the immediate community as well as visitors in projects that usually relate to its four special exhibitions. The museum's permanent collection of paintings and sculpture is particularly strong on works from the 1960s and 70s.

Museum of the City of New York ❾

Address: 1220 Fifth Avenue (at 103rd Street), www.mcny.org
Telephone: 212-534 1672
Opening Hours: daily 10am–6pm
Entrance Fee: charge
Subway: 103rd Street

Founded in 1923 and originally housed in Gracie Mansion (now the mayor's home), the museum has amassed a collection of over 1 million artifacts and artworks related to the city's ever-changing character and phenomenal growth. Antiquated fire trucks, antique toys, elegant bedroom furniture that once belonged to the Rockefellers – this is no dry and dusty slog through history, but a museum as vibrant and exciting as the city it chronicles.

WEST HARLEM TO WASHINGTON HEIGHTS

West Harlem extends from around Amsterdam Avenue to Riverside Drive, taking in the Convent Avenue and Sugar Hill areas, along with Hamilton and Morningside Heights. Many of Harlem's white residents live in this district, which encompasses **Columbia University** ❿ and **Barnard College**, as well as the Jewish Theological and Union Theological seminaries. All these are located on or near upper Broadway.

At 112th Street and Amsterdam Avenue, the impressive **Cathedral of St John the Divine** ⓫ is home to the city's largest Episcopal congregation; it is said to be the world's second-largest Gothic cathedral. At

Apollo Theater exhibition at the Museum of the City of New York.

Grant's Tomb.

Riverside Drive and 120th Street, the non-denominational **Riverside Church** has the world's largest bell carillon atop its 22-story tower. Both churches host special religious and cultural events throughout the year.

Grant's Tomb ⓬

Address: Riverside Drive (at 122nd Street), www.nps.gov/gegr
Telephone: 212-666 1640
Opening Hours: Wed–Sun 10am–11am, noon–1pm, 2–3pm and 4–5pm.
Entrance Fee: free
Subway: 116th Street

Officially the General Grant National Memorial, this granite mausoleum is the final resting place of Civil War general and former president Ulysses S. Grant and his wife, Julia; it was dedicated in 1897 as a national park site, and is said to be inspired by Les Invalides in Paris, which contains Napoleon's tomb.

Parks and historic homes

Farther north on Riverside Drive, Manhattan's only state park opened in 1993 on the 28-acre (11-hectare) site of a former sewage-treatment plant alongside the Hudson between 137th and 145th streets. Today, the swimming pools, skating rink, and

The external wall of El Museo del Barrio.

St John the Divine.

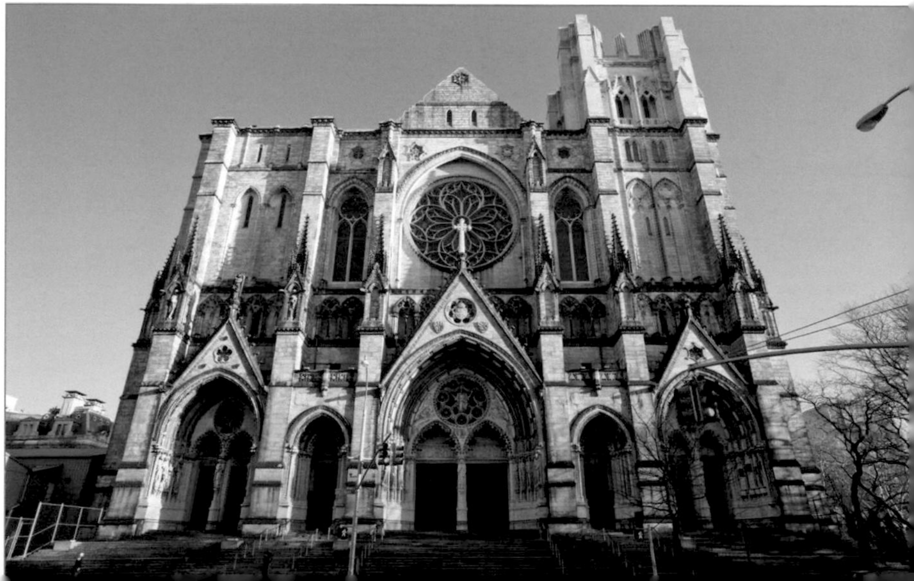

EAT

Among the upscale eateries thriving uptown is Billie's Black (271 West 119th Street; www.billiesblack.com). The menu is soul food, and the prices are relatively moderate. In keeping with the neighborhood, there are jazz and soul performances on many nights.

The interior of Grant's Tomb.

spectacular views of **Riverbank State Park** ⓭ are enjoyed by an estimated 3 million people every year.

West and North Harlem have many other historical attractions. Around 160th Street is the **Jumel Terrace Historic District**, built up in the 1880s and 1890s. **Jumel Terrace** itself is a street of 20 beautifully presented row houses; the famous singer and activist Paul Robeson had a home nearby, on **Sylvan Terrace** at 161st.

Morris-Jumel Mansion ⓮

Address: 65 Jumel Terrace (at 162nd Street), www.morrisjumel.org
Telephone: 212-923 8008
Opening Hours: Tue–Sun 10am–4pm, until 5pm Sat–Sun
Entrance Fee: charge
Subway: 163rd Street

Built in 1765, this lovely Palladian-style mansion served as George Washington's headquarters during the American Revolution, and was visited by Queen Elizabeth II during the American Bicentennial of 1976.

Cultural complex

Audubon Terrace, back on Broadway between West 155th and 156th streets, is lined by two stately neo-classical structures built as cultural institutions between 1905 and 1923. Admission to both of them is free: the **American Academy**

IVY ON THE HUDSON

NYU students share their campus with their fellow West Villagers. At Columbia, coeds have their own private swatch of the city, a quad that may not compete with the grassy stretches of their Ivy League peers, but is still unique in Manhattan.

There are more than two dozen buildings in the quad alone, and dozens more in the surrounding Morningside Heights neighborhood making up Columbia, Barnard, and Teacher's College. The Low Memorial Library is the star. A granite-domed structure evoking classical Greek architecture, it sits within a series of lawns, its steps and plaza doubling as a meeting place and as a venue to watch outdoor concerts and theater. The library is flanked to the east and west by St Paul's Chapel and Earl Hall, which serve as spiritual and religious anchors. Uris Hall, home to the lauded business school, is to the north; it was considered so ugly when completed in 1961 that students picketed its dedication. The Joseph Pulitzer-funded Journalism Hall, where countless media giants have studied, is to the south, and the enormous Butler Library, part of one of the 10 biggest academic collections in the country, dominates the far southern end.

Columbia University.

and Institute of Arts and Letters (tel: 212-368 5900; www.artsandletters.org), whose members have included luminaries from Mark Twain to Toni Morrison; and the **Hispanic Society of America** (tel: 212-926 2234; www.hispanicsociety.org), with a superb collection including El Greco and Goya. The Hispanic Society was renovated in early 2010; additions included new decorative arts galleries and early 20th-century masterworks by Spanish artists such as Sorolla.

Once mainly Irish, today far-northern **Washington Heights** is pleasantly ethnically mixed, as Dominicans, Puerto Ricans, Haitians, and others claim it for their own. New York's largest Jewish educational institution, **Yeshiva University** (www.yu.edu), has a campus on 185th Street. The tiny **Bennett Park**, between 183rd and 185th streets, was named after a Scottish immigrant and holds the honor of being the highest point on the island at a whopping 265ft (81 meters) above sea level.

On West 192nd Street, Frederick Law Olmsted's son designed lovely **Fort Tryon Park** (67 acres/27 hectares), a hilly patch of lawns and gardens with meandering paths, unobstructed views of the Hudson River, and perfect spots for shady picnics. This is not the park for a game of softball or to watch a concert. It's for relaxation and contemplation, a reminder of a New York when there were quiet getaways. It is no wonder that here you will find The Cloisters, a stately and serene branch of the Metropolitan Museum of Art.

The Cloisters ⓯

Address: Fort Tryon Park, www.metmuseum.org
Telephone: 212-923 3700
Opening Hours: daily 10am–5.15pm, Nov–Feb until 4.45pm
Entrance Fee: charge
Subway: 190th Street

Fort Tryon Park.

EAT

Eat well and do good: the New Leaf Restaurant & Bar (www.newleafrestaurant.com), nestled in the wooded approach to The Cloisters, serves New American food in a rustic setting. A portion of the profits goes toward the upkeep of Fort Tryon Park.

The famous unicorn tapestry at The Cloisters.

The Cloisters is an inspiring spot, built to showcase the Metropolitan's collection of medieval art. French and Spanish monastic cloisters, a 12th-century chapterhouse, and Gothic and Romanesque chapels were shipped from Europe and reassembled on this site, stone by stone. The prize of the collection is the six hand-woven 15th-century Unicorn Tapestries. Visiting is as much about exploring the building and its grounds as it is about the art. Your admission to the Met will get you access to The Cloisters on the same day, and both are covered by the CityPass.

In Inwood

The parks don't end there. Farther north, in **Inwood**, the wild and woolly Inwood Hill Park is home to nature trails and bald eagles. It reaches as far as the Spuyten Duyvil Creek, which separates Manhattan from the Bronx and connects the Hudson to the Harlem River Canal. While you are in the area, stop by the pretty **Dyckman Farmhouse Museum** (tel: 212-304 9422; http://dyckmanfarmhouse.org; Thu–Sun 11am–4pm, until 3pm on Sun; voluntary donation). A Dutch-Colonial cottage from 1785, it was restored in 1915.

The Cloisters.

The Harlem Gospel Choirs

While many are sleeping off a raucous night, or sipping mimosas to nurse a hangover, early morning singing is filling the churches uptown.

In Harlem, Sunday means church and church means gospel. Originating from hymns and the negro spirituals sung during the days of slavery, gospel music is an essential part of the African-American, primarily Baptist, church service. It is also profoundly moving and entertaining. Sunday church services are drawing crowds you might find at the Beacon Theatre or Radio City Music Hall on a Friday night, and entrance fees are much more competitive (that is, free).

An early morning subway ride to 125th Street will put you right in the thick of things. You can easily walk south to Mount Neboh Baptist Church (tel: 212-866 7880; www.mountneboh.org) on 1883 Adam Clayton Powell Jr. Blvd. This is where soul singer Freddie Jackson first found his voice, and the choir continues to entrance audiences. Or you can venture north to Abyssinian Baptist Church (tel: 212-862 7474; www.abyssinian.org) at 132 Odell Clark Place (formerly 138th Street) and Adam Clayton Powell Jr Boulevard, which was founded in 1808 by a group of African-Americans in protest at segregated seating in the First Baptist Church of New York. Civil rights activist Adam Clayton Powell Jr was minister here in the 1930s, and today noted religious thinker Reverend Calvin Butts III carries on the tradition. On 125th Street itself, neighboring the Studio Museum, is The Greater Refuge Temple (tel: 212-866 1700; www.greaterrefugetemple.org), a Pentecostal church housed in a former movie theater. The atmosphere is still theatrical, with a guitar, organ, drums, and more than 50 singers filling the room with spirit.

Before You Go

There are a few things to remember. Not all the churches can accommodate every new visitor. Lines to enter fill up early, and seating is given first to members of the congregation. You should always contact churches in advance if you plan on visiting with a large group and to confirm that there will indeed be a gospel performance that day. It goes without saying that you should never forget that these are places of worship and should be treated as such. Gentlemen should remove hats, cell phones should be silenced, and the utmost respect should be shown to the local parishioners.

To take some of the guesswork out of where and when to visit, you can consult http://harlemonestop.com. You could also sign onto a tour with Harlem Spirituals-New York Visions (tel: 212-391 0900; www.harlemspirituals.com) or another bus service that will pick you up in Midtown and ferry you northward to the music and worship. Many Harlem eateries, such as the legendary Sylvia's (tel: 212-996 0660; www.sylviasrestaurant.com), host Gospel brunches for those who prefer their songs with a side of bacon.

Women worshipers at a gospel service.

Brooklyn Bridge as seen from DUMBO.

THE OUTER BOROUGHS

Some come for the art and music, some for the lower rent, while others have lived here their entire lives. For 6.5 million New Yorkers, the boroughs of Brooklyn, Queens, the Bronx, and Staten Island are home.

Staten Island, Queens, Brooklyn, the Bronx: these are places some visitors to Manhattan simply don't go to, except maybe to see the zoo or a ballgame, or to take the ferry.

But they're really missing out. The Outer Boroughs offer parks, cafés and gourmet restaurants, museums, and history. Cool bars buzz around Williamsburg in Brooklyn; woodlands and the Verrazano-Narrows Bridge beckon on Staten Island; New York's oldest – and thriving – movie studios are in Queens; and the home of Edgar Allen Poe stokes the imagination in the Bronx. There are architectural sites of Old New York. As well as the zoo, botanical gardens, and Yankee Stadium, of course.

So often overlooked, many of these attractions – all less than an hour from Broadway, and accessible by public transportation – have the added plus of being (with few exceptions) uncluttered by other out-of-towners.

Neighborhoods

The key word in the Outer Boroughs is 'neighborhood.' Neighborhoods change, overlap, and can be a bazaar of ethnic delight. Stroll through Middle Eastern stores selling frankincense, order pasta in Italian, and have *kasha* served in Yiddish.

Some new neighbors are artists and young professionals in search of affordable rents. Since prices in Manhattan have soared, new generations have turned to former industrial zones, like Long Island City in Queens and Williamsburg in Brooklyn, to live. Co-ops flourish where warehouses once thrived. Burned-out buildings become galleries or restaurants. Then real-estate values skyrocket, and the artists turn their sights elsewhere.

Main Attractions

- Brooklyn Academy of Music
- Brooklyn Museum of Art
- Prospect Park
- Red Hook and Williamsburg
- Coney Island
- Flushing Meadows Corona Park
- Museum of the Moving Image
- Historic Richmond Town
- Edgar Allan Poe Cottage

Map

Page 242

The Queens building called 5 Pointz, a labor of love by local writer Meres.

Amid the new is the older side of the boroughs: the avenues, parks, and palazzi built as grand civic projects in the late 19th century. Architects like Frederick Law Olmsted and Calvert Vaux found open space here unavailable in Midtown. With sweeping gestures, they decked the boroughs with buildings inspired by the domes and gables of Parisian boulevards.

Despite this grandeur, however, one thing 'the boroughs' lack is Manhattan's easy grid system. Off the parkways, they are a maze of streets and expressways. With a little attention, though, it's easy to uncover neighborhoods that can be explored at a comfortable pace on foot – places where the boroughs really breathe.

BROOKLYN ❶

More than 70 sq miles (180 sq km) at the southeast tip of Long Island encompasses the most populous borough of New York City, Brooklyn. More than 2.6 million people live here, which would make it the fourth-largest metropolis in the United States if it weren't a part of New York City. Just a 20-minute ride on the subway from the heart of Manhattan will take you out to Williamsburg or Prospect Park.

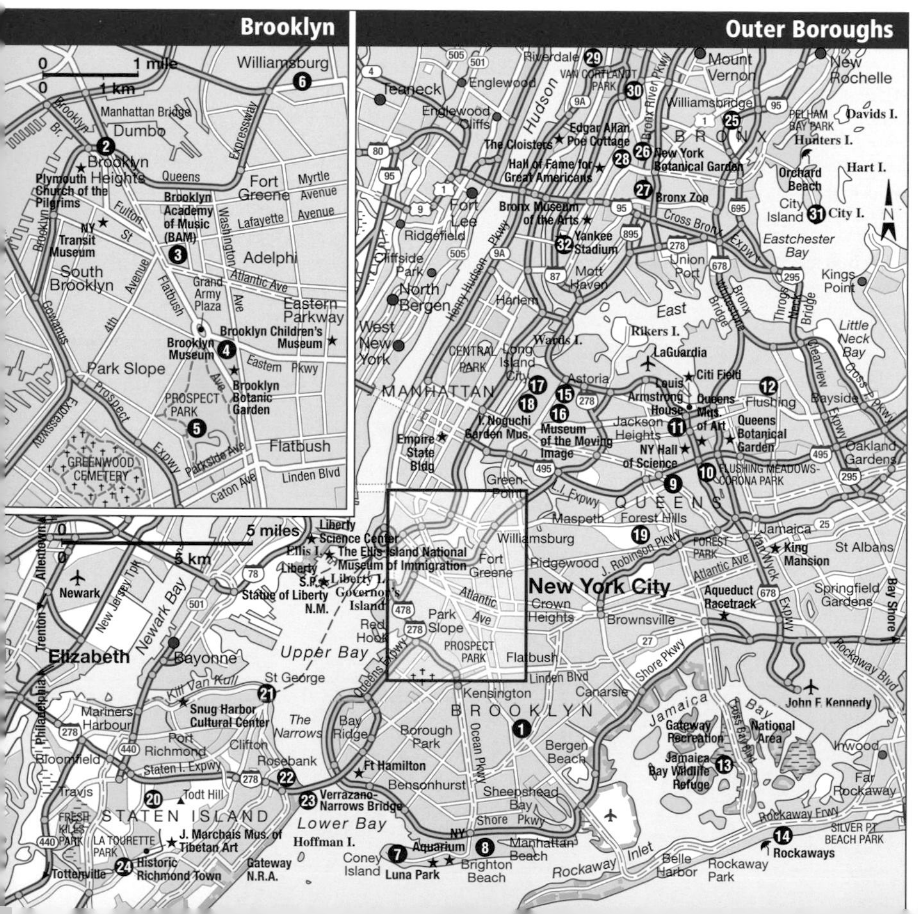

Another scenic way to escape from Manhattan is via the **Brooklyn Bridge**. A stroll across the walkway leads to **Fulton Ferry Landing**, where cobblestoned streets have come back to life after lying dormant for decades. It was here that the borough inaugurated its first mass transit, carrying Brooklynites to Wall Street. In 1814 Robert Fulton's steam ferry, the *Nassau*, replaced the East River's earlier rowboats, sailboats, and vessels powered by horses on treadmills. Ferries remained the main way to cross until the Brooklyn Bridge opened in 1883.

DUMBO

Brooklyn's modern-day renaissance began in now-classic New York style – following the trail of artists. When Soho became too expensive, they moved over the water to lofts in **DUMBO** (for **D**own **U**nder the **M**anhattan **B**ridge **O**verpass), now a thriving neighborhood that includes the innovative cultural hubs **St Ann's Warehouse** (45 Water Street; tel: 718-834 8794; www.stannswarehouse.org).

Young families followed – so many that recently revitalized **Brooklyn Bridge Park** incorporated into its design a 'destination playground,' a carousel, open grass fields, and a rock beach on the East River where the Brooklyn Bridge Park Conservancy holds ecology classes for curious minds of all ages. The conservancy has been doing all it can to attract people to the glorious new spaces, and it's working. Outdoor movies are always big draws, as is the pop-up pool that opens in the summer. In autumn, there are fall foliage tours; in the winter, ice-skating. Construction concluded with piers containing sporting fields, lawns, and river access.

When DUMBO became too expensive, the artists moved to Williamsburg, and when they were priced out of Williamsburg, they colonized Red Hook (and just about every other corner of the metropolis where the cost of studio space wasn't extortionate). Like-minded creative types always followed.

Wherever artists went, they left behind a series of neighborhood

TIP

Brooklyn's East River waterfront has been undergoing the same upscale transition as the Hudson River in Manhattan. Oh-so-cool Red Hook (and the city's only Ikea) is hard to reach by subway or bus, but it's easy by water taxi. Go to www.nywatertaxi.com.

Brooklyn street scene.

revivals after they moved on. For instance, you can listen to chamber music, jazz, and avant-garde music at **Bargemusic** (Fulton Ferry Landing, Brooklyn; tel: 718-624 4924; www.bargemusic.org), a converted old coffee barge that's moored at the end of Old Fulton Street.

It's on the other side of the Fulton Ferry Landing from the **River Café** (), considered one of the city's most romantic restaurants. Around the bend to the east is the old **Brooklyn Navy Yard** (now an industrial park, not open to visitors), where ships like the USS *Missouri* were built during World War II.

Brooklyn Heights ❷

Directly inland from the Fulton Ferry, the property has always been hot. In **Brooklyn Heights**, where streets are lined with narrow row houses, brownstones change hands for sums in the millions of dollars.

Along the river edge is the **Brooklyn Heights Promenade**, a walkway that overlooks the East River and the Brooklyn Bridge, and offers a movie-star view of the Manhattan skyline.

The neighborhood of DUMBO stands for Down Under (the) Manhattan Bridge Overpass.

A stroll along here and through the Heights can be extremely pleasant. Each block is iced with wrought-iron flourishes, stained-glass windows, stone busts, and fancy trims. On the corner of **Willow Street** and

Brownstones on Henry Street, Brooklyn Heights.

Middagh is the oldest wooden house in the district, dating to 1824.

Before the Civil War, **Plymouth Church of the Pilgrims** (tel: 718-624 4743; www.plymouthchurch.org; tours available by appointment on weekdays, without an appointment after Sunday morning service), on **Orange Street** between Henry and Hicks, served as a stop on the Underground Railroad, while Henry Ward Beecher (Harriet Beecher Stowe's brother) preached abolitionism to the congregation.

Many streets in the Heights, like Middagh and Hicks, take their names from the neighborhood's early gentry. Five, however, are named after flora – **Pineapple**, **Cranberry**, **Orange**, **Poplar**, and **Willow** streets.

The **Brooklyn Historical Society** (128 Pierrepont Street; tel: 718-222 4111; www.brooklynhistory.org; Wed–Sun noon–5pm; charge) is in a landmark building. Browse and enjoy its rich mix of 'Old Ebbett's Field' baseball memorabilia, maritime artifacts, and Coney Island exhibitionism. A block away is **St Ann and the Holy Trinity** church. Dating to the 1840s, it has the oldest stained-glass windows made in the US.

On the southern slope of Brooklyn Heights is the **Civic Center**, with its Greek Revival **Borough Hall** (209 Joralemon Street; tel: 718-802 3820; http://brooklyn-usa.org). From here, it's a short walk down Boerum Place to the fun **New York Transit Museum** (Boerum Place and Schermerhorn Street; tel: 718-694 1600; http://web.mta.info/mta/museum; Tue–Fri 10am–4pm, Sat–Sun 11am–5pm; charge). In a classic 1930s-era subway station, the museum has exhibits on the city's transportation systems, along with vintage subway cars and buses.

Keep walking south past State Street and turn right on **Atlantic Avenue**. Between Court and Henry streets, stores bulge with imported spices, dried fruits, olives, and halvah. Some bakeries cook their filo pastries in coal-burning ovens. This Middle Eastern bazaar shares the sidewalk with a number of antiques shops. These have plenty of interesting stock (Victorian, Art Deco, 1930s, 1940s), and are usually open on weekends, if not every day.

The Brooklyn Heights Promenade provides amazing view of Manhattan.

Fort Greene

On the other side of Brooklyn's not terribly attractive downtown is another cache of worthwhile sights. From Brooklyn Heights, walk east on Atlantic Avenue, and turn left on Flatbush Avenue.

Just a few blocks down, you'll find **Junior's** (www.juniorscheesecake.com), home to Brooklyn's original claim to cheesecake fame, and BAM, the Brooklyn Academy of Music.

The indoor **Brooklyn Flea Market** alternates between different venues in summer and winter (including Fort Greene on Saturdays in the summer), and while you're always guaranteed an eclectic mix of hundreds of stalls, vendors do change from week to week so it's best to check the website (http://brooklynflea.com) before setting out.

Brooklyn Winter Flea Market.

Brooklyn Academy of Music (BAM) ❸

Address: Peter Jay Sharp Building, 30 Lafayette Avenue, www.bam.org
Telephone: 718-636 4100
Opening Hours: box office Mon–Sat noon–6pm (different in summer)
Entrance Fee: charge
Subway: Atlantic Avenue, Nevins Street, Fulton Street

At the corner of Lafayette Avenue and Ashland Place is this innovative school and performance space for music, film and the performing arts. Its spectrum has included

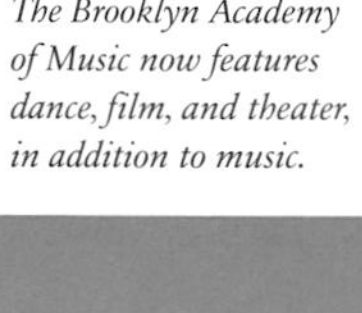

The Brooklyn Academy of Music now features dance, film, and theater, in addition to music.

multimedia maestro Laurie Anderson, Martha Clarke's performance art, and the music of minimalist composer Philip Glass. Home to the experimental **Next Wave Festival** since 1982, it includes the beautifully restored **BAM Harvey Theater** (formerly known as the Majestic Theater), the **lively BAM Café**, and four screening rooms, known as the **BAM Rose Cinemas**. Close by is **BRIC House** (647 Fulton Street; www.bricartsmedia.org), which presents contemporary art and runs community media programs celebrating Brooklyn's creativity and diversity. Just around the corner is a massive shopping mall, **Atlantic Terminal**.

Prospect Heights and Park Slope

Follow Flatbush Avenue in the other direction from Fort Greene, and you'll make your way on the road that separates **Park Slope**, to your right, and **Prospect Heights**, to your left. Here you'll find, at Grand Army Plaza, the entrance to Brooklyn's green lung, Prospect Park. The neighborhood of Park Slope runs along Prospect Park's western border, and is filled with Victorian row houses, many of which have been divided up into apartments. It has become a popular neighborhood for Manhattan defectors and young families. Seventh Avenue, wall-to-wall with stores and restaurants, is two blocks west of the park.

Make a left from Grand Army Plaza onto Eastern Parkway, and you'll see a number of cultural attractions lining the boulevard.

Brooklyn Museum of Art ❹

Address: 200 Eastern Parkway, www.brooklynmuseum.org
Telephone: 718-638 5000
Opening Hours: Wed–Sun 11am–6pm, Thu until 10pm
Entrance Fee: charge
Subway: Eastern Parkway/Brooklyn Museum

This marvelous museum – the second largest in New York after the Metropolitan – has an Egyptian collection considered by many the best outside of Cairo and London.

Grand Army Plaza and the Soldiers' and Sailors' Memorial Arch.

Prospect Park.

TIP

If you plan on spending significant time in Brooklyn, or even a couple of days, consider booking a hotel in the borough. Many are much more affordable, but just as nice as what you'll find in Manhattan. Ideally located hipster haven the NU Hotel (85 Smith Street; tel: 718-852 8585; www.nuhotelbrooklyn.com) offers apartment-style accommodations.

Wonderfully eclectic, the Brooklyn museum displays an array of world-class exhibits, including 23 period rooms and an unusual outdoor sculpture garden of New York building ornaments. There are many other highlights in addition to its celebrated Egyptian relics. A global museum, it has lovely artifacts from Polynesia, Africa, and Southeast Asia, Japanese ceramics, and an *Art in the Americas* section with highlights from ancient Peruvian textiles to modern bowls from New Mexico's Pueblos.

American art

The kaleidoscope of American art continues with Colonial decorative art, including a reconstructed 1675 Dutch interior from Brooklyn itself, and a comprehensive display of paintings with masterpieces by artists such as Georgia O'Keeffe. There's an impressive stock of European – especially French and 19th-century – art, including sculptures by Rodin and major paintings by Degas, Cézanne, Monet, and Matisse. The photography collection is also excellent.

The Wilbour Plaque, Egyptian 18th Dynasty (c.1567–1320 BC), Brooklyn Museum of Art.

Grand Army Plaza

Bordering the museum is the **Brooklyn Botanic Garden** (1000 Washington Avenue; tel: 718-623 7200; www.bbg.org; Tue–Fri 8am–6pm, Sat–Sun 10am–6pm, until 4.30pm in winter; charge, but free on Tue), covering 52 acres (21 hectares). The Japanese gardens alone are worth a visit, especially when the cherry blossoms arrive in spring, but it's pleasant in any month.

The huge traffic circle at the western end of the Parkway is **Grand Army Plaza**, where the **Soldiers' and Sailors' Memorial Arch** – a Civil War memorial designed by John H. Duncan, architect of Grant's Tomb, with sculptures by Frederick MacMonnies – provides a formal entrance to the 585 acres (237 hectares) that make up **Prospect Park** ❺. The park, plaza, and boulevards were all designed by Frederick Law Olmsted and Calvert Vaux, and some consider it to be their best work, even better perhaps than Central Park.

Prospect Park

Grand Army Plaza is their most literal tribute to Paris – an Arc de Triomphe at the focal point of the borough. Roam dreamily through the romantic park: the **Long Meadow**, the Ravine, and Nethermead. For details, check www.prospectpark.org, tel: 718-965 8951. At the **Children's Corner** (near Prospect Park Subway), as well as an antique carousel, there is the **Lefferts Historic House** (tel: 718-789 2822 x301; Sat–Sun noon–4pm; suggested donation), a two-story Dutch farmhouse built in 1777–83. Interactive exhibits portray African and Native American life in 19th-century Flatbush.

Williamsburg

North of the Manhattan Bridge, up the East River, there's another connection to Manhattan, the **Williamsburg Bridge**, which is, naturally, also

The Outlier (1909) by Frederic Remington, Brooklyn Museum of Art.

the entryway to **Williamsburg ❻**. At the foot of the bridge is the **Peter Luger Steakhouse**, Brooklyn's oldest restaurant. Across Broadway, the lovely, Renaissance-style **Williamsburg Savings Bank** building was constructed in 1875, while north up Driggs Avenue, the onion-domed Russian Orthodox **Cathedral of the Transfiguration** (228 North 12th Street; tel: 718-387 1064; www.roct.org), dating from 1922, evokes the area's ties to Eastern Europe. This part of Brooklyn is hopping right now. **Bedford Avenue** is the main drag, with clothing stores and cafés vying for attention.

One block west is **Berry Street**, another place with hip eateries, intriguing street-corner galleries and eclectic stores. Williamsburg has a vibrant arts community, and some of the outdoor murals and graffiti are exquisite. The center for all this creativity is the **Williamsburg Art & Historical Center** (135 Broadway at Bedford; tel: 718-486 7372; www.wahcenter.net).

Crown Heights and East Brooklyn

East of central Brooklyn in **Crown Heights**, Hasidic Jews and immigrants from the West Indies are building communities that are

Brooklyn Botanic Garden.

DRINK

Play bocce ball, relax in a library, sing karaoke, try a microbrew, or catch a hip new band? You don't have to choose. You can do it all at Park Slope's Union Hall (702 Union Street at Fifth Avenue; tel: 718-638 4400; www.unionhallny.com).

worlds apart, but only separated by a few doorsteps. They share their home with the **Brooklyn Children's Museum** (145 Brooklyn Avenue, at St Mark's Avenue; tel: 718-735 4400; www.brooklynkids.org; Tue–Sun 10am–5pm; charge). Founded in 1899, this is the oldest children's museum in America, a hands-on learning center with thousands of interesting objects to ogle – and almost as many buttons and knobs to twiddle. Child-powered vehicles, too.

Even farther east is **Brownsville**. Before World War II, this was a mainly Jewish slum. Local legend places the headquarters for Murder Inc. – the notorious 1930s gangster ring – in a candy store on Livonia Avenue. (For a Brownsville classic book, check out *A Walker in the City* by Alfred Kazin.)

Coney Island ❼

On the coast to the south is Coney Island, which is not actually an island, but a peninsula. The famous name can be traced back to its days as New York's premier vacation center—urbanites have been escaping here ever since the summers of the 1840s. Get a **Nathan's Famous** hot dog at the enormous stand on Surf and Stillwell. The grills, first fired up in 1916, can sizzle more than 1,500 dogs an hour on a hot summer's day.

Tempt fate aboard the **Cyclone**, the granddaddy of roller coasters, where cars speed at 68mph (109kph) over 2,640ft (805 meters) of steel-and-wood track. Along with **Deno's Wonderwheel** (www.wonderwheel.com), a giant Ferris wheel surrounded by quaint rides for young children, this is all that remains of the old Coney Island amusements. Some boisterous new neighbors, the **Scream Zone** and **Luna Park** (www.lunaparknyc.com), arrived in 2009. Their more than 20 rides, a combination of whimsical retro designs and stomach-churning modern engineering, are categorized as Mild, Moderate, High, or Extreme Thrill.

For years, it seemed that the age of the amusement park was over in Coney Island, but it is back with a vengeance, and it has been part of the revitalization of the entire neighborhood. The 2001 establishment of the minor league **Brooklyn Cyclones** (www.brooklyncyclones.com) baseball team, which plays at nearby MCU Park, certainly helped kick-start the revival. The boardwalk, once a seedy stretch of planks, is now a (mostly) pleasant place to stroll, cycle and watch the seagulls swooping over the ocean.

The popular **New York Aquarium** (tel: 718-265 3474; www.nyaquarium.com; daily 10am until at least 4.30pm, depending on season; charge) is located just behind the beach, at West 8th Street and Surf Avenue. With an outdoor theater where frisky and lovable sea lions perform, this metropolitan home for ocean life is one of the borough's best-known attractions.

Shopping on Bedford Avenue.

Farther east on the boardwalk is **Brighton Beach** ❽, which for years was an enclave of elderly Jews, made famous by playwright Neil Simon. But in the 1970s a new wave of migrants, mainly Russians and Ukrainians, began moving into the area, which soon became known as '**Little Odessa**.' Today Russian restaurants, bookstores, markets, and other businesses have infused the neighborhood with vitality. Dance the night away at one of the exuberant nightspots on **Brighton Beach Avenue**.

QUEENS ❾

Visitors taking taxis from JFK International Airport into Manhattan pass as swiftly as traffic allows through Queens, but the borough is more than just a point of arrival. Named for Queen Catherine of Braganza, wife of Charles II of England, it is a diverse community, with one of the largest Greek neighborhoods outside of Athens, and immigrants from all around the world.

The area between **Northern Boulevard** and **Grand Central Parkway**, once a swamp and later the 'Corona Garbage Dump,' ended up as the glamorous grounds for the 1939 and 1964 World's Fairs. Now known as **Flushing Meadows-Corona Park** ❿, it is an expanse of 1,255 acres (508 hectares) that includes museums, sports facilities, and botanical gardens. Indoor and outdoor skating rinks are part of a

Flushing Meadows-Corona Park.

Nathan's Famous hot dogs are a Coney Island tradition.

TIP

Queens was the home of Louis Armstrong, Dizzy Gillespie, Count Basie, Billie Holiday, Ella Fitzgerald, and John Coltrane. Off-the beaten-path walking tours through Queens and Brooklyn can be booked at BQE Tours (www.bqetours.com).

new state-of-the-art recreational facility in the northeastern section, and there are also aquariums, a zoo, football fields, skate parks, and barbecue areas in the park. On display in what was the World's Fair's New York City Building – now the vastly extended and refurbished **Queens Museum** (tel: 718-592 9700; www.queensmuseum.org; Wed–Sun noon–6pm; charge) – is the **Panorama of the City of New York**, a scale replica of the city in meticulous detail.

The **New York Hall of Science** (tel: 718-699 0005; www.nysci.org; Mon–Fri 9.30am–5pm, Sat–Sun 10am–6pm; charge), near the park's 111th Street entrance, is well known for its hands-on exhibits and rocket ships in the outdoor Rocket Park.

Close by are two nationally recognizable sports arenas, the **USTA Billie Jean King National Tennis Center**, open to public players but also home of the US Open every September; and the **Citi Field**, which became the home of the Mets in 2009 (http://newyork.mets.mlb.com). Also in the neighborhood, the 38-acre (15-hectare) **Queens Botanical Garden** (43–50 Main Street; tel: 718-886 3800; www.queensbotanical.org; Tue–Sun 8am–6pm, until 4.30pm in winter; charge, but free Nov–Mar) has the largest rose garden in the northeast, and is a good spot for weddings.

South of Corona Park at 90-02 168th Street in Downtown Jamaica, the famous **Queens International Night Market** (http://queensnightmarket.com; Sat 6pm–midnight) features independent vendors selling merchandise, art, and food. In winter there is a craft market (Sat 10am–7pm).

Louis Armstrong House ⓫

Address: 34–56 107th Street (at 34th and 37th avenues), Corona, www.louisarmstronghouse.org
Telephone: 718-478 8274
Opening Hours: Tue–Fri 10am–5pm, Sat–Sun noon–5pm
Entrance Fee: charge
Subway: 103rd Street/Corona Plaza

Louis and Lucille Armstrong came to live in this modest house in 1943,

The Museum of the Moving Image is a fun, stylish ride through aspects of modern visual culture.

MOVIE MUSEUM

The Museum of the Moving Image was the first institute in the US devoted to exploring all aspects of film, TV, and video. It is part of the Kaufman Astoria Studios complex – Paramount Pictures' East Coast facility in the 1920s. Along with nearby Silvercup Studios, this is the largest production facility between London and Hollywood, favored by Woody Allen and Martin Scorsese, and was substantially expanded in 2011.

The museum has plenty of early film and TV equipment, as well as legendary props and costumes. Modern exhibits include interactive workstations where you can select sound effects for famous movies, or insert your own dialogue into classic scenes.

The more than 400 yearly film screenings are held most Friday evenings and weekend afternoons.

Nearly one quarter of Queens is reserved for parkland.

FACT

Barnum's Circus (later the Barnum & Bailey Circus) opened in Brooklyn in 1871. 'The Greatest Show on Earth' was an instant success. By taking the circus on tour (in 65 railcars), the show was playing to 20,000 people a day by 1874.

a year after they were married, and stayed here for the rest of their lives, despite Louis being one of the world's most famous faces. Louis died in his sleep here in 1971, and Lucille stayed on until her own death in 1983.

Lucille had much more to do with the decoration of the house than Louis did – he was often on tour – but 'Satchmo's' den has been restored to look exactly as it did in his lifetime. Also part of the museum are the **Louis Armstrong Archives** (Queens College, 65–30 Kissena Boulevard; www.queenslibrary.org/research/special-collections/louis-armstrong; weekdays by appointment; free), the first stop for hundreds of jazz researchers from all over the world.

Flushing and its Little Asia

East of the park, **Flushing** ⓬ is packed with history, and perked up by **'Little Asia**,' with one of the

Louis Armstrong House.

Staten Island Ferry.

biggest Hindu temples in North America, on **Bowne Street**.

The **Quaker Meeting House**, built in 1696, is the oldest place of worship in New York City. A good place to learn about the area is the **Queens Historical Society** (143–35 37th Avenue; tel: 718-939 0647; www.queenshistoricalsociety.org; Tue and Sat–Sun 2.30–4.30pm; charge).

Kayakers in the Fresh Kills former landfill site, Staten Island.

Most people assume the largest stretches of land in Queens belong to **JFK** and **LaGuardia airports**. These sprawling terminals with their long runways are huge, but an even more impressive acreage remains undeveloped – nearly a quarter of the borough of Queens is kept as parkland, under preservation orders.

South of the JFK runways, **Jamaica Bay Wildlife Refuge** ⓭ (Cross Bay Boulevard; tel: 718-318 4340; www.nps.gov/gate; free) gives a home to more than 300 species of birds, as well as scores of small creatures like raccoons, chipmunks, and turtles.

Trail maps, available from National Park Rangers at the visitor center, guide hikers to some beautiful routes through luscious groves of red cedar and Japanese pine trees. Workshops about birds are also available year-round. The birds of Jamaica Bay avoid tangling with passing jets thanks to an innovative program using falcons to chase them away from the danger areas.

Big beach

Along the southernmost strip of Queens, **The Rockaways** ⓮ form the biggest municipal beach in the country and are easy to reach by subway from Midtown Manhattan. To the east is **Far Rockaway**; to the west is **Neponsit**, where old mansions echo the bygone salad days when wealthy New Yorkers vacationed here. Sadly, **Belle Harbor** was the site of the tragic incident on November 13, 2001, when American Airlines Flight 587 crashed shortly after take-off from JFK, killing 260 people, including some residents and rescue workers from 9/11. To add insult to injury, many of the beachside homes were destroyed in 2012 from the Hurricane Sandy storm surge.

Astoria and movieland

On the opposite end of Queens, facing Manhattan across the East River, **Astoria** ⓯ is a modest section of small apartment buildings and semi-detached homes. Traditionally a Greek enclave, Astoria has lately attracted migrants from across the world. Along main drags like **Steinway Street** and **Broadway** are Greek delis, Italian bakeries, Asian markets, and restaurants. And despite the movie stars working nearby, the side streets remain pretty quiet.

Astoria has also regained its old status as the center of New York's film industry. The motion-picture business here dates back to the 1920s, when the Marx Brothers and Gloria Swanson were among those working at what was then the Famous Players-Lasky Studios. The **Kaufman Astoria Studios** (www.kaufmanastoria.com) now occupy the old site. Films, TV shows and commercials are rolling again, here and at **Silvercup Studios** (www.silvercupstudios.com) in nearby Long Island City.

Museum of the Moving Image ⓰

Address: 35th Avenue (at 37th Street), Astoria, www.movingimage.us
Telephone: 718-777 6888
Opening Hours: Wed–Thu 10.30am–5pm, Fri 10.30am–8pm, Sat–Sun 11.30am–7pm

Innovative P.S.1, affiliated with the Museum of Modern Art, has its premises in an old schoolhouse.

FACT

Long Island City promotes itself as the eastern counterpoint to Chelsea, with more light, more space, and less glamour. But glamour does come its way: *The Sopranos*, *30 Rock* and *Sex and the City* were all made at LIC's Silvercup Studios.

Entrance Fee: charge, free Fri 4–8pm
Subway: Steinway Street

This museum evokes the glory days of early New York filmmaking, when Astoria's studios were known as 'Hollywood on the Hudson.' It also has fascinating and fun exhibits that demonstrate how movies are made and the possibilities of new technologies, and hosts regular film screenings (Fri–Sun) in some of the city's newest screening rooms.

Long Island City ⓱

West of Astoria, Long Island City also has much to offer visitors. An aging industrial district, it was discovered in the 1980s by the arts community. From 2002–4, MoMA was relocated here, while it awaited the completion of its improved premises in Manhattan. **P.S.1 Contemporary Art Center** (22–25 Jackson Avenue, at 46th Avenue; tel: 718-784 2084; http://momaps1.org; Thu–Mon noon–6pm; charge) is an exuberant exhibition space attached to the Museum of Modern Art that's dedicated to showing the work of emerging artists, and one of the city's most exciting venues.

Sculpture parks

A lovely, leafy landmark is **the Isamu Noguchi Garden Museum** ⓲ (9-01 Vernon Boulevard at 33rd Road; tel: 718-204 7088; www.noguchi.org; Wed–Fri 10am–5pm, Sat–Sun 11am–6pm; charge, free on the first Friday of each month). Almost 250 works by the Japanese sculptor are displayed in 13 galleries created from a converted factory building, while others encircle a garden of the artist's design. The overall effect is one of harmony and serenity, a far cry from Manhattan's screaming streets.

Just up Vernon Boulevard, more outdoor art can be enjoyed in the 4.5-acre

A day at Aqueduct Racetrack can be fun.

FRESH KILLS PARK

Formerly the site of an immense landfill that made Staten Island the target of far too many jokes, Fresh Kills (http://freshkillspark.org) is on track to be the biggest park built in the city in over 100 years, with 2,200 acres (890 hectares) available for development. Some projects on the park's outskirts, including Owl Hollow Soccer Fields and Schmul Park (with a children's playground, and handball and basketball courts), have already been completed and are open to residents of adjacent neighborhoods, but work may continue on the park until 2036. Even though it is officially closed for the public, it's possible to book free education, nature, or kayak tours led by its staff members through the park's website. Once the transformation is completed, visitors will be able to enjoy nature trails through wetlands and woods, memorials, sports fields, waterfront access, art installations, and just about everything that makes the kind of park that any city in the world would envy. And those jokes will soon be a distant memory.

The New York City Marathon starts on Staten Island's Verrazano-Narrows Bridge.

(2-hectare) **Socrates Sculpture Park** (tel: 718-956 1819; www.socratessculpturepark.org; daily 10am–sunset; free). Started by artists, this grass expanse has been made an official city park. The view across to Manhattan, through giant sculptures, is delightful.

Garden suburb

A neighborhood worth exploring is **Forest Hills** 19. Best known for the West Side Tennis Club (www.foresthillstennis.com, tel: 718-268 2300), once host to the US Open, this part of Queens was inspired by the English 'Garden Suburb' movement. Planning began in 1906 with a low-cost housing endowment, but in 1923, the project only half completed, residents took over management and began vetting newcomers. The mock-Tudor district turned fashionable, and styled itself 'lawn-tennis capital of the western hemisphere.'

For a change of pace, a day at the races can be fun. Events at **Aqueduct Racetrack** (110-00 Rockaway Boulevard; tel: 718-641 4700; www.nyra.com/aqueduct) include the Wood Memorial and the Gotham Stakes.

STATEN ISLAND 20

Once upon a time in New York, there was an island with roads paved by oyster shells, where yachts swayed by resort hotels, European-style finishing schools were founded, and where Americans first played tennis.

TIP

The quickest way to get to the Isamu Noguchi Garden Museum from Manhattan is to take subway N, Q (exit at the Broadway stop, Queens) or 7 (exit at the Vernon-Jackson stop) and then public bus Q104 or Q103 respectively. Check www.mta.info for schedules.

Demonstrating 18th-century skills in Staten Island's Historic Richmond Town.

Could this be Staten Island, the least-known borough? To most New Yorkers, this is just the place where the famous ferry goes. As the poet Edna St Vincent Millay wrote: 'We were very tired, we were very merry – we had gone back and forth all night on the ferry.' Yes, come for the ride, but try to reserve some time for Staten Island itself.

The ferry lands at **St George** ㉑, where part of the extensive ferry collection is shown at the **St George Ferry Terminal** (1 Bay Street). Two blocks away is the **Staten Island Museum** (tel: 718-727 1135; http://statenislandmuseum.org; Mon–Fri 11am–5pm, Sat 10am–5pm, Sun noon–5pm; charge), in a dignified 1918 building at 75 Stuyvesant Place.

Snug Harbor Cultural Center (1000 Richmond Terrace, tel: 718-448 2500; www.snug-harbor.org; general grounds open daily dawn to dusk) is a short bus ride from St George. The handsome visitor center first opened in 1831 as a home for retired seamen. Now its 83 acres (34 hectares) of wetlands and woodlands are a Smithsonian affiliate. Within the center's grounds is the **Staten Island Botanical Garden** (free), with an orchid collection and Chinese Scholar's Garden (charge). Here, too, is the fun **Staten Island Children's Museum** (tel: 718-273 2060; http://sichildrensmuseum.org; Tue–Sun 11am–5pm; charge), an interactive experience for kids.

Rosebank ㉒

East of the ferry is Rosebank, home to Staten Island's first Italian-American community. The **Garibaldi-Meucci Museum** (420 Tompkins Avenue; tel: 718-442 1608; www.garibaldimeucci museum.org; Wed–Sat 1–5pm; charge), commemorates Antonio Meucci, who invented a type of telephone years before Alexander Graham Bell. Exhibits focus on this and his other inventions, and his friendship with Italian hero Giuseppe Garibaldi, who stayed here on his 1850 visit to New York. This simple house was Meucci's home until his death in 1889.

A bus or taxi ride away, the **Alice Austen House Museum** (2 Hylan

New York Botanical Garden.

Boulevard; tel: 718-816 4506; www.aliceausten.org; Tue–Sun 11am–5pm; charge) is a 1690s cottage surrounded by a pretty garden that was the home of a pioneering woman photographer from 1866 to 1945.

Verrazano-Narrows Bridge ㉓ features in many of the island's easterly views. When built in 1964, it was the longest suspension bridge in the world. The Verrazano connects Staten Island to Brooklyn and brought great change to the island. The traffic that poured across its magnificent span brought Staten Island's fastest, least controlled construction boom. Now, laws are in place to prevent this from happening again.

Taking to the Staten hills

Because a glacier ridge runs through the middle of the island, Staten's six hills – **Fort, Ward, Grymes, Emerson, Todt**, and **Lighthouse** – are the highest points in New York City. Handsome mansions with breathtaking views stand on the ridge of Todt Hill, the highest point on the eastern seaboard south of Maine. Take a taxi up **Signal Hill**, a narrow hairpin lane. Along the way, alpine homes peek out of the cliff, half-hidden by rocks and trees. At the top, beyond the wonderful views from the ridge, is the core of the island. Called the **Greenbelt** (tel: 718-667 2165; http://sigreenbelt.org; for information on walking trails), this enormous expanse of meadows and woodland has been preserved by a civic plan that tightly controls or prohibits development. **High Rock Park** is a 90-acre (36-hectare) open space.

On **Lighthouse Hill** is an idyllic corner imported from the Himalayas, the **Jacques Marchais Museum of Tibetan Art** (338 Lighthouse Avenue; tel: 718-987 3500; www.tibetanmuseum.org; Wed–Sun 1–5pm; charge).

Historic Richmond Town ㉔

Address: 441 Clarke Avenue, www.historicrichmondtown.org
Telephone: 718-351 1611
Opening Hours: Wed–Sun 1–5pm
Entrance Fee: charge
Bus: Bus S74 from Staten Island Ferry Terminal

Less than a mile from Lighthouse Hill on Richmond Road is a restored 17th- and 18th-century village, showcasing 300 years of life on Staten Island. On a 100-acre (40-hectare) site, more than 15 buildings have been restored. The former County Clerk's and Surrogate's office, from 1848, was the first part of Richmond brought back to life. Staff in period garb conduct tours, and old-fashioned skills are demonstrated in this local 'living museum.'

THE BRONX ㉕

In 1641, a Scandinavian, Jonas Bronck, bought 500 acres (200 hectares) of the New World from Native Americans. After building his home on virgin land, he and his family found the area

EAT

The most historic restaurant in New York City is on Staten Island: The Old Bermuda Inn opened in 1832. This landmark Colonial house – said to be haunted – is at 2512 Arthur Kill Road, Rossville (www.theoldbermudainn.com; tel: 718-948 7600). The Wedding Cottage on the grounds is a high-end B&B.

The Verrazano-Narrows Bridge seen from the Staten Island Ferry.

remote and lonely, so they threw parties for friends.

The Indian land was called Keskeskeck (or Rananchqua, the native Siwanou name), but the name was changed, the story goes, by Manhattanites asking their neighbors, 'Where are you going on Saturday night?' and being answered, 'Why, to the Broncks.'

The tale is certainly questionable, but the Bronx *had* been virgin forest, and *did* begin with Jonas's farm. Idyllic woods seem unimaginable in today's Bronx, but a part of its original hemlock forest remains untouched in the 250-acre (100-hectare) **New York Botanical Garden** ㉖ (200th Street and Kazimiroff Boulevard; tel: 718-817 8700; www.nybg.org; Tue–Sun 10am–6pm, until 5pm in winter; charge).

The **Enid A. Haupt Conservatory,** constructed in 1902, is the botanical garden's grandest structure, a veritable crystal palace with a central Palm Court and connecting greenhouses. There are plenty of outdoor gardens to explore, which are particularly wonderful in the springtime, such as the Everett Children's Adventure Garden, which has kid-size topiaries and mazes.

Bronx Zoo ㉗

Address: Bronx River Parkway (at Fordham Road), www.bronxzoo.com
Telephone: 718-220 5100
Opening Hours: daily 10am–4.30pm (later in summer)
Entrance Fee: charge
Subway: Pelham Parkway (#2)

This 265-acre (107-hectare) park is the country's largest urban zoo – and shares **Bronx Park** with the Botanical Garden. Popular exhibits include the **African Plains**, the **Baboon Reserve, the Aquatic Bird House**, and the **Butterfly Garden**. There's a **Children's Zoo**, a monorail ride through **Wild Asia**, and a 40-acre (16-hectare) complex with moats to keep the big cats away from their prey – that would be you. The **Congo Gorilla Forest** has acres of forest, bamboo thickets, and families of lowland gorillas, while **Madagascar!** has lemurs galore.

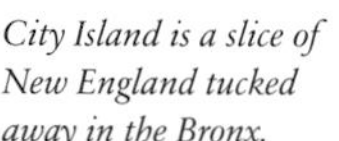

City Island is a slice of New England tucked away in the Bronx.

Along the Grand Concourse

The zoo is at the geographic heart of the Bronx, but its architectural and nostalgic heart may be the **Grand Concourse**. This Champs-Elysées-inspired boulevard began as a 'speedway' through rural hills. As the borough became more industrialized, it achieved a lofty role as the Park Avenue of the Bronx, stretching as it does for more than 4 miles (6km).

On the Grand Concourse, at 165th Street, is the **expanded Bronx Museum of the Arts** (tel: 718-681 6000; www.bronxmuseum.org; Wed–Sun 11am–6pm, Fri until 8pm; free), which hosts exhibitions reflecting the multicultural nature of the Bronx.

Edgar Allan Poe Cottage ㉘

Address: 2640 Grand Concourse (at Kingsbridge Road), www.bronxhistoricalsociety.org
Telephone: 718-881 8900
Opening Hours: Thu–Fri 10am–3pm, Sat until 4pm, Sun 1–5pm
Entrance Fee: charge
Subway: Kingsbridge Road

At the north end of the Grand Concourse, writer Edgar Allan Poe's cottage sits humbly among the high-rise apartment blocks on Kingsbridge Road. Poe moved here in 1846, hoping the then-country air would be good for his consumptive young wife, Virginia. But she died at an early age, leaving Poe devastated; the haunting poem *Annabel Lee* was a reflection of his distress. The cottage has been a museum since 1917, run by the Bronx Historical Society.

The West and North Bronx

Farther up is **Riverdale** ㉙. It's hard to believe this is the Bronx, as the curvy roads wind through hills lined with mansions. A drive down Sycamore Avenue to Independence Avenue leads to **Wave Hill** (tel: 718-549 3200; www.wavehill.org; Tue–Sun 9am–5.30pm, until 4.30pm in winter; charge). This once-private estate, now a city-owned environmental center, has greenhouses and gardens overlooking the Hudson. It's a pretty spot, and the site of outdoor concerts and dance performances.

East of Riverdale, **Van Cortlandt Park** ㉚ stretches from West 240th to West 263rd streets, and includes stables, tennis courts, and acres of playing fields. The **Van Cortlandt House Museum** (Broadway at West 246th Street; tel: 718-543 3344; www.vchm.org; Tue–Fri 10am–4pm, Sat–Sun 11am–4pm; charge, but Wed free/voluntary donation) overlooks the park's lake. Built in 1748 by Frederick Van Cortlandt, a wealthy merchant, it is filled with some of the family's original furnishings and possessions.

On the park's east side, **Woodlawn Cemetery** (Webster Avenue; tel: 718-920 0500; www.thewoodlawncemetery.

TIP

Don't miss the Jacques Marchais Museum of Tibetan Art. Built in the style of a Himalayan mountain temple and surrounded by tranquil gardens, the museum was the vision of a Victorian-era actress who wanted to bring Tibetan culture to New York. It's usually open Wed–Sun 1–5pm.

City Island lighthouse

org; daily 8.30am–4.30pm) is permanent home to about 300,000 New Yorkers. Herman Melville, Duke Ellington, and five former mayors are just a handful of the celebrities at rest in the elaborate mausoleums. Over 400 acres (162 hectares) of trees, hills, and streams have made this a place for strolling since it opened in 1863.

Farther east is Pelham Bay Park. Three times the size of Central Park, it is currently the city's largest park. It offers an 18-hole golf course, tennis courts, and **Orchard Beach**, the Bronx's only public beach and a favorite summer destination for the borough's residents. On the way, the road passes Co-Op City, a sprawling 1960s housing development that looms over the horizon like a massive urban beehive.

The road ends at **City Island** ❸❶, a little slice of New England. Accessible by car, bus, or boat, this 230-acre (93-hectare) island off the Bronx coast has remained quietly detached from the rest of the city. The boatyards along **City Island Avenue** yielded masterworks like *Intrepid*, twice winner of the America's Cup. Today, the street has fishing-gear emporia and craft shops, along with galleries and seafood restaurants. Be sure to see stately **Grace Church**.

The South Bronx

The opposite end of the borough – in location and reputation – is the **South Bronx**. Its best-known landmark is the baseball stadium with the nickname The House That Ruth Built, though actually, this is the house built for Ruth; its shortened right field was originally designed to make Babe Ruth's home-run slugging a little easier.

More World Series championship flags and American League pennants have flown over **Yankee Stadium** ❸❷ (tel: 646-977 8400; http://newyork.yankees.mlb.com) than any other baseball field in the US.

Since Babe Ruth, other stars of the field have included Joe DiMaggio, Lou Gehrig, Mickey Mantle, and Derek Jeter. But, just like Shea Stadium, it too was replaced by a new stadium in 2009. As a result, tickets are more expensive. Fortunately, the team still justifies the extra fees – they won their last World Series in 2009.

Wave Hill in the fall.

Bronx Bombers or the Amazin's?

New York is very much a baseball town, and from April through October eyes are fixed on two very important diamonds.

New York-based baseball-lovers are literally divided into two groups – Yankee fans and Mets fans. It's not the most congenial of competitions, either. The Yankees, regarded by their fans as the primary hometown team, are proud of their endless winning streaks and an incredible 27 World Series titles; the Mets, who see themselves as the inheritors of the Brooklyn Dodgers mantle, a team that moved to LA in 1958, have a less glowing record with only two World Series titles to their name, but just as much pride. Fans spar often, in offices and bars around the city.

But both had reason to be proud in 2009: at the beginning of the baseball season, both of New York City's major league teams opened new stadiums. It was the first time in America that two teams had done so in the same town at the same time. Both fields are open-air, and have natural grass; both are right across from the old stadiums, and therefore still reached by most attendants by subway.

Citi Field replaced the Mets' previous stadium, Shea, in Flushing, Queens. The architecture of the new building makes a lot of references to the Dodgers, including a rotunda named for Jackie Robinson, the first modern-day African-American major league baseball player. Yankee Stadium, which had opened in 1923, was replaced by a new site with the same name at 161st Street in the Bronx. The architects also managed to keep some aspects of the old stadium that fans were sentimental about, such as the view of the elevated subway line from the bleachers.

Subway series

As members of separate leagues – American League for the Yankees and National League for the Mets – the teams had merely a cordial rivalry for many years, meeting only during exhibition games. The 1990s brought inter-league play, and things have gotten far more heated. Every year since 1999, they face off six times during the regular season, split between three-game stretches at each ballpark. They call them 'Subway Series,' a reference to the legendary World Series of yesteryear when the Yankees would play the New York Giants or New York Dodgers and a subway fare was the only travel expense for fans of the 'away' team. It's been over 50 years since the Giants and Dodgers slipped away to California, and the only true Subway Series since occurred in 2000. The Yankees won, as they so often do.

The rivalry will continue for years to come, but the acrimony will always be a bit tempered. There are bigger enemies out there. Ask a Yankee fan what team they hate the most and you will always get the same answer: the Boston Red Sox. Ask a Mets fan the same question and they're likely to say the Philadelphia Phillies... or perhaps the Yankees.

Former Mets' player Johan Santana pitches.

Hasidic Jewish families in Williamsburg.

Bear Mountain Bridge in the Hudson River Valley.

EXCURSIONS

A trip outside of the city presents a variety of distractions, from visiting vineyards and perusing art galleries, to hiking in the mountains or braving the frosty Atlantic.

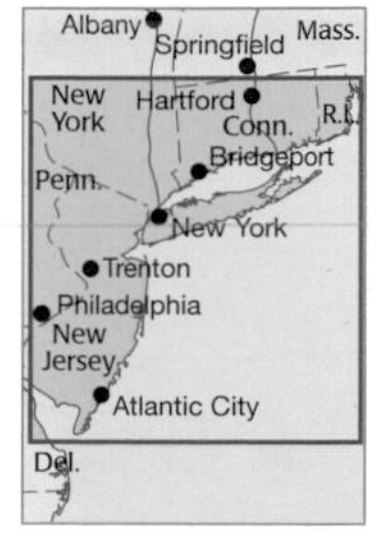

Main Attractions

The Hamptons
Fire Island
North Fork
The Hudson Valley
Sleepy Hollow
The Jersey Shore
Long Beach Island
Atlantic City
Cape May

Map

Page 269

Beyond the boroughs, in what is commonly known as the tri-state area of New York, Connecticut, and New Jersey, is where much of the city's workforce lives. They settle down here for the grassy lawns, garages, and school systems. Even though Manhattanites gently tease these suburbanites – aka the 'bridge-and-tunnel' crowd – they also envy them a bit. Why else would city folk escape to quieter shores on the weekends? As big and wonderful as New York City is, there are things that you just can't find there. For those, you hop a train or rent a car and go on an adventure. The best times to venture out into these wilds are May, September, and October, when the crowds are thinner and the days bright, warm, and pleasant.

LONG ISLAND

It's home to Brooklyn and Queens, two international airports, another domestic one, a professional hockey team, a national seashore and nearly 8 million people. It's the biggest island in the contiguous United States. It's technically in New York State, but it's a singular place, tethered to the mainland by a handful of bridges and tunnels and proud of its own slang, accent, and cuisine. Long Island ice tea, anyone?

The Hamptons

Some would have you believe that everyone in Manhattan owns a house in the Hamptons, and come summertime they all scoot off on the weekends for beachside parties at the mansions of Billy Joel, Jerry Seinfeld, and Martha Stewart. For a select group of the wealthy, this may be true, but the majority of New

Long Island winery, Calverton.

TIP

Arrive in the Hamptons by train or bus and you'll have to rely on your feet or taxis. The ambitious start-up Hamptons Free Ride (tel: 646-504 3733; http://thefreeride.com/hamptons) in East Hampton is dedicated to providing a less tiring, more affordable option. They offer free rides to and from the beach aboard their advertisement-plastered electric vehicles. Time will tell if their business model is truly sustainable.

Yorkers only pop in for an occasional visit or weekly house rental.

Most know that the Hamptons are located on the southern shores of Long Island, but their exact borders can be a bone of contention. The most liberal interpretation has them stretching from the relatively humble hamlet of **Westhampton**, 80 miles (129km) west of the city, all the way to lovely **Montauk**, 50 more miles (80km) to the east at the island's tip, and from the sandy Atlantic coast to the northern bays near preppy **Sag Harbor**. The towns of **Southampton** ❶ and **East Hampton** ❷, and the hamlets and villages contained within the center of each, make up what everyone would agree is the heart of the region, and this is where you'll find the majority of inns, restaurants, and high-end shopping that distract visitors when they're not sunbathing.

Locals have a love-hate relationship with summer denizens. On one hand, visitors provide a well-needed jolt to the local economy. On the other, they transform these sleepy places into raucous playgrounds for the privileged. The debate is somewhat pointless. With white sand beaches this alluring, it would be impossible to keep them away. The beaches are the natural attraction, of course, and **Coopers Beach** in Southampton Village is among the best patches of sand to lounge with the well-to-do, while **Hither Hills** showcases the windswept beauty and seaside wildlife of Montauk. Historical and cultural attractions are lower on the totem pole, but a visit to the **Pollock Krasner House & Study Center** ❸ (830 Springs-Fireplace Road; tel: 631-324 4929; http://sb.cc.stonybrook.edu/pkhouse; June–Aug Thu–Sat 1pm–5pm, May and Sep–Oct by appointment; charge) in East Hampton is a must for any student of art history. This is where, from 1946 to 1952, Jackson Pollock created many of his masterpieces.

The easiest way to get to any major town in Long Island is to catch a **Long Island Railroad** (aka

Shinnecock Bay in the Hamptons.

LIRR; tel: dial 511 in New York City; www.mta.info/lirr) train out of Penn Station. The Hamptons are serviced by the Montauk Branch, and each of the seven Hampton stations is within a few miles of the nearest beach. There are only three or four departures daily and trains can be packed on weekends, so plan ahead and arrive early. Many New Yorkers, especially young ones, choose to ride the **Hampton Jitney** (tel: 212-362 8400; www.hamptonjitney.com) instead. It's a bus – albeit a comfortable one deemed worthy by picky Upper East Siders – that stops along Lexington Avenue between 80th and 40th streets, runs out to Queens, and then moves onto the Hamptons. The advantage: it departs daily, at least once an hour. The disadvantage: it costs more than the train and is subject to traffic jams.

To the west

Not part of the Hamptons, but closer to Manhattan is **Jones Beach State Park** ❹ (tel: 516-785 1600; www.nysparks.com/parks/10/details.aspx), where the city comes to swim and see outdoor concerts. It's definitely not the best beach around and crowds can

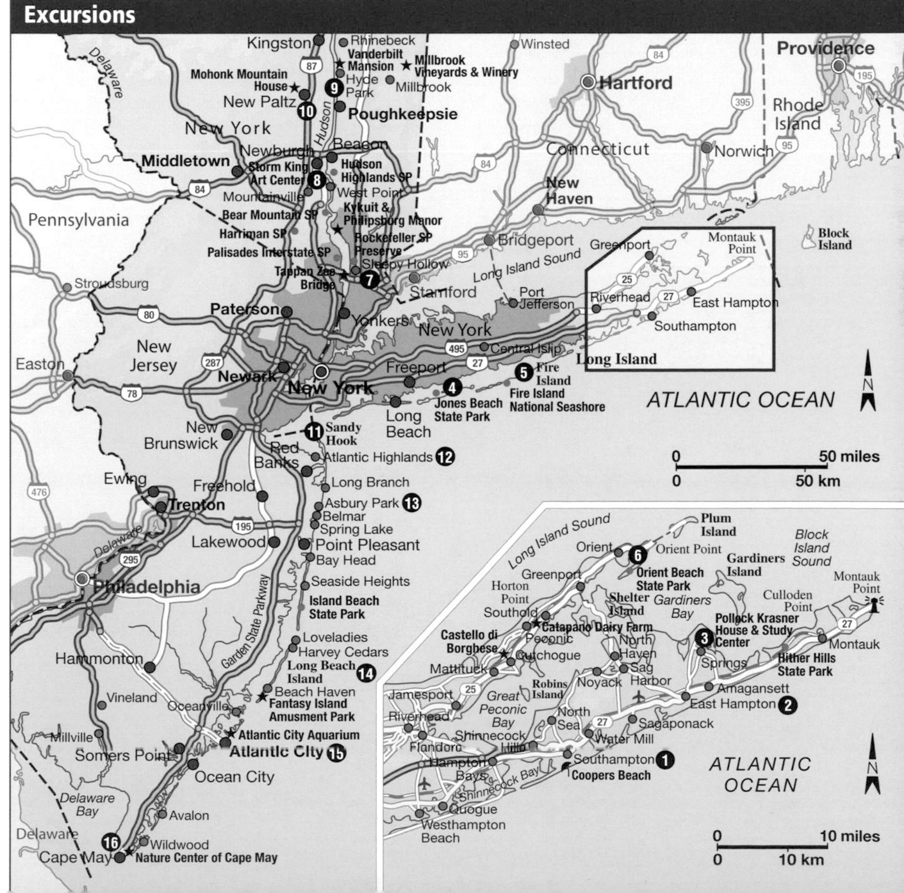

TIP

Car rental rates in Manhattan are staggeringly high. If venturing beyond the reaches of public transportation, consider taking a train or bus to a suburban rental location with lower prices. Many companies, including Enterprise (www.enterprise.com), are willing to pick customers up at stations and bring them to their lots.

be suffocating, but it's a quick drive from Manhattan. Further east is **Fire Island** ❺, a skinny – and buggy – barrier island, with a well-established gay community and New York's only national seashore (tel: 631-687 4750; www.nps.gov/fiis). Most of the island is without roads, which means you must arrive by ferry, and groceries and luggage must be transported along boardwalks with little red wagons. It's charming, to be sure, but accommodations for visitors are few and far between.

The North Fork

The shape of Long Island is a bit like the forked tongue of a lizard. Its eastern end is split between two pointed peninsulas separated by a bay. The South Fork is where the Hamptons bask in the sun. The North Fork is a more rural getaway, where farmers still work the land and vintners ply the rich soil.

Agricultural businesses, such as **Catapano Dairy Farm** (33705 North Road, Peconic; tel: 631-765 8042; www.catapanodairyfarm.com; daily 10am–5pm), are often open to the public and sell fresh produce on site. Catapano is along Route 48, one of only two thoroughfares on the North Fork. The scenic drives along it and Route 25 will yield numerous farmstands and the fork's main attraction: vineyards.

One of the most important winemaking states in the country, New York has growing regions in the Hudson Valley and the Finger Lakes, but Long Island is where the state's most diverse wine varieties are produced. Merlots get the primary praise, but there are Cabernets, Syrahs, Chardonnays, sparkling wines and more to sample. With more than 40 vineyards in all, **Castello di Borghese** (17150 County Route 48; tel: 631-734-5111; http://castellodiborghese.com; tastings daily 11am–5pm) in Cutchogue claims the title of the oldest and, arguably, the best. Consult the **Long Island Wine Council** (tel: 631-722 2220; www.liwines.com) for listings and general information.

The Fire Island Lighthouse.

Thomas Cole (1801–48), painter of the Hudson River School, c.1845.

There are beaches here too, situated along the Long Island Sound, with views of Connecticut to the north. The beach at **Orient Beach State Park** ❻ (tel: 631-323 2440; http://parks.ny.gov/parks/106/details.aspx) forms a ring around a rare maritime forest at the tip of the fork, and is a gorgeous place for a walk. Most of the area's accommodations and restaurants are split between the towns of **Southhold** and **Greenport**, both accessible by public transportation. For train service, use LIRR's **Ronkonkoma Branch**. The Hampton Jitney offers bus service to the North Fork as well, but not as frequently as it does to its namesake. Taxis are harder to find and the area isn't exactly walkable, though it is a cyclist's dream. Your best bet is to drive or, if you're spending the day sampling wine, have someone else drive for you. **North Fork Wine Tours** (tel: 631-723 0505; www.northforkwinetours.com; charge) has some popular shuttle options.

HUDSON VALLEY

Travel north of Long Island and past the Tappan Zee Bridge, which spans the Hudson River between Nyack and Tarrytown, and the urban sprawl will be behind you. More wine awaits, as well as art, nature, cuisine,

SHELTER ISLAND

Wedged between the forks of Long Island is a friendly and isolated community with families who can trace their local routes back hundreds of years, to when the Quakers came here to avoid persecution. Shelter Island's Mashomack Preserve, run by the Nature Conservancy (www.nature.org), has 12 miles (20km) of coastline and covers more than 2,000 acres (800 hectares) with hiking trails through forests, beaches, and saltwater marshes. There are only two ways to get here: from the North (www.northferry.com) and South (www.southferry.com) forks, and only by ferry. Of course, you'll have to get out to the ends of Long Island first.

Shelter Island Ferry.

EAT

The Hudson Valley's Blue Hill at Stone Barns (630 Bedford Road, Pocantico Hills; tel: 914-366 9600; www.bluehillfarm.com; Wed–Sat 5–10pm, Sun 1–11pm) harvests ingredients at their local farm and is better than almost all the restaurants in the city.

and some of the country's most historically important homes.

History and hiking

Washington Irving's Headless Horseman haunted **Sleepy Hollow** ❼. The cute little town of the same name, along Route 9 North on the southeastern banks of the Hudson, will remind you of that early and often, especially during the Halloween season. At the **Old Dutch Church and Burying Ground** (tel: 914-631 4497; www.odcfriends.org) you can read gravestones marked with names familiar from Irving's tales, as well as visit New York's oldest church. Pair it with a trip to **Kykuit** (tel: 914-631 8200; www.hudsonvalley.org; see website for timings; charge), former home to four generations of Rockefellers with stunning gardens, art and architecture on display. A living-history museum, **Philipsburg Manor** (tel: 914-631 8200; www.hudsonvalley.org/historic-sites/philipsburg-manor; Wed–Sun, timed tours only; charge) is Kykuit's neighbor and an intriguing window into 18th-century America. Stretch your legs at nearby **Rockefeller State Park Preserve** (tel: 914-631 1470; http://parks.ny.gov/parks/59/details.aspx), where immaculate carriage roads are perfect for a stroll or jog, or even a horseback ride.

On the opposite bank of the river, the cliffs of **Palisades Interstate Park** serve up some grueling climbs for cyclists, while **Harriman State Park** (tel: 845-786 2701; http://parks.ny.gov/parks/145/details.aspx) has lakes and hiking in the closest patch of significant forest to the city. The **Appalachian Trail** snakes through Harriman and into **Bear Mountain State Park**, before crossing the Hudson at the Bear Mountain Bridge and entering **Clarence J. Fahnestock Memorial State Park** (tel: 845-225 7207; http://parks.ny.gov/parks/133/details.aspx), where a popular campground is a draw for high-rise dwellers.

Art and wine

Fahnestock connects to the **Hudson Highlands State Park** in charming

Mark Di Suvero's sculpture Mother Peace at Storm King Art Center.

HUDSON RIVER ART

This 'school' was actually an art movement, made up of 19th-century American landscape painters. When Thomas Cole's romantic paintings of a trip to the Hudson River and the Catskills caught the eye of wealthy patron Daniel Wadsworth, the style began to dominate the New York City art scene. Painters such as Frederic Church, Asher Durand, Albert Bierstadt, and Sanford Gifford would set out into the wilderness to capture billowing clouds, raging waterfalls, and towering mountains in oil. Then they'd bring their exaggerated depictions back to the city, where enthusiastic collectors would snatch them up.

These days, you can view many of the masterpieces at the Albany Institute of Art (www.albanyinstitute.org) and the Wadsworth Atheneum (www.thewadsworth.org) in Hartford, Connecticut.

Cold Spring, where you can look back west across the river and see the **United States Military Academy at West Point** (tel: 845-561 2671 ext. 103; www.westpointtours.com; daily; charge), which can be visited on a guided tour. You will see the cliffs of Storm King State Park. Just beyond the park is **Storm King Art Center** 8 (Old Pleasantville Road, Mountainville; tel: 845-534 3115; www.stormking.org; Apr–Nov Wed–Sun 10am–4.30pm) where art, not nature trails, are the lure. Explore acres of grassy fields and lightly forested areas decorated with modern sculptures, some as big as small buildings.

North of Storm King, post-industrial Newburgh is a rare raggedy town on the picturesque river, but back east across the Newburgh-Beacon Bridge is even more modern art, housed inside at the **Dia: Beacon** (tel: 845-440 0100; www.diabeacon.org; Jan–Mar Fri–Mon 11am–4pm, Apr–Oct Thu–Mon 11am–6pm, Nov–Dec until 4pm; charge). Be warned, this tends to be modern art in its most contentious form, focusing on shapes and large installations.

The core of the **Hudson Valley Wine Country** (www.hudsonvalleywinecountry.org) is north of Newburgh and Beacon. **Millbrook Vineyards & Winery** (26 Wing Road, Millbrook; tel: 845-677 8383; www.millbrookwine.com; daily noon–5pm) is one of the most visited, but over a dozen other producers are nearby, and over a dozen more are further up and down the river. **Little Wine Bus** (tel: 917-414 7947; http://thelittlewinebus.com) organizes weekend trips out of Midtown Manhattan for those who don't have a designated driver.

Mansions

Traveling to the eastern banks of the Hudson is easy by commuter rail. The **Hudson Line** on Metro-North Rail (tel: in Manhattan dial 511; www.mta.info) out of Grand Central Terminal runs right along the river and makes frequent stops until reaching Poughkeepsie north of Beacon. Out of Penn Station, the **Port Jervis Line** of

Vanderbilt Mansion.

FACT

Jersey Shore locals refer to two types of visitors: Bennies and Shoobies. A Benny is rabble-rouser from up north, particularly the urban communities of Bayonne, Elizabeth, Newark, or New York. A Shooby is a day-tripper, typically from the regions near Philadelphia, the type of person who brings his lunch in a shoebox and doesn't contribute to the local economy.

New Jersey Transit (tel: 973-275-5555; www.njtransit.com) makes a few stops in New York State west of the Hudson.

To get farther north, **Greyhound** (tel: 800-231 2222; www.greyhound.com) has various bus routes and **Amtrak** (tel: 800-872 7245; www.amtrak.com) trains stop a few times on their way to Albany, but a car is definitely your best bet. On the east side of the Hudson, be sure to visit Hyde Park ❾, home to the **Culinary Institute of America** and its associated restaurants (tel: 845-452 9600; www.ciachef.edu), as well as the **Presidential Library of Franklin Delano Roosevelt** (4079 Albany Post Road; tel: 800-337 8474; www.fdrlibrary.marist.edu; daily 9am–5pm). This is also where the Vanderbilts lived, and the **Vanderbilt Mansion** (4079 Albany Post Road; tel: 845-229 9115; www.nps.gov/vama/index.htm; charge) is perhaps the most notable of the many gilded-age estates that line the water. Upriver, Rhinebeck is a pretty country getaway beloved by harried office workers and the site of September's **Hudson Valley Wine & Food Fest** (www.hudsonvalleywinefest.com).

On the west side of the Hudson, **New Paltz** ❿ brims with galleries and shops, and is the last major town before the gateway to the **Catskill Mountains**. And the breathtaking – and breathtakingly expensive – **Mohonk Mountain House** (1000 Mountain Rest Road; tel: 855-883 3798; www.mohonk.com) with its spa, golf course, and acres of sprawling grounds and nature trails is the grand gatekeeper.

THE JERSEY SHORE

While the Hudson Valley has always attracted praise for its bucolic beauty, New Jersey has been battling a bad reputation for decades. Television shows like *The Real Housewives of New Jersey* and *The Jersey Shore* have done little to rehabilitate that reputation, but a visit to the Garden State's beach towns – or 'Down the Shore' – is sure to change a few minds with the coastline's diverse natural beauty.

Without a car

As the seagull flies, it's barely 15 miles (24km) from the northern tip of the Jersey Shore at **Sandy Hook** ⓫ to

The beach at Long Branch.

Downtown Manhattan. However, driving between the two can take upwards of two hours. In the summer, the **Seastreak Ferry** (tel: 800-262 8743; www.seastreak.com) makes the trip in a third of the time, with the bonus of gorgeous views. The ferry lands at **Fort Hancock** in Sandy Hook, part of the Gateway National Recreation Area (tel: 718-354 4606; www.nps.gov/gate). Explore the grounds, where more than 100 former military buildings still stand, as well as the country's oldest surviving lighthouse. A museum explains the history, while the interiors of some former officers' homes are often open to the public.

Atlantic Highlands ⓬, the only other Jersey Shore town accessible by ferry, is to the south, and has stately Victorian homes and parks with paths for walkers, runners, and cyclists, including the seaside Henry Hudson Trail. To reach points farther south, a ride on along **North Jersey Coast Line** (tel: 973-275 5555; www.njtransit.com) train from Penn Station is the simple choice. It will bring you to **Long Branch**, once a favorite resort of 19th-century commanders-in-chief who worshiped at the **Church of the Presidents** (1260 Ocean Avenue; tel: 732-233 0905; www.churchofthe presidents.org). Two train stops later and you'll be in **Asbury Park** ⓭. Made famous by Bruce Springsteen, the town has seen better days – and worse ones – but people still come for shows at **The Stone Pony** (913 Ocean Avenue; tel: 732-502 0600; www.stone ponyonline.com), where 'The Boss' cut his teeth over 35 years ago. It's a rite of passage for any New Jersey band to play this legendary room.

The train continues through **Belmar**, where college students and 20-somethings sleep shoulder-to-shoulder in summer-share houses and party into the night, much to the chagrin of the more buttoned-up and affluent neighboring communities of **Spring Lake** and **Sea Girt**. The last stop is at Bay Head, just after **Point Pleasant**, a family-friendly town with a bustling boardwalk and a very popular beach.

Peninsulas and islands

To visit the nicest shore towns you'll need a car. The **Garden State Parkway**, which runs 173 miles (278km) along

A Victorian-era bed & breakfast in Cape May.

coastal New Jersey, was built in 1952 to offer residents better beach access and a leafy, truck- and advertisement-free route north-to-south. Sixty years later, it's clogged with cars on summer weekends, and if your vehicle isn't equipped with an E-Z Pass, you'll need to carry quarters to feed the occasional toll plazas. Still, it's by far the best way to get to places like Barnegat Peninsula, home to **Seaside Heights**, the hard-partying community portrayed in *The Jersey Shore* television show. For all the negative attention it receives – some of it deserved – Seaside Heights is often forgotten as the entryway to **Island Beach State Park** (tel: 732-793 0506; www.nj.gov/dep/parksandforests/parks/island.html), a pristine 10-mile (16km) stretch of beach and dunes enjoyed by swimmers, walkers and surfers.

At the southern tip of the park and peninsula, it's less than 1,000ft (300 meters) across Barnegat Bay to **Long Beach Island** ⓮ and its iconic red and white **Barnegat Lighthouse** (tel: 609-494 2016; www.state.nj.us/dep/parksandforests/parks/barnlig.html), but unless you have a boat, you'll have to drive back to the Parkway and loop around to get there. A skinny barrier island, it is commonly referred to as LBI, and families come here to escape the boardwalks and all-night parties. There are nightclubs on the island, as well as mini-golf and the **Fantasy Island** amusement park (320 Seventh Street, Beach Haven; tel: 609-492 4000; www.fantasyislandpark.com), but they are sprinkled sparsely throughout the 18-mile (29km) length.

The northern half of the island – where towns wear colorful names like **Loveladies** and **Harvey Cedars** – has very little commercial development. It consists almost exclusively of sprawling beach- and bay-side seasonal homes for the rich. The southern half, anchored by **Beach Haven**, is where most day-trippers come, and with miles of beach access, it's usually easy to find a private stretch of sand. The beaches are considered public land but, as with many shore towns, there is a small charge during peak season. Don't be surprised if a teenager checking and selling 'beach badges' approaches you.

Blackjack and B&Bs

The most famous Jersey Shore town is also its most contradictory one.

Boardwalk casinos in Atlantic City.

Atlantic City ⓯, the skyline of which can be seen to the south of LBI on a clear day, is both a glittering home to gambling and entertainment and a sad display of urban decay. Casinos like the Borgata, the Tropicana, Caesars, Harrahs, and the Trump Taj Mahal can compete with those in Las Vegas, but if you step off the immense and instantly recognizable boardwalk and stroll a few blocks, you will find dilapidated streets that haven't aged well since being immortalized on the *Monopoly* game board. Come for cards and dice, boxing matches, and the **Atlantic City Aquarium** (800 North New Hampshire Avenue; tel: 609-348 2880; www.acaquarium.com; daily 10am–5pm), but not for sightseeing. Greyhound offers daily bus service on the **Lucky Streak** (tel: 800-231 2222; www.luckystreakbus.com), a wiser choice than the offers of free transport aboard sketchy shuttle buses you might see advertised on utility poles. Like many towns on the shore, Atlantic City suffered significant damage during Hurricane Sandy. But also like those towns, it quickly rebounded. Jersey pride is strong indeed.

South of Atlantic City, the island town of **Avalon** is a quaint community with high sand dunes. It was also the setting of an eponymous 1990 film directed by Barry Levinson. If you're looking for a cocktail, it's a little difficult to find in **Wildwood**, where the boardwalk is packed with amusements geared toward families, but alcohol is only starting to be served near the beach after a 100-year ban. The town's reputation for good clean fun goes back to the days when Dick Clark's *American Bandstand* visited for a summer, doo-wop bands performed outside, and Bill Haley and the Comets debuted the immortal Rock Around the Clock.

Driving down the Parkway, you're bound to see bumper stickers reading 'Exit 0.' These cars will belong to fans of **Cape May** ⓰, the southernmost point in the state, where brightly colored Victorian homes sit along tree-lined streets and the pace of life is leisurely. For the B&B experience on the shore, Cape May has no peers. It is also an ornithologist's delight, with enthusiasts flocking to the **Nature Center of Cape May** (1600 Delaware Avenue; tel: 609-898 8848; www.njaudubon.org/centers/nccm) to spot shore and seabirds.

Victorian houses in Cape May.

New York apartments.

INSIGHT GUIDES TRAVEL TIPS
NEW YORK CITY

Transportation

A – Z

Further Reading

TRANSPORTATION

GETTING THERE AND GETTING AROUND

GETTING THERE

By Air

Airports

New York's two major airports, **John F. Kennedy International** (**JFK**) and **LaGuardia** (**LGA**), are both in Queens, east of Manhattan on Long Island, 15 and 8 miles (24 and 13km) respectively from Midtown. Driving time to/from Kennedy is estimated at 30–40 minutes, but heavy traffic can more than double this, so leave lots of time if you're catching a flight. LaGuardia is used for shorter US domestic and some Canadian routes, and does not have any intercontinental flights.

New York's third airport, **Newark Liberty International** (**EWR**), is used by a growing number of international flights. It's really in New Jersey, but, although a little bit farther from Manhattan than JFK, it's often quicker to reach. It's also newer, cleaner, and less chaotic than Kennedy.

Between the three, you will have access to just about every major airline in the world, or at least a connecting partner. Domestic coach fares can range from $100–750, while international fares are generally $500 and up, and include applicable taxes. You will not need to pay any additional arrival or departure taxes at the airport.

Airport to City Transportation

AirTrain is an airport rail system that connects **JFK** and **Newark** airports with the subway and rail networks. Howard Beach (A train) and Sutphin Boulevard (E, J, and Z train) subway stops and the Jamaica station of the Long Island Rail Road (LIRR) connect to JFK (www.airtrainjfk.com, tel: 877 535 2478), and a special airport rail station connects to Newark (www.airtrainnewark.com, tel: 973-961 6000). At each airport, AirTrain runs every few minutes 24 hours a day and takes about 10 minutes from each terminal. The trip between AirTrain JFK and Midtown Manhattan takes 20 minutes by LIRR and about 45 minutes by subway. It's 25 minutes from AirTrain Newark to Penn Station.

The reasonably priced NYC Airporter (www.nycairporter.com) buses run between both LaGuardia and JFK airports and Manhattan. Pick-up and drop-off points include: Port Authority Bus Terminal and Grand Central Terminal, with a transfer service available to or from Midtown hotels. Buses from JFK run 6.15am–11.10pm.

From LaGuardia, the **M60** bus (now also offering a faster service with fewer stops) to upper Manhattan subway stations operates 24 hours/7 days a week, while the fast **Q70 Limited** bus runs to Woodside-61st Street LIRR and 74th Street subway stop in Jackson Heights, Queens, from which various trains run to Manhattan. For exact schedules check www.mta.info or dial 877-690 5114 or 511 in New York City.

Newark Airport Express (https://newarkairportexpress.com, tel: 877-894 9155) operates express buses daily between Newark airport and Manhattan, stopping along 42nd Street. Buses run every 15 minutes 4am–1.45am.

There are several **minibus** services from all three airports to Manhattan. A big plus is that they take you door-to-door, direct to hotels or private addresses, but this can be slow, with many stops. **Super Shuttle** (www.supershuttle.com tel: 800-258 3826) offers a frequent service. It can be booked online, at airport ground transportation centers, or from courtesy phones at the airports.

The **cheapest routes** from JFK to the city are by AirTrain, or by MTA bus to one of several subway stations in Queens. If you have a group of 3 or 4, a taxi can be an affordable and easy option.

Each airport has a busy taxi stand, and you rarely have to wait more than a few minutes. From

LaGuardia to Manhattan, drivers will charge the metered rate, which will generally be in the $30–35 range, excluding a tip. A trip from JFK to Manhattan is a flat rate of $52, excluding a tip and tolls. At Newark, the taxi stand determines your rate depending on the exact destination. Expect to pay around $55, plus the tunnel tolls (currently $13) and a tip, to get to Midtown.

Don't forget to leave plenty of time getting to and from the airports if traveling by road; the traffic can be very bad, especially during rush hours on business days, and on holidays.

By Rail

Trains arrive and depart from two railroad hubs in Manhattan: **Grand Central** Terminal at Park Avenue and 42nd Street (lines to the northern suburbs, upstate New York and Connecticut), **and Pennsylvania Station** at Seventh Avenue and 33rd Street (for Long Island, New Jersey, and destinations serviced by Amtrak). City buses stop outside each terminal, and each has a subway station. Amtrak information: www.amtrak.com, tel: 800-872 7245.

By Road

Driving

From the south, the **New Jersey Turnpike** leads into lower Manhattan via the Holland (Canal Street) or Lincoln (Midtown) tunnels and offers access farther north via the George Washington Bridge. From the north, the **New York State Thruway** and Interstate 95 connect with Henry Hudson Parkway or the Bruckner Expressway toward northern Manhattan. Driving in from the Long Island airports, access is via either the **Midtown Tunnel** or the **Triborough Bridge**, and down Manhattan's FDR (East River) Drive.

On a Bus

The busy **Port Authority Bus Terminal** (625 Eighth Avenue, at

Hailing a cab.

40th and 42nd streets) sits atop two subway lines and is used by long-distance companies, including **Greyhound**, (www.greyhound.com, tel: 800-231 2222), and local commuter lines, including New Jersey Transit (www.njtransit.com, tel: 973-275 5555). City buses stop outside. A modern terminal with stores and other facilities, it nevertheless tends to attract more than its share of shady individuals; though well policed, and cleaner than in years past, it's not a place to trust strangers or to leave bags unguarded.

Upstarts MegaBus (http://us.megabus.com, 877-462 6342) and BoltBus (www.boltbus.com, tel: 877-265 8287) provide transit between almost 20 cities in northeastern US and Canada on comfortable coaches equipped with Wi-Fi and electrical outlets. If you book early for off-peak travel, rates can be as low as a few dollars. Most buses pick up and drop off at locations within a couple blocks of Penn Station.

By Sea

Stretching along the Hudson from 46th to 54th streets in Manhattan (at Twelfth Avenue), the **Manhattan Cruise Terminal** (www.nycruise.com, tel: 212-641 4440) has customs facilities and good bus connections to Midtown. There is also a **Brooklyn Cruise Terminal** (www.nycruise.com, tel: 718-855 5590) and a port at Cape Liberty (www.cruiseliberty.com, tel: 201-823 3737) in Bayonne, NJ, just 15 minutes from Newark Airport.

GETTING AROUND

On Arrival

Orientation

From the song *On the Town* comes the saying: 'The Bronx is up and the Battery's down – New York's geography makes it easy to get around,' which pretty much sums things up. The layout of Manhattan couldn't be simpler, with a grid of numbered streets through most of the island that makes it near-impossible to get lost.

Generally, avenues in Manhattan run north to south; streets east to west. North of Houston Street, streets are numbered, which makes orientating oneself very easy. Below Houston navigating can be tricky, but as long as you know the general location of some major stretches of pavement – Broome, Canal, Chambers, Worth and Fulton on the horizontal; Hudson, Broadway, Lafayette, Bowery and Allen on the vertical – you'll never go astray more than a few blocks. Even-numbered streets tend to have one-way eastbound traffic; odd-numbered streets, westbound. There are very few exceptions. Most avenues are one-way, north or south, the major exception being Park Avenue, which is wide enough for two-way traffic.

Buses do not stop on Park Avenue but they do on most other avenues, as well as on major cross-streets (most two-way): Houston, 14th, 23rd, 34th, 42nd, 57th, 66th, 86th, 116th, 125th, and a few others. Subway trains run crosstown at 14th and 42nd streets, but there is no north–south line east of Lexington Avenue (until the long-gestating Second Avenue subway arrives) or west of Eighth Avenue and Broadway above 59th Street.

Public Transportation

Subways and Buses

Subways and buses run 24 hours a day throughout the city, although they are less frequent after midnight. There are many subway routes, identified by letters or numbers; some share the same tracks, so be careful to get the right train. Detailed directions between any two addresses – including both train and bus options – are available online at www.mta.info.

The standard single fare for a subway or local bus journey (no matter how far you travel) is currently $2.75 if you buy a SingleRide ticket, or $2.50 if you buy a MetroCard. You can add as much money as you want to a **MetroCard**, and for every $5.50 or more spent, a 11 percent bonus is added. Discounted unlimited-ride cards are also available, valid for seven or 30 days. SingleRide tickets are found only at station vending machines, but MetroCards and passes can also be bought at some newsstands and hotels. Vending machines are located at all stations and accept cash and credit or debit cards. They have easy-to-follow touch-screen instructions and dispense new MetroCards or add money to your existing card.

Transfers between subways and buses are free. Buses do accept cash in the form of coins, but you will need exact change and you will not receive reduced rates. Express buses, which operate during rush hour on weekdays, charge $6.50. Of course, fares are always subject to change.

For general **bus and subway** information, check www.mta.info or tel: 718-330 1234 or 511 in New York City. Every station should include a subway map, but only a quarter of the 422 stations are wheelchair-accessible.

PATH (Port Authority Trans-Hudson) trains run under the river between Manhattan and Hoboken, Jersey City, and Newark in New Jersey. The Downtown line leaves from the World Financial Center. The Midtown line stops along Sixth Avenue at 33rd, 23rd, 14th, and 9th streets and at the corner of Christopher and Hudson streets. It's a slightly cheaper and sometimes quicker alternative to the 1 or F trains and it accepts MetroCards, though not unlimited ones. For more information check www.panynj.gov, tel: 800-234 7284.

Subways operate 24 hours a day.

Private Transportation

Bicycling

Riding a bike in New York is easier and safer than ever, with the number of bike lanes doubling in the last few years. In 2015 NYC's bike network was over 1,000 miles long. Bike-only greenways along the Hudson and East rivers make north–south travel a breeze and, except for in Midtown, there are lanes almost every 10 blocks to make crossing the island less death-defying. For an interactive map of bike lanes visit www.nycbikemaps.com. Remember to wear a helmet (although not a legal requirement for adults), stay off sidewalks and highways, and obey all traffic signs and signals. Just because it's safer, doesn't mean there still aren't plenty of dangers.

Bike lane.

If you don't bring your own wheels, you can rent some, either from the ubiquitous vendors in Central Park or from a local bike shop. Operating since 1969, Toga Bike Shop (110 West End Avenue at 64th Street; tel: 212-799 9625; http://togabikes.com) has affordable options right starting from around $35 per day. The newest option is to join the CitiBike bike-sharing program (http://citibikenyc.com), which will give you unlimited access to bikes throughout the city for a single day or an entire week. All you need to bring is a credit card and a helmet. For additional maps and safety tips, visit the Department of Transportation at www.nyc.gov/html/dot/html/home/home.shtml.

Car Services

You can hail a yellow cab, but you can't book one. For that, you'll need a car service. These can range from limousines and town cars to shuttle vans and sedans. You may be solicited by drivers of 'gypsy cabs,' usually nondescript black cars used by local car services, but you would be wise to call a trusted service. A few reliable ones include luxury-minded **Allstate** (www.allstatelimo.com, tel: 212-333 3333), Downtown's **Delancey** (http://delanceynyc.com, tel: 212-228 3301), and airport specialists **Dial 7** (www.dial7.com, tel: 212-777 7777).

Driving in New York

Driving around Manhattan is not fun. Visitors arriving by car would do well to leave their vehicle parked in a garage and use public transportation, as traffic and scarce parking space make driving in the city a nightmare.

If you must drive, remember certain rules of the city: the speed limit is 30mph (50kph) unless otherwise indicated; the use of seat belts is mandatory; the speed limit on most highways in New York is 55mph (90kph) and is strictly enforced – look out for signs, as on some major highways this has now been raised to 65mph (105kph). Right turns are prohibited at red lights throughout the city.

Parking

While street parking is at least possible in some areas outside of Midtown, a garage or parking lot is the safer (though far more expensive) choice. You can find garages and lock-in discounted rates at www.nyc.bestparking.com and www.iconparkingsystems.com. If you happen to find a parking spot on the street, obey posted parking regulations, which may include parking only on one side of the street on alternate days, or call **311** for more information. Never park next to a fire hydrant and don't leave your car over the time limit, or it may be towed away.

Buying Gas

Service stations are few and far between (Eleventh and Twelfth avenues on the West Side are good hunting grounds). They are often open in the evening and on Sundays.

Breakdowns

Your car rental company should have its own emergency numbers in case of breakdown. Otherwise, the **Automobile Club of New York** (ACNY), a branch of the American Automobile Association (AAA, www.aaa.com), will help members and foreign visitors affiliated with other recognized automobile associations. In case of a breakdown, or for other problems along the way, call their Emergency Road Service (tel: 800-222 4357) or wait until a police car comes along.

Car Rental

Since New York City has the highest car rental and parking rates in the US, we don't recommend you rent a car unless you plan to leave the city a few times. If you do need a car, you'll find it's generally cheaper to rent at the airport than in Manhattan, and cheaper still to rent a car outside of New York City, where prices are more competitive. It's a good idea to make car rental reservations online before you leave home. (A curious twist is that weekend rentals in Manhattan are more expensive than weekday rates, since most New Yorkers do not own cars and rent when they go away for weekends.)

You will need a major credit card to rent a car, plus your driver's license. The minimum age for renting a car is 21, but some companies will not rent to drivers under 25, or when they do will impose a high, additional fee.

Taxis

Taxis, all metered, cruise the streets and must be hailed, although there are official taxi stands at places like Grand Central and Penn Station. Hail with an outstretched arm, from near an intersection if possible, so they can see you and have ample space to pull over. If the number on the roof is lit, it means the taxi is available. Be sure to flag down an official, yellow cab, not an unlicensed 'gypsy' cab. Flat fares to and from the airports can usually be negotiated, but bridge and tunnel tolls, and the tip, of course, will be extra.

One fare covers all passengers up to four (five in a few of the larger cabs). The meter starts at $2.50 plus $0.50 state tax and increases by 50¢ every fifth-of-a-mile (or 50¢ for waiting time). There is a 50¢ surcharge from 8pm to 6am and a $1 surcharge for peak hours (4–8pm weekdays). Taxis are now able to accept credit cards. A list of your rights as a passenger should be posted in the vehicle and can be read at www.nyc.gov/html/tlc/html/passenger/taxicab_rights.shtml. To request a wheelchair-accessible taxi call 311 or 646-599 9999 (dispatch center) or order online at www.nycaccessibledispatch.org.

24-hour hotline: telephone 212-692 8294 or 311 in New York City.

BORO TAXIS

Much to the chagrin of drivers of yellow cabs, the city has introduced 15,000 new lime green 'Boro Taxis' that will serve Upper Manhattan and the outer boroughs. If you see one on your adventures farther afield, hail it just as you would a yellow cab.

CAR RENTAL

Alamo, www.alamo.com:
US 1-888 233 8749
International 1-800 522 9696
Avis, www.avis.com:
US 1-800 633 3469
International 1-800 331 1084
Budget, www.budget.com:
US 1-800-218 7992
International 1-800-472 3325
Dollar, www.dollar.com:
US 1-800 800 5252
International 1-800-800 6000
Enterprise, www.enterprise.com:
US 1-800-266 9289
International 1-800 325 8007
Hertz, www.hertz.com:
US 1-800 654 3131
International 1-800 654 3001
National, www.nationalcar.com:
US 1-800 826 6890
International 1-800 227 3876
Thrifty, www.thrifty.com:
US 1-800 334 1705
International 1-918 669 2168

A – Z

AN ALPHABETICAL SUMMARY OF PRACTICAL INFORMATION

A

Accommodations

A good percentage of accommodations, especially chains, are located in Midtown, for the obvious advantage that most attractions are only a short taxi or subway ride away. Affordable chains Comfort Inn, La Quinta, Days Inn, Holiday Inn and Best Western all have quality properties in the city. One place for budget-minded travelers to start is by searching the collection of five centrally located hotels managed by Apple Core Hotels (http://applecorehotels.com). Some may prefer to simply pick a favorite mid-range brand (Hilton, Hampton Inn, Marriott, etc.) and go there.

Of course, the New York experience can be about choosing accommodations that are exclusive to the city. Many of the classic hotels (The Waldorf Astoria, The Plaza, The Algonquin, etc.) are clustered between Central Park South and 42nd Street. They aren't necessarily the city's most luxurious options any more (though they are very nice, and very expensive), but for a quintessential New York experience, you can't go wrong booking one of their rooms, or at least bellying up to one of their bars. And the city has just as good options in every neighborhood. You may want to be in the thick of things, looking out on Times Square from a high-rise or out on the Hudson River from a swank new room in the Meatpacking District. Perhaps you'd prefer an inn on a leafy residential street on the Upper West Side or just bed and a shared bathroom in the Lower East Side or Greenwich Village so you can save your cash for dining and playing. It's all here.

When making reservations, ask about special weekend rates and package deals. Better prices are often available via the hotels' websites, or from hotel aggregators like www.priceline.com, www.hotels.com, and www.kayak.com, especially if you pay upfront. It's always a good idea to book by credit card to secure a guaranteed late arrival. In addition to regular hotels, we've included a few 'suite hotels,' and guesthouses. The former are basically apartments, available from a few nights up to a month; the latter are modeled on those in the UK and Europe. Of late, the city has been cracking down on popular services, such as www.AirBnB.com, that list apartments as weekly or nightly vacation rentals. Booking a room through these websites can save you some money and place you in neighborhoods where hotels are in short supply, but do your research because quality varies widely (New Yorkers tend to live in very small apartments).

As far as standard hotels go, make room reservations as far in advance as possible, and remember that the prices listed here are for low season, and rates go up over holidays and peak travel times. In New York, the low season is January–March, as well as July–August. Most of all, don't stress. There's never a room shortage in New York, and wherever you land, you'll find restaurants, bars, museums, and historic sites, within a few blocks.

Admission Fees

Fees to attractions range from about $10–20. A few museums, like the MoMA or the Met, charge more. At some public museums such as the Met, the entry fee is not strictly obligatory, but there is a 'suggested donation.' On Thursday or Friday evenings, some museums are free.

B

Budgeting for Your Trip

Your biggest expense will be your hotel room. Expect to pay $199 for a room at a budget hotel during the low season; $325 for a moder-

Bloomingdale's, New York.

ate establishment; and $525 at a deluxe hotel. It's possible to eat out cheaply in New York, with main courses ranging from $10 at the lower end to $20 at a moderate place and $30+ at an expensive venue. The average cost of a beer is $6 and a glass of wine $10 – and remember to tip $1 per drink. A taxi from JFK Airport to Manhattan costs $52, plus tip and tolls. A single bus or subway ride is $2.75 and a 7-day unlimited MetroCard will set you back $31.

C

Children

At museums you'll find strollers, kid-friendly exhibits, and discounts galore. Navigating the stairs in the subway system with strollers and small children can be tricky, so splurge on taxis when possible.

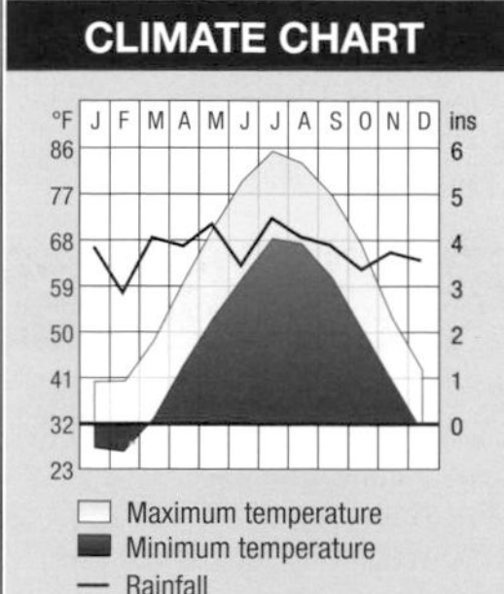

Climate

New York has four distinct seasons, and is at its best during the spring and fall months. Summer temperatures hover in the mid-70s to mid-80s°F (24–29°C), although heat waves where the mercury rises to 100°F (38°C) may occur, and uncomfortable humidity is often the rule, especially in July and August.

September and October sometimes usher in a balmy, dry 'Indian summer' that fills parks and office plazas with sun worshipers. Winter temperatures can drop below 10 or 15°F (–12 or –9°C), with the average for January closer to 32°F (0°C). The average annual rainfall is 44ins (112cm) and the average snowfall is 29ins (74cm). Raincoats and umbrellas are a good idea year-round.

What to Wear

Except for casual wandering, dress tends to be a little bit more formal compared to other US cities. It's a good idea to ask about proper dress codes for restaurants, clubs, etc.

Crime and Safety

Despite its post 9/11 reputation as 'caring, sharing New York,' parts of the city are still unsafe, and visitors should not be lulled into any false sense of security. Adopt the typical New Yorker's guise of looking street-smart and aware at all times.

Ostentatious displays of jewelry or wealth invite muggers; excursions into deserted areas at night (such as Central Park or Battery Park) are equally unwise. Lock your hotel door even when you are inside, and travel to places like Harlem and the Bronx in a group. And even though Times Square has thrown off its seedy mantle, the streets around it attract pickpockets.

The subways are much safer than they were, but when traveling alone at night, stay on alert. Once through the turnstile, stay within sight of the ticket booth. **In emergencies, dial 911 for police, fire, or ambulance.**

Police Precincts

Downtown
1st, 16 Ericsson Place (West Canal Street), tel: 212-334 0611.
5th, 19 Elizabeth Street (Chinatown), tel: 212-334 0711.
6th, 233 West 10th Street (Greenwich Village), tel: 212-741 4811.
7th, 19½ Pitt Street (Lower East Side), tel: 212-477 7311.
9th, 321 East 5th Street, tel: 212-477 7811.
10th, 230 West 20th Street, tel: 212-741 8211.
13th, 230 East 21st Street, tel: 212-477 7411.

Midtown
South, 357 West 35th Street, tel: 212-239 9811.
17th, 167 East 51st Street, tel: 212-826 3211.
North, 306 West 54th Street, tel: 212-767 8400.

Uptown
19th, 153 East 67th Street, tel: 212-452 0600.
20th, 120 West 82nd Street, tel: 212-580 6411.
Central Park, Transverse Road at 86th Street, tel: 212-570 4820.

23rd, 162 East 102nd Street, tel: 212-860 6411.
24th, 151 West 100th Street, tel: 212-678 1811.
25th, 120 East 119th Street, tel: 212-860 6511.
26th, 520 West 126th Street, tel: 212-678 1311.
28th, 2271–2289 Eighth Avenue (near 123rd Street), tel: 212-678 1611.
30th, 451 West 151st Street, tel: 212-690 8811.
32nd, 250 West 135th Street, tel: 212-690 6311.
33rd, 2207 Amsterdam Avenue, tel: 212-927 3200.
34th, 4295 Broadway, tel: 212-927 9711.

Customs Regulations

For a breakdown of up-to-date US Customs and Border Protection regulations, visit www.cbp.gov, tel: 877-CBP 5511.

D

Disabled Travelers

Disabled travelers can obtain information about rights and special facilities from the **Mayor's Office for People with Disabilities**, 100 Gold Street, 2nd Floor, New York, NY 10038, www.nyc.gov/html/mopd, tel: 311, TTY: 711.

E

Electricity

The US uses a 110-volt current. Electrical adapters are available in hardware and appliance stores and some drugstores.

Embassies and Consulates

Embassies are located in Washington D.C. but most countries have consulates or missions to the United Nations in New York.
Australia: Consulate General, 150 East 42nd Street, www.newyork.consulate.gov.au, tel: 212-351 6500.
Canada: 1251 Avenue of the Americas, between 49th and 50th streets, http://can-am.gc.ca/new-york, tel: 212-596 1628.
Ireland: 345 Park Avenue, www.dfa.ie/irish-consulate/new york/, tel: 212-319 2555.
New Zealand: 295 Madison Avenue, 41st floor, www.nzembassy.com/usa, tel: 212-832 4038.
South Africa: 333 East 38th Street, www.southafrica-newyork.net, tel: 212-213 4880.
UK: 845 Third Avenue, www.gov.uk/government/world/organisations/british-consulate-general-new-york, tel: 212-745 0200.

Motorcycle cop.

Emergencies

Telephone Numbers

For all emergencies: police, fire, ambulance, dial **911**. For non-emergency assistance, dial **311**.

Etiquette

Contrary to popular opinion, New Yorkers are generally a polite bunch, but the one thing you don't want to do is slow them down. Never cut in line, steal a taxi, step into traffic, block a subway door with your arm, or stop on stairs or busy sidewalks. Stand to the right on escalators, so people can pass on the left, and don't stare.

You will see every manner of dress on the streets, but that doesn't mean they are all appropriate for religious buildings. All the usual international practices regarding hats, sunglasses, shoes, and clothing apply to the churches, temples, synagogues, and mosques of New York. If you are unsure what those are, contact the establishment and ask. Always silence cell phones when attending a religious service or any type of performance.

On public transportation, seating preference should be given to the elderly, disabled, and pregnant. If visiting someone's home for dinner, it never hurts to bring a bottle of wine or, perhaps, freshly baked goods as a gift. New Yorkers love to talk, but it's considered tacky to discuss what they pay in rent or what they are paid in salary. Most honking of car horns is considered rude and unnecessary in much of the country, but that would come as news to New York City taxi drivers.

Hold doors, say 'thank you,' and exercise common courtesy and you will do just fine.

G

Gay and Lesbian

The Gay, Lesbian, Bisexual, and Transgender National Hotline, tel: 888-843 4564 or 212-989 0999, provides information to gay men and women about all aspects of gay life. Locally, GMHC (Gay Men's Health Crisis), 446 West 33rd Street, offers walk-in counseling and a useful hotline, tel: 800-243 7692, and website: www.gmhc.org. The **Lesbian, Gay, Bisexual, and Transgender Community Center**, 208 West 13th Street, tel: 212-620 7310, is another helpful local organization. Its website is www.gaycenter.org.

H

Health and Medical Care

Medical services are extremely expensive; always travel with comprehensive travel insurance to cover any emergencies. **New York House Call Physicians**, tel: 646-957 5444, make house calls on a non-emergency basis, for $400 and up. Their website is www.doctorinthefamily.com.

To find a local pharmacy, go to www.cvs.com or www.walgreens.com. Both drugstores have many locations throughout the city, with varying hours. Some are open 24 hours.

Hospitals with Emergency Rooms

Downtown/Midtown

Bellevue Hospital, 462 First Avenue and East 27th Street, www.nychhc.org/bellevue, tel: 212-562 4141.

Mount Sinai Beth Israel Hospital, First Avenue at East 16th Street, www.mountsinaihealth.org, tel: 212-420 2000.

NYU Langone Medical Center, 550 First Avenue at 33rd Street, http://nyulangone.org, tel: 212-263 7300.

Mount Sinai St Luke's Hospital, 1111 Amsterdam Avenue, www.stlukeshospitalnyc.org, tel: 212-523 4000.

Uptown

New York-Presbyterian Hospital/Columbia University Medical Center, 630 West 168th Street, http://nypemergency.org, tel: 212-305 2500.

Lenox Hill Hospital, 100 East 77th Street at Park Avenue, www.northshorelij.com, tel: 212-434 2000.

Mount Sinai Hospital, 1 Gustave L. Levy Place, www.mountsinai.org, tel: 212-241 6500.

New York-Presbyterian Hospital/Weill Cornell Medical Center, 525 East 68th Street, http://nypemergency.org, tel: 212-746 5454.

I

Internet

Wi-Fi is available in Union Square and other parts of Manhattan, including at least 10 city parks. More and more hotels provide free Wi-Fi, too. For the latest update check out www.wififreespot.com or www.nycgo.com/articles/wifi-in-nyc. Email can be sent from most branches of FedEx copy shops or from branches of the New York Public Library, including the **Science, Industry, and Business Library**, 188 Madison Avenue at 34th Street, www.nypl.org, tel: 917-275 6975.

Starbucks offers free Wi-Fi and so most other coffee shops and fast food joints have followed suit.

L

Left Luggage

Options for luggage storage are limited. Terminal 1 at JFK has a luggage storage service for $4–16 per bag per day, depending on dimensions, tel: 718-751 2947. It's open 7am–11pm. Penn Station has luggage storage for Amtrak passengers only, located near the Eighth Avenue entrance, tel: 800-872 7245. In proximity to Penn Station, Port Authority and Grand Central, Schwartz Travel (http://schwartztravel.com, tel: 212-290 2626) has two locations with luggage lockers for $7–10 per bag, per day.

Lost Property

The chances of retrieving lost property are low, but items may be turned in to the nearest police precinct. To inquire about items left on public transportation (**subway** and **bus**) visit http://advisory.mtanyct.info or call 511 or **311**.

WHAT'S ON

A calendar of events is included in the *Official NYC Guide*, which can be downloaded or ordered by phone (www.nycgo.com/official-nyc-guides, tel: 212-397 8222; free). For week-by-week details, check the local media and freebie listings publications, and the searchable databases at www.nycgo.com.

Tickets can be booked in advance for live TV shows.

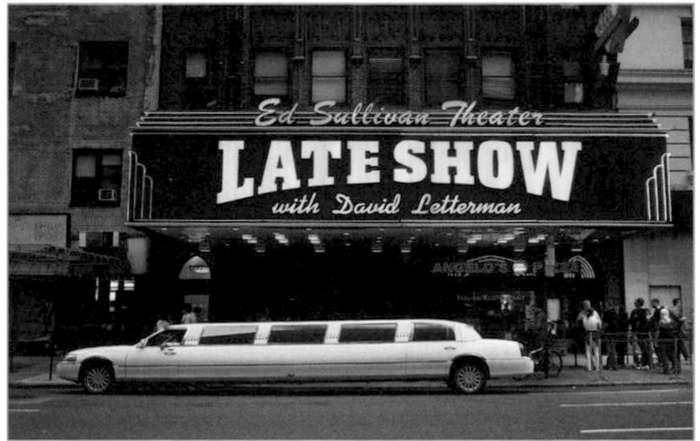

M

Maps

The official **NYC & Co.** provides good maps at its visitors' center (810 Seventh Avenue between 52nd and 53rd streets) and online through its website: www.nycgo.com. Subway and bus maps are available at subway station booths, or from the New York City Transit Authority booth in Grand Central and the Long Island Rail Road information booth in Penn Station. Maps may also be obtained by calling 718-330 1234 (dial 511 in New York City) or online through the Metropolitan Transit Authority website: www.mta.info.

The *Insight Fleximap to New York City* is laminated and immensely durable. The most detailed street map is a book called *Manhattan Block by Block*, published by Tauranac Maps.

Media

Print

The internationally known *New York Times* is the paper of choice for many well-informed readers, with its bulky Sunday edition listing virtually everything of consequence. On a daily basis, two tabloids compete for the rest of the audience: the *New York Post*, famed for its garish headlines and down-market appeal; and the *Daily News*. There are two 'commuter' dailies distributed free in the mornings: *AM New York* and *New York Metro*. The best sources of information for what's on in the city are the *magazines New York*, the *New Yorker*, and *Time Out New York*, but there are also two useful free weeklies, the *Village Voice* and the *New York Press*.

Television

The three major networks – all with NY headquarters – are **ABC**, 77 West 66th Street, tel: 212-456 2700; **CBS**, 524 West 57th Street, tel: 212-975 3525; and **NBC**, 30 Rockefeller Plaza, tel: 212-664 4444. **Fox Broadcasting** has national offices at 1211 Sixth Avenue, tel: 212-301 3000, and **CNN** has offices at the Time Warner Center at Columbus Circle, tel: 212-275 7800.

The **Public Broadcasting System** (**PBS**) can be found on channels 13 and 21 on the VHF band (for those without cable). Other local stations are affiliated with the **Fox** (Channel 5), **UPN** (9), and **WB** (11) networks. These channels broadcast nationally aired shows as well as local programming. In addition, there are half a dozen UHF stations that broadcast in Spanish and other languages.

Cable companies in the city offer hundreds of movie channels, although the exact ones differ depending on the provider.

HOW TO SEE A TELEVISION SHOW

With advance planning, it's possible to join the audience of a New York-based TV show. For more details, go to the NYC & Co. Information Center or www.nycgo.com. Here's a selection:

The Daily Show with Trevor Noah
These very popular satirical shows have been so overwhelmed by ticket requests that the producers occasionally have to stop offering them to the public. Tickets can only be ordered online at www.showclix.com. Audience members must be 18 or older. Mon–Thu at Comedy Central Studios, 733 Eleventh Avenue; doors open at 2.30pm.

Late Show with Stephen Colbert
Tapings of this classic talk show are Mon–Fri at 5pm. Audience members must be 18 or older; proper ID required. Tickets can be applied for online, or by visiting the theater. Standby tickets may be available if you're at the box office by 9.30am on the day of broadcasting. Ed Sullivan Theater, 1697 Broadway, New York, NY 10019, www.cbs.com, tel: 212-975 8800.

Late Night with Seth Meyers
Tapings Mon–Thu at 6.30pm, and audience members must be at least 16. Reserved tickets are only available by calling tel: 212-664 3056, for a maximum of four. Standby tickets are available on the morning of the show – arrive by 9am at NBC Studios at Studio 8G, 30 Rockefeller Plaza. More info at www.nbc.com/late-night-with-seth-meyers.

NBC Today Show
Tapings of this show are Mon–Fri 7–10am. An audience is encouraged to watch from the streets outside, but you must get there by dawn. The best place to stand is the southeastern corner. Go to kiosks at 30 Rockefeller Plaza for information or check www.today.com.

Saturday Night Live
Tapings of this venerable comedy show are on Saturday at 8pm (rehearsal) and 11.30pm. Audience members must be 16 or older. A ticket lottery is held each August. Only one email per person will be accepted, for two tickets each. Standby tickets are given out at 7am on the 49th Street entrance for the dress rehearsal and the live show, but do not guarantee admission. Email to: snltickets@nbcuni.com. *NBC Tickets*, www.nbc.com/saturday-night-live, tel: 212-664 3056.

NBC Studio Tour
At least to see the studios of *Saturday Night Live* and other shows (as long as they're not taping), tag along on the NBC Studio Tour. Attractions include blue-screens to let you 'join' presenters on the sets. Tours start at the NBC Experience Store at 30 Rockefeller Plaza, every 15 or 30 minutes, 7 days a week (www.nbcstudiotour.com, tel: 212-664 3700; charge).

New York's religious community is large and diverse.

Most hotels offer cable in their guest rooms in addition to – for a fee – recent Hollywood movies.

Money

Most ATMs will charge a fee for withdrawing cash. Credit cards are accepted almost everywhere in the city, although not all cards are accepted at all places.

There are numerous outlets for exchanging currency in New York, but a few banks still charge a fee to cash traveler's checks, and a passport must be produced. Dollar traveler's checks are accepted in many hotels, restaurants, and stores in the US, so long as they are accompanied by proper identification, so it's generally easier just to use them as cash rather than change them at a bank.
Travelex, www.travelex.com, tel: 516-300 1622; 1578 Broadway at 48th Street, tel: 212-265 6063; 1271 Broadway at 32nd Street, tel: 212-679 4365; and 30 Vesey Street, tel: 212-227 8156. All Travelex offices sell and cash traveler's checks as well as exchange money, as do the many **American Express** offices around town, such as 374 Park Avenue, www.amextravelresources.com, tel: 212-421 8240.
Citibank offers exchange facilities at most of its 200 or so branches around the five boroughs. Visit www.citigroup.com or call 800-285 3000.

O

Opening Hours

New Yorkers work long and hard in a city where this is generally seen to be an advantage. Normal business hours are 9am–6pm, but stores, in particular, tend to stay open later. They can get crowded at lunchtime. Many shops also open on Sundays. Banking hours are nominally 9am–5pm but increasingly, banks are opening as early as 8am and staying open until early evening – ATM machines are everywhere.
Port Authority Bus Terminal (Eighth Avenue at 42nd Street, www.panynj.gov) stays open 24 hrs, tel: 212-502 2200
Penn Station (Seventh Avenue at 32rd Street) is open 24 hrs. Long Island Rail Road Information: www.mta.info/lirr, tel: 718-264 6880; New Jersey Transit Info: www.njtransit.com, tel: 973-275 5555.
Grand Central Terminal closes at 1.30am. MetroNorth Information: www.mta.info, tel: 212-532 4900.

P

Postal Services

Manhattan's main post office on Eighth Avenue between 31st and 33rd streets is open 24 hours a day for stamps, express mail, and certified mail. To send a letter or postcard internationally will cost approximately $1.20. To find out where post office branches are located throughout the five boroughs, and to inquire about other mailing rates and methods, call the Postal Service Consumer Hotline: 800-275 8777, or go to www.usps.gov.

R

Religious Services

New York is approximately 60 percent Christian, 8 percent Jewish, 8 percent Muslim, 24 percent non-affiliated, with Buddhists, Hindus, and others also represented. Around 6,000 churches, temples, and mosques are scattered throughout the five boroughs. Ask at the desk of your hotel for the nearest place of worship.

S

Smoking

There is now a no-smoking law in effect in virtually all New York City parks, bars, restaurants, offices, and public buildings. A few hotels still have rooms for smokers; ask when booking.

TIPPING

Most New Yorkers in the service industries (restaurants, hotels, transportation) regard tips as a God-given right, not just a pleasant gratuity. The fact is, many people rely on tips to make up for what are often poor hourly salaries. Therefore, unless service is truly horrendous, you can figure on tipping everyone from bellmen and porters (usually $1 a bag; or $2 if only one bag) to hotel doormen ($1 if they hail you a cab), hotel maids ($1–2 a day, left in your room when you check out), restroom attendants (at least 50¢), and room-service waiters (approximately 15 percent of the bill unless already added on). In restaurants, one way to figure out the tip is to double the tax (which adds up to a little more than 16 percent), but the standard restaurant tip is inching closer to 20 percent these days. For parties of six or more, tips are often added to the bill, usually at a rate of 18 percent. In taxis, tip as much as 15 percent of the total fare, with a $1 minimum.

Tourist information.

T

Telephones

International calls, dial: 011 (the international access code), then the country code, city code, and local number.

Most Manhattan numbers have the **212** area code, which has been in existence for decades; newer places might use the **646** or **917** prefix. Brooklyn, Queens, Staten Island, and Bronx numbers are prefixed by **718** (or the newer **347** or **917**). Regardless of the number you are calling from, the area code of the number being called must be used: eg, in a 212 area, if you are calling another 212 number, the 212 prefix must still be used.

Toll-free calls are prefixed by **800**, **888**, **866**, or **877**.

Public phones are few and far between but **telephone dialing cards**, available from newsstands and corner stores, are still an inexpensive way to make calls, especially international ones.

Cell phones are ubiquitous. International travelers staying for more than a few days, or who makes repeated trips to NY, might consider buying a disposable cell phone or SIM card: prices are cheap compared to those in many cities.

Useful Numbers

New York has a three-digit number that can be dialed for information on a range of services, whether the caller is a New York resident or just a visitor. Calls to **311** are answered by a live operator, 24 hours a day, seven days a week, and information is provided in over 170 languages.

The purpose of a call can be as wide-ranging as tourist destination inquiries, making a complaint about noise or a taxi; finding out about the tax-free shopping weeks held several times a year, or locating lost and found items on public transportation.

Directory help, including toll-free numbers, dial: 555-1212 preceded by the area code you are calling from.

Wrong number refunds, dial: 211.

Time Zone

New York is in the Eastern Standard Time zone (EST). This is five hours behind GMT, one hour ahead of Chicago, and three hours ahead of California.

Tour Operators

Among the dozens of operators offering sightseeing trips around the city, one of the most popular is **Gray Line New York**, www.grayline.com, tel: 212-445 0848, which features double-decker buses with hop-on, hop-off itineraries.

Manhattan is, of course, an island, so there's a big choice of boat tours, including: **Circle Line**, www.circlelinedowntown.com, tel: 212-742 1969, which operates boat trips around Manhattan and harbor cruises from South Street Seaport; **NY Waterway**, www.nywaterway.com, tel: 800-533 3779, featuring harbor cruises and entertainment cruises; **New York Water Taxi,** www.nywatertaxi.com, tel: 212-742 1969, with stops near the 9/11 Memorial, in Brooklyn, and at Yankee Stadium during the baseball season; **Manhattan by Sail**, www.manhattanbysail.com, tel: 212-619 6900, which cruises near the Statue of Liberty in a beautiful 1929 double-masted schooner; and **Spirit Cruises**, www.spiritcruises.com, tel: 866-483 3866, which offers luxury cruises with dinner and entertainment afloat.

Other interesting or off-the-beaten track options include:

Art Horizons International, www.art-horizons.com, tel: 212-969 9410. Visits to galleries, museums, and artists' studio lofts.

Big Onion Walking Tours, www.bigonion.com, tel: 888-606 9255. Historic, ethnic neighborhood tours with zing.

Central Park Sightseeing, www.centralparksightseeing.com, tel: 212-257 0417. Guided bike, carriage, and walking tours, including cycle rentals, through the park.

Central Park Carriage Rides, www.centralparkcarriages.com, tel: 212-736 0680.

Central Park Conservancy, www.centralparknyc.org, tel: 212-

PUBLIC HOLIDAYS

As with many other countries in the world, the United States has gradually shifted most of its public holidays to the Monday closest to the actual dates, thereby creating a number of three-day weekends. Holidays that are celebrated no matter what day they fall are:

New Year's Day (January 1).
Independence Day (July 4).
Veterans' Day (November 11).
Christmas Day (December 25).

Other holidays are:

Martin Luther King Jr Day (third Mon in Jan).
President's Day commemorating Lincoln and Washington (third Mon in Feb).
Memorial Day (last Mon in May).
Labor Day (first Mon in Sept).
Columbus Day (second Mon in Oct).
Election Day (first Tue in Nov, every four years for Presidential races).
Thanksgiving (fourth Thu in Nov).

310 6600. Free walking tours. Also **Urban Park Rangers Tours**, tel: 311 or 212-639 9675.
Elegant Tightwad Shopping Tours, www.theeleganttightwad.com, tel: 800-808 4614. Designer showroom tours, sample sales.
Harlem Heritage Tours, www.harlemheritage.com, tel: 212-280 7888. Walk around the streets with a local resident.
Harlem Spirituals/New York Visions, www.harlemspirituals.com, tel: 212-391 0900. Gospel tours.
Hush Tours, http://hushtours.com, tel: 212-714 3544. Hip-hop tours.
Lower East Side Tenement Museum, www.tenement.org, tel: 212-982 8420, offers walking tours, led by local historians.
Municipal Art Society, www.mas.org, tel: 212-935 3960. Architectural walks.
Museum of Chinese in the Americas, www.mocanyc.org, tel: 212-619 4785; another walking tour of the immigrant experience.
On Location Tours, www.screentours.com, tel: 212-913 9780. See the locations of *Sex and the City*, *The Sopranos*, *Gossip Girl*, and various movies that have been filmed in NY.
Radio City Music Hall, www.radiocity.com, tel: 212-247 4777. Go behind the gold curtain to find out who plays the gigantic Wurlitzers.
Real New York Tours, http://realnewyorktours.com, tel: 917-572 7017. Experience the city with friendly and knowledgeable local guides.

Tourist Information

NYC & Company Visitor Information Center, 810 Seventh Avenue (at 52nd and 53rd streets), New York, NY 10019, www.nycgo.com, tel: 212-484 1200, has an abundance of maps, brochures, and information about special hotel packages and discounts at various attractions.

They also publish the *Official NYC Guide*, a listing of activities, hotels, tours, and restaurants. NYC & Co. are able to provide information online, by mail, over the phone, or you can drop by the information center in person (Mon–Fri 8.30am–6pm, Sat–Sun 9am–5pm).

There are also official information kiosks in Chinatown, and at the southwestern tip of City Hall Park.
Greater Harlem Chamber of Commerce, 200A West 136th Street, New York, NY 10030, http://greaterharlemchamber.com, tel: 212-862 7200. Information on tours, events, and landmarks in Harlem. There's also an information kiosk at 163 West 125th Street.
Bronx Tourism Council, 851 Grand Concourse, Bronx NY 10451, www.ilovethebronx.com, tel: 718-590 3518. Information about art, music, and other events.
Brooklyn Tourism and Visitors Center, 209 Joralemon Street, Brooklyn, NY 11201, http://brooklyn-usa.org, tel: 718-802 3846. Information on culture, shopping, history, parks, events, and historic sites.
Queens Tourism Council, 120-55 Queens Blvd, Kew Gardens, NY 11424, www.discoverqueens.info, tel: 718-263 0546 Provides museum and attraction information and tours.
Council on Arts and Humanities for Staten Island (COAHSI), 10 Ferry Terminal Drive, Staten Island, NY 10301, www.statenislandarts.org, tel: 718-447 3329. Lists cultural events and places of interest.

CITY WEBSITES

Several boroughs have their own websites, listed here under 'Tourist Information.' Other websites that provide helpful information include:
www.newyork.citysearch.com for listings and reviews of current arts and entertainment events, and restaurants and shopping. It's excellent for links to every conceivable aspect of New York City.
www.nyc.gov, the official site of the City of New York, contains news items, mayoral updates, city agency information, and parking regulations.
www.nycgo.com, the NYC & Co. Visitor Information site, which also has useful links.
www.nypl.org is where you'll find everything you ever wanted to know about the New York Public Library. There's also an online information service.

V

Visas and Passports

Due to increased security, the precise regulations for entry to the United States change often, and vary for citizens of different countries. It's a good idea to check on the current situation before you travel on www.cbp.gov or via a US embassy or consulate in your home country.

Currently, Canadians traveling by air must present a valid passport for entry. Visitors from the UK, Australia, New Zealand, and Ireland qualify for the visa waiver program, and therefore do not need a visa for stays of less than 90 days, as long as they have a valid 10-year machine-readable passport and a return ticket. However, they must apply online for authorization at least 72 hours before traveling at https://esta.cbp.dhs.gov. Citizens of South Africa need a visa. All foreign visitors will have their two index fingers scanned and a digital photograph taken at the port of entry. The process should take only 10–15 seconds.

W

Weights and Measures

The United States uses the Imperial system.

FURTHER READING

FICTION

The Age of Innocence by Edith Wharton. A classic, scathing depiction of New York high society in the 1870s.
Breakfast at Tiffany's by Truman Capote. The charming little novel made famous by the Audrey Hepburn film.
Bright Lights, Big City by Jay McInerney. A tale of fast times and big money in 1980s New York.
The Catcher in the Rye by J.D.Salinger. An all-time classic with Manhattan as a symbol of loneliness and alienation.
Let the Great World Spin by Colum McCann. A dizzying novel revolving around a cast of New York characters in 1974, including the man who walked on a tightrope between the World Trade Center towers.
Ragtime by E.L. Doctorow. A complex, polyphonic, and colorful tale of the city's society at the beginning of the 20th century with a great political and economic transformation in the background.
Time and Again by Jack Finney. A man time travels to 1880s New York and gets a whole new perspective on the city.
Writing New York: A Literary Anthology edited by Philip Lopate. Observations about life in New York by such literary greats as Henry David Thoreau, Walt Whitman, Maxim Gorky, and F. Scott Fitzgerald. Required reading for city-philes.

GUIDES

From Abyssinian to Zion, A Guide to Manhattan's Houses of Worship by David W. Dunlop. Listings of churches, temples, synagogues, mosques and all other major religious buildings.
New York: The Movie Lover's Guide by Richard Alleman. A detailed primer on famous film locations in the city.
The WPA Guide to New York City: the Federal Writers Project Guide to 1930s New York, edited by the Federal Writers Project. The classic guide to New York, compiled during FDR's New Deal.
111 Places in New York That You Must Not Miss by Jo-Ann Elikann. A quirky trip through lesser known but interesting places around the city, including a Coney Island sideshow, Louis Armstrong's home, and a Central Park croquet court.

HISTORY AND CULTURE

Gotham: A History of New York to 1898 by Mike Wallace and Edwin G. Burrow. Pulitzer Prize-winning narrative about the city's early years; in-depth, with an emphasis on some of its characters.
The Great Bridge by David McCullogh. An exhaustive and thrilling history of the building of the Brooklyn Bridge.
The Island at the Center of the World by Russell Shorto. An account of the city in its early days, when it was called New Amsterdam.
Low Life by Luc Sante. Everything you always wanted to know about the gangs, gangsters, and general riff-raff who thrived at the edge of New York's society in the 19th century.
Lower East Side Memories: A Jewish Place in America by Hasia R. Diner. A cultural history of the Lower East Side and its Jewish community.
Manhattan '45 by Jan Morris. A speculative portrait of a thriving city in the wake of World War II.
New York: An Illustrated History by Ric Burns. Coffee-table history, with brilliant photographs.
New York Characters by Gillian Zoe Segal. An exuberant and sympathetic account of 66 New Yorkers, photographed in their distinctive environments.

MEMOIR

Gone to New York by Ian Frazier. A collection of essays about the city from the 1970s to the 2000s.
Here is New York by E.B. White. An ode to the city in 1948 from the master stylist and author of *Charlotte's Web*.
Liar's Poker by Michael Lewis. A portrait of life on Wall Street in the 1980s.
Waterfront, A Journey Around New York by Phillip Lopate. A combination of memoir and cultural history – with a little nature thrown in – centered on the city's waterfront.
Lucking Out: My Life Getting Down and Semi-Dirty in Seventies New York by James Wolcott. A paean to a time and place by the former cultural critic for *Vanity Fair* and contributor to *The New Yorker*.

NEW YORK STREET ATLAS

The key map shows the area of New York covered by the atlas section. An index of street names and places of interest shown on the maps can be found on the following pages. For each entry there is a page number and grid reference

Map Legend

Freeway with Exit
Freeway (under construction)
Divided Highway
Main Road
Secondary Road
Minor Road
Track
International Boundary
State/County Boundary
National Park/Reserve
Airport
Church (ruins)
Monastery
Castle (ruins)
Archaeological Site
Cave
Place of Interest
Mansion/Stately Home
Viewpoint
Beach
Freeway
Divided Highway
Main Roads
Minor Roads
Footpath
Railroad
Pedestrian Area
Important Building
Park
Subway
Bus Station
Tourist Information
Post Office
Cathedral/Church
Mosque
Synagogue
Statue/Monument
Tower

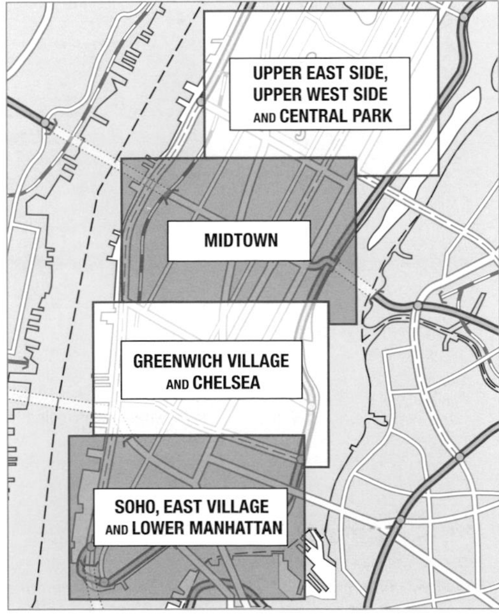

UPPER WEST SIDE
CENTRAL PARK
Zabar's
79th St
Congregation Rodeph Sholom
81st St
Rose Center for Earth & Space
American Museum of Natural History
Eleanor Roosevelt Memorial
Promenade Theatre
Beacon Theatre
Verdi Square
72nd St
New-York Historical Society
San Remo Apts
The Dakota
72nd St
The Lake
Strawberry Fields
Con-Edison
Spanish and Portuguese Synagogue
Bethesda Fountain
Juilliard School
V. Beaumont Theater
American Folk Art Museum
A. Tully Hall
66th St Lincoln Center
Lincoln Square
Metropolitan Opera
Lincoln Center
David Geffen Hall
Tavern on the Green
Sheep Meadow
David H. Koch Theater
Fordham University
Carousel
St Luke's Roosevelt Hospital
59th St Columbus Circle
Trump International Hotel & Tower
The Dairy Visitor Center
Maine
Time Warner Center
Columbus Circle
Wollman Rink
Zoo
Children's Zoo
Museum of Arts & Design
Newsweek Bldg
Hearst Tower
The Pond
57th St
Grand Army Plaza
5th Ave
Carnegie Hall
57th St
Solow Bldg
1700 B'way Bldg
7th Ave
General Motors Bldg
Alliance Capital Bldg
Trump Tower
50th St
American Folk Art Museum
Former IBM Bldg
CBS Bldg
Museum of Modern Art (MoMA)
Sony Bldg
50th St
West Side Highway (Joe Di Maggio Highway)
Riverside Drive
West End Avenue
Amsterdam Avenue
Columbus Avenue
Central Park West
Broadway
Ninth Avenue
Eighth Avenue
Seventh Avenue
Central Park South
Transverse Rd No 1
Centre Drive
West Drive
Bridle Path
The Mall
Riverside Blvd
Freedom Place

Jacqueline Kennedy Onassis Reservoir
Transverse Rd No.3
GREAT LAWN
Jewish Museum
Cooper-Hewitt National Design Museum
National Academy Museum
Guggenheim Museum
Neue Galerie New York
Park Ave Synagogue
Cleopatra's Needle
Metropolitan Museum of Art
Turtle Pond
East Drive
American Irish Historical Society
Ukrainian Institute of America
Alice in Wonderland
Harkness House
Conservatory Water
Lenox Hill Hospital
77th St
86th St
UPPER EAST SIDE
Frick Collection
St James
Asia Society
Americas Society
Hunter College
68th St Hunter College
Seventh Regiment Armory
China Institute
Society of Illustrators
63rd St Lexington Ave
Bloomingdale's
Holy Trinity Cathedral
JOHN JAY PARK
Franklin D. Roosevelt Drive
East End Avenue
York Avenue
First Avenue
Second Avenue
Third Avenue
Lexington Avenue
Park Avenue
Madison Avenue
Fifth Avenue
East 96th St
0 100 200 300 400 yds
0 100 200 300 400 m
D
E
1
2
3
4

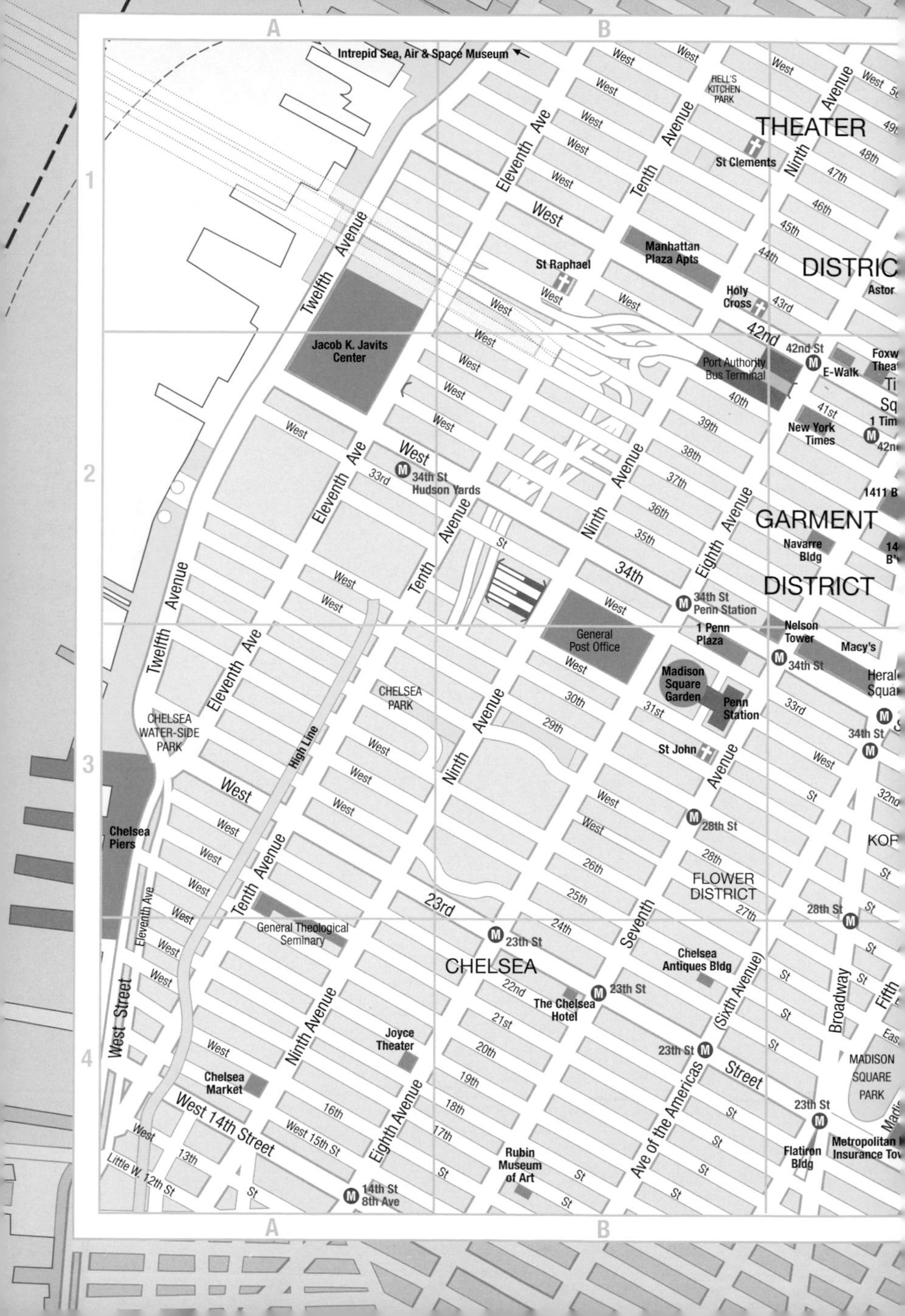
A
B
1
2
3
4
Intrepid Sea, Air & Space Museum
HELL'S KITCHEN PARK
THEATER
DISTRIC
St Clements
Ninth Avenue
Tenth Avenue
Eleventh Ave
Twelfth Avenue
West
49th
48th
47th
46th
45th
44th
43rd
42nd
Manhattan Plaza Apts
St Raphael
Holy Cross
Astor
Jacob K. Javits Center
42nd St
E-Walk
Port Authority Bus Terminal
Foxw
Thea
Ti
Sq
1 Tim
41st
40th
39th
38th
37th
36th
35th
34th
33rd
New York Times
42n
34th St Hudson Yards
1411 B
GARMENT
Navarre Bldg
14 B'
DISTRICT
Eighth Avenue
St
34th St Penn Station
General Post Office
1 Penn Plaza
Nelson Tower
Macy's
34th St
Herald Squar
Madison Square Garden
Penn Station
CHELSEA PARK
CHELSEA WATER-SIDE PARK
30th
29th
31st
33rd
34th St
St John
High Line
Chelsea Piers
32nd
28th St
KOR
28th
FLOWER DISTRICT
26th
25th
27th
28th St
24th
23rd
Seventh
General Theological Seminary
23th St
Chelsea Antiques Bldg
CHELSEA
22nd
The Chelsea Hotel
23th St
(Sixth Avenue)
Broadway
Fifth
21st
20th
19th
18th
17th
16th
West 15th St
13th
Eleventh Ave
West Street
Ninth Avenue
Joyce Theater
23th St
Ave of the Americas
Street
MADISON SQUARE PARK
Chelsea Market
West 14th Street
Eighth Avenue
23th St
Little W. 12th St
Rubin Museum of Art
Flatiron Bldg
Metropolitan Insurance Tov
14th St 8th Ave

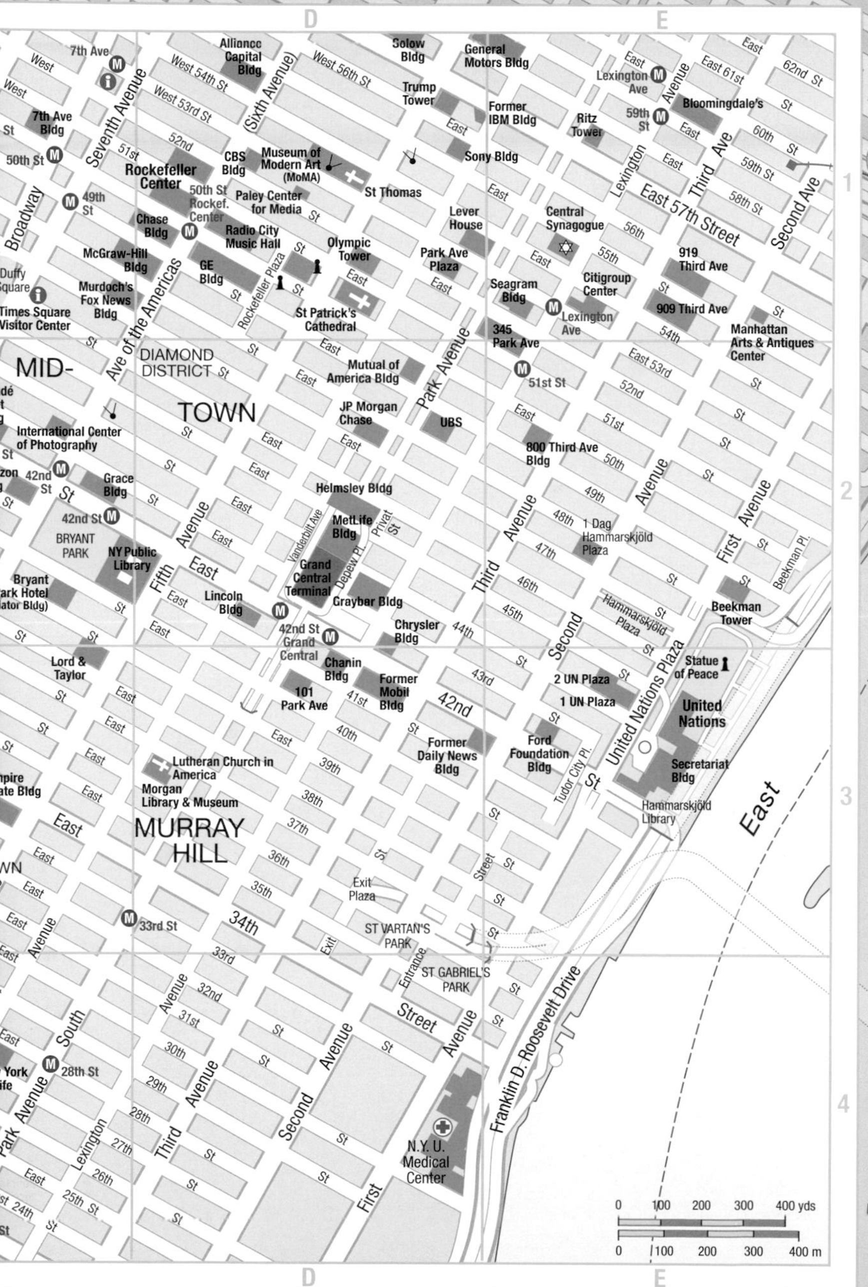
D
E
1
2
3
4
MID-
TOWN
DIAMOND DISTRICT
MURRAY HILL
Alliance Capital Bldg
Solow Bldg
General Motors Bldg
Trump Tower
Former IBM Bldg
Sony Bldg
Ritz Tower
Bloomingdale's
7th Ave Bldg
Rockefeller Center
CBS Bldg
Museum of Modern Art (MoMA)
St Thomas
Paley Center for Media
50th St Rockef. Center
Radio City Music Hall
Chase Bldg
McGraw-Hill Bldg
GE Bldg
Olympic Tower
Lever House
Park Ave Plaza
Central Synagogue
919 Third Ave
Seagram Bldg
Citigroup Center
909 Third Ave
Murdoch's Fox News Bldg
Times Square Visitor Center
Duffy Square
St Patrick's Cathedral
345 Park Ave
Manhattan Arts & Antiques Center
Mutual of America Bldg
JP Morgan Chase
UBS
800 Third Ave Bldg
International Center of Photography
Grace Bldg
Helmsley Bldg
MetLife Bldg
BRYANT PARK
NY Public Library
Grand Central Terminal
1 Dag Hammarskjöld Plaza
Bryant Park Hotel
Lincoln Bldg
Graybar Bldg
Chrysler Bldg
Beekman Tower
Lord & Taylor
Chanin Bldg
Former Mobil Bldg
101 Park Ave
Statue of Peace
2 UN Plaza
1 UN Plaza
United Nations
Former Daily News Bldg
Ford Foundation Bldg
Secretariat Bldg
Lutheran Church in America
Morgan Library & Museum
Hammarskjöld Library
East
Exit Plaza
ST VARTAN'S PARK
ST GABRIEL'S PARK
N.Y.U. Medical Center
Franklin D. Roosevelt Drive
7th Ave
50th St
49th St
Lexington Ave
59th St
Lexington Ave
51st St
42nd St
42nd St
42nd St Grand Central
33rd St
28th St
Seventh Avenue
Broadway
Ave of the Americas
(Sixth Avenue)
Fifth Avenue
Park Avenue
Lexington Avenue
Third Avenue
Second Avenue
First Avenue
United Nations Plaza
Rockefeller Plaza
Vanderbilt Ave
Depew Pl.
Privat St
Tudor City Pl.
Beekman Pl.
Hammarskjöld Plaza
West 56th St
West 54th St
West 53rd St
East 57th Street
East 61st
62nd St
60th St
59th St
58th St
East 53rd
42nd
34th
0 100 200 300 400 yds
0 100 200 300 400 m

MEATPACKING DISTRICT
GREENWICH VILLAGE
WEST VILLAGE
SOHO
NOLITA
LITTLE ITALY
TRIBECA
Chelsea Market
Joyce Theater
Whitney Museum of American Art
Fire Boat Station
Rubin Museum of Art
Yivo Institute for Jewish Research
Jackson Square
Abingdon Square
Westbeth
Village Vanguard
St Vincent's Hospital
New School for Social Research
Forbes Magazine Galleries
Jefferson Market Library
Church of the Ascension
Lucille Lortel Theater
Sheridan Square
St-Luke-in the-Fields
Cherry Lane Theatre
Provincetown Playhouse
Washington Square Arch
WASHINGTON SQUARE PARK
Minetta Lane Theater
Our Lady of Pompeii
Father Demo Square
Judson Mem. Church
NY University
Astor Place Theatre
Children's Museum of the Arts
University Plaza
Dia Center for the Arts
New York City Fire Museum
Station A
Soho Cast-Iron Historic District
Little Singer Bldg
Dean & Deluca
Ohio Theater
St Patrick's Old Cathedral
Performing Garage
Grunther Bldg
Bloomingdale's SoHo
Haughwout Bldg
New Museum of Contemporary Art
Museum of Chinese in America
Old Police Bldg
Tribeca Film Center
Manhattan Community College
Mercantile Exchange Bldg
HUDSON RIVER PARK AND GREENWAY
Holland Tunnel (Toll)
ALBERT CAPSUTE PARK
Merchant's House Museum
14th St 8th Ave
14th St
23th St
Christopher St Sheridan Sq.
W 4th St
Houston St
Spring St
Canal St
Prince St
Bleecker St
Broadway Lafayette
8th St
Bowery
Grand St
West Street
Tenth Ave
High Line
Ninth Ave
Eighth Avenue
Seventh Avenue
Avenue of the Americas (Sixth Avenue)
Fifth Avenue
Broadway
Canal Street
West Houston Street
Kenmare St
Bowery
Chrystie
A
B
1
2
3
4
53
52
51
46
45
40
34
9A

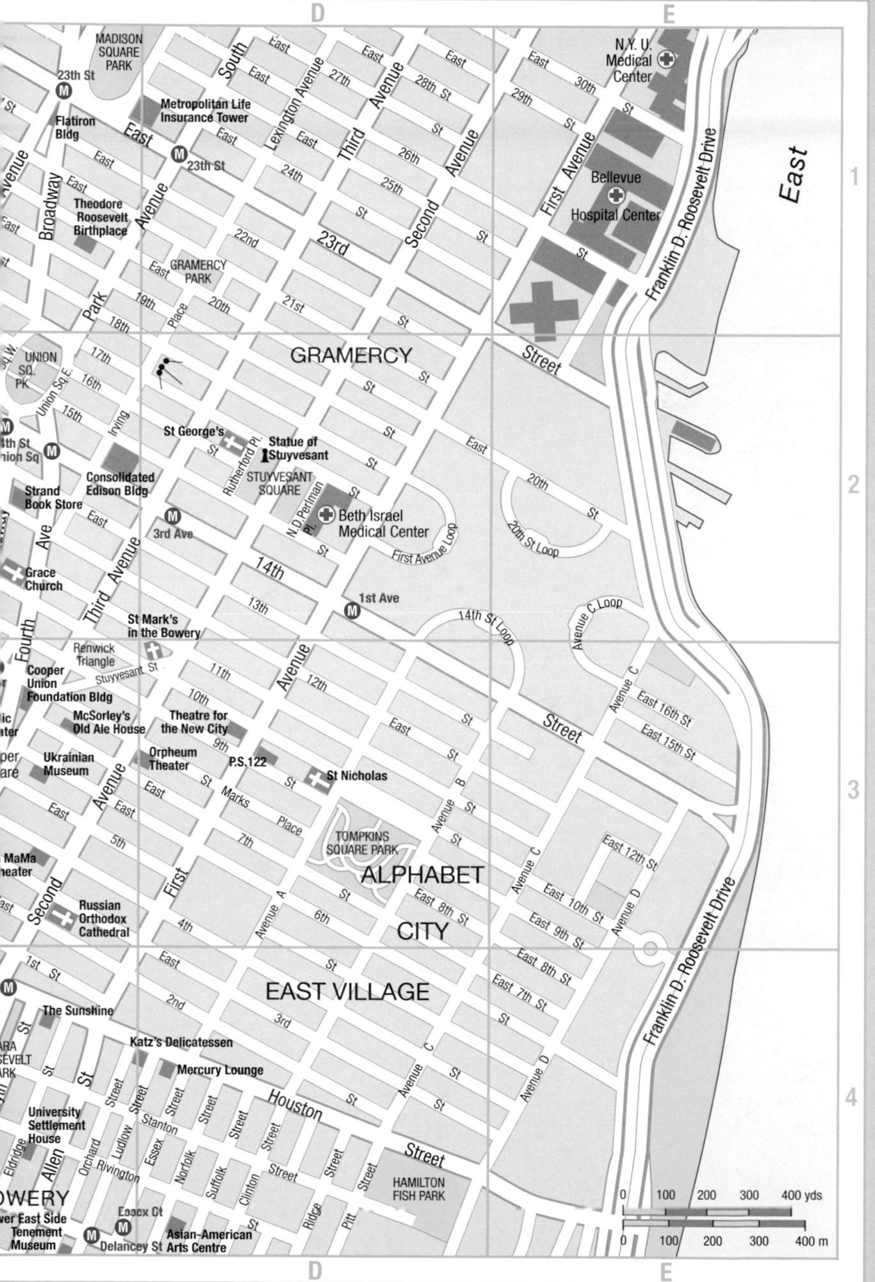
D
E
1
2
3
4
MADISON SQUARE PARK
23th St
Metropolitan Life Insurance Tower
Flatiron Bldg
23th St
Theodore Roosevelt Birthplace
GRAMERCY PARK
N.Y. U. Medical Center
Bellevue Hospital Center
Franklin D. Roosevelt Drive
East
GRAMERCY
UNION SQ. PK
St George's
Statue of Stuyvesant
STUYVESANT SQUARE
Consolidated Edison Bldg
Strand Book Store
Beth Israel Medical Center
3rd Ave
First Avenue Loop
20th St Loop
Grace Church
1st Ave
14th St Loop
Avenue C Loop
St Mark's in the Bowery
Renwick Triangle
Cooper Union Foundation Bldg
McSorley's Old Ale House
Theatre for the New City
Ukrainian Museum
Orpheum Theater
P.S.122
St Nicholas
TOMPKINS SQUARE PARK
ALPHABET CITY
Russian Orthodox Cathedral
EAST VILLAGE
The Sunshine
Katz's Delicatessen
Mercury Lounge
University Settlement House
HAMILTON FISH PARK
Asian-American Arts Centre
Delancey St
0 100 200 300 400 yds
0 100 200 300 400 m

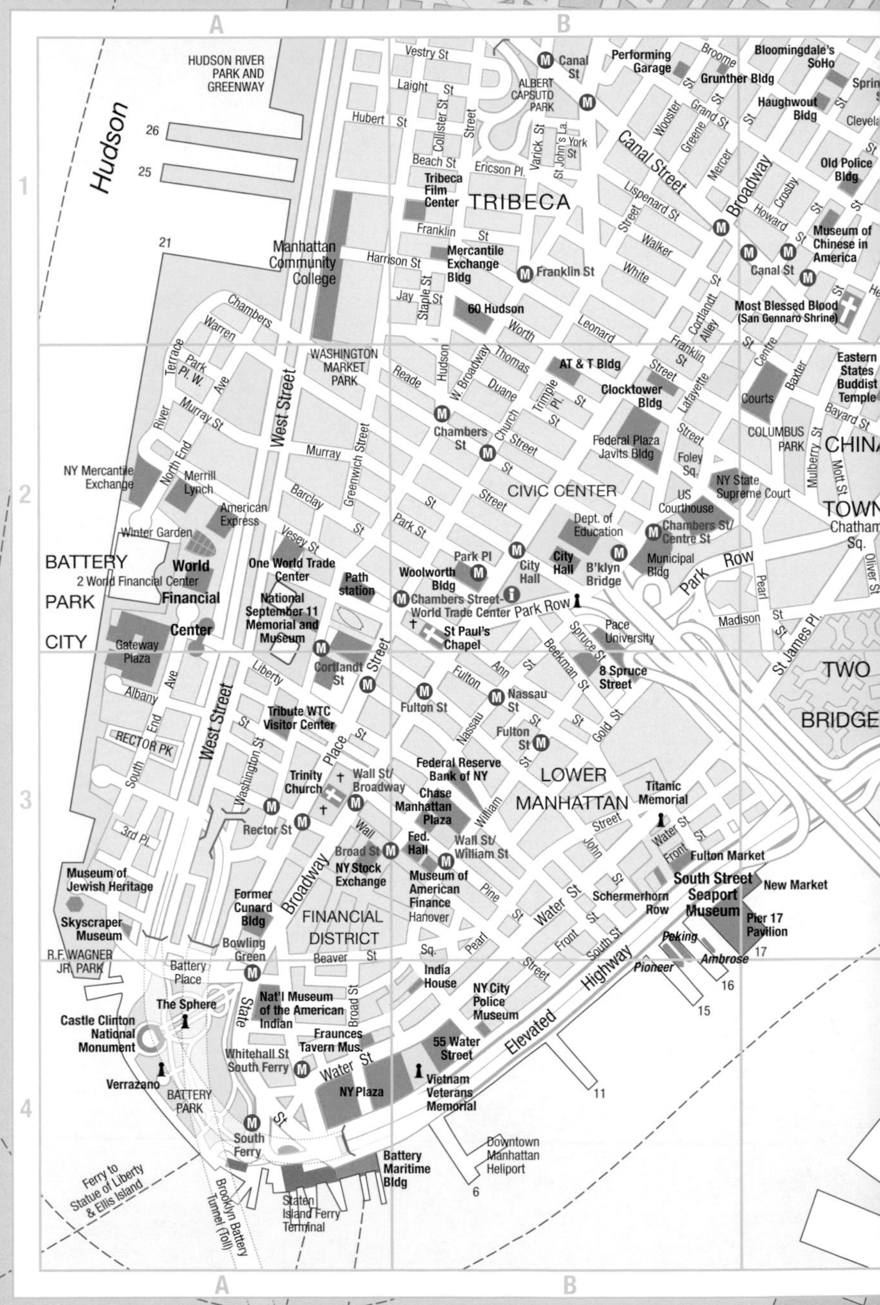
A
B
1
2
3
4
Hudson
HUDSON RIVER PARK AND GREENWAY
TRIBECA
Canal St
Performing Garage
Bloomingdale's SoHo
Grunther Bldg
Haughwout Bldg
Old Police Bldg
Museum of Chinese in America
Canal St
Most Blessed Blood (San Gennaro Shrine)
ALBERT CAPSUTO PARK
Tribeca Film Center
Mercantile Exchange Bldg
Franklin St
60 Hudson
Manhattan Community College
WASHINGTON MARKET PARK
AT & T Bldg
Clocktower Bldg
Eastern States Buddist Temple
Courts
COLUMBUS PARK
CHINA
TOWN
Chatham Sq.
Chambers St
Federal Plaza Javits Bldg
Foley Sq.
NY State Supreme Court
US Courthouse
CIVIC CENTER
Dept. of Education
Chambers St/ Centre St
Municipal Bldg
NY Mercantile Exchange
Merrill Lynch
American Express
Winter Garden
BATTERY PARK CITY
World Financial Center
2 World Financial Center
Gateway Plaza
One World Trade Center
Path station
National September 11 Memorial and Museum
Woolworth Bldg
Park Pl
City Hall
City Hall
B'klyn Bridge
Chambers Street-World Trade Center
St Paul's Chapel
Pace University
TWO BRIDGES
Cortlandt St
8 Spruce Street
Fulton St
Nassau St
Fulton St
Tribute WTC Visitor Center
RECTOR PK
Federal Reserve Bank of NY
LOWER MANHATTAN
Titanic Memorial
Trinity Church
Wall St/ Broadway
Chase Manhattan Plaza
Rector St
Broad St
NY Stock Exchange
Fed. Hall
Wall St/ William St
Museum of American Finance
Fulton Market
South Street Seaport Museum
New Market
Schermerhorn Row
Pier 17 Pavilion
Museum of Jewish Heritage
Skyscraper Museum
Former Cunard Bldg
FINANCIAL DISTRICT
Bowling Green
Hanover Sq.
Peking
Ambrose
Pioneer
R.F. WAGNER JR. PARK
Battery Place
India House
NY City Police Museum
The Sphere
Nat'l Museum of the American Indian
Castle Clinton National Monument
Fraunces Tavern Mus.
55 Water Street
Whitehall St South Ferry
NY Plaza
Vietnam Veterans Memorial
Verrazano
BATTERY PARK
South Ferry
Battery Maritime Bldg
Downtown Manhattan Heliport
Ferry to Statue of Liberty & Ellis Island
Brooklyn Battery Tunnel (Toll)
Staten Island Ferry Terminal
Elevated Highway
West Street
Broadway
Canal Street
Park Row
Water St
State St

EAST VILLAGE
BOWERY
LOWER EAST SIDE
New Museum of Contemporary Art
Katz's Delicatessen
Mercury Lounge
SARA ROOSEVELT PARK
University Settlement House
Lower East Side Tenement Museum
Essex St
Delancey St
Asian-American Arts Centre
HAMILTON FISH PARK
Lower East Side Business Improvement District Visitor Center
SEWARD PARK
E Broadway
Straus Sq.
Former Daily Forward Bldg
Dickstein Place
Williamsburg Bridge
EAST RIVER PARK
Franklin D. Roosevelt Drive
Elevated Highway
Corlears Hook
Circle Line Boat Tour
35
East River
Manhattan Bridge
Brooklyn Bridge
Queens Expressway
York St
High St
Bowery
Grand St
Houston Street
Delancey Street
East Broadway
Henry Street
Madison Street
Grand St
Cherry St
Water St
South St
John Street
Plymouth Street
Water Street
Front Street
York Street
Prospect St
Sando Street
278
0 100 200 300 400 yds
0 100 200 300 400 m
D
E
1
2
3
4

STREET INDEX

ART AND PHOTO CREDITS

Alamy 31T, 35, 54L, 54R, 55B, 55TR, 55MR, 104B, 104T, 105, 114B, 114T, 115, 121, 125B, 146, 171MR, 194B, 207B, 214B, 219, 222/223T, 232, 235B, 239, 253B, 254B, 271T, 272
American Museum of Natural History 227T, 227TC
Art Archive 29B
AWL Images 18, 56, 135B, 142, 186, 228, 268, 270
Bigstock 138, 161B, 225M
Britta Jaschinski/Apa Publications 6ML, 11B, 21, 23, 24B, 24T, 25B, 25T, 26, 58, 59, 69T, 69B, 78, 80, 81T, 87, 94B, 95M, 95TC 101T, 101B, 109BR, 109M, 111, 116, 117, 120B, 123, 127, 130, 131T, 132, 133T, 133B, 134B, 136, 139, 144, 145, 161T, 164T, 164B, 165B, 166, 170B, 170T, 171TC, 173, 175T, 175B, 177T, 178T, 179, 184ML, 192B, 193, 194T, 207T, 208T, 210R, 210L, 218T, 223BR, 224TL, 224ML, 224BR, 224BL, 225BR, 227M, 235TR, 241, 243, 244T, 246B, 252, 253T, 255, 260, 261, 282B, 285, 286, 287, 289, 290
Brooklyn Museum 248
Children's Museum of the Arts 102
Corbis 9BL, 28B, 30B, 31B, 33, 37, 43, 45, 85, 90, 92, 205B, 234, 263, 266
Dreamstime 1, 9M, 10T, 52/53, 60MR, 61M, 75T, 81B, 88/89, 94T, 95T, 103B, 109TC, 113, 118, 126, 154, 156, 162, 163, 165T, 167B, 167T, 172, 181, 182MR, 182MR, 182BL, 183B, 183T, 184ML, 184MR, 185M, 185T, 185MR, 187, 191B, 203, 208B, 209T, 211BR, 211T, 212, 213, 237, 240, 244B, 245, 246T, 247T, 247B, 251B, 251T, 256, 267, 273, 277
Getty Images 4/5, 12/13, 14/15, 16/17, 36, 38, 38/39, 40/41, 48, 49, 50, 51, 62/63, 64/65, 68, 72, 91, 106, 141, 147B, 150, 154/155T, 157, 159, 160, 168, 205T, 211M, 221, 222, 225TC, 229, 231, 233, 257T, 278
Gramercy Park Hotel 143
Hotel Gansevoort 8
Illustrated London News 32
iStock 6TL, 7M, 7B, 22, 61T, 67, 88, 93BR, 107, 128, 129, 131B, 147T, 152, 169, 178B, 180T, 189, 192T, 197, 199, 216, 218B, 235T, 271B, 275, 292
Juillard School 224/225T
Keiko Niwa/Lower East Side Tenement Museum 119T, 120T
Library of Congress 29T, 93TC, 190
Marcus Wilson-Smith/Apa Publications 155TC
Mark Read/Apa Publications 108L, 135T
Mary Evans Picture Library 30T
Maya Lin Studio/MCA 124
Merchant's House Museum 112T, 112B
Metropolitan Museum of Art 209TC, 209M, 209BR
Metropolitan Opera 223M, 223TR
Mockford & Bonetti/Apa Publications 7ML, 7BR, 93B, 184MR, 195B
Morgan Library 188B, 188T
Museum of Modern Art 171ML, 170/171T, 170/171B
National Museum of the American Indian 79TR
New York City Ballet 214/215
New York Public Library 34
Nowitz Photography/Apa Publications 6MR, 6B, 7T, 9TR, 19T, 19B, 20, 57, 60BL, 60MR, 73, 75B, 76T, 76B, 77, 79BR, 79T, 83B, 83T, 84, 86, 93T, 96, 97, 99B, 99T, 103T, 108R, 110, 119B, 125T, 134T, 137, 140, 148B, 148T, 151B, 151T, 153, 155M, 155ML, 177B, 180B, 191T, 195T, 204B, 204T, 206, 211TC, 211ML, 217B, 236B, 236T, 254T, 259, 280, 281, 282T, 284
NPS Photo 95BR
PA/EPA 44
Public domain 174, 28T, 248/249T
Rex Features 40T, 42, 54/55T, 109B, 108/109T, 220
Rickshaw Dumplings 61BR
Robert Harding 27, 214T, 274
Rubin Museum of Art 149
Shutterstock 7MR, 11T, 82, 258
Sony 196
Superstock 10B, 46/47, 122, 176, 198, 249B, 250, 257B, 262, 265, 276
The American Museum of Natural History 226B, 226T, 227BR
The Frick Collection 201B, 201T, 202
The Kobal Collection 55M
The Metropolitan Museum of Art 238B, 238T
Tips Images 216/217T
Topfoto 40B, 155BR
Tribeca Film Festival 52
Tribeca Grand Hotel 100
Wafels & Dinges 61TR

Cover Credits

Front cover: NYC skyline *Shutterstock*
Back cover: Statue of Liberty *iStock*
Front flap: (from top) Times Sq *Shutterstock*; Brownstones *iStock*; view from Brooklyn Bridge *Dreamstime*; the Highline *iStock*
Back flap: Manhattan Bridge and Empire State Building from Dumbo *Dreamstime*

INDEX

N

T

ABOUT THIS BOOK

This fully updated edition of Insight Guide New York was commissioned by **Rachel Lawrence** and edited by **Tim Binks**. The book was comprehensively updated by **Maciej Zglinicki** an experienced travel writer and editor.

This new edition builds on earlier editions produced by **John Gattuso**, **Kathy Novak**, **Mimi Tompkins**, **Tom Cavalieri**, **Joanna Potts**, **Aaron Starmer**, **Divya Symmers**, **Nick Rider**, **David Whelan**, **A. Peter Bailey**, **Michele Abruzzi**, **John Wilcock**, and **John Strausbaugh**.

The principal photographers were **Abe Nowitz** and **Britta Jaschinski**, both regular contributors to Insight Guides. Special thanks also to **Ed Yourdon**. The index was compiled by **Penny Phenix**.

SEND US YOUR THOUGHTS

We do our best to ensure the information in our books is as accurate and up-to-date as possible. The books are updated on a regular basis using local contacts, who painstakingly add, amend, and correct as required. However, some details (such as telephone numbers and opening times) are liable to change, and we are ultimately reliant on our readers to put us in the picture.

We welcome your feedback, especially your experience of using the book "on the road". Maybe we recommended a hotel that you liked (or another that you didn't), or you came across a great bar or new attraction that we missed.

We will acknowledge all contributions, and we'll offer an Insight Guide to the best letters received.

Please write to us at:
Insight Guides
PO Box 7910, London SE1 1WE
Or email us at:
hello@insightguides.com

INSIGHT GUIDES
NEW YORK

Editor: Rachel Lawrence
Updater: Maciej Zglinicki
Head of Production: Rebeka Davies
Update Production: AM Services
Pictures: Tom Smyth
Cartography: original cartography Berndtson & Berndtson, updated by Carte

Distribution

UK, Ireland and Europe
Apa Publications (UK) Ltd
sales@insightguides.com

United States and Canada
Ingram Publisher Services
ips@ingramcontent.com

Australia and New Zealand
Woodslane
info@woodslane.com.au

Southeast Asia
Apa Publications (SN) Pte
singaporeoffice@insightguides.com

Hong Kong, Taiwan and China
Apa Publications (HK) Ltd
hongkongoffice@insightguides.com

Worldwide
Apa Publications (UK) Ltd
sales@insightguides.com

Special Sales, Content Licensing and CoPublishing

Insight Guides can be purchased in bulk quantities at discounted prices. We can create special editions, personalised jackets and corporate imprints tailored to your needs.
sales@insightguides.com;
www.insightguides.biz

Printing

CTPS-China

First Edition 1991
Tenth Edition 2016

www.insightguides.com

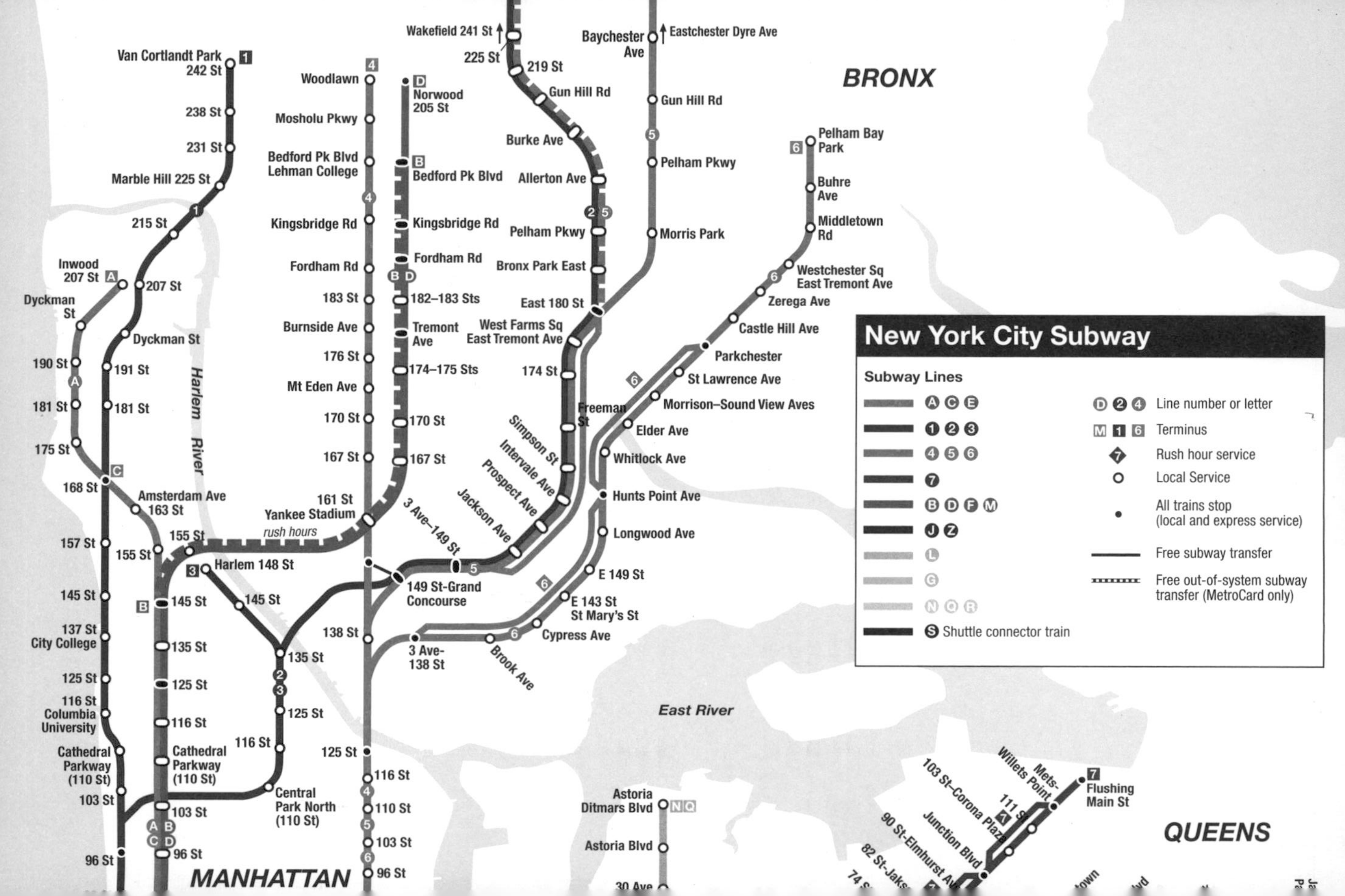
New York City Subway
Subway Lines
A C E
1 2 3
4 5 6
7
B D F M
J Z
L
G
N Q R
S Shuttle connector train
D 2 4 Line number or letter
M 1 6 Terminus
7 Rush hour service
Local Service
All trains stop
(local and express service)
Free subway transfer
Free out-of-system subway transfer (MetroCard only)
BRONX
MANHATTAN
QUEENS
Harlem River
East River
Van Cortlandt Park 242 St
238 St
231 St
Marble Hill 225 St
215 St
207 St
Dyckman St
191 St
181 St
168 St
157 St
145 St
137 St City College
125 St
116 St Columbia University
Cathedral Parkway (110 St)
103 St
96 St
Inwood 207 St
Dyckman St
190 St
181 St
175 St
Amsterdam Ave 163 St
155 St
135 St
116 St
Harlem 148 St
Central Park North (110 St)
Woodlawn
Mosholu Pkwy
Bedford Pk Blvd Lehman College
Kingsbridge Rd
Fordham Rd
183 St
Burnside Ave
176 St
Mt Eden Ave
170 St
167 St
161 St Yankee Stadium
rush hours
138 St
110 St
Norwood 205 St
Bedford Pk Blvd
182–183 Sts
Tremont Ave
174–175 Sts
3 Ave–149 St
149 St-Grand Concourse
Wakefield 241 St
225 St
219 St
Gun Hill Rd
Burke Ave
Allerton Ave
Pelham Pkwy
Bronx Park East
East 180 St
West Farms Sq East Tremont Ave
174 St
Freeman St
Simpson St
Intervale Ave
Prospect Ave
Jackson Ave
Baychester Ave
Eastchester Dyre Ave
Morris Park
Pelham Bay Park
Buhre Ave
Middletown Rd
Westchester Sq East Tremont Ave
Zerega Ave
Castle Hill Ave
Parkchester
St Lawrence Ave
Morrison–Sound View Aves
Elder Ave
Whitlock Ave
Hunts Point Ave
Longwood Ave
E 149 St
E 143 St St Mary's St
Cypress Ave
Brook Ave
3 Ave-138 St
Astoria Ditmars Blvd
Astoria Blvd
Flushing Main St
Mets-Willets Point
111 St
103 St–Corona Plaza
Junction Blvd